May I Quote You on That?

May I Quote You on That?

A Guide to Grammar and Usage

STEPHEN SPECTOR

OXFORD
UNIVERSITY PRESS

OXFORD

UNIVERSITY PRESS

Oxford University Press is a department of the
University of Oxford. It furthers the University's objective
of excellence in research, scholarship, and education
by publishing worldwide.

Oxford   New York

Auckland   Cape Town   Dar es Salaam   Hong Kong   Karachi
Kuala Lumpur   Madrid   Melbourne   Mexico City   Nairobi
New Delhi   Shanghai   Taipei   Toronto

With offices in

Argentina   Austria   Brazil   Chile   Czech Republic   France   Greece
Guatemala   Hungary   Italy   Japan   Poland   Portugal   Singapore
South Korea   Switzerland   Thailand   Turkey   Ukraine   Vietnam

Oxford is a registered trade mark of Oxford University Press
in the UK and certain other countries.

Published in the United States of America by
Oxford University Press
198 Madison Avenue, New York, NY 10016

Library of Congress Cataloging-in-Publication Data
is available

ISBN 978-0-19-021528-6

1 3 5 7 9 8 6 4 2

Printed in the United States of America
on acid-free paper

*For Mary, who makes everything possible
and everything better*

Contents

(∗)
Acknowledgments

I want to thank first of all the great scholars who taught me the history of the English language. My deep gratitude and warm appreciation go to Marie Borroff. I found her course on the history of the language to be inspirational, I've valued her mentorship, and I've treasured her friendship. I'm profoundly indebted to Talbot Donaldson. His brilliance and humor in reading Chaucer made Middle English a delight. I'm very grateful to John Pope, Traugott Lawler, and Dorothee Metlitzki for sharing their immense knowledge of Old and Middle English and for modeling personal kindness and generosity. I deeply appreciate Norman Davis's patience and good humor in advising me when I was just out of graduate school, in the hope that I wouldn't embarrass the Early English Text Society too badly. Some of them are gone now, but what I learned from all of them enlivens this little book.

Through the entire process of writing this book, my wife, Mary, has been a wise and loving support and comfort, as she always is. My son, Dave, and my daughter-in-law, Şebnem, gave me great advice from first to last, drawing on their experience in English language instruction and their excellent judgment and cleverness. I'm very grateful to Leigh Ann Hirschman and Betsy Amster for helping me find the right voice for the book. It turned out to be my own voice, the one in which I actually speak to my students. After I'd written the manuscript, I couldn't have asked for more talented, learned, and helpful friends than the ones who kindly read it and suggested changes: Henry Abelove, Paul Dolan,

Traugott Lawler, Lila Naydan, Roger Rosenblatt, and Howie Schneider. I'm very grateful to the terrific editors at Oxford University Press, Cynthia Read, who encouraged me to submit the book to OUP, and Hallie Stebbins, who believed in it, edited it wisely, and shepherded it to publication. Thanks also to Marcela Maxfield, my former student who now works at OUP, for reading the manuscript and making comments that made the book better and saved me from big and small mistakes.

(❊)

Introduction

Imagine for a moment that your boyfriend, girlfriend, or spouse went away for a week and forgot to call you. You're pretty annoyed. What kind of language will the two of you use when you see each other? Your significant other might begin with something loving, in a very informal, intimate style, like this:

"Hey, sweetheart. Love you. Miss me?"

You might reply in a similar style, but a lot less sweetly, like this:

"Yeah, right! How come you didn't call or text, you jerk?"

Now imagine how you'd talk in a job interview at Google. You'd probably use a much more formal level of speech. You might say,

"Good morning. It's a pleasure to meet you. Thanks so much for inviting me here today."

The interviewer might respond,

"We're very impressed with your credentials."

We all use language in different styles, depending on the situation.[1] You wouldn't talk to a congressman the same way that you would to a misbehaving child, for example—though that depends on the congressman, of course. And if you write a college application essay, your language should be a lot more formal than it would be if you and your friends were watching your team blow a lead in the ninth inning of a playoff game. The more formal the context, the more appropriate it is to use a formal level of Standard English, the style of writing and speech that we'll explore in this book.

My goal is to make the conventions of formal English easier and more fun to learn than traditional approaches usually do. It's the product of my forty years of teaching courses on the English language, and it differs from most other usage and style guides in several ways:

- It teaches by example, so you can learn from context. The lessons start with quotations, not with rules or definitions. Reading these sentences may be enough for you to infer the usage rules or the word meanings for yourself.[2] You may find that some of these quotations are memorable. That's good, because if you remember them, you can model your own sentences on them. An incidental benefit is that these illustrations can be useful for new learners of English.
- Many of the quotations are funny, interesting, or instructive (I hope). Most are from celebrities, great writers, or historical figures. Mark Twain is cited often. Jerry Seinfeld appears, as do Groucho Marx, Woody Allen, Billy Crystal, Jon Stewart, and Stephen Colbert. Lady Gaga and Taylor Swift are quoted, as are Jennifer Lawrence, Scarlett Johansson, and George Clooney. Chaucer, Shakespeare, Hemingway, and Tolkien are represented. So are Benjamin Franklin, Abraham Lincoln, Sigmund Freud, Winston Churchill, Mahatma Gandhi, John F. Kennedy, Martin Luther King Jr., and the Dalai Lama. Babe Ruth, Yogi Berra, and Michael Jordan appear. So do Marilyn Monroe, Steve Jobs, Oprah Winfrey, and many others.

- Each lesson includes a mini-essay telling the history of the rules or the words being discussed. These discussions are written in a clear, accessible style. They put the traditional rules in the context of historical changes and informal or nonstandard speech today. And they illustrate the fact that the "right" usage is often a moving target and a personal choice. A living language changes over time, and so do ideas about what is appropriate in formal use. You may be surprised by what you learn about the current views on some of the usage rules.

- This is a book for the twenty-first century, and it includes many frequently misunderstood words that are relevant today. Just as H. W. Fowler's old standby, *A Dictionary of Modern English Usage,* included terms that were especially significant for its time (1926), such as *atom, electron, communism,* and *anarchism,* this book addresses tricky words that are part of our current experience. It covers, for example, the difference between extremism and fanaticism, the Holocaust and a holocaust, the Internet and the Web, and the terms *Islamic* and *Islamist.* It also discusses the history and meaning of words like *avatar, fundamentalism, jihad, metadata, racism, schizophrenia,* and *terrorism.*

- The book has a dedicated website containing practice drills. You can find it at www.oup.com/us/MayIQuoteYou. To master and retain Standard English grammar and usage rules, most of us need to learn them, then relearn them, with practice and guidance. In that sense, writing a Standard English sentence is like doing a ballroom dance. Both involve graceful, varied, rhythmic movement. Done right, both can be beautiful. But each has patterns that aren't familiar from everyday experience. When writers or dancers become technically skillful, we describe them as literate. Those moves don't always come naturally, though, so both require practice and guidance. I've had over thirty ballroom dance lessons (to please my wife, who's a literate dancer). At the start of every lesson my wife has had to remind me about the basic steps. When she whispers in my ear as we begin to dance, she's not saying sweet nothings; she's giving me the rhythm: "Quick, quick, slow. Quick, quick, slow." Then I catch the beat and the dance moves come back to me. Many of my students have a similar experience with grammar and usage: through relearning, guidance, and practice they gain confidence, grace, and mastery.

This book is for anybody who wants to write well. It's for you if you're composing an essay or a report, taking the SAT, or applying to a college or graduate school. It's for anyone who's answering an ad for a good job or writing a school assignment, a formal presentation, or a publication. Teachers and editors certainly have to know the traditional rules and the tricky word meanings that are covered in this book. And many everyday writers want to know how to select the precise word or phrase that Standard English requires, the right choice between words that look alike, the plural form of a noun, etc., in order to communicate clearly and effectively.

GOOD GRAMMAR AND FINDING LOVE

Here's something that you probably didn't expect to see: this book also may be for you if you're looking for love. A national survey in 2013 found that both single men and single women say that good grammar is one of the most important qualities they judge in a romantic partner.[3] That's actually not surprising if you think about it. Your writing shows your ability to communicate, your style, and your level of education, and those things can be very important to a potential mate.

Yet forty years ago, when I was first asked to teach my department's required course on the English language, many of our students dreaded a course in which they'd have to learn grammar and usage. Very bright English majors, including many who wanted to teach or do graduate study, had never been taught formal Standard English. They often weren't confident about when to say *who* as opposed to *whom*, for example. Now, it's true that people don't say *whom* very often nowadays, especially in conversation. The humorist Calvin Trillin said this about the word:

> "*Whom* is a word that was invented to make everyone sound like a butler. Nobody who is not a butler has ever said it out loud without feeling just a little bit weird."
> "Whom Says So?" *The Nation,* June 8, 1985

What would a stranger think if he knocked on your door and you asked, "Whom do you wish to see?" He might be impressed and a little surprised. Or he might think you're a pretentious nerd. But there are times when *whom* is natural and appropriate in formal writing, so it's important to know when to use it. My students also had problems choosing between *less* and *fewer, as* and *like, imply* and *infer,* and *lay* and *lie.* They frequently weren't sure if *either, neither,* and *each* are singular or plural. Most of them had never even been taught what the subjunctive mood is, much less how and when to use it. Sometimes they confused *I* and *me* in their essays, and they employed other casual, nonstandard, and awkward usages that don't belong in formal writing.

I found that the solution was to try to make learning grammar and usage fun. I immersed the class in funny or interesting sentences that illustrated the formal English usages. Only then did I teach the standard rules. And I learned to use only the grammar terms that were absolutely necessary. The result was surprising, especially to the students: they learned the standard usages and developed a sense of confidence about their writing. A lot of them said that they loved the experience. The course became one of the most popular in the department, and many students from other departments tried to enroll, specifically to learn grammar and usage. I've taught nearly five thousand students in that course over the years, and in their course evaluations very many of them have said that they wished they'd had the grammar and usage instruction earlier in their college careers. In response, my department changed the rubric of the course so it would be one of the first courses our majors take.

I use the same approach in this book. It's based on these principles:

(1) People learn more naturally and more happily from reading funny, instructive, or engaging illustrations of good writing than from memorizing grammar and usage rules.

(2) Most people don't like having to learn grammar terms. So this book avoids jargon as much as possible.

(3) The definitions of tricky words are easier to recall when people see memorable quotations that exemplify them. And look-alike words are easier to distinguish when interesting sentences illustrate the differences between them.

(4) When you remember these illustrations of the usages and meanings, you can use them as models in your own writing.

THE SPAT WITH YOUR SIGNIFICANT OTHER

As you probably noticed, the spat between romantic partners at the top of this introduction includes incomplete sentences and other very informal usages, including *hey; love you; miss me?; yeah, right; how come;* and *jerk.*

That's fine in an intimate conversation. But when you write in a more formal style, adjust your linguistic choices appropriately. The style you choose depends on the social setting, the audience, the topic, whether you're speaking or writing, and your mood. I'm writing this book, for instance, in a conversational tone. I employ the standard usages that I teach in the lessons, but my style is more casual than it would be if this were an academic publication. For example, I'm using contractions, which usually are inappropriate in very formal writing.

APPLE PREDICTS YOUR STYLE!

Have you ever been embarrassed (and maybe horrified) by a change that the autocorrect function on your computer or phone made in one of your electronic messages? Many grandmothers reportedly have been stunned to learn that Facebook's interface automatically changed "Love, Grandma" at the close of their postings to "Love,

Grandmaster Flash" (a hip-hop artist). Well, the latest devices are smarter and better attuned to you personally. In fact, Apple says that its iOS 8 operating system adjusts its suggestions and corrections to the style of language that it predicts you'll use in different contexts. It expects you to use casual word choices when you text and more formal language when you send email. What's more, it assumes that your style probably will be more informal when you write to your friends or your spouse than to your boss. It also bases its choices on the words and phrases that you've actually used in the past.[4]

HOW SHOULD YOU USE THIS BOOK?

The first few chapters of the book are divided into lessons, with quotations at the start of each. I suggest that you read the quotations carefully and pay close attention to the underlined words. They illustrate the point of the lesson, so you may be able to see the patterns even before you get to the rules.

Then read the mini-essays. **They state the rules in boldface**, but they also show that usage experts don't always agree. **Look for my suggestions, also in boldface, to see my best judgment about what to do in those cases.** These short essays use basic grammar terms. If you're not sure what they mean, check their definitions in Chapter 2.

Do the exercises that appear at the bottom of most lessons, to be sure that you can apply the rules. Then do the exercises on the website. They'll serve as both practice and diagnostic tools, so you can see if you need to go back to the lessons in the book for review.

Then make your own decisions as you do your own writing, depending on the style you're aiming for and the audience you're addressing.

SOME THOUGHTS BEFORE WE BEGIN

After a quick look at Standard English in Chapter 1 and a brief review of some basic terms in Chapter 2, Chapter 3 deals with tricky word meanings, usage, and grammar. It includes words that are disputed, misunderstood, confused, or frequently looked up in online dictionaries. Chapter 4 focuses on examples of those issues that arose or became especially significant in the twentieth century and later. Chapter 5, called "Look-Alikes," addresses fine distinctions between similar-looking words that are often confused. The final chapter is on plurals, including curious native English forms and words that were borrowed from other languages.

The quotations in each lesson illustrate the standard usage or word meaning, unless otherwise noted. And when you're asked to choose between two versions of a passage, the actual quotation is the one that properly illustrates the standard usage.

You may want to look up specific entries. That's good, but I suggest that you also browse. Even if you're pretty sure you already know the rules, you might find that current opinion in some cases is more liberal or more conservative than you expect. And keep in mind that some lessons address only the most important meanings of words, or the main distinctions between look-alikes, and may not give a complete set of meanings. So supplement those lessons with a good dictionary when appropriate.

One more tip: even when you write in a formal style, always do your best to keep your writing natural, relaxed, and above all, clear. That sounds very bland and general, I know, but it's actually a main point of many of the lessons in this book. If you're a little anxious about all of this, don't worry: that's understandable. It's hard to write formal English with precision and clarity and still sound natural. It takes practice, then more practice. It's easier to learn how, though, if you're having fun. And the good news is that a lot of people want you to succeed. Every teacher I know likes to see good, clear writing. In my experience, admissions officers, job search directors, and editors feel exactly the same way. Here's hoping that this book helps you to write well, and that your writing helps you to be a huge success.

(*)

About the Companion Website

www.oup.com/us/MayIQuoteYou

Oxford has created a password-protected website to accompany *May I Quote You on That?*

The reader is encouraged to consult this resource for a workbook with additional practice exercises.

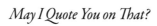

May I Quote You on That?

CHAPTER 1

What Is Standard English, and Who Gets to Decide What's Proper English Today?

Standard English consists of the grammar, vocabulary, and spelling that have the most prestige in any English-speaking country. It's the level of communication that people normally use in the news media, government, and other leading national institutions, and it's the type of English that we learn in school. As the distinguished linguist David Crystal points out, Standard English is English on its best behavior. It's widely understood, but people use it mainly in writing, not speech. When we speak, most of us use a regional English, or a mixture of regional and standard Englishes.[1]

NONSTANDARD ENGLISH

Using nonstandard forms isn't lazy, immoral, or inherently wrong. Most of us do it in informal contexts.[2] And nonstandard language can be rich, creative, and eloquent. Does that mean that it's okay to say a sentence like "I ain't hungry"? Well, I'm a stuffy English professor and I wouldn't say that, of course. But many linguists will tell you that it's not wrong if the people you're talking with say it in casual conversation. It's a question of context—and, strangely enough, of history. The word *ain't* is condemned in Standard English use today, so you may be surprised to hear that it once was considered perfectly acceptable. Educated Englishmen and women said *an't*, a form of *ain't*, colloquially in the seventeenth century. In the eighteenth century, though, Jonathan Swift and others disparaged abbreviated words, and by the nineteenth century, grammarians specifically denounced the word *ain't*. Jane Austen, Charles Dickens, and others put it in the speech of uneducated and vulgar characters.[3] So when people say *ain't* today, they're simply using a word that once was part of "polite usage" but has gone out of style in standard use today.

Ain't still survives in nonstandard speech, though. Here's a classic example by the great and beloved former New York Yankee Yogi Berra:

> "Slump? I ain't in no slump.... I just ain't hitting."
> Yogi Berra, *The Yogi Book* (1998)

THE PRESCRIPTIVE APPROACH

The history of *ain't* shows one of the ways in which usage rules became part of Standard English. As the Harvard linguist and psychologist Steven Pinker observes, there's nothing inherently wrong with *ain't*. But in the nineteenth century, grammarians preferred *isn't* because it had been part of the dialect spoken around London hundreds of years earlier.[4] This decision was really a matter of style: it involved a choice between usages. Grammarians judged *isn't* (and *aren't*, *hasn't*, etc.) to be appropriate to "polite" or formal English, while dismissing *ain't* as substandard.

They made decisions like this because they wanted to refine and correct English, which, like other languages, is naturally messy. Their dictums are called *prescriptive* because they prescribe how to speak and write (the way that a doctor prescribes a medicine).[5] The grammarians enshrined the polite usage of a privileged language community, and they tried to stifle new usages. That can never work: no one can freeze a living language. But many people in the rising middle class in the eighteenth century and later were eager to learn the prescriptive rules. They wanted the status that came with speaking and writing like the social group they aspired to join, so they bought huge numbers of these books. One eighteenth-century grammar book alone sold nearly two million copies during the next one hundred years.[6]

The fascination with books that prescribe proper usage has continued. A prime example is Fowler's *Modern English Usage*. Published in 1926, it quickly became so popular that people didn't even feel the need to cite the title. They just called it "Fowler." Its appeal cut across social classes. Winston Churchill, for example, quoted from it often. Churchill was a great orator, a man who "mobilized the English language and sent it into battle" during World War II.[7] He insisted on the precision in language that he thought Fowler provided. While planning the invasion of Normandy, for example, he reportedly snapped a command at an aide to check a word in Fowler. As prime minister he quoted *Modern English Usage* in the margins of official documents and even sent a copy to Buckingham Palace as a Christmas present. Linguists today criticize Fowler for basing decisions on his personal prejudices and for often being judgmental about nonstandard usage. They're right on both points. But no book had a greater influence on attitudes toward English in Britain in the twentieth century.[8]

WHO DECIDES WHAT'S PROPER ENGLISH TODAY?

Many of the prescriptive decisions stuck and are part of Standard English. As Pinker notes, though, the stylistic choices that dictate proper usage are only conventions. A virtual community of literate speakers and writers implicitly agrees to follow those rules, and the rules serve an indispensable purpose: they govern the ways that words agree with each other, fine distinctions in meaning, punctuation, and more. They "lubricate comprehension, reduce misunderstanding, provide a stable platform for the development of style and grace, and credibly signal that a writer has exercised care in crafting a passage."[9]

These choices of proper expression aren't necessarily permanent, though. They depend on a consensus among literate users. And because educated people don't all use language in the same way, that consensus may change. Some so-called rules are what Pinker calls *bubbe meises*, a Yiddish term meaning "grandmother's fables." They're linguistic old wives' tales, patterns of usage that came from a false consensus. The rules that are likely to endure for a time, by contrast, are the ones that represent the common knowledge of careful speakers.[10]

Since this consensus shifts, how can we be sure which stylistic choices are in favor right now? Well, one way is to read recent usage and style guides and grammars, including ones that track the actual usage of educated speakers and writers. We also can check the usage notes in the *Oxford English Dictionary* and the major American dictionaries. And we can look at the opinions of large usage panels consisting of professional authors, scholars, journalists, teachers, editors, and others. The mini-essays in this book review those sources in order to get a sense of current opinion about some of the most common usage choices and distinctions in word meanings. That way, you'll be able make your own informed decisions about them as you write.

CHAPTER 2

Some Really Basic Grammar Terms

If you're like most people, you probably don't love grammar terms. So this book uses only the terms that you really need in each lesson. The mini-essays include definitions of those terms, but here are some basic ones that aren't defined in the discussions, along with fuller coverage of a few that are.

GRAMMAR

Do you worry that your grammar isn't good? People often think that grammar consists of the conventions of educated speech and writing, and they're afraid that they don't know the prescriptive rules well enough. In this book, we'll define grammar much more broadly. And in that sense, if people understand you when you speak, and you understand what you're reading here, then you do know English grammar.[1]

The grammar of a language is how that language works. It consists of the rules that let us make sense to each other in a sentence. Our grammar tells us, for example, how to change the structure of words to show how they function. It also tells us how to put words together in the right order, and how to make them agree with each other. We learn the basic grammar rules of our language as children, and we learn more as adults. That lets us invent grammatical sentences that have never been said before, and it allows us to know intuitively when a sentence is ungrammatical. We know without having to think about it, for instance, that "Call maybe me" isn't in natural English word order. But we all understand Carly Rae Jepsen when she sings "Call Me, Maybe," because the grammar makes sense to us.[2]

USAGE

Usage is the way that people actually speak or write, depending on the circumstances, the audience, the purpose, and the dialect. Since this is a book about expressing yourself in a formal style, it focuses on a particular type of usage: the linguistic choices that literate writers and speakers make in formal contexts.

NOUNS

"<u>Man</u> was made at the end of the <u>week</u>'s <u>work</u>, when <u>God</u> was tired."
   Mark Twain (pen name of Samuel Langhorne Clemens), American
   author and humorist (1835–1910), *Notebook,* 1903

"<u>I</u>'m not a <u>member</u> of any organized <u>party</u>—I am a <u>Democrat</u>."
   Will Rogers, American humorist, actor, and cowboy (1879–1935),
   quoted in P. J. O'Brien, *Will Rogers: Ambassador of Goodwill,
   Prince of Wit and Wisdom* (1935)

"You can lead a <u>man</u> to <u>Congress</u>, but you can't make him think."
   Attributed to Milton Berle, Emmy Award–winning American
   comedian and actor (1908–2002), quoted on The Official Site of
   Milton Berle

"<u>Cricket</u> is basically <u>baseball</u> on <u>Valium</u>."
   Robin Williams, award-winning American actor and comedian,
   quoted in "Robin Williams, Comedy Genius: His 50 Greatest
   Jokes," nypost.com, Aug. 12, 2014

The word *noun* derives from the Latin word for "name," and that's what a noun does: it names. A **noun** names or identifies a person, place, thing, idea, or quality:[3]

man	party
week	cricket
work	baseball
	member

Some nouns name particular people, places, or periods of time, or specific businesses, groups, organizations, products, and so forth. They're called **proper nouns**, and they're usually capitalized:

God
Democrat
Congress
Valium

PRONOUNS

"If <u>you</u> tell the truth, <u>you</u> don't have to remember anything."
Mark Twain, *Notebook,* 1894

"This is not an easy time for humorists because the government is far funnier than <u>we</u> are."
Art Buchwald, Pulitzer Prize–winning American humorist and writer (1925–2007), in a speech at an international meeting of satirists and cartoonists, 1987

"I'm over the hill, but <u>nobody</u> prepared <u>me</u> for what was going to be on the other side."
Jane Fonda, award-winning American actress, writer, fitness expert, activist, and model, quoted in *Mail on Sunday,* Jan. 6, 2008

Lady Gaga, on not wanting to be grounded in reality: "In <u>my</u> show <u>I</u> announce, 'People say Lady Gaga is a lie, and <u>they</u> are right.'"

Lady Gaga (stage name of Stefanie Joanne Angelina Germanotta), award-winning American singer-songwriter, businesswoman, and actress, quoted in Fiona Sturges, "Lady Gaga: How the World Went Crazy for the New Queen of Pop," independent.co.uk, May 16, 2009

"<u>We</u> used to lead the world in making things. But…<u>we</u> don't make <u>anything</u> anymore. <u>I</u> miss that. [But] Hollywood still makes things."

George Clooney, Academy Award–winning American actor, film director, producer, and screenwriter, quoted in Cal Fussman, "George Clooney's Thoughts for Today," esquire.com, Dec. 13. 2012

"If <u>you</u>'re trying to achieve, there will always be roadblocks. <u>I</u>'ve had them. <u>Everybody</u> has had them. But obstacles don't have to stop <u>you</u>."

Michael Jordan, American professional basketball player and team owner, quoted in Ben Frederick, "Michael Jordan: 10 Quotes from His Airness, the King," csmonitor.com, Feb. 19, 2013

The word *pronoun* derives from the Latin meaning "in place of a noun or a name," and a **pronoun** is a word that you can use instead of a noun.

Personal pronouns refer to specific people or things:

I, you, he, she, it, we, you, they
me, you, him, her, it, us, you, them
my, your, his, her, its, our, your, their

Some pronouns don't refer to anyone or anything specific. Since they're not definite about whom or what they refer to, they're called **indefinite pronouns**. They include *anybody, anyone, anything, each, everybody, nobody, none,* and *somebody:*

"<u>nobody</u> prepared me"
"we don't make <u>anything</u> anymore"
"<u>Everybody</u> has had them"

You can use a pronoun to replace a group of words that act like a noun.

"We all want to be in love and find <u>that person who is going to love us</u>."

> Will Smith, Grammy Award–winning American actor, rapper, and producer, quoted in Stella Papamichael, "Will Smith, Hitch," bbc. co.uk, Mar. 2005

In this passage, *her* or *him* could replace "that person who is going to love us."

ADJECTIVES

"To my mind, Judas Iscariot was nothing but a <u>low, mean, premature</u> congressman."

> Mark Twain, letter to the editor, *New York Daily Tribune,* Mar. 10, 1873

An **adjective** describes a noun or a pronoun:

"low, mean, premature"

VERBS

"No one can make you <u>feel</u> inferior without your consent."

> Eleanor Roosevelt, U.S. First Lady, 1933–1945, attributed in *Reader's Digest,* Sept. 1940

"I <u>think</u> crime <u>pays</u>. The hours <u>are</u> good; you <u>travel</u> a lot."

> Woody Allen, Academy Award–winning filmmaker, actor, comedian, and writer, in the 1969 film *Take the Money and Run*

"You <u>look</u> *mah*velous!"

> Billy Crystal, award-winning American actor, writer, comedian, producer, and director, as Fernando, telling guests that they look *marvelous,* on NBC-TV's *Saturday Night Live,* 1980s

"No one <u>washes</u> a rented car."

> Attributed to former Harvard president Lawrence Summers, but used widely in the 1990s

"A single Beyoncé video is capable of staggering the senses; the simultaneous release of 17 of them … was a lot to process."

> Jody Rosen, "The Woman on Top of the World," tmagazine.blogs. nytimes.com, June 3, 2014

Verbs describe actions and occurrences:

think
pays
travel
washes

Verbs also describe states of being and sensations:

feel
are
look
was
is

See the discussion of linking verbs on pages 81–84.

ADVERBS

"Bessie, my dear … you are <u>disgustingly</u> ugly. But tomorrow I shall be sober and you will still be <u>disgustingly</u> ugly."

> Winston Churchill, British prime minister (1874–1965), to Bessie Braddock, MP, who accused him of being "disgustingly drunk," 1946

"Writing is <u>very</u> pleasurable, <u>very</u> seductive, and <u>very</u> therapeutic."

> Woody Allen, quoted in Michiko Kakutani, "Woody Allen, The Art of Humor, No. 1," *Paris Review,* Fall 1995

"If a man watches three games of football in a row, he should be declared <u>legally</u> dead."

> Attributed to Erma Bombeck, American humorist, columnist, and author (1927–1996), in A. J. Maikovich and M. Brown, eds., *Sports Quotations* (2000)

"I am an actor. But you can't take things <u>too</u> seriously."
> Scarlett Johansson, BAFTA- and Tony Award–winning American
> actress, model, and singer, quoted in star-magazine.co.uk, June 7, 2011

"People will say a movie bombed at the box office, but I couldn't
care <u>less</u>."
> Johnny Depp, Golden Globe Award–winning American actor, film
> producer, and musician, quoted in "'I Don't Want My Kids to
> Google Me and Read Lies and Rumours," mirror.co.uk, May 9, 2012

About Robin Williams: "Mr. Williams was one of the most
<u>explosively</u>, <u>exhaustingly</u>, <u>prodigiously</u> verbal comedians who
<u>ever</u> lived."
> A. O. Scott, "Robin Williams, an Improvisational Genius, Forever
> Present in the Moment," nytimes.com, Aug. 11, 2014

Also about Robin Williams: "He made us laugh—<u>hard</u>, every
time you saw him."
> Billy Crystal, Emmy Awards, Los Angeles, Aug. 25, 2014

Adverbs modify verbs, as the word *adverbs* suggests:

"care <u>less</u>"
"<u>ever</u> lived"
"laugh—<u>hard</u>"

Adverbs also modify adjectives:

"<u>disgustingly</u> ugly"
"<u>very</u> pleasurable, <u>very</u> seductive, and <u>very</u> therapeutic"
"<u>legally</u> dead"
"<u>explosively</u>, <u>exhaustingly</u>, <u>prodigiously</u> verbal"

And adverbs modify other adverbs:

"<u>too</u> seriously"

Adverbs can be used to negate:

"Happiness <u>never</u> decreases by being shared."

> Buddha, spiritual leader on whose teachings Buddhism is based (ca. 6th–4th century BC), quoted in *The Teachings of Buddha,* ch. 1, Bukkyo Dendo Kyokai (2005)

"I have <u>never</u> been lost, but I will admit to being confused for several weeks."

> Daniel Boone, American frontiersman, pioneer, soldier, politician, and folk hero, quoted in Rick Burke, *Daniel Boone* (2003)

"My job is <u>not</u> to be skinny.... My job is to act."

> Jennifer Lawrence, Academy Award–winning American actress, quoted in Lynn Hirschberg, "The Brave Ones," *W Magazine,* Sept. 2010

Adverbs also can modify phrases, clauses, or whole sentences. They can, for example, express a speaker's attitude, or the likelihood or truth of an event:

"I believe there is something out there watching us. <u>Unfortunately</u>, it's the government."

> Attributed to Woody Allen

"With age, you see people fail more. You see yourself fail more. How do you keep that fearlessness of a kid? You keep going.... <u>Luckily</u>, I'm not afraid to make a fool of myself."

> Hugh Jackman, award-winning Australian actor and producer, quoted in Mike Zimmerman, "The Hugh Jackman Workout: The X Factor," menshealth.com, June 2006

"<u>Maybe</u> my fairy tale has a different ending than I dreamed it would. But that's OK."

> Kim Kardashian, American TV and social media celebrity, fashion designer, model, and actress, quoted in "Kim Kardashian's Guide to Love," huffingtonpost.com, Feb. 10, 2014

"I have flabby thighs, but <u>fortunately</u> my stomach covers them."

> Joan Rivers, Emmy Award–winning American comedian, actress, writer, TV host, and producer (1933–2014), attributed on healthline.com, Sept. 5, 2014

Adverbs usually end in *-ly*, but some don't, including *very* and *hard* in the passages above.

PREPOSITIONS

A preposition shows a relationship between other words in a sentence.

Many prepositions indicate **position or direction**. One way to remember them is to fill in the blank in this passage:

Iron Man flew _____ the clouds.

How many prepositions can you think of to complete the sentence?

Here are several possibilities: *above, across, against, along (with), among, around, at, behind, below, beneath, beside, between, beyond, by, from, in, inside (of), into, near, next to, off of, on, onto, on top of, out (from), out of, outside, over, past, through, to, toward, under, underneath, up, upon, with,* and *within.*

Prepositions also relate to **time.** They include *about, after, before, during, following, since, throughout, till,* and *until.*

Prepositions can indicate many other kinds of relationships as well: *for* indicates support, for example, while *against* shows opposition and *with* denotes accompaniment.

Other prepositions that show relationships include *according to, as, as for, aside from, because of, concerning, despite, except, except for, in addition to, in front of, in spite of, instead of, like, of, on account of, plus, regarding, unlike,* and *without.*

PREPOSITIONAL PHRASES

Prepositions appear in **prepositional phrases.** A **phrase** is a small group of related words that lacks a **subject**, a **verb**, or both.

The **subject** either does something or is described or discussed in a sentence:

"One morning I shot an elephant <u>in my pajamas</u>. How he got <u>in my pajamas</u>, I don't know."

> Groucho Marx, Academy Award–winning American comedian, film and TV star, and writer (1890–1977), in the 1930 film *Animal Crackers*

In Groucho's quotation, *I* is the subject of the first sentence because that person did something: he shot an elephant.

He (the elephant) is a subject in the second sentence, because he, too, did something: he got into Groucho's pajamas.

The words *in my pajamas* form a phrase. Since it includes the preposition *in,* it's a **prepositional phrase**.

Prepositional phrases can appear anywhere in a sentence. Here are a few at the start of sentences:

"<u>At fifty</u>, everyone has the face he deserves."

> George Orwell, English writer, journalist, and critic (1903–1950), notebook, Apr. 17, 1949

"<u>In the future</u>, everybody will be world famous for 15 minutes."

> Andy Warhol, American artist (1928–1987), quoted in the catalogue for his exhibit in a museum in Stockholm, 1968

Here's one in the middle of a sentence:

"A sore-faced baby, <u>with a neglected nose</u>, cannot be conscientiously regarded as a thing of beauty."

> Mark Twain, "Answers to Correspondents" (1865), quoted in *Early Tales and Sketches: 1864–1865* (1981)

These prepositional phrases appear at or near the end of sentences:

"I kept putting my wife <u>underneath a pedestal</u>."

> Woody Allen, quoted in "Woody Allen: Rabbit Running," time. com, July 3, 1972

"I have come <u>to the conclusion</u> there is an afterlife."
"An afterlife?"
"Right. I think life goes on <u>after the children are grown</u>."

> Erma Bombeck, *The Grass Is Always Greener over the Septic Tank,* ch. 10 (1976)

"She was the people's princess, and that is how she will remain <u>in our hearts</u> and <u>in our memories</u> forever."
> British prime minister Tony Blair, speaking of Lady Diana, Aug. 31, 1997

George Clooney, referring to his role as Batman in the 1997 film *Batman and Robin:* "I'm not going to do any more films <u>in rubber suits</u>."
> Quoted in Linda Holmes, "George Clooney on Acting, Fame, and Putting Down Your Cellphone Camera," npr.org, Feb. 9, 2012

Many words that are used as prepositions also can be used as adverbs, depending on the context. For example, *up* is a preposition in *They climbed up Mount Everest.* But it's an adverb in *They woke up,* since it's part of the phrase *woke up.*

A challenge for you: how many prepositional phrases are in the sentence below?

Lady Gaga said in an interview with Howard Stern on July 18, 2011, that she lives in Brooklyn, in a tiny $1100-a-month apartment.
> "Lady Gaga Opens Up to Howard Stern," huffingtonpost.com, July 19, 2011

The answer is five: "in an interview," "with Howard Stern," "on July 18, 2011," "in Brooklyn," and "in a tiny $1100-a-month apartment."

The word that the preposition connects a noun or pronoun to is called the **object of the preposition**. If the object of a preposition is a personal pronoun, it should be *me, you, him, her, it, us,* or *them:*

"If that plane leaves the ground and you're not <u>with him</u>, you'll regret it."
> Humphrey Bogart, American actor (1899–1957), in the 1942 film *Casablanca*

"Winning an Oscar is an honor, but, <u>between you and me</u>, it does not make things easier."

Robin Williams, interview in "Não Me Contem Piadas,"
Veja (Brazilian magazine), Nov. 11, 1998, translated in
Anderson Antunes, "'Don't Tell Me Jokes,'" forbes.com,
Aug. 12, 2014

See the lesson on "I or Me" on pages 94–103.

CLAUSES

A **clause** is a unit of words that has a subject and a verb.

A **main clause** makes a complete statement and can stand as a sentence by itself. Since it can exist independently, it's also known as an **independent clause**. Often a sentence consists of a single **main clause**, such as these two by Mark Twain:

"Clothes make the man. Naked people have little or no influence in society."

Mark Twain, quoted in *More Maxims of Mark,* ed. Merle Johnson (1927)

And here's a short but sweet one by Lady Gaga:

"I love glamor."

Lady Gaga, in John Dingwall, "Lady Gaga Used Tough Times as Inspiration for Her New Album," *Daily Record* (Scotland), Nov. 27, 2009

MOOD

The grammatical term *mood* is a different word from the *mood* that describes how you're feeling. It's actually a variant of *mode,* which refers to the manner in which something is done or expressed. And yet these two words overlap in meaning. Grammatical mood is a verb form that indicates your attitude. It tells whether your sentence expresses a fact, a wish, uncertainty, a command, etc. That can reflect your emotional mood, which may be matter-of-fact, wishful, doubtful, or demanding.[4]

We use the **indicative mood to** indicate a fact or an opinion, as in this passage by Woody Allen:

> "The message is, God is love, and you should lay off fatty foods."
> Woody Allen, quoted in *Time* magazine, July 3, 1972

Another grammatical mood is the **imperative**, which we use to give commands or exhortations, and to make requests:

> "Always obey your parents, when they are present."
> Mark Twain, "Advice to Youth," 1882

> "When in doubt, tell the truth."
> Mark Twain , *Following the Equator,* ch. 2 (1897)

> "Never give a sucker an even break."
> Popularized by W. C. Fields, American comedian, actor, juggler, and writer (1880–1946), in the 1923 play *Poppy*

> "If at first you don't succeed, try, try again. Then quit. There's no use being a damn fool about it."
> W. C. Fields, quoted in *Reader's Digest,* Sept. 1949

> "When you['ve] got it, flaunt it!"
> Zero Mostel, American actor and comedian (1915–1977), in Mel Brooks's 1967 film, *The Producers*

> "Eat my shorts!"
> Bart Simpson, on Matt Groening's TV series *The Simpsons,* Jan. 14, 1990

> "Don't make me come down there!"—God
> Sign in front of Cornerstone Christian Church, quoted in "Funny Church Signs," beliefnet.com

The **subjunctive mood** conveys a wish or a desire, or it states hypothetical or contrary-to-fact conditions. You also can use it to suggest, urge, or require something. See "If I Were a Rich Man" on pages 103–11.

CHAPTER 3

Tricky Words, Usage, and Grammar

A or AN

"Suppose you were <u>an idiot</u>. And suppose you were <u>a member</u> of Congress. But I repeat myself."[1]

    Mark Twain, quoted in Albert B. Paine, *Mark Twain: A Biography* (1912)

"If <u>a man</u> could be crossed with <u>a cat</u> it would improve the man, but it would deteriorate the cat."

    Mark Twain, *Notebook*, 1894

"I want...people in the universe, my fans and otherwise, to essentially use me as <u>an escape</u>....I am the jester to the kingdom. I am the route *out*."

    Lady Gaga, quoted in Jonathan Van Meter, "Lady Gaga, Our Lady of Pop," *Vogue,* Mar. 2011

Jack Nicholson, breaking in on <u>an interview</u> with Jennifer Lawrence: "You look like <u>an old</u> girlfriend of mine."
Lawrence: "Oh really? Do I look like <u>a new</u> girlfriend?"

    Jack Nicholson is an Academy Award– and Golden Globe Award–winning American actor, director, producer, and writer; this interview aired on ABC-TV, Feb. 24, 2013

Let's start this book with one of the easiest lessons in it. If you're a native English-speaker, you almost always know when to use *a* or *an* without thinking about it. If you're not, here's a general rule. It's pretty simple, except for several words that begin with *h:*

Use *a* before words beginning with a consonant sound.

Use *an* before words beginning with a vowel sound.[2]

<u>a</u> member of Congress	<u>an</u> idiot
<u>a</u> man	<u>an</u> escape
<u>a</u> cat	<u>an</u> interview

Remember, it's the first <u>sound</u> (not the first letter) of the next word that matters. For example, the word *unicorn* begins with the vowel *u* but is pronounced with a *y-* sound in this context (*YOU-ni-corn*). So we say *a unicorn*. We also say <u>an</u> *H-bomb, an MBA, an NCAA record,* and *a united front.*

✳ A *or* An *Before Words That Start With* H-

<u>an</u> heir
<u>an</u> honor
<u>an</u> hour

Languages are messy, and much of the confusion about whether to say *a* or *an* before words that begin with *h* is a result of the messy way that English developed over time. Words like *honor, heir,* and *hour* came into English from medieval French with the *h* silent. In fact, Middle English scribes often wrote those words without an *h*. Other words, including *hereditary,* were borrowed directly from Latin with the *h* pronounced. And some, like *historian,* had a silent *h* that people later started to pronounce.

Speakers commonly said *an* before words beginning with *h* when the first syllable was unstressed. By the late nineteenth century, though, educated people generally pronounced the *h* in those words, and began to write *a* before them. But the truth is that even today many people, including some very famous historians, still say *an historian* and *an historic(al)*. Some people also say *an* before *habitual, hereditary, heroic, hotel, hysterical,* and a few other words beginning with *h-*.

So where does that leave us? Several language critics and usage guides insist that we should say *a historian.* Some of them call *an historian* a vestigial or pedantic usage, or a stylistic oddity with no phonetic justification.

My advice is that you can't go wrong saying *a historian, a historic(al), etc.*

In American English, *herb* is pronounced *erb,* so Americans say "an herb." The British pronounce the *h* in *herb,* so the right form for them is "a herb." *Herbal* has traditionally been pronounced with the *h-* sound, but most Americans now say *erbal.* So "an herbal tea" is correct for them. But speakers who pronounce the *h* in *herbicide* should say "a herbicide."

Which version of the sentence below is correct?

(A) An X-Man is a superhero mutant who is part of a group founded by Professor Charles Francis Xavier.
(B) A X-Man is a superhero mutant who is part of a group founded by Professor Charles Francis Xavier.

Since we pronounce the letter *x* as *ex,* it begins with a vowel sound. So precede "X-Man" with *an,* as in version A.

A and *an* go so naturally with the words that follow them that the *n-* sound sometimes has jumped from one to the other. A *nickname,* for example, should be an *ickname.* In early English it was *an eke-name* (an "additional name"). In everyday speech over time, though, the *-n* from *an* became attached to the phrase that came after it. Our word *umpire* is another case. It was originally *a noumpere,* but the *n* attached to the *a* that preceded it. So *a noumpire* became *an umpire.*

AIN'T

"If it <u>ain't</u> broke, don't fix it."
> Bert Lance, director of the Office of Management and Budget
> under President Jimmy Carter (1931–2013), quoted in *Nation's
> Business,* May 27, 1977 (*OED*)[3]

"The future <u>ain't</u> what it used to be."
> Yogi Berra, American major league baseball catcher and manager,
> in *The Yogi Book* (1998)

Don't use *ain't* in formal speech and writing. It's considered a classic example of substandard usage.

The word *ain't* first appeared in writing in the early eighteenth century, and educated speakers had used an earlier form of the word even before that. But since the nineteenth century, *ain't* has been denounced as an illiterate vulgarism. *Webster's Third New International Dictionary* (1961) was widely mocked because it said that many "cultivated" American speakers say *ain't,* especially in the phrase *ain't I* ("am I not?"). *The Chicago Daily News,* for example, reviewed that dictionary under the sarcastic headline "Good English Ain't What We Thought."[4] Many people still say *ain't* in conversation, though.[5] It flourishes in Cockney British usage and in Black English in the United States. *Ain't* also is common in song titles and lyrics. It appears in folk expressions, catchphrases, and much informal speech. People sometimes use the word humorously, playfully, or for effect, but otherwise *ain't* isn't appropriate in Standard English.

ALLUDE, ALLUSION

✳ *Allude*

> On the influence of *Star Wars:* "People can't offhandedly <u>allude</u>
> to the Bible, or Milton, or Shakespeare anymore with certainty
> that everyone's going to know what we're talking about, but

everybody instantly understands 'these aren't the droids you're looking for'…or 'a great disturbance in the Force.'"

> Douglas Wolk, "What Star Wars Means to Me," time.com, Aug. 11, 2010

In his book *Mickey and Willie,* sports journalist Allen Barra "continually <u>alludes</u> to the similarities of these Hall of Fame centerfielders."

> *Kirkus Reviews,* Feb. 15, 2013

The phrase "loss of innocence" <u>alludes</u> to the Garden of Eden story in Genesis.

✳ *Allusion*

"Brevity is the soul of lingerie" was Dorothy Parker's playful <u>allusion</u> to Shakespeare's line "brevity is the soul of wit" in *Hamlet* (act 2, sc. 2).

> Dorothy Parker, American poet, critic, and satirist, in *Vogue,* 1916, quoted by Alexander Woollcott, *While Rome Burns* (1934)

Quarterback Tim Tebow threw for exactly 316 yards in the Denver Broncos' upset victory in the AFC wildcard game in 2012. Some people took that to be a mystical <u>allusion</u> to John 3:16, a biblical verse that has special meaning to the evangelical Tebow.

"May the odds be ever in your favor" is an <u>allusion</u> to the *Hunger Games.*

How is an *allusion* different from any other kind of reference? The short answer is that it's a reference that you make indirectly or in passing. *Allude* comes from the Latin for "play with, touch lightly upon." In English, it once referred to playful punning. Though it no longer has that meaning, *allude* still has the sense of touching lightly on something:

To *allude* is to hint at or suggest, or to mention indirectly.

That's the strict definition that language critics gave these words in the nineteenth century, and many usage handbooks still adhere to it. In practice, though, there's often ambiguity about how direct or indirect a reference is when someone speaks of it as an *allusion*.

To *allude to* also can have the sense of mentioning something in passing.

***Allusion* is the noun form.**

ALTERNATE or ALTERNATIVE

✳ *Alternate*

"I never had the courage to talk across a long, narrow room. . . . If I attempt to talk across a room I find myself turning this way and that, and thus at <u>alternate</u> periods I have part of the audience behind me. You ought never to have any part of the audience behind you; you never can tell what they are going to do."

Mark Twain, "Courage," speech in New York City, Apr. 18, 1908

His children stay with him on <u>alternate</u> weekends and some holidays.

✳ *Alternative*

"Men and women do behave wisely, once all other <u>alternatives</u> have been exhausted."

Israeli foreign minister Abba Eban (1915–2002), quoted in *Vogue*, Aug. 1, 1967

"Most allopathic doctors think practitioners of <u>alternative</u> medicine are all quacks. They're not."

Dr. Mehmet Oz, Turkish American surgeon, author, and TV personality, quoted in Jane E. Brody and Denise Grady, *The New York Times Guide to Alternative Health* (2001)

If you're not sure which of these words to use, that's easy to understand, because more and more, *alternate* is replacing *alternative* as an adjective, especially in American English. The traditional difference is that *alternate* refers to something that alternates, in the sense that it happens or appears by turns. *Alternative,* by contrast, refers to having a choice. But since the 1940s, Americans have used the word *alternate* to refer to a choice. It's become so common that most Americans probably don't think twice about it. Book clubs, for example, offer *alternate* selections, and Americans often speak of taking an *alternate* route when they drive.[6]

Alternate as an adjective means "one after the other, alternating in a regular pattern."

at <u>alternate</u> periods

Alternate also can mean "every other, every second (one)."

on alternate weekends

In North America, *alternate* is often used in the sense of *alternative*:

<u>alternate</u> universes

Other examples include an *alternate route,* an *alternate school,* an *alternate reality game,* and *alternate technologies.*

The British are more likely to say *alternative* in contexts like these.

As a noun, an *alternate* is someone who alternates with somebody else in doing something.

In North American English, an *alternate* also can be a substitute or reserve for someone else:

"Being snubbed for the Pro Bowl didn't really bother veteran strong safety Bernard Pollard. Named as a first <u>alternate</u>, Pollard could still be added to the AFC Pro Bowl squad if another player bows out due to injury or other reasons."

Aaron Wilson, "Bernard Pollard, Named First <u>Alternate</u> to Pro
Bowl, Not Bothered by Snub," baltimoresun.com, Dec. 27, 2012

Alternative comes from the Latin for "the other of two," so the traditional view is that an *alternative* is one of only two possibilities. But the English word has referred to choices between three or more things for more than 150 years, and most usage guides accept this broader meaning.[7]

As an adjective, *alternative* refers to a choice between two or more things.

Since the early 1960s, *alternative* also has been used to describe something that you prefer to something else, or that you at least accept as a choice:

alternative energy sources
alternative medicine
alternative rock

As a noun, too, an *alternative* is a possible choice between two or more things.

once they have exhausted all other <u>alternatives</u>

Keep in mind that the word *alternative* may suggest an obligation to make a choice. If someone tells you that you have two alternatives, for example, you might feel obliged to choose one. Also, saying that something is one *alternative* may imply that it's a good choice, or at least that it's good enough.

Which version of the sentence below is correct?

(A) Because of <u>alternate</u>-side parking laws in Manhattan, I have to move my car every Tuesday and Thursday morning.
(B) Because of <u>alternative</u>-side parking laws in Manhattan, I have to move my car every Tuesday and Thursday morning.

Alternate-side parking rules require drivers to keep one side of many streets clear for cleaning at certain times on alternating days. I used to park overnight on or near East 95th Street in Manhattan, and two days a week I had to move my car by 7:00 a.m. and hope to find another spot. I hated it. Version A is correct.

AMONGST

"Reality is the leading cause of stress <u>amongst</u> those in touch with it."

> Jane Wagner, playwright, actress, and writer for Lily Tomlin, in *The Search for Signs of Intelligent Life in the Universe,* pt. 1 (1987)

Every now and then, one of my students uses the word *amongst* in a paper. Sometimes one of them even throws in *amidst* or *whilst.* These forms ending in *-st* may seem archaic and quaint to Americans, who are much more likely to say *among, amid,* and *while.* But **most commentators consider both forms to be grammatically correct.** And one word of this kind has turned out to be a winner on both sides of the Atlantic today: *against.*[8]

AMOUNT or NUMBER

✳ *Amount*

"Hugs can do a great <u>amount</u> of good—especially for children."

> Diana, Princess of Wales (1961–1997), quoted in *Diana Remembered, 1961–1997* (1997)

"I don't feel comfortable taking my clothes off. . . . I wouldn't wear tiny <u>amounts</u> of clothing in my real life, so I don't think it's necessary to wear that stuff in photo shoots."

> Taylor Swift, award-winning America singer-songwriter, quoted in usmagazine.com, Apr. 11, 2011

"My father ran for Congress in 2004, and I got a sense that there is no way to achieve much success without a certain <u>amount</u> of compromise."

George Clooney, quoted in "10 Questions for George Clooney," time.com, Oct. 24, 2011

"Every day, three times per *second*, we produce the equivalent of the <u>amount</u> of data that the Library of Congress has in its entire print collection, right? But most of it is like cat videos on YouTube or 13-year-olds exchanging text messages about the next *Twilight* movie."

Nate Silver, American statistician, elections analyst, and writer, quoted in John Heilpern, "Silver Streak," vanityfair.com, Nov. 2012

"It's amazing that the <u>amount</u> of news that happens in the world every day always just exactly fits the newspaper."

Jerry Seinfeld, award-winning American comedian, actor, writer, and TV and film producer, quoted in "What's the Deal with…: 15 Jokes from Jerry Seinfeld on His Birthday," wcbsfm.cbslocal.com, Apr. 29, 2013

"Athletes and musicians make astronomical <u>amounts</u> of money…. Shouldn't we all take less and pass some of that money on to others? Think about firefighters, teachers, and policemen. We should celebrate people that are… trying to make this world a better place."

Kid Rock, American musician, music producer, and actor, quoted in Andy Greene, "Kid Rock on his $20 Tour and 'Dumbass Republicans,'" rollingstone.com, Apr. 10, 2013

✳ *Number*

In a "grain of salt there are about… 10 million billion atoms…. Now, is this number more or less than the <u>number</u> of things which the brain can know?"

Carl Sagan, award-winning American astronomer, cosmologist, astrophysicist, and writer (1934–1996), in *Brokaw's Brain: The Romance of Science* (1979)

"New York now leads the world's great cities in the <u>number</u> of people around whom you shouldn't make a sudden move."

Award-winning American TV host David Letterman, *Late Night with David Letterman,* CBS, Feb. 9, 1984

"A lot of the younger Indian generation are either IT geniuses or doctors. The <u>number</u> of doctors I've seen in LA who are Indian is just crazy."

> Freida Pinto, award-winning Indian actress and model, quoted in "Freida Pinto's Love 'Understanding,'" timesofindia.com, Aug. 1, 2011

"I don't pay attention to the <u>number</u> of birthdays. It's weird when I say I'm 53. It's just crazy that I'm 53. I think I'm very immature. I feel like a kid."

> Ellen DeGeneres, award-winning American comedian, TV host, and actress, quoted in David Hochman, "Ellen DeGeneres: Nice Girls Finish First," goodhousekeeping.com, Oct. 2011

Amount **refers to things that can't be counted.** It means "quantity." Use it with singular nouns that you think of as a mass. These nouns often are abstractions, but not always.

a great <u>amount</u> of good
tiny <u>amounts</u> of clothing
a certain <u>amount</u> of compromise
astronomical <u>amounts</u> of money

Say *number* **to refer to people or things that can be counted individually. These nouns are plural.**

the <u>number</u> of things
the <u>number</u> of people
the <u>number</u> of doctors
the <u>number</u> of birthdays

People increasingly are saying *amount* when they think of countable things as an aggregate or collection ("a large <u>amount</u> of jelly beans," "a huge <u>amount</u> of calories," etc.). According to the traditional rule, they should say *number* in these cases. Some usage guides complain about this use of *amount* but acknowledge that it's becoming pervasive. *Merriam-Webster's Dictionary of English Usage* sees no reason to condemn it.

Here's an illustration of, first, the standard use of the word *amount,* then its controversial use in a single quotation by the inimitable Louis C.K.:

> "I'm still editing Season 3. There's still a tremendous amount of work to do. I have a crazy amount of different jobs, so the way I manage that is to not do more than one at a time."
>
> Louis C.K., Emmy Award– and Grammy Award–winning American comedian, screenwriter, actor, director, producer, and film editor, quoted in Dave Itzkoff, "Emmy Nominees: Louis C.K.," nytimes.com, July 19, 2012

I suggest that, in formal speech and writing, you follow the traditional rule distinguishing between *amount* and *number*. It's a useful distinction, and many traditionalists insist on maintaining it.

So say "the amount of gratitude," meaning the quantity of it, which can't be counted or put in numbers. But say "the number of things to be grateful for," which you can count.

Say "the amount of success" but "the number of victories."

Which word do we use with *money*? When we speak of "counting your money," that's really a figure of speech. You can count dollars, quarters, dimes, euros, liras, etc. But the word *money* is a singular noun and an abstract concept that can't be counted in individual units. So we say "the amount of money," not "the number of money."

Some nouns take *amount* when they are singular but *number* when they are plural and can be counted.

Say "the amount of success" but "the number of successes."

Which version of the sentence below is correct?

(A) An amazing number of fans waited for hours for the Monster Ball concert.

(B) An amazing amount of fans waited for hours for the Monster Ball concert.

Since the fans can be counted, the right choice is *number*, as in version A.

AND/OR

This construction first appeared in the middle of the nineteenth century in a maritime shipping contract, and it wasn't long until two parties went to court because they disagreed about what it meant in a contract. *And/or* is usually said to be restricted to legal and business writing. It sometimes does appear in general contexts, though, and since the 1920s, stylists have attacked it as ugly and possibly ambiguous. If *and/or* refers to only two people or things, the meaning is usually clear. Things can get confusing, though, if three or more are involved. This construction can be economical, but many purists will object to it. I do when students use it in papers. **So unless you're writing a business or a legal document, I suggest that you don't say *and/or* in formal contexts. Instead, use the construction *A or B, or both*:**

I'm in the mood for <u>chocolate or vanilla ice cream, or both</u>.

ANXIOUS

"Love is a thing full of <u>anxious</u> fears."
    Ovid, *Heroides*, I, 12 (first century B.C.)

"Recently I was directing an episode of *Glee* and I lost my cell phone—and I didn't have time to buy a new one for three weeks. Well, the first two days I was <u>anxious</u> as hell, suffered the delirium tremens, didn't think I could make it through, etc. Then something kind of curious happened—I began to feel great, really great."
    Eric Stoltz, award-winning American actor, director, and producer, quoted in guardian.co.uk, Jan. 14, 2011

"I get <u>anxious</u>—[I feel] that lovely Jewish guilt that comes with ancestry."

Maya Rudolph, America actress and comedian, quoted in Dave Itzkoff, "Juggling a Comedy Series About Juggling Life's Tasks," nytimes.com, Sept. 9, 2011

"A dog makes [your] feelings tangible by mirroring them back to you. 'The dog is imitating the energy that is in your bubble.... If you feel <u>anxious</u>, the dog becomes <u>anxious</u> with you.'"

Cesar Millan, Mexican American dog trainer known as the "Dog Whisperer," quoted in Lisa Yeung, "Cesar Millan Teaches Me How to Trust My Instincts," huffingtonpost.ca, Nov. 26, 2012

Anxious comes from a Latin word meaning "to choke, squeeze, strangle, inflict pain." You have to admit, that's a pretty disturbing and graphic image of what anxiety feels like. The word is related to *anguish* and to its German cousin *angst*.

Anxious came into English in the seventeenth century, meaning "troubled, distressed." The quotations above illustrate that meaning of the word.

A little over a hundred years later, *anxious* took on a new meaning: "eager, full of desire," as in the phrase *anxious to please*. This may seem to be a very far cry from the original meaning of the word *anxious* and its linguistic ancestry in "painful distress." Since the early twentieth century, a number of American usage books have rejected this new meaning of *anxious*. Some complain that it obscures the sense of stress and anxiety in the earlier meaning of the word. In fact, though, this use of *anxious* often blends worry with eagerness.

Careful speakers, including at least one prime minister and a queen of England, have used the word *anxious* in its more recent sense. Here are some examples:

"Something unpleasant is coming when men are <u>anxious</u> to tell the truth."

Benjamin Disraeli, English politician, writer, wit, and prime minister, *The Young Duke* (1831)

"The Queen is most <u>anxious</u> to enlist everyone who can speak or write to join in checking this mad, wicked folly of 'Woman's

Rights,' with all its attendant horrors, on which her poor, feeble sex is bent, forgetting every sense of womanly feeling and propriety."
     Queen Victoria, correspondence, May 29, 1870

"We are always more <u>anxious</u> to be distinguished for a talent which we do not possess than to be praised for the fifteen which we do possess."
     Mark Twain, *The Autobiography of Mark Twain*, vol. 1 (2010)

"A woman who is very <u>anxious</u> to get children always reads 'storks' for 'stocks.'"
     Sigmund Freud, Austrian father of psychoanalysis (1856–1939), *The Psychopathology of Everyday Life* (1904)

"I try to stay fit and eat healthily, but I'm not <u>anxious</u> to starve myself and become unnaturally thin....I don't find that look attractive [in] women."
     Scarlett Johansson, quoted in heraldsun.com, Sept. 19, 2006

Both of these meanings of *anxious* are well established. To avoid ambiguity in formal writing, though, **I suggest that you say *anxious* when the situation you're describing mainly involves worry or stress, and *eager* to describe happy anticipation and enthusiasm.**

AS or LIKE

✻ *As*

<u>As</u> You <u>Like</u> It.
     Shakespearean comedy (1599–1600)

"If the man doesn't believe <u>as we do</u>, we say he is a crank, and that settles it. I mean it does nowadays, because now we can't burn him."
     Mark Twain, *Following the Equator* (1897)

"Then Oz got into the basket and said to all the people in a loud voice: 'I am going away to make a visit. While I am gone the Scarecrow will rule over you. I command you to obey him <u>as you would</u> me.'"

> L. Frank Baum, American writer (1856–1919), *The Wonderful Wizard of Oz* (1900)

"They cry a lot during the show, <u>as do I</u>."

> Lady Gaga, speaking of her fans, on *The Ellen DeGeneres Show,* Apr. 28, 2011

Of Taylor Swift: "<u>As</u> she <u>puts</u> it, 'I think I am smart unless I am really, really in love, and then I am ridiculously stupid.'"

> Jonathan Van Meter, "Taylor Swift: The Single Life," vogue.com, Jan. 2012

The little word *as* is one of the most frequently used words in our language, but are you always sure whether to use it or to say *like* instead?

Use *as* when it is followed by a clause (a group of words including a subject and a verb). The passages at the top of this lesson illustrate this: in each, *as* is followed by a subject and a verb:

As You Like It
as we do
as you would
as do I
as she puts it

✳ *Like*

"Nothing <u>helps</u> scenery <u>like ham and eggs</u>."

> Mark Twain, *Roughing It* (1872)

"Women <u>are like teabags</u>: you never know how strong they are until they get into hot water."

> Eleanor Roosevelt, attributed by Hillary Clinton, quoted in *New York Times Magazine,* Aug. 26, 2007

"Float like a butterfly, sting like a bee."

> Muhammad Ali, American three-time heavyweight boxing champion, quoted in George Edward Sullivan, *The Story of Cassius Clay* (1964)

Hemingway "uses those short, sharp words just like hooks and uppercuts. You always know what he's saying because he always says it very clearly."

> Mike Tyson, American heavyweight boxing champion, who read Hemingway while in prison, quoted in *Independent on Sunday,* Feb. 13, 1994

"Man! I Feel Like a Woman!"

> Title of Shania Twain's 1999 hit song, written with Mutt Lange

"I always acted like a star long before I was one."

> Madonna, award-winning American singer-songwriter, actress, author, and director, quoted in Andrew Morton, *Madonna* (2002)

"Resentment is like drinking poison and waiting for the other person to die."

> Carrie Fisher, American actress, writer, and performance artist, in *Wishful Drinking* (2008), citing an old proverb

"I'm like Tinker Bell.... You know how she dies if you don't clap for her?... Scream for me!"

> Lady Gaga, quoted in Christine Spines, "Lady Gaga Wants You," *Cosmopolitan,* Apr. 2010

"Do I feel like a loser sometimes? Yes, of course I do. We all feel like losers sometimes."

> Lady Gaga, on *The Ellen DeGeneres Show,* Apr. 28, 2011

Many women in New York are getting nose jobs to make themselves look like Kate Middleton.

Use *like* after a verb when it's followed by a noun or a pronoun but not by another verb. In other words, use *like* when what comes next isn't a clause.

are like teabags
float like a butterfly, sting like a bee
feel like a woman
acted like a star

Some common idioms use *like* in this way, including:

drinks like a fish
fits like a glove
looks like a million dollars
runs like the wind
selling like hotcakes
sings like an angel

That's the rule in formal English. Since the fourteenth century, though, writers have followed *like* with a clause. Chaucer did it. Shakespeare did, too, though not often. That usage became more common in the nineteenth century and is widespread today. *The New Yorker,* for example, printed it in an article that described a legendary disk jockey: "Murray the K tells it like it really is" (even though the rule calls for "as it really is").[9] The colloquial expression "tell it like it is" was popular in the 1960s and later, as we aging fans of Murray the K remember.

There's no clear linguistic reason for the rule requiring *as* before a clause, and it's not certain who introduced it, or when. But for more than a century language critics and usage guides have strongly condemned using *like* in that context, and very many traditionalists still do, including me. Over 90 percent of the *Harper Dictionary* Usage Panel, for example, objected to that usage in writing, and about 80 percent rejected it even in conversational speech. Panel member Isaac Asimov joked that he wouldn't accept it until someone puts on a version of Shakespeare's *As You Like It* and calls it *Like You Like It.*[10] Still, *like* before a clause is very widely used in formal as well as informal contexts.

You can use *like* within a phrase set off by commas, even when there's no verb in front of it in the phrase:

"You've got to find what you love. And that is as true for your work as it is for your lovers.... Don't settle. As with all matters of the heart, you'll know it when you find it. And, <u>like any great relationship</u>, it just gets better and better."

>   Steve Jobs, American pioneer of the personal computer revolution, co-founder, chairman, and CEO of Apple, Inc. (1955–2011), in commencement address at Stanford, June 12, 2005

Like can mean "such as, for example":[11]

"I have been looking at your report card & find it remarkable. Why, I never was marked up 100 in my life, when I was a boy, except for one or two commonplace things, <u>like Good Spelling & Troublesomeness</u>. You seem to be tolerably slim in the matter of History (5), but you make up for it in other things."

>   Mark Twain, letter to a young student, Mar. 20, 1880

"Poems are made by fools <u>like me</u>,
But only God can make a tree."

>   Joyce Kilmer, American poet (1886–1918), "Trees" (1914)

But be careful to avoid ambiguity. _There aren't many great actors <u>like Robert De Niro</u>_, for example, could mean either "resembling Robert De Niro" or "such as Robert De Niro." **If there can be any doubt about your meaning, it's a good idea to say _such as_ instead.**

Like is gaining ground in some contexts where the standard rule requires _as_ or _as if_. It can have the sense of "as if," especially in casual speech. It appears in constructions like _She was spending money like there was no tomorrow_ and _I remember it like it was yesterday_. Some traditionalists prefer _as if_ in formal writing, but _like_ in this context is widespread, especially in America and Australia:

"When I was on _SNL_ [_Saturday Night Live_], people would walk up to me and talk to me <u>like</u> they were old friends of mine. Now that I'm just doing movies, they act nervous, <u>like</u> they don't know what to do around me."

>   Eddie Murphy, American comedian, actor, writer, musician, and director, quoted in interviewmagazine.com, Sept. 1987

"I tend to sleep in the nude. I'm an innately tactile person and a very sensual-leaning woman. You have to use the word 'leaning' or it <u>sounds like I'm boasting</u>!"

> Padma Lakshmi, Emmy Award–winning Indian-born cookbook author, actress, model, and TV host, quoted in *Allure* magazine, May 2009, reprinted in hindustantimes.com, Apr. 14, 2009

"I'm far from fearless. I'm afraid of everything. But maybe when you're afraid of everything, it sort of <u>seems like you're scared</u> of nothing."

> Natalie Portman, Academy Award–winning Israeli American actress, quoted in *Interview Magazine,* Sept. 2009

"Confidence is key. Sometimes you need to <u>look like you're confident</u> even when you're not."

> Vanessa Hudgens, American actress and singer, quoted in seventeen.com, Apr. 8, 2010

Like before verbs is becoming more acceptable, or at least neutral, in three other main senses as well:

(1) Meaning "in the way that" (*If you knew Susie <u>like I know</u> Susie*)
(2) Used interchangeably with "as" in some fixed phrases (*<u>like</u> I <u>said</u>*)
(3) In comparisons (*<u>like</u> you <u>always used to do</u>*)

Although these uses are very common in casual English, they aren't accepted in formal writing, at least not yet.

Casual: This turned out just <u>like I expected</u>.
Formal: This turned out just <u>as I expected</u>.

The famous mid-twentieth-century advertising slogan quoted below contained this casual usage. It got a lot of attention because it broke the formal rule for *as*, and that must have pleased the advertising company that created it:

"Winston tastes good, <u>like</u> a cigarette <u>should</u>."

In formal English, this would have been:

"Winston tastes good, <u>as</u> a cigarette <u>should</u>."

"AS GOOD AS . . . OR BETTER THAN"

When you use a construction like "<u>as</u> good <u>as</u>" followed by "or better than" in formal speech or writing, be sure to include the second *as*.

Strunk and White suggest rewriting a sentence that doesn't have the second *as*:

My opinion is as good or better than his

   can be revised to

My opinion is as good as his, or better.[12]

Here are some more examples:

Colloquial	Formal
<u>as fast or</u> faster than her	<u>as fast as</u> she is, or faster
<u>as tall or</u> taller than him	<u>as tall as</u> he is, or taller
<u>as useful or</u> more useful than that	at least <u>as useful as</u> that
<u>as bad or</u> worse than them	<u>as bad as</u> they are, or worse

Which version of the sentence below is correct in Standard English? (More than one may be right.)

(A) I think *Toy Story 3* was <u>as good or better than</u> the earlier *Toy Story* movies.

(B) I think *Toy Story 3* was <u>as good as or better than</u> the earlier *Toy Story* movies.

(C) I think *Toy Story 3* was <u>as good as</u> the earlier *Toy Story* movies, <u>or better than</u> they were.

Version A of the statement about *Toy Story 3* is nonstandard because it omits the second *as*. Version B is fine. Version C is a perfectly acceptable variation.

BEGGING THE QUESTION

"Begging the question is the fallacy of assuming what you are supposed to be proving.... Such a 'proof' proves nothing."
William Safire, American author, columnist, and presidential speechwriter (1929–2009), "Brother, Can You Spare a Question?," *New York Times*, Nov. 16, 1986

An example of begging the question:

Parallel lines will never meet because they are parallel.

Have you ever heard someone say that an answer "begs the question," meaning that it invites another question? That sense is pretty common in casual use, but it's not what *begging the question* actually means traditionally. The phrase, which dates from the sixteenth century, is a bad translation of a Latin term that refers to a specific logical fallacy: the error of assuming that something is true even though it hasn't been proved.

So **begging the question means "trying to prove something by using an argument that itself hasn't been proved."** A person typically *begs the question* when he makes a circular argument, claiming that an idea is true because it's true. Here's an example:

"YOU: I can't understand why the news media give so much coverage to Lindsay Lohan. It's ridiculous. She's not that important or newsworthy.

ME: What? Of course she's important and newsworthy! Lindsay Lohan is a big deal. Why, just look at the newsstand. [She's in] *People* magazine, *The Post,* you name it. She's everywhere.

YOU: That <u>begs the question</u>.

ME: Huh?"

> Philip B Corbett, "Begging the Question, Again," blogs.nytimes. com, Sept. 25, 2008

In this conversation, you doubted that Lindsay Lohan is newsworthy and I begged the question by saying that she's newsworthy because she's in the news a lot. In other words, I claimed that she deserves to be a celebrity because she's a celebrity.

Since that sort of reasoning dodges a question, many people conclude that if you *beg the question* you're being evasive. That's true in a way, but it misses the point of the phrase, which refers to a logical failure.

Also, if people think of the word *begging* in its familiar sense of "asking for something," it's natural for them to misconstrue *begging the question* to mean "asking for a question." That's how the phrase often is used today: to mean "inviting a question that no one has addressed yet," or "raising another question." That usage is very common, but traditionalists object to it.[13]

In formal speech or writing, when you say *begs the question,* be conservative and stick to its original sense of "assumes something is true without proof." Keep in mind, though, that the phrase can be confusing.

BETWEEN or AMONG

✴ *Between*

> "As long as you are in your right mind, don't you ever pray for twins. Twins amount to a permanent riot. And there ain't any real difference <u>between</u> triplets and an insurrection."
>
> Mark Twain, "The Babies" toast, Chicago, Nov. 1879 (obviously, if this were formal English, "ain't" should be "isn't")

"The difference <u>between</u> the right word and the almost-right word is the difference <u>between</u> lightning and the lightning bug."
　　Mark Twain, correspondence, Oct. 15, 1888

"One of the most striking differences <u>between</u> a cat and a lie is that a cat has only nine lives."
　　Mark Twain, *Pudd'nhead Wilson* (1894)

"<u>Between</u> two evils, I always pick the one [I've] never tried before."
　　Mae West, American actress, singer, writer, and sex symbol (1893–1980), in the 1936 film *Klondike Annie*

Jerry Seinfeld, joking that he couldn't make up his mind <u>between</u> Miss USA and Miss Universe: "I didn't know whether to go for the entire nation or the galaxy."
　　Jerry Seinfeld, quoted in Toby Young, "Has Jerry Seinfeld Lost His Sting?" telegraph.co.uk, Dec. 16, 2007

On the Internet comedy series <u>*Between Two Ferns,*</u> Zach Galifianakis insults his celebrity guests and often has them removed from the stage. He told Jennifer Lawrence that she was "off-putting." She quickly responded that he should be "off pudding"—because he's fat.
　　"Between Two Ferns: Oscar Buzz Edition Part 1," funnyordie.com, Feb. 12, 2013

✳ *Among*

"He who is without sin <u>among</u> you, let him throw a stone at her first."
　　John 8:7 (KJV)

"Indecency, vulgarity, obscenity—these are strictly confined to man; he invented them. <u>Among</u> the higher animals there is no trace of them."
　　Mark Twain, "The Lowest Animal"

"If a star, or studio chief, or any other great movie personages find themselves sitting <u>among</u> a lot of nobodies, they get frightened—as if somebody [is] trying to demote them."

> Marilyn Monroe, American model, actress, and singer (1926–1962), in Marilyn Monroe and Roger G. Taylor, *Marilyn Monroe in Her Own Words* (1983)

Lupin said that he'd been living <u>among</u> his fellows: werewolves.

> J. K. Rowling, British novelist, *Harry Potter and the Half-Blood Prince* (2005)

Newt Gingrich was <u>among</u> the winners in a lottery to get Google Glass, a wearable computer with a head-mounted display.

"The instrument that I never learned how to play was my fans. You know, they are the part of the story that nobody teaches you....I want to be a voice with them, <u>among</u> them."

> Lady Gaga, quoted in Jackie Huba, *Monster Loyalty: How Lady Gaga Turns Followers into Fanatics* (2013)

The traditional rule is that you should use *between* with two people or things and *among* with three or more. That's what almost all of my students were taught at some point, and maybe you were too. The root *-tween* is related to the Old English word for "two," after all, and *between* does show a relationship involving two people or things. But for over a thousand years, since its first appearance in English, *between* also has applied to more than two. Many of the leading usage guides agree that *between* applies when three or more people or things are thought of individually rather than as a group.[14]

Here are guidelines for using *between*.

The first rule is easy. **Say *between* when you're talking about two people or things:**

The rivalry <u>between</u> the Yankees and the Red Sox is legendary.
Let's divide this carrot cake <u>between</u> you and me.
<u>between</u> a cat and a lie
<u>between</u> two evils

I suggest that you also feel free to say *between* with reference to three or more people or things if you're thinking of them individually, not as a group:

Keep this <u>between</u> you, me, and the lamppost.
To make a billion dollars after college, I'll decide <u>between</u> English, philosophy, and fine arts as my major.
Nothing has changed <u>between</u> my mother, my father, and me.

Say *between* to describe the limits or endpoints of a location or range:

"The distance <u>between</u> the pitcher's plate and home base (the rear point of home plate) shall be 60 feet, 6 inches."
   Official Rules, MLB.com

Ohio is located <u>between</u> Pennsylvania, Indiana, and three other states.

Now, here are rules for *among*:

Say *among* to refer to relationships involving people or things that you think of collectively, not as individuals.
   ***Among* also means "in the group, number, or class of":**

Newt Gingrich was <u>among</u> the winners in a lottery.

There is honor <u>among</u> thieves.

"... they are endowed by their Creator with certain unalienable rights; that <u>among</u> these are life, liberty, and the pursuit of happiness."
   Declaration of Independence, July 4, 1776

"There is a strange pecking order <u>among</u> actors. Theatre actors look down on film actors, who look down on TV actors. Thank God for reality shows, or we wouldn't have anybody to look down on."
   George Clooney, quoted in nzherald.co.nz (*New Zealand Herald*), May 10, 2008

Among can mean "in the midst of, in the company of." It also can show location in a general area.

sitting <u>among</u> a lot of nobodies
living <u>among</u> his fellows
the terrorists hid <u>among</u> the civilian population

She was <u>among</u> friends means that she was with a group of friends. But *She was <u>between</u> jobs* means that one job was over for her and another hadn't yet begun.

Among also can mean "preeminent in a group, above the others."

He was a man <u>among</u> men.

Which version of the sentence below is correct?

(A) "I agree with you that there is a natural aristocracy <u>among</u> men. The grounds of this are virtue and talents."

(B) "I agree with you that there is a natural aristocracy <u>between</u> men. The grounds of this are virtue and talents."
Thomas Jefferson, U.S. president 1801–9, letter to John Adams, Oct. 28, 1813

Because Jefferson refers to a quality shared by men as a group, the right choice is *among,* as in version A.

CAN or MAY

✳ *Can*

"I <u>can</u> live for two months on a good compliment."
Mark Twain, quoted in Albert Bigelow Paine, *Mark Twain: A Biography*

"All I <u>can</u> say about the United States Senate is that it opens with a prayer and closes with an investigation."

> Will Rogers, quoted in Lewis Paul Todd and Merle Curti, *Triumph of the American Nation* (1997)

"You gain strength, courage, and confidence by every experience in which you really stop to look fear in the face. You are able to say to yourself, 'I lived through this horror. I <u>can</u> take the next thing that comes along.'"

> Eleanor Roosevelt, *You Learn by Living* (1960)

"Sometimes I'm so sweet even I <u>can't</u> stand it."

> Attributed to Julie Andrews, Academy Award– and Tony Award–winning English, actress, singer, author, director, and dancer, in *Orange Coast* magazine, Oct. 1984

"I'm shy, paranoid, whatever word you want to use. I hate fame. I've done everything I <u>can</u> to avoid it."

> Johnny Depp, quoted in "From Shy to Stardom," glamourmagazine.co.uk, Sept. 2012

✳ *May*

"<u>May</u> I Quote You, Mr. President?"

> "A Selection of 50 Quotes from President George W. Bush, for Entertainment or Meditation," Rodrigue Tremblay, globalresearch. ca, Nov. 19, 2006

<u>May</u> I take your coat?

Here's a rule that I'll bet you've heard: if you *can* do something, you have the ability to do it; if you *may* do it, you have permission. For generations parents have told their children to say *May I?* (when they're asking for a second piece of chocolate cake, for example). This distinction between *can* and *may* is a traditional part of American education, and many of the books that teach it are aimed at schoolchildren. Then, after school, both the kids and the adults often happily ignore it.

Saying *can I* instead of *may I* to request permission is common in casual use today, especially when people ask a question like *Why can't I?* But *can I* in this sense is a relatively recent addition to the language. The phrase didn't appear in print with this meaning until the second half of the nineteenth century. Even now it's far more common in speech and informal writing than in edited prose.

Say *can* to refer to physical or mental ability or capacity.

I <u>can</u> live for two months
even I <u>can't</u> stand it

In polite or formal contexts, use *may* to ask for permission.

<u>May</u> I quote you?
<u>May</u> I take your coat?

Both *can* and *may* can indicate that something is possible. Sometimes they can be used almost interchangeably:

Anything <u>can</u> happen
Anything <u>may</u> happen

When it means that something is possible, *can* keeps its sense of "being able." It means that a thing is able to happen or that people may be able to do something:

> "To those of you who received honors awards and distinctions I say, well done. And to the C students I say, you too <u>can</u> be President of the United States."
>> George W. Bush, U.S. president 2001–9, commencement address, Yale University, May 21, 2001

> "Never doubt that a small group of committed people <u>can</u> change the world. Indeed, it is the only thing that ever has."
>> American cultural anthropologist Margaret Mead (1901–1978), attributed in *Christian Science Monitor*, June 1, 1989

May **indicates a certain measure of likelihood:**

It <u>may</u> snow again tomorrow.

"You <u>may</u> marry the man of your dreams, ladies, but fourteen years later you're married to a couch that burps."

> Roseanne Barr, American actress, comedian, writer, producer, director: *Roseanne*, ABC-TV series, 1988

"We <u>may</u> be surprised at the people we find in heaven. God has a soft spot for sinners. His standards are quite low."

> Desmond Tutu, Nobel Peace Prize–winning South African retired Anglican bishop and opponent of apartheid, quoted in *Sunday Times,* Apr. 15, 2001

Which version of the sentence below is correct according to the traditional rule?

(A) Mom, <u>can</u> I go to the movies tonight?
(B) Mom, <u>may</u> I go to the movies tonight?

Since this passage refers to permission rather than ability, *may* is correct, as in version B.

CANNOT BUT or CANNOT HELP

"I <u>cannot but conclude</u> the bulk of your natives to be the most pernicious race of little odious vermin that nature ever suffered to crawl upon the surface of the earth."

> A description of the English in Jonathan Swift's *Gulliver's Travels* (1726)

"For we <u>cannot help agreeing</u> that no living human being
Ever yet was blessed with seeing bird above his chamber door...
With such name as 'Nevermore.'"

> Edgar Allan Poe, "The Raven" (1845)

Both of these idioms mean "I have no choice; I have to (do something)." The construction *cannot but* has been used since the sixteenth century and appears in the work of many fine writers, including Samuel Johnson, Jane Austen, and Lord Byron.

cannot but conclude
cannot but be
cannot but think

Cannot <u>help</u> but is a more recent addition to the language. It seems to be only a little over a hundred years old, but it has become common in casual speech and good writers have used it. Some usage authorities consider *but* unnecessary after *help,* though, so they disapprove of the phrase.

Strunk and White say, for example, that

He <u>could not help but see</u> that

should be

He <u>could not help seeing</u> that.[15]

Phrases like *cannot help seeing* and *cannot but see* are accepted in formal English. Go ahead and use them if you want to, but they may seem stilted to many people.

COMPARISONS: "MAGIC MIRROR ON THE WALL, WHO IS THE FAIREST ONE OF ALL?"

In everyday conversation, it probably wouldn't bother you at all to hear someone say, "Put your best foot forward." And you might not think twice to hear "May the best man win" when only two guys are competing. Those statements are so natural that even stuffy professors like me wouldn't object to them in informal use. But in formal contexts they violate a traditional rule:

When comparing two people or things, say *better, fairer, faster, taller, more interesting,* **etc.**

When comparing three or more, say *best, fairest, fastest, tallest, most interesting,* **etc.**

This wasn't a formal rule until the eighteenth century. Shakespeare, for instance, wrote, "Prove whose blood is <u>reddest</u>, his or mine."[16] About 250 years ago, though, grammar commentators began to express a preference for restricting *best, fastest,* etc. to three or more things. Gradually that hardened into a rule. Not all grammarians have accepted it, and many splendid writers have ignored it. The truth is that this distinction doesn't serve a useful function, and no one will be confused if you say that somebody was the strongest, the tallest, or the prettiest of two. What's more, this rule has never reflected the way people actually speak. But many style guides insist on it in formal contexts, and many careful readers will expect you to observe it in your writing.

May the best man win is a common idiom in casual use, though Standard English calls for the word *better* when it refers to only two men. *Put your best foot forward* is another exception to the rule. Since each of us has only two feet, *better* would be formally correct. But it would sound pretentious to try to correct such a well-known idiom. In addition to these two instances, it's quite common in casual speech to hear that one of two is the <u>best</u>, the <u>fastest</u>, the <u>smartest</u>, etc.[17] **The standard rule is well established among many stylists, though. I suggest that you observe it in formal speaking and writing:**

This one is better than that one.	This is the best of the three.
You are prettier than she is.	You are the prettiest of them all.
She was more generous than he was.	She was the most generous of all.

Which version of the sentence below is correct in formal English?

(A) "Mom always liked you <u>best</u>!"
(B) "Mom always liked you <u>better</u>!"
Tommy Smothers, *The Smothers Brothers Comedy Hour*

To choose the right answer, you need to know some background. Tommy and Dick Smothers did a brilliant comedy routine in the 1960s in which Dick criticized Tommy, who finally complained, "Mom always liked you best!" Since Tommy was comparing himself to his brother, the right choice in formal English would be *better*. However, the Smothers brothers had a sister. If Tommy was including her in the supposed contest for their mother's love, *best* would be formally correct.

COMPOSED OF or COMPRISE

✳ *Is Composed Of*

"When written in Chinese, the word *crisis* is <u>composed of</u> two characters. One represents danger, the other represents opportunity."
> Senator (later President) John F. Kennedy, speech to United Negro College Fund, Indianapolis, Apr. 12, 1959

✳ *Comprises*

British pop legend David Bowie's 2013 album *The Next Day* <u>comprises</u> 14 song tracks.
> *Radio & Music,* Feb. 19, 2013

The *Oxford English Dictionary* <u>comprises</u> twenty volumes.

Let's start this lesson on a high intellectual note: Is a straight flush in poker *composed of* five cards of the same suit in sequence, or is it *comprised of* those cards? Do three matching cards of one rank plus two matching cards of another rank *comprise* a full house or does a full house *comprise* them?

Here's the traditional rule:

A whole *comprises* its parts. *Comprise* means "to consist of," "to contain." A whole *is composed of* its parts.

The *Oxford English Dictionary* <u>comprises</u> twenty volumes
David Bowie's album *The Next Day* <u>comprises</u> 14 songs
A deck <u>comprises</u> 52 cards

So a straight flush *comprises* five cards of the same suit in sequence. And a full house *comprises* three matching cards of one rank plus two matching cards of another rank. You also can say that a straight flush and full house *are composed of* those cards. Just remember, the whole *comprises* its parts, not the other way around.

About two hundred years ago, some writers began to say that the parts *comprise* the whole. That became common over the course of the twentieth century, and it continues today. Many usage books firmly condemn that usage, though, and insist on the traditional rule. So do a lot of stylists. A majority of the *American Heritage Dictionary* Usage Panel in 1996, for example, rejected sentences in which the parts *comprise* the whole. But resistance is weakening: only about a third of the panel members objected to the idea that something can be *comprised of* its parts.

In formal speech and writing, remember that the whole *comprises* its parts.

You're probably on safe ground if you say *is comprised of,* though even that is disputed. You can always say *is composed of* instead.

Here are a few more examples of the traditional usage:

A year <u>is composed of</u> twelve months.
A week <u>comprises</u> seven days.
The Lord of the Rings trilogy <u>comprises</u> *The Fellowship of the Ring, The Two Towers,* and *The Return of the King.*

DECIMATE

Japan consumes half of the tuna catch in the world and has exceeded its fishing quota. Overfishing now threatens to <u>decimate</u> the tuna population.

> Toko Sekiguchi, "Why Japan's Whale Hunt Continues," time.com, Nov. 20, 2007

A recent study in New Zealand concluded that housecats are such effective hunters that they may <u>decimate</u> the local bird and animal population.

> Kharunya Paramaguru, "The Biggest Threat to U.S. Wildlife? Cats," time.com, Jan. 13, 2013

Decimate is a gruesome word that describes a serious loss of life. If you use it, keep in mind how harsh this word really is. To *decimate* literally means "to take or kill a tenth." The ancient Romans did that to soldiers who had mutinied, choosing one in ten by lot and executing them. So, since the time that the word came into English, in the seventeenth century, to *decimate* has meant "to kill, destroy, or remove one in ten people or things." It also has referred to a 10 percent tax. *Decimate* has rarely been used in those ways, though, except in historical writing.

Decimate is widely used more loosely, to mean "to kill a large number of."

threatens to <u>decimate</u> the tuna population
they may <u>decimate</u> the local bird and animal population

In formal writing, feel free to use *decimate* in this looser sense. Most careful writers will approve. In 2005, for example, over 80 percent of the *American Heritage* Usage Panel accepted a sentence stating that the Jewish population of Germany was *decimated* by the Holocaust, even though many more than 10 percent of the Jews were killed.

Decimate is also widely use to mean "to cause great harm or destruction." Be careful about applying the word this way, though. Many stylists will object if you use *decimate* to refer to the destruction of crops, for example, or anything else that doesn't involve killing people or animals.[18]

Keep in mind that *decimate* refers to the destruction of a significant portion of a population. I suggest that you don't use the word to describe more or less than that. Don't apply it to a small proportion of deaths or a trivial defeat. And, at the other extreme, don't use it to refer to a total annihilation. Over 80 percent of the *Harper Dictionary* Usage Panel said that they only used the word to refer to the destruction of a large part of a group of people.

DIDACTIC or PEDANTIC

✻ *Didactic*

Edgar Allan Poe believed that poetry should exist for its own sake. He called it a "heresy" to require poetry to be <u>didactic</u>: a poem should be judged by its value as art, not by the moral truth that it teaches, said Poe.

Edgar Allan Poe (1809–1849), American writer and author, in "The Poetic Principle" (1850)

"In a study published this month in *Developmental Science*, 16-month-old children were taught new names for foods like jelly and syrup.... The conclusion? The toddlers learned better if they... played with their foods.... 'They literally taste the world by putting things in their mouths.... <u>Didactic</u> information just falls flat.... They have to figure [it] out for themselves, and the only way they can do this is by messing around.'"

Perri Klass, "18 & Under: To Smoosh Peas Is to Learn," nytimes .com, Dec. 24, 2013

✻ *Pedantic*

"A man who has been brought up among books, and is able to talk of nothing else, is... what we call a <u>pedant</u>."

English essayist, poet, playwright, and politician Joseph Addison and Irish writer and politician Richard Steele, *Spectator* no. 105 (1711)

"Do not be bullied out of your common sense by the specialist; two to one, he is a <u>pedant</u> [and will display] his knowledge … if it will give him chance to show off his idle erudition."

Oliver Wendell Holmes Sr., American physician and poet (1809–1894), *The Writings of Oliver Wendell Holmes: Over the Teacups* (1895)

"Science-fiction is as profound as you want it to be, or it can be very simple entertainment. … We tend to just steer clear of being <u>pedantic</u>; it's entertainment first; otherwise we'd be on a lecture circuit."

Joe Flanigan, American TV actor, speaking of the TV series *Stargate Atlantis,* quoted in "In Sheppard's Care" in *Stargate SG-1: The Official Magazine,* Jan. 2005

Gail Collins: "Politics is … more fun than watching Texas beat Duke in the Chick-fil-A bowl."

David Brooks: "Not to be <u>pedantic</u>, but that was Texas A&M over Duke."

"Happy New Year, Politicians. Seriously," nytimes.com, Jan. 4, 2014

Both of these words can describe annoying behavior, and when they do, they can shade into each other. But something that is *didactic* also can be potentially helpful and instructive, while *pedantry* is almost always obnoxious.

Here's how to distinguish *didactic* from *pedantic:*

Didactic means "intended to teach," "instructive," or "having the character or manner of a teacher." When being *didactic,* it's possible to overdo it and to slip into pedantry.

If somebody is *pedantic,* he's excessively concerned with minutiae, and he's showing off his academic or technical knowledge. That kind of obnoxiously ostentatious person is called a ***pedant.***

A pedant can be someone who is narrowly concerned with formal rules. He might even write an entire book on grammar and usage! Uh-oh. Let's do the review question below, then move on to the next lesson quickly.

Which version of the sentence below is correct?

(A) In Woody Allen's film *Midnight in Paris,* Rachel McAdams plays a sexy, shallow woman who is attracted to her friend, "a <u>pedantic</u> know-it-all who won't shut up."

(B) In Woody Allen's film *Midnight in Paris,* Rachel McAdams plays a sexy, shallow woman who is attracted to her friend, "a <u>didactic</u> know-it-all who won't shut up."
        David Denby, "The Better Life," *New Yorker,* May 23, 2011

Since the professor is a know-it-all who won't shut up, he fits the textbook definition of *pedantic*. Version A is correct.

I wouldn't have expected it, but people seem to be curious about the meaning of *didactic* and *pedantic*. They're among the most looked-up words in the history of the Merriam-Webster online dictionary.

DIFFERENT FROM, DIFFERENT THAN, or DIFFERENT TO, DIFFERENTLY FROM or DIFFERENTLY THAN

✻ *Different From*

"Let me tell you about the very rich. They are <u>different from</u> you and me."
        F. Scott Fitzgerald, American writer (1896–1940), "Rich Boy," in *All the Sad Young Men* (1926)

"Take calculated risks. That is quite <u>different from</u> being rash."

> General George S. Patton, commander of the Third United States Army during World War II (1885–1945), quoted in *The American Heritage College Thesaurus* (2004)

"I'm no <u>different from</u> anybody else with two arms, two legs, and 4200 hits."

> Pete Rose, major league baseball player and manager, quoted by Cheryl Lavin, *Chicago Tribune,* July 5, 1992

"The battles against loneliness that I fought when I was 16 are very <u>different from</u> those I fought when I was 27, and those are very <u>different from</u> the ones I fight at 44."

> Tom Hanks, American actor, producer, writer, and director, quoted in theguardian.com, Jan. 11, 2001

"It's <u>different from</u> being 21.... At 33, the ending is much, much closer."

> Kobe Bryant, American professional basketball player, on his eventual retirement, quoted in Brian Kamenetzky, "Shelburne on Kobe's 'Unfamiliar Territory,'" espn.go.com, May 23, 2012

"The truth about the women in rock and roll is that their experience is completely <u>different from</u> the experience that the men have."

> Bette Midler, award-winning American singer-songwriter, comedian, actress, and producer, interviewed by David Steinberg on the Showtime TV series *Inside Comedy,* Feb. 17, 2014

✳ *Different Than*

"I mean, honestly, we have to be clear that the life for many Afghan women is not that much <u>different than</u> it was a hundred years ago."

> Hillary Clinton, former U.S. senator and secretary of state, quoted in Gini Reticker, "Our Interview with Secretary of State Clinton," pbs.org, Oct. 25, 2011

"I am wired in a <u>different</u> way <u>than</u> this event requires."
> Barack Obama, 44th U.S. president, before the second debate with
> Mitt Romney, quoted in Mark Halperin and John Heilemann,
> "The Intervention," *New York Magazine,* Nov. 11, 2013

✳ *Differently From*

"Women artists are still treated <u>differently from</u> men."
> Yoko Ono, Japanese artist, musician, filmmaker, and peace activist,
> quoted in Kate Kellaway, "When Sam Taylor-Wood Met Yoko
> Ono," theguardian.com, June 16, 2012

✳ *Differently Than*

Jack Nicholson learned in real life that the woman he thought
was his older sister was actually his mother. That explained why
she had always doted on him: a mother relates <u>differently than</u> a
sister does.
> Jack Nicholson, interview in *Playboy,* Jan. 2004

"Somehow, men understand other men's need for respect
<u>differently than</u> they understand it for a woman."
> Carly Fiorina, American former CEO of Hewlett-Packard,
> speaking on *60 Minutes,* quoted in Del Jones and Michelle Kessler,
> "Dunn Calls Allegations in HP Scandal a 'Myth,'" usatoay.com,
> Oct. 8, 2006

Of Lena Dunham and Kristen Wiig: "With both Lena and
Kristen…you do get the sense that they approach all of the work
<u>differently than</u> men [do].…There's more of a vulnerability to
how they go about their lives."
> Judd Apatow, Emmy Award–winning American film producer,
> director, comedian, actor, and screenwriter, on how women write
> for TV and film, quoted in "In *This Is Forty,* Family Life in All Its
> Glory," npr.org, Dec. 6, 2012

"I might sing a gospel song in Arabic or do something in Hebrew. I want to mix it up and do it <u>differently than</u> one might imagine."

> Stevie Wonder, Grammy Award–winning American singer-songwriter, musician, and record producer, quoted in Associated Press, Oct. 30, 2013

Should you say *different from* or *different than*? How about *different to*? The answer depends on who you are, where you live, and the context in your sentence. Historically, writers have said *different to, different from, different than,* and even *different against* and *different with*. But since the eighteenth century, grammarians often have favored *different from.* It's the usual idiom in Britain today and it's widespread in American English. Both the Americans and the British also say *different than,* though Americans say it more often and many British speakers consider it an Americanism. *Different to* is standard in British English. It sounds odd to most Americans, though.

In formal speech and writing, you usually can't go wrong saying *different from.*

They are <u>different from</u> you and me.
That is quite <u>different from</u> being rash.
I'm no <u>different from</u> anybody else.

Different than often has been condemned in formal use, and there's still opposition to it. More than half of the *American Heritage* Usage Panel in 2004 rejected this phrase in several contexts, for example. But many fine authors have said *different than,* and this phrase can be useful, especially when it's followed by a clause (a group of words including a subject and a verb).

Notice that in each of the passages below, *different than* is followed by a clause.

<u>different than</u> it was a hundred years ago
wired in a <u>different</u> way <u>than</u> this event requires
are <u>different</u> for hipsters <u>than</u> they were for their parents

In this passage, *different...than* isn't followed by a clause, but it's more economical than saying *different...than they were:*

are <u>different</u> for hipsters <u>than</u> for their parents

Different to is common and acceptable in British English.[19]
Differently from is often recommended:

Women artists are still treated <u>differently from</u> men.

But *differently than* has been used since the seventeenth century, and it's natural and economical before a full clause:

<u>differently than</u> a sister does
<u>differently than</u> they understand it for a woman
<u>differently than</u> one might imagine

I suggest that you say *differently than* before a clause.

DOUBLE NEGATIVES

"Two million people were killed in the north-south war in Sudan before 2005. I <u>wasn't</u> going to stand on the sidelines and <u>not</u> participate."
    George Clooney, quoted in David Gergen, "What Drives George Clooney," *Parade,* Sept. 25, 2011

We all know that two negatives result in an affirmative statement, right? Well, yes, that's the rule in Standard English, but it hasn't always been. Before the eighteenth century, some of the best English writers felt free to use multiple negative markers for emphasis. Chaucer, for example, could pile on two, three, or even more negatives when he really wanted to be negative. He did it four times in one sentence in his description of the noble knight on the *Canterbury Tales* pilgrimage:

"He <u>never</u> yet <u>no</u> vileynye <u>ne</u> sayde … unto <u>no</u> maner wight."

("He never yet no wickedness didn't say … to no sort of person," or, translated into today's Standard English, "He had never spoken wickedly or unkindly … to any sort of person.")
  Chaucer, *General Prologue,* late 14th century

Two hundred years later, Shakespeare could put together an impressive string of negatives, too. But by the middle of the eighteenth century, this linguistic fashion was changing in both writing and speech, especially among the educated. By the late eighteenth century, a grammarian recommended against using double negatives. The rule opposing it in formal contexts is firmly established today.[20]

Even during Shakespeare's lifetime, the point was being made that two negatives make a positive. Sir Philip Sidney's humorous sonnet 63 in *Astrophel and Stella* has a lady say "No, no" to an ardent suitor. He tries to turn the tables on her when he replies, "Grammar says … two negatives affirm"—so since she said no twice, she's really saying yes.

In formal writing, use double negatives only to express a positive thought, especially an unenthusiastic one:

My blind date <u>wasn't</u> <u>unattractive</u>.
Congress <u>isn't</u> entirely <u>nonfunctional</u>.

In this quotation, Albert Einstein managed to throw in *three* negatives:

"I <u>don't</u> think it's <u>impossible</u> that dreams are suppressed wishes, but I'm <u>not</u> convinced."
  Quoted in Johanna Fantova, "Conversations with Einstein," Nov. 5, 1953

Why is a sentence like *I don't got no money* nonstandard? It's not because somebody introduced a sloppy new form into English. Actually, the opposite seems to have happened: this is the survival of a historical form that went out of fashion in literate circles. Although the use of double negatives started to die out in Standard English after Shakespeare's time, it persisted in nonstandard speech. The fact that "(I Can't Get No) Satisfaction" is nonstandard English didn't prevent that song from being a massive hit for the Rolling Stones. The 1966 Motown hit song "Ain't No Mountain High Enough" also has a double negative in its title, as does Christina Aguilera's 2006 Grammy Award–winning song "Ain't No Other Man."

E.G. or I.E.

✳ *E.g.*

Dennis Farina to John Travolta (threateningly): "Let me explain something to you: Momo is dead, which means that everything he had now belongs to Jimmy Cap, including you.... When I speak, I speak for Jimmy. E.g., from now on, you start showing me the proper [expletive] respect."

John Travolta: "'E.g.' means 'for example.' What I think you want to say is 'i.e.'"
> Dennis Farina as Ray "Bones" Barboni and John Travolta as Chili Palmer in the 1995 film *Get Shorty*

Several top-tier players will be eligible for the Baseball Hall of Fame soon, e.g., Billy Wagner and Ken Griffey Jr.

✳ *I.e.*

"I have had a 'call' to literature, of a low order—i.e., humorous. It is nothing to be proud of, but it is my strongest suit."
> Mark Twain, correspondence, Oct. 19, 1865

"There are times when you have to obey a call which is the highest of all, <u>i.e.</u>, the voice of conscience."

> Mahatma Gandhi, Indian nationalist leader and advocate of non-violence (1869–1948), quoted in the Official Mahatma Gandhi eArchive

Confusing these two sets of pesky Latin initials is one of the main mistakes that editors see at publishing houses. Here's a simple guideline for how to use them:

Say *e.g.* before examples.

Say *i.e.* before you clarify something that you've just said.

***E.g.* means "for example, such as," so it should precede a list that illustrates what you've just referred to. That list should be partial or representative, not complete, since it's only giving examples.**

By contrast, *i.e.* means "in other words." So when you write *i.e.*, rephrase your complete point in a clearer or more specific way.

For the record, *e.g.* comes from *exempli gratia* ("for the sake of an example") in Latin and *i.e.* comes from *id est* (which means "that is").

Many editors and style manuals follow the rule that you should use these two abbreviations only in scholarly writing, footnotes, lists, or parentheses. Everywhere else, say *for example, such as,* or *including* instead of *e.g.* Say *in other words, that is,* or *namely* instead of *i.e.* Some usage guides let authors decide this for themselves, though.

Here are some more suggestions for using these initials:

- There's no need to italicize them unless your editor requires it. (I italicize them in this section because I italicize all of the terms that I discuss in this book.)
- If you start a list with *e.g.*, don't end it with *etc.*
- American authorities usually want *e.g.* and *i.e.* to have a period after each letter. The British often don't require it.
- Both *i.e.* and *e.g.* normally should be preceded by a comma, or by another punctuation mark or a parenthesis. The *Chicago Manual of Style* says that *e.g.* and *i.e.* must be followed by commas, too, though many style guides don't require that.

- Finally (and with no disrespect to Bones Barboni in *Get Shorty*) I suggest that, as a matter of style, you use *e.g.* and *i.e.* only in writing, not speech.

Which version of the passage below is correct?

(A) I'd like a new car as my birthday present this year, <u>i.e.,</u> a BMW or a Jaguar. But I'll probably get a tie.
(B) I'd like a new car as my birthday present this year, <u>e.g.,</u> a BMW or a Jaguar. But I'll probably get a tie.

Version B of the passage above is the right choice. Since the list of cars is partial or representative, *e.g.* should precede it.

EITHER or NEITHER

<u>Either is</u> perfectly fine with me.

<u>Does either</u> of them like lemon meringue pie?

<u>Neither</u> dessert <u>seems</u> very appealing.

Every once in a while, the word *either* or *neither* is the subject of a clause. When that happens, here's the traditional rule:

The pronouns *either* and *neither* are normally singular and take singular verbs.

either has
either says
neither wants
neither asks

When *either* is followed by *of* and a plural noun or pronoun, though, people often think of the whole phrase as plural, so they use a plural verb.[21] That's especially true in questions ("Are either of them coming?") or when *either* or *neither* is the first word of a phrase ("<u>Neither of the girls are</u> here yet"). But this is widely considered nonstandard, and a whopping 89 percent of the *American Heritage* Usage Panel rejected it in 2009. **You won't go wrong by following the traditional rule that *either of* and *neither of* should take singular verbs:**

> "Biofuels such as ethanol require enormous amounts of cropland and end up displacing either food crops or natural wilderness, <u>neither of which is</u> good."
>> Elon Musk, South African–born Canadian American founder of SpaceX, Tesla Motors, and PayPal, quoted in Michael Kanellos, "Elon Musk on Rockets, Sports Cars, and Solar Power," news.cnet.com, Feb. 15, 2008

Which version of the passage below is correct according to the traditional rule?

(A) Neither of the candidates <u>seem</u> to care about much, except being elected.
(B) Neither of the candidates <u>seems</u> to care about much, except being elected.

Neither is singular and takes a singular verb ("Neither...seems"), as in version B.

EITHER...OR, NEITHER...NOR

※ *Either...Or*

> "<u>Either</u> he's dead <u>or</u> my watch has stopped."
>> Groucho Marx, in the 1937 film *A Day at the Races*

> "Every nation in every region now has a decision to make. <u>Either</u> you are with us <u>or</u> you are with the terrorists."
>> President George W. Bush, address to joint session of Congress, Sept. 20, 2001

"You're <u>either</u> in my corner <u>or</u> you're with the trolls."
> Golden Globe Award–winning American actor Charlie Sheen,
> webcast, Mar. 5, 2011

✳ *Neither...Nor*

"These people...are a very gentle race, without the knowledge of any iniquity; they <u>neither</u> kill, <u>nor</u> steal, <u>nor</u> carry weapons."
> Christopher Columbus, Italian explorer and colonizer (ca.
> 1450–1506), quoted in *Journal of the First Voyage to America,
> 1492–1493,* entry for Nov. 12, 1492

"Those who would give up essential liberty to purchase a little temporary safety deserve <u>neither</u> liberty <u>nor</u> safety."
> Benjamin Franklin, American founding father, politician, author,
> diplomat, scientist, inventor (1705/6–1790), written for the
> Pennsylvania Assembly, Nov. 11, 1755

"France has <u>neither winter nor summer nor morals</u>. Apart from those drawbacks it is a fine country."
> Mark Twain, *Mark Twain's Notebooks* (1935)

Here are a few traditional rules for how to use *either...or*:

The words that follow *either* should be balanced by the words that follow *or*, especially in edited English. If an adjective follows *either*, for example, an adjective should follow *or*. If a clause (a string of words including a subject and a verb) follows *either,* a clause should follow *or,* etc. **The same guideline applies to the word or words that follow *neither* and *nor*.**

Each of the passages at the top of this lesson illustrates this. In Groucho's quotation, *either* is followed by a clause, "he's dead"; *or* is followed by a clause, too: "my watch has stopped."

President Bush's declaration is parallel in the same way. Both *either* and *or* are followed by clauses containing a prepositional phrase: "<u>you are with us</u>" and "<u>you are with the terrorists</u>."

Charlie Sheen's passage is balanced, too, as both *either* and *or* are followed by clauses containing prepositional phrases: "<u>in my corner</u>" and "<u>with the trolls</u>."

Columbus's quotation is parallel in a different way, with *neither, nor,* and *nor* each followed by verbs: "neither kill, nor steal, nor carry."

Franklin's statement has *neither* followed by the noun *liberty* and *nor* followed by the noun *safety*.

Twain's passage also places nouns after *neither, nor,* and *nor:* "neither winter nor summer nor morals."

Another rule is that if you put a verb immediately <u>before</u> *either*, you don't need to repeat that same verb after *or*.

In this example, the word *it's* needs to appear only once:

> "When a man opens the car door for his wife, <u>it's either a new car or a new wife</u>."
>> Prince Philip, Duke of Edinburgh, husband of Queen Elizabeth II, on *Today,* Mar. 2, 1968

Because he said *it's* <u>before</u> *either,* Prince Philip didn't need to say it again after *or*.

If he had said "<u>either it's</u> a new car," he would ideally have ended the sentence with "<u>or it's</u> a new wife."

The same rule applies if you put a verb before *neither:*

> "I <u>like neither new clothes nor new kinds of food</u>."
>> Albert Einstein, German-born theoretical physicist and Nobel Prize winner (1879–1955), quoted in Abraham Pais, *Subtle Is the Lord*

Because Professor Einstein put the verb *like* in front of *neither,* he didn't need to repeat it after *nor*.

Many *either… or* constructions have two subjects: one after *either* and the other after *or*.

Either Ben or Jerry is…
Either Simon or Garfunkel was…

Here's the general rule. It comes in two parts:

(1) **If both subjects are singular, the verb is singular. If both subjects are plural, the verb is plural.**[22] That's easy enough, but the second part of the rule is more complicated:

(2) **If one of the subjects is singular and the other is plural, there's no definite rule about what to do with the verb. Many careful writers agree that the subject closer to the verb determines if the verb is singular or plural.** That means that if the second subject (the one after the word *or*) is singular, the verb should be singular too. But if the second subject is plural, the verb should be plural.

The same rules apply to *neither ... nor.*

In the sentences below, the noun that comes right after *or* is singular, so the verb is singular:

Either his family **or he is** there.
Either John's parents **or his brother has** the car.
Either the Kardashians **or Jennifer Lawrence is** on Jimmy Fallon's show.

In these sentences, the second subject is plural, so the verb is plural too:

Either he **or his brothers are** there.
Either John **or his parents have** the car.
Neither Kim **nor her sisters seek** publicity.

I follow this pattern in my own writing, and I teach it. Some of the major style guides simply state it as a rule. But the truth is, the situation is messy. There's not a total consensus about it. Still, **if the second subject is plural, I recommend that you make the verb plural, too.** Most stylists will accept it.[23] Luckily, this construction is pretty rare, so the problem shouldn't come up too often, and you can always rewrite the sentence to avoid it if you want to.

One more thing: be consistent in saying *neither ... nor,* NOT *neither ... or.*

Which version of the passage below is correct?

(A) Neither Leo nor Kate <u>was</u> impressed by the differences in their backgrounds.

(B) Neither Leo nor Kate <u>were</u> impressed by the differences in their backgrounds.

Both *Leo* and *Kate* are singular, which means that the verb is singular, too, as in version A.

ENDING A CLAUSE OR A SENTENCE WITH A PREPOSITION: "PEDANTIC NONSENSE UP WITH WHICH I WILL NOT PUT"

"No problem is so big or so complicated that it can't be run away <u>from</u>."
　　Charles Schulz, *Peanuts* comic strip, Feb. 27, 1963

"What I want to talk about tonight is, why are your friends so annoying? It doesn't make any sense. These are the people you have picked to be <u>with</u>."
　　Jerry Seinfeld, on *Late Show with David Letterman,* CBS, 2010, quoted in salon.com, Dec. 20, 2012

Let's start this lesson by reviewing what a preposition is:

A preposition is a word like *after, for, from, in, on, to, under,* or *with* that relates nouns or pronouns to other words. Prepositions often indicate position, direction, or time. Examples are underlined in these movie titles:[24]

The Day <u>After</u> Tomorrow
Midnight <u>in</u> Paris
Star Trek <u>into</u> Darkness
The Girl <u>with</u> the Dragon Tattoo

Now let's get to the rule.

You may have heard that it's ungrammatical to end a clause or a sentence with a preposition. That's pretty famous as grammar rules go, but it's actually just a myth. In 1672, the writer John Dryden seems to have been the first to criticize ending a sentence with a preposition, and this idea remained controversial into the nineteenth century.[25] It became well known because schoolteachers enforced it as a rule. But in the last hundred years major usage authorities have dismissed it. H. W. Fowler, for example, called it a "cherished superstition." The reasoning behind the "rule" was that Latin doesn't "strand" prepositions that way, so English shouldn't either. Yet it's been natural in English to strand prepositions since Old English times, and a long and distinguished list of writers have done it. Fowler noted that almost all great English writers have stranded prepositions, and he insisted that everyone should be free to do this (1926). As if to prove the point, he often dangled prepositions at the end of clauses in his own writing.[26] You're free to do the same. It's a matter of style, not grammar.

Whether to end a sentence with a preposition is a stylistic choice for you to make. Some traditionalists still insist that you shouldn't do it when you write on a sophisticated level. But most stylists won't object. In fact, 80 percent of the *Harper Dictionary* Usage Panel had no problem with stranding a preposition. So you may want to ignore this so-called rule, as long as the result is natural and graceful. Still, keep in mind that 20 percent of the *Harper Dictionary* panel didn't accept it. So in some types of formal writing, when a lot is at stake (college applications or job inquiries, for example), you may choose to be ultraconservative and not end sentences with prepositions. That's up to you.

Always aim for clarity and natural expression, though. Feel free to strand prepositions in order to achieve that.

In the lines from *Peanuts* and Seinfeld's passage at the top of this lesson, the prepositions sound natural at the end. Placing them earlier would have seemed stilted—and would have ruined the rhythm of the jokes.

These other examples that end with prepositions also sound natural:

Who are you talking about?
That was the moment I was waiting for.
What did I just step in?

Of course, you also could rewrite them to say:

About whom are you talking?
That was the moment for which I was waiting.
In what did I just step?

Those versions are grammatically correct, but they sound like something a butler would say in a 1930s Hollywood movie about high society. In very formal writing, you may choose to say something like *This is the essay about which I told you,* rather than the more natural *This is the essay I told you about.* But that's matter of style, and many readers may find it pretentious.

Here's another stylistic point: **Omit a preposition at the end of a sentence (or anywhere else) if it's superfluous.**

Where did you go to? should be *Where did you go?*
Where is the book at? should be *Where is the book?*

Which version of the sentence below is correct?

(A) What is the world coming to?
(B) To what is the world coming?

Both versions are acceptable. *To what is the world coming* is technically correct but artificial and awkward. *What is the world coming to* is more natural.

Several usage books note that Winston Churchill wrote this famous sentence as a witty way of mocking the rule that prohibits final prepositions:

> "This is the kind of pedantic nonsense up with which I will not put."
> Attributed to Winston Churchill, in *Washington Post,* Sept. 30, 1946

The point here is that rigidly following the rule about stranding prepositions can produce a silly, pretentious sentence. It's certainly true that putting a preposition at the end would have sounded much more natural here: "This is the kind of pedantic nonsense I will not put up with." There are two things wrong with the story, though. First, there's no evidence that Churchill ever said this line. Second, *put up with* isn't technically an instance of preposition stranding. It's what grammarians call a phrasal verb.[27] So if the speaker had ended this sentence with *put up with,* he wouldn't have stranded a preposition. Even so, if this quotation sticks in your mind, it's a very clever way to remember that strictly forbidding preposition stranding is pedantic and restrictive.

EQUALLY AS

"I was accepted rather readily at Princeton and <u>equally as</u> fast at Yale."

> U.S. Supreme Court justice Sonia Sotomayor, quoted in Antonia Felix, *Sonia Sotomayor: The American Dream* (2010)

Language commentators have been denouncing this idiom for about 150 years. The attacks reached a crescendo in 1926, when Fowler called it an illiterate repetition of words. Their point is that you could drop the word *equally* or the word *as* in many cases and the sentence would still function just as well. *Equally as* is fairly common in speech, in which the word *equally* adds emphasis that would be missing if you just said *as.* That's true in the quotation at the top of this lesson.

Despite the hostility of usage critics, this phrase is harmless in informal contexts. Even a Supreme Court justice uses it. But it's rare in edited texts, except in quotations of speech.

Avoid it in formal speech and writing. Say *equally* or *as* instead. Or, to be emphatic, you might want to say *just as.*

ET AL. or ETC.

✳ *Et Al.*

"The major developments in the late 1990s and early 21st century have included a new exploration of love as an emotion...and the dramatic new developments in the biology of love...(e.g., Carter et al., 1997)."

> Arthur Aron, Helen E. Fisher, and Greg Strong, "Romantic Love,"
> *Cambridge Handbook of Personal Relationships* (2006)

✳ *Etc.*

"When I sit, you sit. When I kneel, you kneel, et cetera, et cetera, et cetera."

> Yul Brynner, Academy Award– and Tony Award–winning
> Russian-born actor in American films (1920–1985), as the King of
> Siam in the 1956 film *The King and I,* quoted by imdb.com

In the near future, apps for computerized eyewear could be used in medicine, police work, transportation, etc.

> Tim Bajarin, "A Killer App for Google's Glasses," time.com, Mar.
> 25, 2013

Et al. **means "and others." It normally refers to people**. It's an abbreviation of Latin *et alii* or *et aliae*.[28] Since the second word is being abbreviated, put a period after the *al.* There's no need to put this phrase in italics unless your editor requires it. If your profession uses a style manual, follow its guidance about that.

Usage guides generally tell you to use *et al.* **only in lists, source citations, or parenthetical references**. Style manuals in different fields have different requirements, though. The American Psychological Association, for example, says that when you refer to a work by six or more authors, the first citation in your text should give the first author's name, followed by *et al.* If there are five or fewer authors, list all of their surnames when you first mention them. In references after that, you should give the first author's surname and *et al.*[29] The *Chicago Manual of Style,* on the other hand, says that in your bibliography, if you cite a work written or edited by four to ten people, you should list all of their names. But it suggests a briefer style for footnotes: in those, it says, you should cite only the first author's name, followed by *et al.* (with no comma in between). In the body of your text, if you refer to a publication with multiple authors, you can use the same form as in notes: cite the first author's name followed by *et al.* with no intervening comma. You may want to follow that with the year of the publication:

(Carter <u>et al.</u>, 1997)

Don't confuse *et al.* with *etc.* Unlike *et al.,* which came into our language relatively recently (in the late nineteenth century), *et cetera* has appeared in English texts since the early 1400s. **It's a Latin phrase that we use in English to mean "and others of the same or similar kind, and the rest, and so forth."** It's abbreviated *etc.* (and sometimes *&c.*). Some style guides say that you should use *etc.* only of things, while others let it refer to people, too. **I recommend that you say *etc.* of things and *et al.* of people.** That's what most writers do.

Some language commenters restrict *etc.* to notes and technical writing, but it often turns up in expository prose as well. I think that's fine—and I'm usually pretty conservative about these sorts of rules. I sometimes end sentences with *etc.* in this book, and I wouldn't have a problem if my students did the same in their writing. I would get out my red pen, though, if a student wrote *and etc.* Since the *et* in *et cetera* means "and," the student would be saying "and and others."

Put a comma in front of *etc.*

If you say this phrase aloud, be sure to say ***et-SET*-*er-a***. Some English-speakers mispronounce it ***ek-SET*-*er-a***, with an initial sound like that in *ecstasy* or *exceptional*. French-speakers often do the same. Some people even misspell the word so it starts with *ect-*. **Be sure to punctuate, spell, and pronounce *etc.* correctly.**

EXTREMIST or FANATIC

✳ *Extremist*

"What is objectionable, what is dangerous, about <u>extremists</u> is not that they are extreme, but that they are intolerant. The evil is not what they say about their cause, but what they say about their opponents."

> Robert F. Kennedy, U.S. attorney general and senator (1925–1968), "Extremism, Left and Right," *The Pursuit of Justice* (1964)

"I'm parodied as being some right-wing fundamentalist <u>extremist</u>. It just isn't true. The parody doesn't reflect reality."

> Pat Robertson, founder of the Christian Coalition, the Christian Broadcasting Network, and Regent University, quoted in Wes Rickards, "Pat Robertson: A Life, A Legacy," on cbn.com, 2010

"I understand that it's good tactics to categorize me as a close-minded, un-objective <u>extremist</u>, but nobody that respects me has those views."

> Alan Dershowitz, American lawyer, professor, and political commentator, quoted in Kathryn Schulz, "Alan Dershowitz on Being Wrong," slate.com, May 12, 2010

"An intelligence analyst may attribute an attack to al Qaeda, whereas a policymaker could opt for the more general '<u>extremist</u>.'"

> Michael V. Hayden, former director of National Security Agency and Central Intelligence Agency, "Relax, *Zero Dark Thirty* Is Only a Movie," cnn.com, Dec. 28, 2012

✳ *Fanatic*

"From <u>fanaticism</u> to barbarism is only one step."

> Denis Diderot, French philosopher, art critic, and writer (1713–1784), "Essai sur le Mérite de la Vertu" (1745)

"Fanatics have their dreams, wherewith they weave
A paradise for a sect."
> John Keats, English Romantic poet (1795–1821), *The Fall of
> Hyperion*

"A fanatic is a man that does what he thinks th' Lord wud do if
He knew th' facts iv th' case."
> Finley Peter Dunne, American humorist (1867–1936), parodying
> colloquial speech, "Casual Observations," *Mr. Dooley's Philosophy*
> (1900)

"A fanatic is a man who consciously over-compensates a secret
doubt."
> Aldous Huxley, British writer (1894–1963), "Vulgarity in
> Literature," *Music at Night and Other Essays* (1949)

"A fanatic is one who can't change his mind and won't change the
subject."
> Winston Churchill, quoted in *New York Times,* July 5, 1954

"The seed of fanaticism always lies in uncompromising self-
righteousness, a plague of many centuries.... The essence of
fanaticism lies in the desire to force other people to
change.... Shakespeare can help a great deal. Every extremism,
every uncompromising crusade, every form of fanaticism in
Shakespeare ends up either in a tragedy or in a comedy. The
fanatic is never happier or more satisfied in the end; either he is
dead or he becomes a joke."
> Amos Oz, Israel Prize–winning Israeli writer and professor, *How to
> Cure a Fanatic* (2002)

What makes someone an *extremist,* and at what point do you decide
that he's a *fanatic?* It's usually no great honor to be called either, but
there is a difference between them.

**The *Oxford English Dictionary* defines an *extremist* as someone
who goes to extremes or holds extreme opinions.**

In other words, extremism is a relative concept. It refers to someone or something that isn't moderate or centrist. That's a matter of context and perspective, and it may change over time.

People or groups that are labeled *extremist* are considered possibly immoral, potentially or actually dangerous, and certainly wrong. Many (but not all) extremist groups advocate or practice violence, which they may consider to be self-defense.

The label *extremist* is typically applied by an outsider, but people sometimes use it of themselves to describe their zealous dedication to a cause. Here are a few examples. The second one is famous, at least among people who were adults in the 1960s, but the first one may surprise you:

> "The question is not whether we will be <u>extremist</u>, but what kind of <u>extremist[s]</u> will we be."
> Martin Luther King Jr., Nobel Peace Prize–winning African American pastor and leader of the civil rights movement (1929–1968), "Letter from Birmingham Jail," Apr. 16, 1963

> "<u>Extremism</u> in the defense of liberty is no vice!"
> Senator Barry Goldwater (1909–1998), speech accepting the presidential nomination at the Republican National Convention, San Francisco, July 16, 1964

The word *fanatic* comes from a Latin word meaning "temple," and fanaticism very often has religious associations. *Fanatical* acts or words were thought to result from possession by a demon or deity.

A *fanatic* often is seen as a lunatic, or someone driven by single-minded, unreasoning zeal, especially for a religious or political cause.

The labels *extremist* and *fanatic* are both condemnatory, but *fanaticism* suggests a crazed compulsion that puts someone beyond the reach of reason.

The word *fanatic* also can be used in a weakened sense to describe someone whose behavior is zealous but within the normal range:

"I was never really a comic-book <u>fanatic</u>."

> J. J. Abrams, Emmy Award–winning American TV and film producer, screenwriter, director, actor, and composer, whose work includes *Star Trek* and *Star Wars* films, "10 Questions for J. J. Abrams," time.com, May 18, 2009

"My mother was a P.E. teacher, and she was kind of a <u>fanatic</u> about fitness and nutrition growing up, so it was ingrained in me at a young age. As I get older, I'm finding out it's not about getting all buffed up and looking good. It's more about staying healthy and flexible, and trying to stay athletic."

> Josh Duhamel, Daytime Emmy Award–winning American actor and former fashion model, quoted in Paul Chi, "Josh Duhamel and Fergie Are Workout Rivals," people.com, Apr. 15, 2011

Which version of the hypothetical statement below is more likely?

(A) The president said he was optimistic about negotiating a lasting peace with the <u>fanatics</u>.

(B) The president said he was optimistic about negotiating a lasting peace with the <u>extremists</u>.

Both versions are questionable, but B is the more likely choice. It's not impossible that someone you consider an extremist could reach a reasoned compromise, depending on the circumstances. That's less likely with a fanatic.

The word *fan* is an abbreviated form of *fanatic*. It first appeared in the seventeenth century, and two hundred years later it became popular in the United States as a description of baseball fans. The word is used more broadly today. It captures the loose meaning of a *fanatic* as a zealous or obsessive devotee of something. In the twentieth century terms like *fan club*, *fan mail*, *fan fiction*, and *fanboy* arose.

FARTHER or FURTHER

✳ *Farther*

"'Come back!' she screamed. 'I want to go, too!' 'I can't come back, my dear,' called Oz from the basket . . . and all eyes were turned upward to where the Wizard was riding in the basket, rising every moment <u>farther</u> and <u>farther</u> into the sky."

> L. Frank Baum, *The Wonderful Wizard of Oz* (1900)

"The harder you grip the bat, the more you can swing it through the ball, and the <u>farther</u> the ball will go. I swing big, with everything I've got. I hit big or I miss big. I like to live as big as I can."

> Babe Ruth, American baseball player (1895–1948), quoted in William Safire, *Words of Wisdom* (1989)

"Harry's legs were like lead again. . . . They climbed more staircases . . . and Harry was just wondering how much <u>farther</u> they had to go when they came to a sudden halt."

> J. K. Rowling, *Harry Potter and the Sorcerer's Stone* (1997)

"Mary started to scream, and then the curtains parted <u>farther</u> and a hand appeared, holding a butcher's knife. It was the knife that, a moment later, cut off her scream, and her head."

> Helen Mirren, Academy Award–winning English actor, reading from the 1959 novel *Psycho* in the 2012 film *Hitchcock*. The novel itself actually uses the word *further,* not *farther.*

The distance between Texas and Arizona is getting <u>farther</u>. The Rio Grande Rift is widening, pushing New Mexico's borders apart—by nearly a millimeter a year.

> Nick Carbone, "New Mexico Is Stretching, Slowly but Surely," time.com, Jan. 22, 2012

✻ *Further*

"Each generation goes <u>further</u> than the generation preceding it because it stands on the shoulders of that generation. You will have opportunities beyond anything we've ever known."
> Ronald Reagan, U.S. president 1981–89, commencement address at Notre Dame, May 17, 1981

"The important achievement of Apollo was a demonstration that humanity is not forever chained to this planet, and our visions go rather <u>further</u> than that, and our opportunities are unlimited."
> Neil Armstrong, astronaut and first person on the moon, at Apollo 11 30th Anniversary Press Conference, July 16, 1999

"Thinking even <u>further</u> into the future, I definitely want to make an acoustic record. I want to try lots of different things."
> Katy Perry, American singer, businesswoman, and actress, quoted in seventeen.com, Feb. 5, 2009

"According to a study by researchers at Vanderbilt University, the <u>further</u> the major league baseball season progresses, the more often batters swing at bad pitches."
> Nicholas Bakalar, "As a Season Drags On, Batters Chase More Bad Pitches," nytimes.com, June 24, 2013

Al Capone says in the movie *The Untouchables,* "You can get <u>further</u> with a kind word and a gun than you can with just a kind word."[30] Was he right to say *further* or should he have said *farther*? If you're not sure, don't feel bad. *Farther* and *further* were actually the same word historically. They competed with each other for centuries about which one meant what, and they still do.

Farther came into existence in Middle English as a variant of the older word *further,* and a lot of writers since then have used them as if there were no difference between them. Shakespeare did that, though he used *further* much more often. By the nineteenth century, *further* was becoming dominant, and Fowler predicted in 1926 that *farther* eventually would drop out of the language altogether. That hasn't happened, of course. But *further* is far more common, especially in Britain, and *farther* is declining everywhere.[31] They're still used interchangeably, though Americans often say *farther,* especially to signify physical distance.

For the last century or so, most usage commenters have set it down as a rule that we should say *farther* to represent physical distance and *further* to show quantity or degree. *The Chicago Manual of Style,* for example, cites that distinction as the traditional rule. Many careful American writers follow that rule, or at least they try to.[32]

So in formal contexts, especially if you're writing for American readers, I suggest that you use *farther* only to refer to physical distance.

rising every moment <u>farther</u> and <u>farther</u> into the sky
the <u>farther</u> the ball will go
the curtains parted <u>farther</u>

Say *further* for everything else. Use it to describe time, amount, or figurative movement forward.

each generation goes <u>further</u>
our visions go rather <u>further</u> than that
thinking even <u>further</u> into the future
the <u>further</u> the major league baseball season progresses

So, although Capone was a notorious gangster, his usage near the top of this lesson is strictly law-abiding: it follows the traditional rule for using *further* to speak of figurative progress.

Which version of the sentence below is correct according to the normative rule?

(A) "I don't have a Facebook page because I have little interest in hearing myself talk about myself any <u>further</u> than I already do."
(B) "I don't have a Facebook page because I have little interest in hearing myself talk about myself any <u>farther</u> than I already do."

Jesse Eisenberg, American actor and playwright, quoted in Allie Townsend, "Jesse Eisenberg Doesn't Have a Facebook Page," time. com, Sept. 28, 2010

Since the distance is figurative in this statement, *further* is correct, as in version A. It's what Eisenberg actually said.

FEELING BAD, FEELING WELL, LOOKING MARVELOUS, SMELLING SWEET, ETC.: LINKING VERBS

"What's in a name? That which we call a rose
By any other name would <u>smell</u> as sweet."
  Juliet in *Romeo and Juliet* (1591–95)

"No one can make you <u>feel</u> inferior without your consent."
  Eleanor Roosevelt, attributed in *Reader's Digest*, Sept. 1940

"You <u>look</u> *mah*velous!"
  Billy Crystal, as Fernando, telling guests that they look *marvelous,* on NBC-TV's *Saturday Night Live,* NBC TV, 1980s

"Steve McQueen <u>looks</u> good in this movie. He must have made it before he died."
  Yogi Berra, *The Yogi Book* (1998)

"People are always so surprised when they meet me.... They <u>seem</u> surprised that they're not scared of me. The aggressive side of me comes across in my music, but I'm just a sweet girl."
  Pink, American singer-songwriter and actress, quoted in "Pink: I'm Just a Sweet Girl," starpulse.com, Aug. 12, 2006

"You can't live your life blaming your failures on your parents.... I realized it was a waste of time to be angry at my parents and <u>feel</u> sorry for myself."
  Drew Barrymore, Golden Globe Award–winning American actress, screenwriter, director, producer, model, and writer, quoted in telegraph.co.uk, Aug. 23, 2010

"Horses calm me.... They <u>smell</u> great [and] they are beautiful to look at."

> Shania Twain, Grammy Award–winning American singer-songwriter, quoted in Robin Leach, "Shania Twain Q + A, Part 1," lasvegassun.com, Nov. 19, 2012

If you're unhappy or upset, do you feel *bad* or *badly*? What about when you're sick? Are you feeling *bad* or *badly*? We'll get to the answer in a moment, but let's start with an observation: some verbs don't describe actions. Instead, they refer to emotions, sensations, states of mind, or states of being. They're called **linking verbs**. There are about sixty of them in English, including *feel, seem, look, taste,* and the various forms of *be.* Some of the most common ones are underlined in the quotations at the top of this lesson and the sentences below. Notice that each is followed by an adjective.

she <u>is</u> very clever
I'm <u>feeling</u> sleepy
I <u>was</u> thrilled
they <u>became</u> happier
the fans <u>grew</u> restless
it <u>proved</u> successful
the team <u>remains</u> in first place
he <u>seemed</u> lonely
we <u>sounded</u> good
<u>stay</u> true to yourself
that <u>tastes</u> great
the weather has <u>turned</u> cold

Many of the major style guides and virtually all school usage books give this rule: **Linking verbs normally take adjectives, such as *sweet, good, bad, inferior,* and, of course, *marvelous.*** That's a standard rule in American education.

That hasn't always been the pattern in English usage, though, and not everyone follows it today. In fact, sometimes we have to use an adverb after a linking verb (to *feel strongly* or *differently* about something, for instance). But, aside from exceptions like those, very many careful writers observe the rule about using adjectives after linking verbs. More than three-fourths of the members of the *Harper Dictionary* Usage Panel, for example, reported that they say "I feel bad" (not *badly*) when they're physically ill or unhappy about something.[33] So, to answer the questions at the top of this lesson, when you're upset or you're sick, you *feel bad*. This quotation attributed to President Lincoln illustrates the point nicely:

> "When I do good, I <u>feel</u> good; when I do bad, I <u>feel</u> bad, and that's my religion."
>
> Abraham Lincoln, U.S. president 1861–65, attributed in William H. Herndon and Jesse W. Weik, *Herdon's Lincoln: The True Story of a Great Life* (1889)

By the way, it's perfectly idiomatic to say "I feel well" to mean that you're in good health. Used in that sense, *well* is an adjective, and people have been saying it to mean "healthy" since the thirteenth century. Shakespeare did that several times.[34] It's also standard to say *I feel good*.

If you're not sure whether a word is a linking verb, try substituting a form of the verb *to be* for it. If you can, it's a linking verb and you'll normally follow it with an adjective.

you <u>look</u> marvelous	*becomes*	you <u>are</u> marvelous
he <u>seemed</u> lonely	*becomes*	he <u>was</u> lonely
we <u>sounded</u> great	*becomes*	we <u>were</u> great
<u>stay</u> true to yourself	*becomes*	you are true to yourself
that <u>tastes</u> delicious	*becomes*	that <u>is</u> delicious

Some linking verbs also can be used as **action verbs**, which describe actions and take adverbs, like *badly*. It depends on the context. *Feel* and *smell* are two of those verbs. You may feel <u>bad</u> if you unintentionally hurt someone's feelings. *Feel* in that case is a linking verb. But if someone did a poor job of feeling something with her fingers, that's an action verb, so she'd be correct in saying, "I feel <u>badly</u>." And after playing basketball or working out at the gym, someone might smell really *bad*. In that case, *smell* is a linking verb. But if a bomb-sniffing dog fails to smell an explosive at an airport, *smell* is an action verb, so we can say that the dog smells *badly*.

Which version of the sentence below is correct?

(A) I feel <u>bad</u> about having teased you.

(B) I feel <u>badly</u> about having teased you.

Feel in this sentence describes a state of mind. Version A correctly uses the adjective *bad*.

See also **GOOD**.

GO or SAY

We've all heard people say *go* to mean "say." I couldn't say that myself, of course, but it seems as if I hear it every day. This usage is often said to be a recent development, and it first drew critical attention in the 1970s. It's very common among young people (and some who aren't so young). One theory is that it's an extension of *go* introducing a nonverbal sound, as in "the ducks <u>go</u> quack" in children's stories. Actually, using *go* to mean "say" isn't quite so recent. The *Oxford English Dictionary* cites examples going back to 1836, when Charles Dickens used it in *The Pickwick Papers*. Interestingly, examples in the *OED* from that time until the 1980s use *go* before inarticulate sounds ("'Chip-chip-chip,' she <u>went</u>" [1895], and "They all <u>go</u> lah-de-ah-de-ay" [1939], for example). By 1978, *go* appeared in print in the sense of "say" before a direct quotation consisting of words. The speaker was none other than the great Steve Martin:

> "I'm the last person to admit I've achieved anything.... But now my friends say it to me and I <u>go</u>, 'You're right. I can't deny it [anymore].'"
>
> Steve Martin, Academy Award–, Emmy Award–, and Grammy Award–winning American comedian, actor, musician, writer, and film producer, quoted in *Newsweek,* Apr. 3, 1978[35]

In casual conversation, *go* is now widely used to mean "say," especially before a direct quotation. In formal speech and writing, though, use *say* instead.

Which version of the sentence below is appropriate according to the traditional rule?

(A) "I definitely look at my body and I g<u>o</u>, 'Yuck.'"
(B) "I definitely look at my body and I <u>say</u>, 'Yuck.'"
>   Louis C.K., quoted in "Comedian Louis C.K.: Finding Laughs
>   Post-Divorce," npr.org, July 7, 2010

Version B is the right choice, though Mr. C.K. actually said version A.

GOOD

✳ Good *as an Adjective*

> "Be <u>good</u> and you will be lonesome."
>   Mark Twain's handwritten caption on the photo that opens
>   *Following the Equator* (1897)

> Yogi Berra, speaking about the opera *Tosca:*
> "I really liked it. Even the music was <u>good</u>."
>   Yogi Berra, *The Yogi Book* (1998)

✳ Good *as a Noun*

> "All of you want to do well. But if you do not do <u>good</u>, too, then
> doing well will never be enough."
>   Anna Quindlen, Pulitzer Prize–winning author, commencement
>   address at Villanova University, June 23, 2000

Good describes desirable or approved qualities.

be <u>good</u>
even the music was <u>good</u>

To *feel good* suggests good health and maybe high spirits, too. To *look good* means to be attractive or to be worthy of approval.

Good is also a noun:

do <u>good</u>

✳ *To Do Something "Good":* Good *as an Adverb*

Good has been used as an adverb since the thirteenth century. In the mid-nineteenth century, grammarians began to denounce this usage, and very many style guides now insist that *good* can only be an adjective. It survives as an adverb in nonstandard speech, mainly in America. It's associated with uneducated speakers, but it's also widely used. Here's an illustration by the American legend Davy Crockett:

> "I saw the bear climbing up a large black oak-tree.... [I] shot him the third time, which killed him <u>good</u>."
>
> Davy Crockett, American folk hero, frontiersman, politician, and soldier (1786–1836), *Narrative of the Life of David Crockett, of the State of Tennessee* (1834)

As a longtime (suffering) Mets fan, I've noted that professional athletes and coaches, even educated and articulate ones, often use *good* as an adverb:

David hit the ball really <u>good</u> today.

In formal speech and writing, say *well* **to describe an action.**
   See also **FEELING GOOD.**

HANGED or HUNG

✳ *Hanged*

> "Depend upon it, Sir, when a man knows he is to be <u>hanged</u> in a fortnight, it concentrates his mind wonderfully."
>
> Samuel Johnson, British author, scholar, critic, and lexicographer (1709–1784), in James Boswell's *Life of Samuel Johnson* (1791)

> "One must, it is true, forgive one's enemies—but not before they have been <u>hanged</u>."
>
> Sigmund Freud, *Civilization and Its Discontents* (1930), quoting Heinrich Heine, *Gedanken und Einfälle,* sect. I

Winston Churchill, asked about the large audiences at his speeches: "It is quite flattering, but whenever I feel this way I always remember that if instead of making a political speech I [were] being <u>hanged</u>, the crowd would be twice as big."
> Press conference, Washington, D.C., Jan. 17, 1952.

"Saddam Hussein, the former Iraqi dictator … was <u>hanged</u> before dawn Saturday for crimes committed in a brutal crackdown during his reign."
> "Hussein Executed with 'Fear in His Face,'" cnn.com, Dec. 30, 2006

✳ *Hung*

"The stockings were <u>hung</u> by the chimney with care."
> "A Visit from St. Nicholas," Clement Clarke Moore or Henry Livingston (1823)

"The best thing I have is the knife from *Fatal Attraction*. I <u>hung</u> it in my kitchen. It's my way of saying, 'Don't mess with me.'"
> American actress Glenn Close, quoted in askmen.com

The distinction between *hanged* and *hung* is gruesome but easy to remember: a person is *hanged* to death. Coats, pictures of your sweetheart, and everything else that you suspend from a height are *hung*. A jury can be *hung,* too, if it can't reach a verdict. The different meanings of these words were sorted out long ago, but the authors of virtually all recent usage books have found it necessary to cite the distinction.

Hanged and *hung* come from two different Old English verbs and one verb that came from the Vikings. These words got confused with each other, but by Shakespeare's time *hanged* largely had the special sense of "put to death by hanging." That gave us the quaint old expression "I'll be hanged."

***Hanged* today refers to execution or suicide by hanging.**
If you've *hung* a thing, you've suspended it from an elevated point.

People say *hung* in the sense of *hanged* so often that a minority of the *Harper Dictionary* Usage Panel said that they would accept the phrase "hung without trial." In printed texts, *hanged* is far more common than *hung* in that sense, though.[36]

I recommend that you observe the traditional distinction between these words.

Hung appears in a number or colloquial figures of speech, including *hung out with* in the sense of "kept company with."

> "I had the lunchbox that cleared the cafeteria.... Because I <u>hung out with</u> my grandfather, I started to bring my lunchbox with sardine sandwiches and calamari that I would eat off my fingers like rings.... I was also always reeking of garlic."
>> Rachael Ray, Daytime Emmy Award–winning American TV personality, chef, and author, quoted in Paul Chi, "Rachael Ray: 'I Sat Alone' in the Cafeteria," people.com, Dec. 7, 2007

According to the Urban Dictionary, if you've *hung out with* a friend, that's less serious than dating, but it may have involved exploring the possibility of romance.

Another figurative use of *hung* is *hung up on*, one meaning of which is "thinking about a lot, very caught up in."

> "I don't get <u>hung up on</u> weight."
>> Jack Black, American actor, musician, comedian, and writer, quoted in Susan K. Mitchell, *Jack Black* (2009)

She's so <u>hung up on</u> him!

Still another figurative use of *hung* comes from baseball. Years ago, when I was considering taking a job helping to edit and update a dictionary, I was asked to define *hung a curveball.* I'd guess that millions of Americans can define that phrase: when a pitcher has *hung a curveball,* he hasn't put on enough spin, so the ball comes in slowly and high in the zone where batters can hit it.

HE or THEY after ANYBODY, EVERYONE, SOMEBODY, A PERSON, ETC.

✳ *He, Him, His*

"I have never yet seen <u>anyone</u> whose desire to build up <u>his</u> moral power was as strong as sexual desire."

> Confucius, Chinese philosopher (551–479 B.C.), *Analects*

"<u>Everybody</u> is <u>himself</u> his own foremost and greatest flatterer."

> Plutarch, *Moralia*

"<u>Anybody</u> who is old, who has really lived and felt this life—<u>he</u> knows the pathos of the lost opportunity."

> Mark Twain, speech, "Russian Sufferers," Dec. 18, 1905

"At 50, <u>everyone</u> has the face <u>he</u> deserves."

> George Orwell, last entry in his notebook, Apr. 17, 1949, in *The Collected Essays, Journalism, and Letters of George Orwell* (1968)

"I don't think <u>anybody</u> should write <u>his</u> own autobiography until after <u>he's</u> dead."

> Samuel Goldwyn, American movie studio head (1879–1974), quoted in *Goldwyn: The Man Behind the Myth*, prologue by Arthur Marx (1976)

"<u>Anybody</u> that wants the presidency so much that <u>he'll</u> spend two years organizing and campaigning for it is not to be trusted with the office."

> David Broder, Pulitzer Prize–winning American columnist, *Washington Post*, July 18, 1973

"<u>Everybody</u> has a little bit of Watergate in <u>him</u>."

> Billy Graham, quoted in *And I Quote*, ed. Ashton Applewhite and Tripp Evans (1992)

✳ *They, Their, Them*

"God send <u>everyone</u> <u>their</u> heart's desire."
    Margaret in *Much Ado About Nothing* (1598–99)

"It's enough to drive <u>anyone</u> out of <u>their</u> senses."
    George Bernard Shaw, Irish playwright, journalist, and author
    (1856–1950), *Candida* (1898)

"<u>Everybody</u> ought to have a Lower East Side in <u>their</u> life."
    Irving Berlin, Russian-born American songwriter (1888–1989),
    quoted in *Vogue* magazine, Nov. 1, 1962

"<u>Everybody</u> should have some basic security when it comes to
<u>their</u> health care."
    President Barack Obama, remarks at signing of the Health
    Insurance Reform Bill, Mar. 23, 2010

"<u>Everybody</u> has a plan until <u>they</u> get punched in the mouth."
    Mike Tyson, quoted in Mike Beradino, "Mike Tyson Explains One
    of His Most Famous Quotes," sun-sentinel.com, Nov. 9, 2012

"Before you criticize <u>someone</u>, you should walk a mile in <u>their</u>
shoes. That way, when you criticize <u>them</u>, you are a mile away
from <u>them</u> and you have <u>their</u> shoes."
    Attributed to Jack Handey, Emmy Award–winning writer for
    Saturday Night Live

Should you say *everyone…he* or *everyone…they*? How about *some-body…he* or *somebody…they*? The answer is that English doesn't give us a choice that's completely logical. *Everyone…he* gives us agreement in what grammarians call **number** because both pronouns are singular. But it doesn't necessarily give consistency in **gender** if the people being described include girls or women. *Everyone…they* avoids disagreement in gender but creates it in number.

Let's start this lesson by noting that some pronouns are normally singular. This was presented as a strict rule by eighteenth-century grammarians and has become standard. These pronouns include *anybody, anyone, everybody, everyone, nobody, no one, somebody,* and *someone.* They take singular verbs. So we say *anyone is, everybody goes, no one has, somebody was, someone laughs,* etc.

The question is, how do you refer back to these pronouns later if you don't know the gender of the people they describe? Should you say *his, her,* or *their*? And should you refer back to a singular noun like *person* by saying *he* or *they*?

It's enough to drive <u>anyone</u> out of <u>his</u> senses.
or
It's enough to drive <u>anyone</u> out of <u>her</u> senses.
or
It's enough to drive <u>anyone</u> out of <u>their</u> senses.

English doesn't have a singular pronoun that can represent both genders. So Chaucer, Shakespeare, and many others used the plural *they, their,* or *them* to fill that role. But in the 1740s a new rule was invented: that the word *he* should refer to both boys and girls. This made singular masculine pronouns refer back to other singular pronouns and nouns, which is logical grammatically. The rule has endured, and some major authorities, including Fowler (1926) and Strunk and White (1959), adopted it.[37]

There are problems with this rule, though:

(1) It's sexist to refer to both genders as *he*.[38]
(2) Applying this rule rigidly can be ridiculous, as it is in this sentence:
    "<u>Everyone</u> will be able to decide for <u>himself</u> whether or not to have an abortion."[39]
(3) Most importantly, people ignore this rule, or never knew it: they go right ahead and use *they, their,* and *them* as if they were singular. That's inconsistent grammatically, but it avoids issues of gender. And words like *everybody* and *everyone* may suggest plurality anyway, so it may seem natural to refer to them as *their* or *they*:
    "God send <u>everyone</u> <u>their</u> heart's desire."
    "<u>Everybody</u> ought to have a Lower East Side in <u>their</u> life."

British English often uses the plural *they, their,* or *them* in this way, even in formal contexts. In the passage below, for example, no less an authority than R. W. Burchfield, the former chief editor of the *Oxford English Dictionary,* referred back to *everyone* as *them:*

> "The compilation of the *OED* made it possible for <u>everyone</u> to have before <u>them</u> the historical shape and configuration of the language."
> *Unlocking the English Language* (1989)

The strange fact is that British Standard English follows *everyone, everybody, a person,* etc., with a singular verb and a plural pronoun. That's common in American English, too. Still, many careful American writers consider it illogical and shoddy to use *they, them,* or *their* as if they were singular. The opposition is diminishing quickly, though. In 1996, fully 80 percent of the *American Heritage* Usage Panel opposed using *they* to refer back to the singular noun *person* in the sentence *A <u>person</u> on that level should not have to keep track of the hours <u>they</u> put in.* By 2008, only 62 percent of the panelists were opposed to the same sentence and more than a third of them approved of it. There was more support for saying *them* and *their* to refer back to the pronouns *anyone* and *everyone:* more than half of the 2008 panel members allowed that usage. So the overall trend toward acceptance is clear. The opposition is still very strong, though— and, stodgy English professor that I am, I admit that I agree with it.

In informal use, feel free to say *they* when you refer back to a singular pronoun or to a noun like *person* or *individual*.

In formal contexts, very many educated Americans still consider this usage an error. So, **depending on the situation, I suggest that you be conservative**. The good news is that there are ways around the problem:

(1) **If you know that the people you're referring to are all male, simply say *he, his,* or *him;* if they're all female, say *she* or *her*.**
<u>Everybody</u> on the Giants wore <u>his</u> World Series championship ring.
<u>Each</u> member of the 2012 U.S. women's Olympic gymnastic team wore <u>her</u> gold medal.

(2) If you don't know the group's gender, or if it's mixed, you can say "he or she." That can get annoying if you do it too often, though.

(3) Or you can rewrite the sentence to avoid the problem. Here are some ways to do that:

- Switch from the singular to the plural:
  When someone studies, he can learn a lot.
  becomes
  When people study, they can learn a lot.
- Write the sentence with *you: When you study, you can learn a lot.*
- Simply eliminate the pronoun:
  Studying is a good way to learn a lot.[40]

> The idea that the word *he* should stand for both boys and girls seems to have been invented by a schoolmistress named Ann Fisher, the first woman ever to publish a book on English grammar. It's ironic that it was a woman who introduced this rule, as if English weren't sexist enough already.

HOI POLLOI

"My dear fellows, this is our punishment for associating with the hoi polloi."
　　Moe Howard of the Three Stooges (1897–1975), in their 1935 film *Hoi Polloi,* quoted on imdb.com

Hoi polloi means "the many" in Greek. In British university slang the *hoi polloi* were the students who graduated without honors, and in general use today **the term refers to ordinary people, the masses, the man in the street.** Especially since the 1950s in America, though, some people have thought that *hoi polloi* refers to high society, the elite. That's the opposite of its original meaning. The confusion may have come about because *hoi polloi* sounds a little like *hoity-toity*, which means "self-important, stuck-up."

It's technically wrong to say **the** *hoi polloi*, because *hoi* means "the" in Greek. So *the hoi polloi* is redundant: it means "the the masses." The phrase is so commonly used, though, that it's generally accepted, even by educated speakers.[41]

I or ME: SUBJECT PRONOUNS AND OBJECT PRONOUNS

✳ *It's Not You, It's Me*

> George's girlfriend on *Seinfeld* breaks up with him by saying, "It's not you. <u>It's me</u>." He replies indignantly: "You're giving me the 'It's not you, <u>it's me</u>' routine? I *invented* 'It's not you, <u>it's me</u>.' Nobody tells me it's them. If it's anybody, <u>it's me</u>."
>
> Tony Award–winner Jason Alexander as George, "The Lip Reader," *Seinfeld*, NBC-TV, Oct. 28, 1993

The actual meaning of *It's not you, it's me:*

"I no longer find you attractive, but I can't say that because I'll feel guilty. Oh, by the way, good riddance."

Urban Dictionary

Okay, saying *It's not you, it's me* is a pathetic way to break up with somebody. But is it wrong grammatically? Well, strictly, yes, it is. **If a person or thing is doing something or being described, the pronoun should be *I*, *he*, *she*, *it*, *you*, *we*, or *they* in formal speech and writing.** They're called subject pronouns because they serve as the subject. Here's an example:

> "<u>It was I</u> who allowed the Alliance to know the location of the shield generator. It is quite safe from your pitiful little band."
>
> Emperor Palpatine in the 1983 film *Star Wars Episode VI: The Return of the Jedi,* quoted on imdb.com.

Have you ever noticed that some movie villains have impeccable grammar? Emperor Palpatine certainly does in this passage. But in conversation, unless you're an evil tyrant in a sci-fi film, you'll probably be more comfortable saying *It was me*. True, that breaks the traditional rules, and your grammar checker may mark it with squiggly green underlining. But constructions like *It's me* have become so common that the decision whether to say them is almost a matter of style, not grammar. It may be wrong in formal contexts, but in casual speech and writing, constructions like *It's me, it's them,* and *it should have been us* are nearly universal today.[42]

That wasn't always the case. In fact, constructions like *It's me* and *That's me* are comparative newcomers to English. They showed up only very occasionally in Middle English and didn't appear in print until the end of the sixteenth century. Shakespeare was one of the first to use them in writing when he had characters say, "Oh, the dog is me" and "That's me."[43] Some influential eighteenth-century grammarians denounced constructions like *It is me*, though, and schoolmasters then enforced the rule prohibiting them. So these constructions are wrong by formal standards, but you'd never know that judging from everyday speech.

In informal contexts today, speakers and writers use these constructions without fear of criticism. Did you even notice that George says "Nobody tells me it's them" in the passage above? If not, that tells you how natural this construction sounds to us. In fact, people increasingly are saying things like *It is me* not only in American and British English but also in the many varieties of English that are spoken around the world.[44] Some of these "errors" are a lot preferable in casual use to the "correct" alternatives. Try knocking on someone's door and announcing, "It is I." You'll be formally correct, but see what kind of reception you get.

Here are some more examples:

"I thought of maybe hanging up if my parents answered, but that wouldn't've worked, either. They'd know it was me. My mother always knows it's me."

J. D. Salinger, *The Catcher in the Rye* (1951)

Are You There, God? It's Me, Margaret
    Title of Judy Blume's 1970 young adult novel

Are You There, Vodka? It's Me, Chelsea
    Title of comedienne, actress, writer, TV host, and producer
    Chelsea Handler's 2008 best-selling book

"THIS <u>IS ME</u>, WINSTON CHURCHILL"

Winston Churchill ruffled some feathers when he said, "This is me"
in 1946. He was sending a message to a group of workers in New
Haven who had put in overtime to prepare recording equipment
that he planned to use to dictate his memoirs. To thank them, he
used the recording device to say:

> "This <u>is me</u>, Winston Churchill....I am so glad to be able to
> thank you in this remarkable way."
>   "This Is Me, Churchill," Associated Press, Apr. 1, 1946

At that time, editors didn't approve of such a casual usage, at least
not by a speaker of Churchill's eloquence and stature. The
Associated Press put *[sic]* after "This is me" to indicate that it was
Churchill's error, not theirs. The *New York Times* commented
judgmentally that it was "a remarkable sentence."[45]

✳ *Between You and Me*

"Something was starting <u>between Mr. DiMaggio and me</u>. It was
always nice when it started, always exciting. But it always ended
up in dullness."
    Marilyn Monroe, in Marilyn Monroe and Ben Hecht, *My Story*
    (2006)

"What we talked about will have to remain a secret <u>between him
and me</u>. I spoke to him as a brother whom I have pardoned and
who has my complete trust."

Pope John Paul II (1920–2005), speaking on Dec. 27, 1983, after meeting with the imprisoned man who had shot him, quoted in "Pope John Paul II in Pictures," telegraph.co.uk

Oprah told Sean Combs that she had read that he no longer used the name P. Diddy because of his fans. She asked if the *P* had been getting <u>between him and them</u>.

"Oprah Talks to Sean Combs," Oprah.com, *O, The Oprah Magazine,* Nov. 2006

"Bassem Youssef does my job in Egypt. The only real difference <u>between him and me</u> is that he performs his satire in a country still testing the limits of its hard-earned freedom, where those who speak out against the powerful still have much to fear."

Jon Stewart, award-winning American TV host, comedian, political satirist, writer, and director, in *Time* magazine, Apr. 29–May 6, 2013

It's pretty common for people to say something like *Just between you and I,* even though *Just between you and me* is actually the traditionally correct usage. Here's the rule for formal speech and writing:

Between is a preposition, and if you use a personal pronoun after a preposition, it should be *me, you, him, her, it, us,* or *them.*

between you and me
between her and him
between them
between us and them

This wasn't always a strict rule in English. Shakespeare, for instance, had it both ways: he wrote "between you and <u>I</u>" and "between France and <u>him</u>."[46] Language commentators and schoolteachers subsequently banished *between you and I* from formal English and the phrase rarely shows up in print today. It keeps appearing in speech, though, even among highly educated speakers. Many stylists are fiercely opposed to *between you and I:* nearly every member of the *Harper Dictionary* Usage Panel rejected it, even in casual speech. W. H. Auden, who was one of the panelists, called it "horrible."[47] That was a bit harsh. People may say *between you and I* because they're a little nervous about saying *me*. They know that in some formal contexts, speakers sometimes say *me* when traditional grammar requires *I*. So they overcorrect and do the reverse: they say *I* when they should say *me*. The simple trick is just to keep in mind that *between you and me* is good Standard English and can serve as a model for other phrases that begin with prepositions.

Remember, a **preposition** is a word like *for, from, in, on, to, under,* or *with* that **positions** nouns or pronouns with respect to other words. Prepositions often indicate location, direction, or time.

"Bridge <u>over</u> Troubled Water"
Men <u>in</u> Black
X-Men: Days <u>of</u> Future Past
"<u>In</u> My Life"

See page 13 for a list of prepositions.
Here are some other examples with pronouns following *between:*

There was an agreement <u>between him and her.</u>
An ocean lay <u>between us.</u>

Which version of the sentence below is correct in formal English?

(A) Let's keep this <u>between you and I.</u>
(B) Let's keep this <u>between you and me.</u>

Since *between* is a preposition, "Let's keep this <u>between you and me</u>" is the right choice, as in version B.

✳ You and I *or* You and Me

"This land was made <u>for you and me.</u>"
  Lyric from Woody Guthrie's 1944 song "This Land Is Your Land"

You would never say *This land was made for I*, right? But when people add another person to a sentence, they sometimes think that it sounds better to say *for you and I*. This is another instance of overcorrecting, but don't feel too bad if you've said something like it. The Queen of England has done it, too:

> "It has <u>given my husband and I</u> great pleasure."
> Queen Elizabeth II, telegram, 1958

Here's a two-part rule for when to say *me, him, her, them,* and *us*. It's pretty simple:

(1) The personal pronoun *me, him, her, it, you, us,* or *them* refers to the person or people being acted on in your sentence.

> "Dogs look up to you. Cats look down on you. <u>Give me</u> a pig!
> He looks you in the eye and treats you as an equal."
> Winston Churchill, ca. 1952

> "I believe there is something out there <u>watching us</u>.
> Unfortunately, it's the government."
> Attributed to Woody Allen

These pronouns receive action and they're called object pronouns. Grammarians say that they're in the objective or accusative case.

(2) As we saw with *between you and me,* a personal pronoun that follows a preposition should be *me, him, her, it, you, us,* or *them*.

We use these object pronouns because they're the objects of prepositions.
 (*You* and *it* are the same whether they're the subjects or the objects in a sentence.)
 Here are a few examples of pronouns after prepositions:

> "I went down badly and I was dragged for 25 yards, and in the end the horse jumped <u>over me</u> and just clipped me with his back legs."
> Johnny Depp, on a violent fall from a horse while filming *The Lone Ranger,* quoted in mirror.co.uk, May 9, 2012

"In between segments, Ellen leans over and asks me how I'm really doing and checks in <u>with me</u> about what I talked <u>to her</u> about the last time."

> Taylor Swift, on being interviewed by Ellen DeGeneres, quoted in Lacey Rose, "The Booming Business of Ellen DeGeneres," hollywoodreporter.com, Aug. 22, 2012

So far, so good. When people add another person to the sentence, though, it can get a little tricky. You wouldn't say, "Me kissed a girl," for example—unless you happen to be Cookie Monster, or maybe Tonto. So Katy Perry was right, of course, to title her 2008 hit song "<u>I Kissed</u> a Girl." When they talk about two or more people, however, speakers sometimes casually say *me* when the traditional rule requires *I*. The result is nonstandard English:

Nonstandard: **<u>Me</u> and her** still love each other.
Standard: **<u>She</u> and I** still love each other.
Nonstandard: **<u>Me</u> and my friend were** eating chocolate chip cookies.
Standard: <u>My friend and **I** were</u> eating chocolate chip cookies.

These nonstandard constructions are often associated with the speech of children and less educated adults, but many others have said them, too.

People also do the opposite in casual conversation: they say *I* or *he,* for example, when the traditional rules require *me* or *him.*[48]

Nonstandard: She ordered beers <u>for John and I.</u>
Standard: She ordered beers <u>for John and me.</u>

In formal speech and writing, apply the two-part rule above to all of the pronouns in each sentence.

To double-check, just cross out the noun or the first pronoun and the word *and.* Then you should know the right answer intuitively.

Which version of this sentence is correct?

(A) Mr. Buffett <u>invited I</u> to dinner.
(B) Mr. Buffett <u>invited me</u> to dinner.

Okay, that one is too easy. The correct choice is obviously *invited me*, since the pronoun is receiving the action of being invited. But which version of this next sentence is correct?

> (A) Mr. Buffett invited <u>my brother and me</u> to dinner.
> (B) Mr. Buffett invited <u>my brother and I</u> to dinner.

Mr. Buffett's inviting you and your brother is an action that affects you both, so the pronoun has to be *me,* as in version A.

To double-check, cross out *my brother and.* That leaves *Mr. Buffett invited me.*

Which versions of the passages below are correct in formal writing and speech?

> (A) Jennifer Lawrence "had always wanted to perform in some way, but her parents consistently dissuaded her. <u>Her two older brothers and her</u> were supposed to be athletic and scholarly—not theatrical."
> (B) Jennifer Lawrence "had always wanted to perform in some way, but her parents consistently dissuaded her. <u>She and her two older brothers</u> were supposed to be athletic and scholarly—not theatrical."
> Lynn Hirschberg, "The Brave Ones," *W Magazine,* Sept. 2010

> (A) <u>Me and my boyfriend</u> went to see *Frozen.*
> (B) <u>My boyfriend and I</u> went to see *Frozen.*

In the first passage, nothing is acting on Jennifer Lawrence and her brothers and there's no preposition in front of them, so the right choice in formal usage is *she,* as in version B. To double-check, cross out *her two older brothers and.* That leaves you with *she was supposed to be athletic and scholarly,* which confirms that *she* is the right pronoun.

By the traditional rules, *my boyfriend and I went* in the second passage is the right choice. Nothing in the sentence is acting on the speaker and there's no preposition before these pronouns. The speaker is the subject, doing the action, so *I* is correct. If you double-check by leaving out *my boyfriend and*, you're left with *I went to see* Frozen, which confirms that *I* is right.

✳ Than I *or* Than Me, As I *or* As Me

In the sixteenth century, writers started to say *than me* or *than him* where we would traditionally expect *than I* or *than he*. Shakespeare did it.[49] So did Jonathan Swift and Dr. Johnson in the eighteenth century, and many writers since then. Using Latin and Greek as models, however, some influential eighteenth-century grammarians concluded that this usage was ungrammatical. Their view is still the norm in edited prose.

In casual conversation, though, people very often say things like *She is smarter than **me,** You were faster than **him,*** and *We aren't as brave as **her.***[50] That breaks the formal rules, but even educated speakers do it colloquially. Here's an easy way to get it right in formal contexts:

In comparisons like *faster than* or *as brave as*, when a pronoun appears at the end of a clause or a sentence, try to add a verb after it. If you can, the pronoun should be *I, you, he, she, it, we,* or *they*. If you can't, it should be *me, you, him, her, it, us,* or *them*.

Which versions of the sentences below are correct in formal writing?

(A) She <u>is</u> much <u>better</u> at math <u>than me</u>.
(B) She <u>is</u> much <u>better</u> at math <u>than I</u>.

(A) She <u>liked him better than me</u>.
(B) She <u>liked him better than I</u>.

(A) She <u>isn't</u> as ticklish as <u>him</u>.
(B) She <u>isn't</u> as ticklish as <u>he</u>.

In the first sentence, *I/me* is not receiving action, so the right choice is *I*.

Double-check by supplying a verb at the end of the sentence: "She is much better at math than I <u>am</u>."

The second sentence is a trick: both versions are correct, but they mean different things. Version A means that she liked him better than she liked me. Version B is saying that she liked him better than I *did*. In a case like this, choose the pronoun that makes the sentence mean what you want to say.

In the third sentence, you can add a verb after *he*: "as ticklish as he is." So version B is the right choice,

"IF I WERE A RICH MAN": THE SUBJUNCTIVE MOOD

"Heaven goes by favor. If it went by merit, you would stay out and the dog would go in."
> Mark Twain, "Suggestions to Persons Entering Heaven," 1910, in *Mark Twain's Helpful Hints for Good Living* (2004)

Nancy Astor: "If I were married to you, I'd put poison your coffee."
Winston Churchill: "If I were married to you, I'd drink it."
> Ca. 1912, Blenheim Palace, attributed in *Nancy Astor and Her Friends,* ed. E. Langhorne (1974),

In the song "If I Were a Rich Man," Tevye says what he would do if he were wealthy. It would involve a lot of biddy-biddy-bumming.
> Said of the character Tevye in the 1964 musical *Fiddler on the Roof,* by Sheldon Harnick and Jerry Bock

"If pregnancy were a book, they would cut the last two chapters."
> Nora Ephron, American playwright, screenwriter, journalist, producer, and director (1941–2012), *Heartburn* (1983)

"If I Were a Boy"
> Title of Grammy Award–winning American singer and actress Beyoncé Knowles-Carter's 2008 hit song

"They were like all Jewish parents. They hoped that I would be studious enough to be a doctor or a lawyer, or some professional thing. They were creatures of the Depression — they <u>would have been</u> thrilled <u>if I had been</u> a pharmacist or something reliable."

> Woody Allen, on whether his parents encouraged him to be an entertainer, quoted in interviewmagazine.com, Sept. 2008

Megan Fox, on being compared to Angelina Jolie: "People see a dark-haired girl with tattoos who's in an action movie, and it's 'She's the next Angelina.'...But I have nothing in common with her. <u>If</u> someone <u>were to tell</u> me she's a vampire, <u>I'd [say]</u>, 'Yeah, okay, totally.'"

> Alison Prato, "The Devil in Megan Fox," cosmopolitan.com, Jan. 22, 2010

"So go home tonight and ask yourselves, 'What would I do <u>if</u> I <u>weren't</u> afraid?' And then go do it."

> Sheryl Sandberg, American technology executive, author, and chief operating officer of Facebook, commencement address, Barnard College, May 17, 2011

"There's lotion for your face, for your hands, for your feet, for your body. Why? What <u>would happen if you put</u> hand lotion on your feet? <u>Would</u> your feet <u>get</u> confused and start clapping?"

> Ellen DeGeneres, *Seriously...I'm Kidding* (2012)

"I think that you have to laugh at the absurdity of this entire industry and the absurdity of what it is we do. <u>If</u> I <u>didn't</u>, <u>I'd</u> go crazy."

> Mila Kunis, Ukrainian-born American actress, on movies and acting, quoted in interviewmagazine.com, Aug. 2012

Should Tevye's song in *Fiddler on the Roof* be called "If I <u>Were</u> a Rich Man" or "If I <u>Was</u> a Rich Man"? The answer is that "If I <u>Were</u>" is right, according to the traditional rules. Tevye's song and the other passages at the top of this lesson use the word *if* to introduce an idea that's hypothetical, imagined, or contingent. These statements all refer to something that isn't real or an event that hasn't actually happened, and they're expressed in what's called the **subjunctive mood**. Most of the students who enter my courses have never heard of that term, unless they learned about it while studying a foreign language. But they know that a subjunctive construction like *If I were* exists, even if many of them aren't sure when to use it.

The subjunctive mood was well developed in Old English, but it's largely been crowded out of the language since then, and it's been in a major decline in the last three or four centuries. We use it today only in limited ways and in specific contexts. Here are some guidelines for how and when to use the subjunctive:

✳ *"If I Were an Oscar Mayer Wiener"*

"All my life I've looked at words <u>as though</u> I <u>were</u> seeing them for the first time."
>   Ernest Hemingway, Pulitzer Prize– and Nobel Prize–winning American author and journalist (1899–1961), correspondence, Apr. 9, 1945, quoted in *Ernest Hemingway: Selected Letters,* ed. Carlos Baker (1981)

"People had a habit of looking at me <u>as if I were</u> some kind of mirror instead of a person."
>   Marilyn Monroe, quoted in Marilyn Monroe and Roger G. Taylor, *Marilyn Monroe in Her Own Words* (1983)

"<u>If</u> I <u>were</u> an Oscar Mayer wiener,
Everyone <u>would be</u> in love with me."
>   TV advertisement, 1965

"I don't work out. <u>If</u> God <u>had wanted</u> us to bend over, He <u>would have put</u> diamonds on the floor."
>   Attributed to Joan Rivers

Of Lady Gaga: "In an arena, her music…takes flight. It is <u>as if</u> each song <u>were written</u> for the express purpose of being belted— roared—in front of 20,0000 people on an extravagant stage set with ten dancers taking up the rear."
>   Jonathan Van Meter, "Lady Gaga: Our Lady of Pop," *Vogue,* Mar. 2011

When *if, as if,* or *as though* introduces a hypothetical or other contrary-to-fact statement, something we imagine, or think of as contingent, it's often followed by *were* in the subjunctive. In other cases, it's followed by a verb in the past tense. A word like *would* or *could* often appears later in the sentence:

<u>If it went</u> by merit, you <u>would</u> stay out and the dog <u>would</u> go in.
<u>If I were</u> married to you, <u>I'd</u> put poison your coffee.
<u>If I were</u> married to you, <u>I'd</u> drink it.
<u>If pregnancy were a book</u>, they <u>would cut</u> the last two chapters.

As a matter of style, don't put *would* in the *if* clause.

Casual: "If he would have thrown me a fastball, I'd have hit it out of the park."
Formal: "If he had thrown me a fastball, I'd have hit it out of the park."

✳ *"I Wish I Were in Love Again"*

"I <u>wish</u> I <u>were</u> in love again."
> Song by Lorenz Hart, American lyricist (1895–1943), in the 1937 musical *Babes in Arms*

"I have often said that I <u>wish</u> I <u>had invented</u> blue jeans.... They have expression, modesty, sex appeal, simplicity—all I hope for in my clothes."
> Yves Saint Laurent, French fashion designer, quoted in *Ritz,* no. 85, 1984

"'I miss my wand,'" Hermione said miserably. 'I <u>wish</u> Mr. Ollivander <u>could have made</u> me another one too.'"
> J. K. Rowling, *Harry Potter and the Deathly Hallows* (2007)

Nina: "Daddy, I love Miley Cyrus. What's your favorite song of hers?"
LL Cool J: "'Party in the USA.' ... I just <u>wish</u> my name <u>were</u> on it."
> Quoted in *Redbook,* Oct. 2010

Wishes or suppositions are followed in the subjunctive by *were, had, could (have),* **etc.**

You also can use the subjunctive mood to demand, suggest, urge, or exhort. If you do that, remember that the verb after *he, she,* or *it* lacks a final *-s*. Also, *be* appears where we would normally say *is:*

I insist that he <u>sing</u>
it is important <u>that it be honored</u>
I demand that she <u>listen</u>
we recommended that she <u>get</u> some rest
I propose that she <u>be rewarded</u>
he commanded that it <u>be done</u>
it is desirable that he <u>wear</u> a tux

This is a common usage in North America, Australia, and New Zealand, though less so in Britain.

Sometimes without even thinking about it, we use the subjunctive mood in relics of earlier English, expressions that contain *were* when we'd normally say *was, be* instead of *is, come* instead of *comes,* etc. Here are a few of them:

as it were
if need be
be that as it may
perish the thought
come what may
so be it
far be it from me (to)
suffice it to say

God and heaven appear in several of these venerable old fossils. They include *God bless you, God forbid, God save the queen, heaven help us, so help me God,* and *thy kingdom come.* They also include some choice curses.

❋ *When Not to Use the Subjunctive*

When *If* Refers to Something That Might Be True

When you say *if* or *as if* to talk about something that might be the case, or something that could very well happen, don't use subjunctive forms. Instead, use the "normal" grammar that you do when you describe something that's true or real. That's called the indicative mood.

"If you tell the truth, you don't have to remember anything."
    Mark Twain, *Notebook,* 1894

"The man who is a pessimist before 48 knows too much; if he is an optimist after it, he knows too little."
    Mark Twain, *Notebook,* Dec. 1902

"If anything can go wrong, it will."
    Murphy's Law, probably originated by Edward A. Murphy Jr., ca. 1949

"As they say in poker, if you've been in the game 30 minutes and you don't know who the patsy is, you're the patsy."
    Warren Buffett, American business magnate, investor, and philanthropist, letter to the shareholders of his company, Berkshire Hathaway, Feb. 29, 1988

"If we do not succeed, then we run the risk of failure."
    Dan Quayle, U.S. vice president 1989–93, speech in Phoenix, Mar. 23, 1990

"If it's the Psychic Network, why do they need a phone number?"
    Robin Williams, quoted in *Manly* [Australia] *Daily,* Mar. 30, 2004

"I was the best man at the wedding. If I'm the best man, why is she marrying him?"
    Jerry Seinfeld, quoted in "What's the Deal with . . . : 15 Jokes from Jerry Seinfeld on His Birthday," wcbsfm.cbslocal.com, Apr. 29, 2013

"Now they show you how detergents take out bloodstains—a pretty violent image there. I think <u>if you've got</u> a T-shirt with a bloodstain all over it, maybe laundry <u>isn't</u> your biggest problem."

Ibid.

When You're Just Checking on Something
Also use "normal" indicative forms, not subjunctive ones, to describe the act of checking if something is the case:

"She waited for a few minutes to see <u>if she was</u> going to shrink any further."

Lewis Carroll, pen name of Charles Lutwidge Dodgson, English writer, mathematician, and photographer (1832–1898), *Alice's Adventures in Wonderland* (1865)

I called to ask <u>if she was</u> feeling better.

✳ *The Death of the Subjunctive?*

A little over four hundred years ago, people started to say *was* instead of *were* in wishes and contrary-to-fact conditional statements. Nobody knows why, but by the eighteenth century, this may have been happening quite frequently. This passage by Jonathan Swift contains one example:

"<u>I wish</u> my cold hand <u>was</u> in the warmest place about you."
Journal to Stella, Feb. 5, 1711

In the three centuries since Dr. Swift wrote that naughty line, people often have said things like *I wish I was* and *If I was* when the traditional rules required the subjunctive *were.* That's become so common that for well over a hundred years language commentators have been predicting the demise of the subjunctive mood in everyday spoken English. Some usage books declare it nearly dead already. But the subjunctive still survives in some aspects of speech, and it remains well established in careful formal writing. It's a matter of style in many cases. *I wish I was* and *I wish I were,* are both standard, for example, so you should choose which to use, depending on the level of formality you're aiming for. On the other hand, *If I were you* is standard, and *The Columbia Guide to Standard*

American English notes that many educated speakers consider *If I was you* to be substandard in both speech and writing.

I recommend that in formal contexts you say *If I were*, etc., when expressing hypothetical, imagined, or conditional ideas.

I also suggest that in formal writing and speech you say *I wish I were*, etc.

This is often a judgment call, though. In Britain, the subjunctive is mainly reserved for formal contexts and is rarely obligatory. Even in America, it's on the retreat. One eminent American scholarly publication, for example, instructs writers to use the subjunctive mood in wishes and other contrary-to-fact statements, but not in other contexts.[51]

Which versions of the sentences below are correct in formal English?

(A) "If beauty is truth, why don't women go to the library to have their hair done?"

(B) "If beauty were truth, why don't women go to the library to have their hair done?"

> Lily Tomlin, award-winning American comedian, actress, writer, and producer, quoted in *Woman's Hour Book of Humor* (1993), ed. Sally Feldman

(A) "If I were you, I'd bargain.... I'd go to the store and say, 'Can you do a little better? I mean, it's $89; can you give it to me for $79?'"

(B) "If I was you, I'd bargain.... I'd go to the store and say, 'Can you do a little better? I mean, it's $89; can you give it to me for $79?'"

> Mel Brooks, award-winning American film director, screenwriter, actor, producer, and comedian, advising people how to buy the box set *The Incredible Mel Brooks,* quoted in "Mel Brooks: 'Unhinged' and Loving It," National Public Radio, Jan. 23, 2013 (at the time of this writing, this box set was being offered on Amazon for $56.89)

Version A of Lily Tomlin's passage above is correct. Beauty could be truth, and, in the opinion of many poets, scientists, and philosophers, it is. So *if* is followed by *is* and *don't*.

Mel Brooks's statement is hypothetical and whimsical, so, in formal speech and writing, *If* should be followed by *were*, as in version A.

IMPLY or INFER

✳ *Imply*

"The fact that some geniuses were laughed at does not <u>imply</u> that all who are laughed at are geniuses. They laughed at Columbus, they laughed at Fulton.... But they also laughed at Bozo the Clown."

    Carl Sagan, *Boca's Brain* (1979)

One new super political action committee is called Bearded Entrepreneurs for the Advancement of a Responsible Democracy, or BEARD PAC. As its name <u>implies</u>, it is dedicated to supporting candidates with beards. People with mustaches do not qualify.

    Katy Steinmetz, "New BEARD PAC Supports Only Bearded Candidates," time.com, Apr. 5, 2013

Stephen Colbert, reporting on the Ku Klux Klan's claim to have a high-tech weapon:

"Yesterday I saw a story that made me realize that today's KKK is not your father's Klan. And yes, I'm <u>implying</u> that your father was in the Klan."

    The Colbert Report, Comedy Central, June 24, 2013

✳ *Infer*

Sherlock Holmes told Dr. Watson that he would deduce who was the owner of a battered old hat by using only the clues on the hat itself. Watson examined the hat and said that he couldn't see anything.

Holmes replied, "On the contrary, Watson, you can see everything. You fail, however, to reason from what you see. You are too timid in drawing your inferences."

"Then, pray tell me what it is that you can <u>infer</u> from this hat," said Watson.

Arthur Conan Doyle, Scottish writer and physician (1859–1930), "The Adventure of the Blue Carbuncle" (1892)

I <u>infer</u> that Professor Plum did it in the parlor with a kitchen knife.

"Suppose you'd never seen chess being played. You could, by watching a few games, <u>infer</u> the rules."

Martin Rees, "Back to the Beginning," *Newsweek,* Jan. 2, 2012 (Lexis)[52]

In the last hundred years or so, and especially since the 1950s, many usage books and countless English teachers have said emphatically that *infer* doesn't mean "imply." The difference between these words is that the speaker or writer *implies* and the listener or reader *infers*. Sir Thomas More was the first writer known to have used these two words with those meanings, in the sixteenth century. But Sir Thomas also used *infer* to mean "imply," and so have other writers since then. In the twentieth century this became a heated issue, and careful speakers and writers now usually observe the difference between these words. Nearly three-fourths of the *Harper's Dictionary* Usage Panel insisted on observing it, too. Several major usage guides agree that the distinction is a useful one.[53]

Imply, like many of our English words, is actually a metaphor. It comes from the Latin for "to fold in." So if something is *implied,* it's folded inside a statement or a fact in the sense that it's contained or entangled in it; in other words, it's not open and on the surface. That's the opposite of *explicit,* which comes from the Latin for "unfolded" and means "openly and distinctly expressed" in English.

To *imply* is to say or suggest something indirectly, not plainly or explicitly.

To *infer* is to deduce or form a conclusion from evidence rather than from an explicit statement.

It may help to keep in mind that to **infer** is to draw an **infer**ence. The word is used much less often than *imply* and typically appears in bureaucratic, legal, or academic writing.[54]

Which version of the sentence below is correct?

(A) Do you mean to <u>infer</u> that I'm an idiot?
(B) Do you mean to <u>imply</u> that I'm an idiot?

The speaker suggests, or *implies*, that the listener is an idiot, as in version B.

IRONY or SARCASM

✳ *Irony*

<u>Ironically</u>, in the *Wizard of Oz*, the Scarecrow wants a brain, not realizing that he is actually very clever. The Tin Man wants a heart, not recognizing he is already very emotional. The Cowardly Lion wants courage, though he already has it. And Dorothy wants the Wizard to take her back to Kansas, not knowing that she has the power to go home any time she chooses.

"'Ludicrous enthusiasm' is an apt way to describe a crucial component of Colbert's shtick.... We're aware that Colbert simultaneously occupies both an earnest, defender-of-the-American-faith persona within the space of the interview and also a zone of <u>ironic</u> distance outside of it."
　　Brad Frazier, "Where the Id Was, There Stephen Colbert Shall Be!," in Aaron Allen Schiller, *Stephen Colbert and Philosophy: I Am Philosophy (And So Can You!)* (2009)

✳ *Sarcasm*

Mark Twain once found himself on a train that stopped and hesitated every few hundred yards. He grew so incensed that he gave the conductor a child's fare, which was half of the amount for an adult. "And are you a child?" the conductor asked <u>sarcastically</u>. "No, not any more," Twain replied. "But I was when I got on your damn train!"

The Wit and Wisdom of Mark Twain, ed. Alex Ayres (2005)

"I tweet from bed. I love it because it's so quick. And it's funny. But it also leaves a lot of room for error because new people don't sense the <u>sarcasm</u>. There's no <u>sarcasm</u> font."

American model Chrissy Teigen, esquire.com

✳ *Irony*

Irony assumes two perspectives.[55] One of them is based on appearances or on what we expect or plan for. The other is the reality, which contradicts the appearances or expectations, and often thwarts people's hopes or plans. There are several types and many degrees of irony in English. People use the words *irony* and *ironically* fairly freely, though they may not be completely sure about what they mean. That may be why *irony* is one of the most popular words in the history of the Merriam-Webster online dictionary.

Someone is being *ironic* when he says something that is very different from and often the opposite of what he really means.

This typically involves pretending to praise someone or something that you're actually criticizing. The result may be funny or emphatic. Stephen Colbert's "ludicrous enthusiasm" in the passage above illustrates that very well. Another example is saying "Great!" when you get bad news, or "Nice weather!" during a blizzard.

***Dramatic irony* describes a situation in which the audience or reader realizes something about the plot that the characters don't.**

The passage about the *Wizard of Oz* at the top of this lesson gives an example of dramatic irony.

***Tragic irony* occurs when events happen despite—or because of— characters' attempts to control their fates in tragedies.**

In Sophocles's *Oedipus the King,* Oedipus flees his home to try to escape his fate, <u>ironically</u> setting in motion the events that fulfill it. Later, he tries to find out who killed the king; <u>ironically</u>, he himself was the killer.

More generally, something may seem *ironic* when it contradicts what we might expect or undermines our plans:

"It is an old and <u>ironic</u> habit of human beings to run faster when we have lost our way."
> Rollo May, American psychologist (1909–1994), "Introduction," *Love and Will* (1969)

"The most <u>ironic</u> outcome of the black Civil Rights movement has been the creation of the new black middle class which is increasingly separate from the black underclass."
> Henry Louis Gates, award-winning American literary critic, academic, writer, and public intellectual, quoted in Sean O'Hagan, "The Biggest Brother," guardian.co.uk, July 19, 2003

"Colbert celebrates the <u>irony</u> that his word *truthiness* is named 'Word of the Year' by Merriam-Webster's, even after he told viewers he was sure the 'wordanistas' at Webster's would say that it wasn't a word."
> Caption of a photo in Sophia A. McClennen, *Colbert's America: Satire and Democracy* (2012)

"Intellectual life is <u>ironic</u> because really smart people often do the dumbest things."
> David Brooks, American political and cultural commentator and journalist, "Rhapsody in Realism," nytimes.com, June 23, 2014

***Cosmic irony* involves the sense that the universe has its own plans, which may correct our expectations or mock our efforts. This may involve a divine plan or poetic justice.**

In the Book of Genesis, Joseph reveals that his brothers' bad behavior has <u>ironically</u> advanced God's hidden plan to achieve a greater good.

Many purists object to calling something ironic when it's simply a strange coincidence or a disappointment, with no larger significance about human folly.[56]

***Irony* also can describe a style of living in which people distance themselves from social conventions and norms.[57]**

Here's an illustration of that sense of the word:

> "If <u>irony</u> is the ethos of our age—and it is—then the hipster is our archetype of <u>ironic</u> living."
>   Christy Wampole, "How to Live Without Irony," blogs.nytimes.com, Nov. 17, 2012

Several lines from Alanis Morissette's 1995 hit song "Ironic" have been criticized for not being strictly ironic. They refer, for instance, to rain on your wedding day, the offer of a free ride after you've already bought a ticket, and meeting the man of your dreams but finding that he's already married. These lines use the word *irony* in the casual sense of an unhappy coincidence or a disappointment, so they're not strictly ironic. But by stringing a series of these events together, Morissette implies an ironic vision in which life conspires to frustrate or mock us. The website College Humor published a parody of this song that makes its individual lyrics fit with traditional meanings of *irony*. Here's an example:

> "Meeting the man of my dreams and then meeting his beautiful wife…who happens to be the psychiatrist I recently hired in hopes of improving my luck with the opposite sex."
>   Patrick Cassels, "Lines from Alanis Morissette's 'Ironic,' Modified to Actually Make Them Ironic," collegehumor.com, Dec. 26, 2006

This revised verse illustrates the ironic notion that life mocks our attempts to control our future.

✳ *Sarcasm*

Sarcasm comes from a Greek word meaning "to tear flesh," and sarcasm can hurt. **It often employs the type of irony in which you say the opposite of what you mean, but with a harsh edge that wounds, insults, or expresses irritation.** There's no clear line beyond which irony shades into sarcasm. It's usually a question of how crude and harsh the comment is. In a sentence like "Oh, you're God's great gift to women, you are," the sarcasm is pretty clear, and an exaggerated inflection in the speaker's voice would make it even more obvious.[58] And yet **sarcasm isn't always hurtful; it also can mock gently.** The quotation below, by the talk show host and writer Dick Cavett, gives an example of that. It imagines a sarcastic response to a celebrity who said "perfect for she and I" instead of the traditional usage "perfect for her and me":

> "Being the offspring of English teachers is a mixed blessing. When the film star says to you, on the air, 'It was a perfect script for she and I,' inside your head you hear, in the <u>sarcastic</u> voice of your late father, 'Perfect for *she,* eh? And perfect for *I,* also?'"
>
> Dick Cavett, "It's Only Language," opinionator.blogs.nytimes.com, Feb. 4, 2007

As Chrissy Teigen points out at the top of this lesson, it's not always easy to know when a written comment is sarcastic. But that hasn't stopped the United States Secret Service. In 2014 it posted an online request for computer programs that can identify sarcasm on Twitter. The *Washington Post* ran this sarcastic headline on June 3 of that year:

> "The Secret Service Wants Software That Detects Social Media Sarcasm. Yeah, Sure, It Will Work."

KIND OF, SORT OF

✳ *Kind Of*

> "It was <u>kind of</u> solemn, drifting down the big, still river."
> Mark Twain, *The Adventures of Huckleberry Finn* (1885)

> "My circle is small and tight. I'm <u>kind of</u> funny about making new friends."

Eminem (stage name of Marshall Bruce Mathers III), American rapper, songwriter, record producer, and actor, quoted in Brian Mockenhaupt, "Eminem: What I've Learned," esquire.com, Dec. 18, 2008

✳ *Sort Of*

"Maybe when you're afraid of everything, it <u>sort of</u> seems like you're scared of nothing."
> Natalie Portman, quoted in *Interview Magazine,* Sept. 2009

Kind of and *sort of* in the sense of "in a way, somewhat, more or less" are very common in casual speech and writing, especially in America. **Don't use these phrases in formal writing, though. Say *in a way, somewhat, more or less,* or something similar instead.**

KUDOS

"Some things you must always be unable to bear. Some things you must never stop refusing to bear: injustice, and outrage, and dishonor and shame.... Not for <u>kudos</u> and not for cash."
> William Faulkner, American writer and Nobel Prize laureate (1897–1962), *Intruder in the Dust* (1948)

"In childhood when I first saw <u>kudos</u> dispensed by a journalist ('<u>Kudos to</u> Rodgers and Hammerstein!') ... I told a friend that these two men were so great that they had received <u>kudos</u>. 'How many kudos?' he asked. That started me thinking and watching other bestowals. I soon noticed that ... nobody ever got just one kudo.... Imagine my amazement upon discovering that there was no such thing as a kudo!! There was, however, a <u>kudos</u>!!!"
> Russell Baker, Pulitzer Prize–winning American writer, "No, No!! Not a Kudo!!!" *New York Times,* Sept. 15, 1990 (Lexis)

"This is not to sing the praises of the black woman's stamina. Rather, it is a salute to her as an outstanding representative of the human race. <u>Kudos to</u> the educators, athletes, dancers, judges, janitors, politicians, artists, actors, writers, singers, poets, and social activists, to all who dare to look at life with humor, determination and respect."

Maya Angelou, award-winning American author and poet (1928–2014), *Even the Stars Look Lonesome* (1997)

"And then there's the poor little [word] *kudo*. It's a word *Variety* has used incorrectly—as in 'De Niro received many <u>kudos</u> for his performance—for enough decades that it is now forgotten that *kudos*…was already singular. There never was a *kudo*. Will *Variety* eventually take the word *pathos* and extract a *patho*?"

Dick Cavett, "It's Only Language," opinionator.blogs.nytimes.com, Feb. 4, 2007

Canadian astronaut Chris Hadfield showed a lot of people how cool the International Space Station is. "He recorded his now viral onboard performance of David Bowie's 'Space Oddity,' which totaled 6.6 million views in the first 24 hours after he posted it….So <u>kudos to</u> Hadfield for being so brilliant—and <u>kudos to</u> the bureaucrats for not getting in the way."

Jeffrey Kluger, "Lessons from the Singing Spaceman: What Governments Can Learn from Chris Hadfield," time.com, May 19, 2013

We'd all like *kudos* ("renown" or "praise"), but can you give somebody a *kudo*?

The word *kudos* was adopted into English as British university slang in the nineteenth century. It came from a singular Greek noun meaning "glory, renown," and it kept that meaning in English. Since then, its meaning has expanded, though. It's also been mistaken for a plural, and a new singular form of the word has been invented.

By the 1920s the meaning of *kudos* had extended to "praise given for an achievement." That sense that was popularized by *Time* magazine.

By 1925, because of its *-os* ending, people started to think that the word is plural. That hasn't happened to any other English word of Greek origin: *chaos, cosmos, pathos,* etc., are all understood to be singular despite ending in *-os.*[59] Since some people thought that *kudos* was plural, it was natural that the singular form *kudo* would appear eventually. The word was first recorded in 1941 as slang in a hash house. Then in 1950 the comedian Fred Allen used it in a letter to Groucho Marx, but his tone was clearly playful, just as we might expect in a letter to Groucho: he said that people in a famous Manhattan delicatessen were so enthusiastic about a TV show that a man sitting on a toilet swung open the men's room door to add his *kudo.* Some usage guides accept *kudo* as a new singular form, while others insist that it isn't a word in Standard English. The reality is that *kudo* is almost never used in print anyway.

I suggest that if you say *kudos* in formal English, keep its singular sense and use it with singular verbs:

kudos <u>is</u>
there <u>is</u> kudos

Pronounce it *kyu-dahs* or *kyu-dohs* (with a final *-s* sound, as in *pathos*). People often end the word with the sound *-doze,* though, which makes it sound plural, like *win**dows.***

To remember the standard usage, substitute the word *praise* for *kudos.* "There were praise for" is obviously ungrammatical, but "there was praise for" sounds fine.

Which version of the sentence below is correct in formal English?

(A) "<u>Kudos go</u> to Memphis for losing by only eight."
(B) "<u>Kudos goes</u> to Memphis for losing by only eight."
    Quoted in Philip B. Corbett, "One Kudo, Two Kudos?,"
    afterdeadline.blogs.nytimes.com, June 5, 2012

Version B is the right choice because *kudos* is singular in formal speech and writing.

This isn't the first time that a singular word has come into English from another language and been mistaken for a plural. In early English a *pea* was called a *pease*. (That's where "pease porridge hot" comes from in the nursery rhyme and the game.) Since *pease* sounded plural, a new singular word was invented later: *pea*. Something similar happened with *cherry*. It probably came from the French *cherise,* a singular noun that sounded plural to English ears. That resulted in a new singular word: *cherry. Pea* and *cherry* are now Standard English, of course, but *kudo* isn't (at least not yet).

LAY or LIE

✳ *Lay*

Lay your cards on the table, boys.
The boys are laying their cards on the table.
The boys laid their cards on the table.
The boys have laid their cards on the table.

"Everyone likes flattery; and when you come to Royalty you should lay it on with a trowel."
Benjamin Disraeli, ca. 1880 (attributed to Matthew Arnold), quoted in G. W. E. Russell, *Collections and Recollections* (1898)

"If all the economists were laid end to end, they would not reach a conclusion."
George Bernard Shaw, attributed

"From the moment I picked up your book until I laid it down, I was convulsed with laughter. Someday I intend [to read] it."
Groucho Marx, blurb for S. J. Perelman's *Dawn Ginsberg's Revenge* (1929)

* *Lie*

<u>Lie</u> down, Spot!
Spot <u>lay</u> there for three hours.
That dog <u>has lain</u> there all day.

"You're not drunk if you can <u>lie</u> on the floor without holding on."

> Dean Martin, Grammy Award–winning American singer, actor, comedian, and TV star, quoted in Paul Dixon, *Official Rules* (1978)

"Here Comes September. There <u>Lie</u> the Mets."

> Headline, nytimes.com, Aug. 30, 2014

"On the plus side, death is one of the few things that can be done as easily <u>lying</u> down."

> Woody Allen, *Without Feathers* (1975)

"I do not know what I may appear to the world; but to myself I seem to have been only a boy playing on the shore, diverting myself and now and then finding a smoother pebble or prettier shell than ordinary, whilst the great ocean of truth <u>lay</u> all undiscovered before me."

> Isaac Newton, English physicist, mathematician, and central figure in the scientific revolution (1642–1727), quoted in *Christian Monitor, and Religious Intelligencer,* July 4, 1812

"A biologist claims to have revived microbes that had <u>lain</u> dormant for tens of millions of years."

> Caption accompanying article, time.com, May 29, 1995

The main difference between these two words is that *lay* describes an action that's done to someone or something. It's called a **transitive verb**. *Lie*, by contrast, is an **intransitive** verb: it describes an action that isn't done to anyone or anything else.[60] To *lie* doesn't move, place, or affect anything other than the person or thing that's lying.

Lay **means to "put something down or in place."** It involves moving or arranging something, either literally or figuratively.

Lay **also can refer to producing an egg:**

> "Noise proves nothing. Often a hen who has <u>laid</u> an egg cackles as if she had <u>laid</u> an asteroid."
> Mark Twain, *Following the Equator* (1897)

The normative meaning of *lie* is "to be in a horizontal or resting position" or "to rest flat." It doesn't involve moving anything, except maybe yourself.

Lie **also can mean "to be buried":**

> "Here <u>lies</u> W. C. Fields. I would rather be living in Philadelphia."
> Epitaph suggested for himself by W. C. Fields, quoted in *Vanity Fair,* June 1925

> "Here <u>lies</u> Groucho Marx—and <u>lies</u> and <u>lies</u> and <u>lies</u>.
> P.S. He never kissed an ugly girl."
> Groucho Marx's suggestion for his epitaph, quoted in B. Norman, *The Movie Greats* (1981)

Lie **can mean "be situated":**

The Shire <u>lies</u> in the kingdom of Arnor.

Have you ever told a dog to *lay* down? If you have, it's not a Standard English usage, but don't feel too bad. It's extremely common, even among educated speakers. *Lay* and *lie* have always been distinct, with different meanings. But *lay* has sometimes been used to mean "lie" for seven hundred years. In the eighteenth century, grammarians objected to that, and schoolteachers and usage books then insisted that we observe the distinction between these words. As a result, to use *lay* in the sense of "lie" in formal writing is frequently considered an uneducated mistake. The fact that *lay* is the past tense of *lie* only adds to the confusion. The word *laid* has almost entirely replaced *lain* in everyday use.[61] In formal writing, though, it's still correct to say "have lain."

Which version of the sentence below is correct in Standard English?

(A) "Never stand up when you can sit down. Never sit down when you can <u>lay</u> down."

(B) "Never stand up when you can sit down. Never sit down when you can <u>lie</u> down."

> Mark Twain, quoted in William Lyon Phelps, *Autobiography with Letters* (1939)

In this sentence, Twain recommends that we recline, or *lie* down, whenever we can, rather than sitting. Version B is the right choice.

Why does English have a distinction between *lay* and *lie* at all? Before the Angles, the Saxons, and other Germanic tribes invaded Britain, their ancestors' language let them make verbs transitive. By changing the sound of a verb slightly, they gave the word the meaning of causing something to happen. That ancient grammatical pattern survives in some word pairs today, which is why to *lay* something in place means to make it *lie* there. It's also why to *set* something down is to make it *sit*, and to *fell* a tree means to make it *fall*.[62]

LESS or FEWER

✳ *Less*

"In Hollywood people attach <u>less importance</u> to a girl's virtue than to her hair-do."

> Marilyn Monroe, in Marilyn Monroe and Ben Hecht, *My Story* (2006)

"Laughter and tears are both responses to frustration and exhaustion.... I myself prefer to laugh, since there is <u>less cleaning up</u> to do afterward."

Kurt Vonnegut, American writer (1922–2007), *Palm Sunday: An Autobiographical Collage* (1981)

"I'm not really conservative. I'm conservative on certain things. I believe in <u>less government</u>."

Clint Eastwood, Academy Award–winning American actor, director, film producer, and composer, quoted in Philip French, "I Figured I'd Retire Gradually, Just Ride Off into the Sunset," theguardian.com, Feb. 24, 2007

"I feel more and more at ease, because I think the older I get, the <u>less pressure</u> there is. People say, 'Well, he's not cutting edge because he's not in his twenties.'"

Jude Law, English actor, film producer, and director, quoted in Jessica Punter, "Clean Cut: Jude Law's Grooming Advice," gqmagazine.co.uk, June 1, 2012

"We live as if there aren't enough hours in the day, but if we do each thing calmly and carefully, we will get it done [more quickly] and with much <u>less</u> stress."

Viggo Mortensen, Danish American actor, poet, and musician, whose movie roles have included Aragorn in *The Lord of the Rings,* quoted in Chitra Ramaswamy, "Viggo Mortensen Is Lord of All Things," Scotsman.com, May 25, 2013

✳ *Fewer*

"If we had <u>less statesmanship</u>, we would get along with <u>fewer battleships</u>."

Mark Twain, unpublished notebook, 1905

"Aristotle maintained that women have <u>fewer teeth</u> than men; although he was twice married, it never occurred to him to verify this statement by examining his wives' mouths."

Bertrand Russell, British philosopher, mathematician, historian, and social critic (1872–1970), in *The Impact of Science on Society* (1952)

"I know I'm getting better at golf because I'm hitting <u>fewer spectators</u>."

> Gerald R. Ford, U.S. president 1974–77, quoted in Don Van Natta, *First off the Tee: Presidential Hackers, Duffers and Cheaters from Taft to Bush* (2004)

"I've always felt that the <u>fewer rules</u> a coach has, the <u>fewer rules</u> there are for the players to break."

> John Madden, American former football player, coach, and TV commentator, in John Madden and Dave Anderson, *Hey, Wait a Minute (I Wrote a Book)* (1985)

"Start in a small TV station so you can make all of your embarrassing mistakes early and in front of <u>fewer people</u>."

> Advice on breaking into television journalism, from award-winning American former TV anchor Diane Sawyer, quoted in Gerda Gallop-Goodman, *Diane Sawyer* (2001)

"I'm always being accused of being a Hollywood Republican—but I'm not....I have just as many Democratic ideas as Republican ones....If they could build three <u>fewer bombs</u> every month and give the money to foster care, that would be great."

> Bruce Willis, Emmy Award– and Golden Globe Award–winning American actor, producer, and singer, quoted in Lloyd Grove and Katherine Thomson, "Willis No Die-Hard for the GOP," nydailynews.com, Sept. 16, 2006

"In Hollywood, they put the knife in your front; in D.C., they put it in your back. I found far <u>fewer duplicitous people</u> in Hollywood."

> Jack Abramoff, former lobbyist, convicted of corruption, quoted in Paul Teetor, "LA Life," laweekly.com, Dec. 22, 2011

My students sometimes use *less* to mean "fewer," and they're not alone. The traditional rule is that ***fewer* refers to countable things**. But people have used *less* to describe things that you can count for over a thousand years. In fact, Alfred the Great, the first king of the Anglo-Saxons, wrote "less words" in Old English in the ninth century. The word *fewer* didn't even exist then, and the rule against using *less* in that sense doesn't seem to have been invented until about nine hundred years later.

The normative rule is to use *less* with <u>singular</u> nouns that <u>can't be counted</u>:

less importance
less cleaning
<u>less</u> government
less pressure
less statesmanship

Use *fewer* with <u>plural</u> nouns that represent things that <u>can be counted</u>:

fewer battleships
fewer teeth
fewer rules
fewer people
fewer spectators
fewer bombs
fewer duplicitous people

Another way to say that is that *less* describes <u>how much</u> there is of something, while *fewer* describes <u>how many</u> there are. So use *less* if you can say "not as much" or "not as much as" instead. Use *fewer* if you can say "not as many" or "not as many as" instead. For example, since you say "<u>not as much</u> homework," say "<u>less</u> homework." Since you can say "<u>not as many</u> cookies," say "<u>fewer</u> cookies."

Here are some more examples of *less* (not as much) vs. *fewer* (not as many):

less fun
fewer parties
less homework
fewer exercises to do
less trouble
fewer worries

✳ *Exceptions to the Rule*

> "We don't wake up for <u>less</u> than $10,000 a day."
>> Canadian supermodel Linda Evangelista, speaking of herself and
>> Christy Turlington, quoted in *Vogue*, Oct. 1990

**It's usual to say *less* in reference to units of time, money, distances,
weights, and other measurements that people think of as amounts.**

The GPS says we'll be there in <u>less than</u> twelve <u>minutes</u>.
The bill was for fifty <u>dollars</u> <u>less than</u> I expected.
Her home is <u>less than</u> five <u>miles</u> away.

***Less* is very often used in the place of *fewer* in *no less than*:**

Our golden retriever, Theo, weighed no <u>less than</u> eighty <u>pounds</u>.

**Constructions like *ten words or less* are common and they may
sound better to the ear than the formally correct *ten words or fewer*.**
These exceptions are standard, but others aren't. People may say "less
calories," for example, thinking of them as an amount. Many careful
writers object to that, though. A large majority of the *Harper Dictionary*
Usage Panel was opposed to saying "less calories" in both speech and
writing. They felt that we should maintain the clear and definite difference between *less* and *fewer*. This passage illustrates the traditional rule:

> "'Lean muscle helps the body burn a greater number of calories,
> but as we age our muscle mass drops, along with our metabolism.'
> The result is that our bodies need <u>fewer</u> calories to maintain our
> weight."
>> Peta Bee, "The Secret of Slimness? 300 Fewer Calories," dailymail.
>> co.uk, Aug. 27, 2012

Which version is correct according to the traditional rule?

(A) I'm eating <u>less</u> cheeseburgers than I used to.
(B) I'm eating <u>fewer</u> cheeseburgers than I used to.

Version B is correct. In formal English the right choice is *fewer,* since the noun is plural and you can count cheeseburgers.

> Many supermarket aisles have signs saying, "Use this line if you have twelve items or <u>less</u>." That's wrong according to the traditional rule, but it's very common. Some food markets do say "twelve items or <u>fewer</u>," though. I like to think that their managers were English majors.

LITERALLY

"Among evangelicals, a <u>literalist</u> would insist…that Adam and Eve were historical figures [and] that Jonah was indeed swallowed by a large fish."
　　Randall Balmer, "Literalism," *Encyclopedia of Evangelicalism* (1989)

"Sometimes I say things that I think are obviously sarcastic and people take them quite <u>literally</u>."
　　Megan Fox, American actress and model, asked about her
　　comment in *Esquire* that she is really confident about herself,
　　interview in telegraph.co, Oct. 23, 2009

From its earliest use in English, *literally* has meant "in a literal sense, word for word" or "in a literal way." In other words, it means "not figuratively."

Since the seventeenth century, though, *literally* also has been used to add intensity or emphasis to what follows. In this sense, it means "actually" or "really." This becomes an issue when people say *literally* to add emphasis to a figure of speech—something that isn't literal. That essentially reverses the word's original function, and stylists generally oppose it. In 2004, for example, most of the *American Heritage* Usage Panel objected to "Industrialism was <u>literally swallowing</u> the country's youth." They also rejected "He was <u>literally out of his mind with worry</u>."

But when no metaphor was involved, the panelists were more open: two-thirds of them accepted the phrase "literally no help."

In formal speech and writing, don't use *literally* to intensify figures of speech. When somebody says that he "literally hit the ceiling," that's pretty unlikely but at least theoretically possible. To literally have steam coming out of your ears normally isn't, though. If somebody tells you, "I literally died," and yet he's standing there telling you about it, there's a pretty good chance that it's not literally true.[63]

In the passages below, *literally* is used nonliterally:

> "I literally coined money."
>> British actress and writer Fanny Kemble (1809–1893), *Journal of a Residence on a Georgian Plantation in 1838–1839* (1863)

> "The pond was literally full of fish"; "the ground was literally alive with snakes."
>> Ambrose Bierce, noting that *literally* is often used to mean "figuratively": *San Francisco Examiner,* Sept. 4, 1887

> "OMG, I literally died when I found out!"
>> *Herald-Times* (Bloomington, Indiana), Oct. 22, 2008 (*OED*)

> "I want to show you...the character of a leader who had what it took when the American people literally stood on the brink of a new Depression."
>> U.S. vice president Joe Biden, speaking of President Barack Obama at the Democratic National Convention, Charlotte, N.C., Sept. 6, 2012

> "When things hung in the balance—I mean literally hung in the balance—the president understood this was about a lot more than the automobile industry."
>> Ibid.

Which version of the sentence below employs standard English usage?

(A) "And when the middle of the afternoon came, from being a poor poverty-stricken boy in the morning, Tom was literally rolling in wealth."

(B) "And when the middle of the afternoon came, from being a poor poverty-stricken boy in the morning, Tom was <u>figuratively</u> rolling in wealth."

> Mark Twain, *Adventures of Tom Sawyer* (1876)

Version B is technically correct. But Twain actually wrote version A. In this context, he used *literally* in its loose sense to capture the living language of the time and place, and he wasn't concerned with the rules of formal English.

Lookups of the word *literally* in the Merriam-Webster online dictionary spiked on August 12, 2013, when a Reddit user posted the sentence "Steam was literally coming out of his ears." The title of the post was "We did it, guys. We finally killed English."

MARK TWAIN'S SNORING: GERUNDS

<u>Mark Twain's snoring</u> disturbed his family so much that they tried every remedy to cure him of it, except banishment.

> Alex Ayres, "Snoring," *The Wit and Wisdom of Mark Twain* (2010)

"When a person cannot deceive himself the chances are against <u>his being</u> able to deceive other people."

> Mark Twain, *Autobiography of Mark Twain* (2012)

"<u>Taylor Swift's earning</u> $57 million at the age of 22 made her the highest-paid entertainer under 30, according to *Forbes* magazine."

> Laura Brown, "Taylor Swift Wears the Pants," *Harper's Bazaar*, Jan. 2013

Should we say "Mark **Twain's** snoring disturbed his family" or "Mark **Twain** snoring disturbed his family"? The word *snoring* in this sentence is what grammarians call a **gerund**: a verb form ending in *-ing* that's used as a noun. Like a noun, it can be the subject of a sentence:

Mark Twain's <u>snoring</u> disturbed his family.

And like a verb, a gerund can take an **object**. That means that a gerund can act on or affect people or things: Troy Tulowitzki's <u>hitting</u> a baseball, Pharrell Williams's <u>coaching</u> a singer on *The Voice,* Taylor Swift's <u>writing</u> a new breakup song, etc.

The question in this lesson is, should the subject of one of these *-ing* forms be in the possessive case or not? In other words, which of these should we say?

<u>Elvis's singing</u> thrilled my grandmother (possessive case: *Elvis's*)
or
<u>Elvis singing</u> thrilled my grandmother (non-possessive case: *Elvis*)

And which of these should we say?

<u>Beyoncé's singing</u> thrills me (possessive: *Beyoncé's*)
or
<u>Beyoncé singing</u> thrills me (non-possessive: *Beyoncé*)

Grammarians have disagreed since the eighteenth century about whether we should use the possessive case in these contexts. Noah Webster declared in 1789 that we should, since it's the authentic English idiom.[64] Fowler insisted in 1926 that people who don't use the possessive case in these *-ing* clauses are corrupting the English language. Well, if that's true, many fine writers have been guilty for centuries. Today, both forms are widely used.

People commonly say both *his getting* and *him getting,* for example:

"A baseball park is the one place where a man's wife doesn't mind <u>his getting</u> excited over somebody else's curves."
Brendan Francis, instantactionsports.com

"This is You-Know-Who we're dealing with, so we can't just rely on <u>him getting</u> the date wrong."
J. K. Rowling, *Harry Potter and the Deathly Hallows* (2007)

Here's what I recommend that you do with *-ing* clauses in formal writing:

When the subject is a personal pronoun, use *my, your, his, her, its, our,* or *their.* This is traditionally preferred, and it's common even in casual writing:

<u>my jogging</u> a mile
<u>her laughing</u> at Louis C.K.
<u>your snorkeling</u> in Hawaii
<u>our seeing</u> the Jennifer Lawrence movie
<u>his tickling</u> his grandchild
<u>their playing</u> Angry Birds online

When the subject is a person, use the possessive form. That means you should use it when the subject is someone's name, or when it's a noun like *father,* which identifies a person. This construction is widely used in good writing.

Mark Twain's snoring
Taylor Swift's earning
My father's laughing

When you open a sentence with an *-ing* clause, you can't go wrong using the possessive case. It's well established in that position.

<u>Elaine's</u> awkward <u>dancing</u> on *Seinfeld* embarrassed everyone but her.

Don't use the possessive construction, though, if the result is unnatural or awkward.

Don't use the possessive case when you refer to things (such as the weather or luggage):

Mark Twain spoke of the New England <u>weather being</u> dazzlingly uncertain.
The <u>luggage getting</u> lost stressed us out.

Don't use the possessive case with plural nouns, or groups of nouns:

The <u>students partying</u> at 3:00 a.m. woke me up.
<u>My father and mother arriving</u> was the high point of my day.

Don't use the possessive case if you want to put the emphasis on a person rather than on the action involved. In the first passage below, the focus is on your grandmother. In the second, it's on her breakdancing:

We were amazed by <u>your grandmother</u> breakdancing.
We were amazed by <u>your grandmother's</u> breakdancing.

Many linguists don't use the term *gerund* anymore. I like it and find it useful, but for our purposes there's no need for you to memorize it. If you can remember the phrase "Mark Twain's snoring," you'll have the model in your mind for using the possessive form in *-ing* clauses in formal writing.

NONE

✳ None *with Singular Verbs*

"If anything interferes with my inner peace, I will walk away. Arguments with family members, all that stuff—<u>none</u> of it <u>matters</u>."
> Shirley MacLaine, award-winning American actress, singer, dancer, and author, quoted in Monica Corcoran, "What a Knock-Off," latimes.com, Sept. 7, 2008

"There are some parents who have really done it right and told their kid, 'You know, we have this dough. <u>None</u> of this <u>is</u> for you. You have to get your own.'"
> Robert Downey Jr., Golden Globe Award–winning American actor, quoted in huffingtonpost.com, Apr. 19, 2012

"We all rely on technology to communicate, to survive, to do our banking, to shop, to get informed. But <u>none</u> of us <u>knows</u> how to read and write the code."

> Will.i.am, award-winning American rapper, singer-songwriter, actor, DJ, entrepreneur, and producer, on studying programming, quoted in Carole Cadwalladr, "Will.i.am: 'I Want to Write Code,'" theguardian.com, Dec. 15, 2012

"My doctor told me that I'm old, fat, and ugly, but <u>none</u> of those things <u>is</u> going to kill me immediately."

> Roger Ailes, president of Fox News Channel and chairman of the Fox Television Stations Group, interviewed by Zev Chafets, quoted in Dylan Byers, "Roger Ailes: I'll Be Dead in 10 Years," politico.com, Mar. 6, 2013

"The National Security Agency has been spying on online sexual activity...as part of a proposed plan to discredit a handful of people the agency believes are 'radicalizing' others....<u>None</u> of the six individuals identified in the document <u>is</u> accused of being involved in terrorist plots."

> Nate Rawlings, "NSA Monitored Porn Habits to Discredit 'Radicalizers,'" time.com, Nov. 27, 2013

✳ None *with Plural Verbs*

"We stress humanity....We can't have a lot of dramatics that other shows get away with—promiscuity, greed, jealously. <u>None</u> of those <u>have</u> a place in *Star Trek*."

> Gene Roddenberry, creator of *Star Trek* (1921–1991), quoted in Sandy Hill, "*Star Trek* Showed Us Human Harmony," Knight-Ridder, Oct. 28, 1991

"There's always failure. And there's always disappointment. And there's always loss. But the secret is learning from the loss, and realizing that <u>none</u> of those holes <u>are</u> vacuums."

> Michael J. Fox, award-winning American actor, author, and producer, interviewed by NPR.org, Apr. 17, 2010

Taylor Swift, speaking about her favorite people: "<u>None</u> of them <u>were</u> cool in their younger years."

Taylor Swift, interviewed in vogue.com, Jan. 2012

"<u>None</u> of my actions <u>have</u> ever been [determined] by the search for a husband."

Lena Dunham, Golden Globe Award–winning American filmmaker and actress, star of the HBO series *Girls,* quoted in "Lena Dunham Addresses Criticism Aimed at *Girls,*" npr.org, May 7, 2012

Hugh Jackman on how to raise children: "The moment your kid's born you realize no one knows anything. No one goes to classes. You just have a kid. You can read all the books you like, but unfortunately, <u>none</u> of our kids <u>have</u> read the books, so they don't care. You're basically making it up as you go along."

Hugh Jackman, in John Mather, "Hugh Jackman's 5 Life Lessons," menshealth.com, Sept. 28, 2012

Many usage rules were invented in the eighteenth century or later, often by analogy to Latin grammar. With the word *none,* though, a rule was born mysteriously, adopted by teachers, and accepted as a law—all with no known authority or any good reason. That rule is that *none* is always singular. Nobody knows who decided this, why, or when, but it seems to be a fairly recent idea.

A lot of us have been taught this rule. I was (a long, long time ago). It seems to make sense, since *one* is singular and *none,* meaning "no one, not any," is even less than that. And yet *none* has been both singular and plural since the time of the Anglo-Saxon king Alfred the Great in the ninth century, and it still is.

When *none* refers to a single thing in a phrase like *none of it* and *none of this,* it's singular:

none of this <u>was</u> made up
none of it <u>matters</u>
none of this <u>is</u> for you

Beyond that, though, there's no consistent pattern. *None* **can be either singular or plural, depending on the surrounding words and what you mean to say.**

In many cases, a writer has treated *none* sometimes as singular and other times as plural. It's a matter of style and how you think the word fits into the sense of what you're saying.

If you'd like more guidance, *The Chicago Manual of Style* gives this sensible rule:

(1) **If *none* is followed by a singular noun, it should be singular.**
(2) **If *none* is followed by a plural noun, it should be plural.**

Another way to say this is that if you're saying "none of **it**," you should use a singular verb. If you're saying "none of **them**," use a plural verb:

Singular: None of the <u>pizza is</u> left. *(none of <u>it</u>)*
Singular: None of her <u>sense of humor was</u> lost. *(none of <u>it</u>)*
Plural: None of the <u>pizzas have</u> pepperoni topping. *(none of <u>them</u>)*
Plural: <u>None</u> of his friends <u>like</u> him. *(none of <u>them</u>)*

Remember, though, that the second part of this guideline isn't binding. *The Chicago Manual of Style* tacitly acknowledges that: it adds that it's okay to follow *none* with a singular verb for emphasis, even when it appears with a plural noun.

Absolutely none of these choices <u>appeals</u> to me!

If your profession uses a stylebook, follow it. But don't be surprised if style manuals disagree, even within your field. *The New York Times Manual of Style and Usage,* for example, tells writers to make *none* plural, except when they want to emphasize the idea of "not one" or "no one"—and it advises them to consider using those phrases instead. *The Associated Press Stylebook*, by contrast, tells writers that *none* normally should be singular; they should treat it as plural only when it means "no two" or "no amount of."

NOR

"The world will little note <u>nor</u> long remember what we say here, but it can never forget what they did here."
　President Abraham Lincoln, Gettysburg Address, Nov. 19, 1863

"All this will not be finished in the first 100 days. <u>Nor</u> will it be finished in the first 1,000 days, <u>nor</u> in the life of this Administration, <u>nor</u> even perhaps in our lifetime on this planet. But let us begin."
　President John Kennedy, inaugural address, Jan. 20, 1961

"A wizard is never late, Frodo Baggins. <u>Nor</u> is he early. He arrives precisely when he means to."
　Award-winning English actor Ian McKellen as Gandalf, in the 2001 film *The Lord of the Rings: The Fellowship of the Ring*

"[People say,] 'Oh my God, he's on a show and [acts] stupid, so he must be stupid.' …I can't control that, <u>nor</u> do I try to, <u>nor</u> do I want to.… There's something advantageous about having people underestimate your intellect."
　Ashton Kutcher, American actor, producer, investor, and former model, quoted in Mickey Rapkin, "Nobody's Fool," elle.com, Mar. 20, 2013

Nor can stand alone (without *neither*) to open a phrase or clause. So, despite what you may have learned in school, **I suggest that you feel free to begin a sentence with *nor*. Just don't overdo it.**

PARODY or SATIRE

✳ *Parody*

Here's a <u>parody</u> of a used-car salesman's pitch:

"There's nothing like a minivan to attract good-looking women. Let me tell you, this car is a babe magnet."
　Anonymous

"Satire is a lesson. Parody is a game."
> Vladimir Nabokov, Russian American novelist (1899–1977),
> *Strong Opinions* (1973)

On the end of *The Colbert Report:* "*The Colbert
Report*…premiered in October 2005 as a spoof of the show
hosted by Fox News Channel personality Bill O'Reilly.
…Colbert won…critical acclaim and two Peabody Awards,
which noted that 'what started as a parody of punditry is now its
own political platform.'"
> "Stephen Colbert Retiring His *Report* and the Host He Played,"
> AP, Dec. 28, 2014

✳ *Satire*

"People say satire is dead. It's not dead. It's alive and living in the
White House."
> Robin Williams, quoted in Geoff Martin and Erin Steuter, *Pop
> Culture Goes to War* (2010)

"The rule of a good satirist, from the time of Jonathan Swift until
now, is to make people see uncomfortable truths as he makes
them squirm. On that score, Colbert succeeded.…In the
persona of his right-wing talk show host, he skewered the
powerful on both sides of the partisan aisle, weaving in tough
truths amid the jokes."
> Report on Stephen Colbert's testimony before a House Judiciary
> subcommittee, Frank James, "Stephen Colbert Gives 'Truthiness'
> Jolt on Capitol Hill," npr.org, Sept. 24, 2010

A satirical comment in Colbert's congressional testimony: "I
trust that following my testimony, both sides will work together
in the best interests of the American people, as you always do."
> Ibid.

"The point of satire is to comfort the afflicted by afflicting the
comfortable."

Garry Trudeau, Pulitzer Prize–winning cartoonist of the *Doonesbury* comic strip, Aug. 3, 2014

"<u>Satirists</u> and ridiculers expose our weakness and vanity when we are feeling proud.... They level social inequality by bringing the mighty low.... <u>Satirists</u> expose those who are incapable of laughing at themselves and teach the rest of us that we probably should."
David Brooks, "I Am Not Charlie Hebdo," nytimes.com, Jan. 8, 2015

A *parody* is an imitation of a literary work, song, film, type of news commentary, use of language, etc., with a comical exaggeration of the style or a humorous focus on an unlikely subject.

> The online Oxford Dictionaries reported in early 2015 that *parody* had become one of the five most looked-up words in the United States. It's no coincidence that interest in parody spiked just as *The Colbert Report* went off the air.

A *parody* also can be a bad imitation of something, a travesty:

"A <u>parody</u> of democracy could be more dangerous than a blatant dictatorship, because that gives people an opportunity to avoid doing anything about it."
Aung San Suu Kyi, Nobel Peace Prize–winning Burmese opposition leader who was under house arrest for almost fifteen years, quoted in David Pilling, "Interview: Aung San Sui Kyi," ft.com, Jan. 28, 2011

***Satire* uses humor, exaggeration, irony, or ridicule to mock people's vices, misbehavior, and foolishness.**

Remember, *parody* is aimed at art, but *satire* focuses on society, groups, or individuals. A satirist may use parody as one way to achieve his goals, though. *The Daily Show with Jon Stewart,* for example, is a <u>parody</u> of a news program; it <u>satirizes</u> foolishness and vices in politics and society.

In the passage below, Jon Stewart appears on a <u>satirical</u> Egyptian TV show and <u>parodies</u> a dictator:

"Millions of viewers tuned into Egypt's top <u>satirical</u> TV show watched as a man, his face obscured by a black hood, was led to the set by a pair of security toughs.... TV show host Bassem Youssef—a popular <u>satirist</u> otherwise known as 'Egypt's Jon Stewart'—unmasked the man and exclaimed with a flourish: 'Ladies and gentlemen, Jon Stewart!' 'Thank you, thank you, enough,' said Stewart in Arabic to an audience that could not seem to get enough of him. 'Order!' he continued in heavily accented English reminiscent of an Arab dictator."

Leela Jacinto, "Jon Stewart 'Takes Over' Egyptian Satirical TV Show," france24.com, June 22, 2013

A question: does the passage below illustrate parody or satire?

Sesame Street's Cookie Monster sang a song called "Share It, Maybe" about his search for cookies. It was a spoof of Carly Rae Jepsen's "Call Me, Maybe" and it got more than thirteen million hits on You-Tube.

In this passage, Cookie Monster offers a humorous twist on a work of art, or a *parody*.

PRACTICABLE, PRACTICAL, PRAGMATIC

✳ *Practicable*

In 1803, President Thomas Jefferson authorized the explorers Lewis and Clark to find "the most direct and <u>practicable</u> water route across the continent."

In 2013, the Obama administration proposed a decade-long effort to map the activities of the human brain in the hope of eventually finding cures for diseases like Alzheimer's and epilepsy. Some scientists said, however, that this project would not be <u>practicable</u> in a period of only ten years.

✳ *Practical*

"I have no dress except the one I wear every day. If you are going to be kind enough to give me one, please let it be <u>practical</u> and dark so that I can put it on afterwards to go to the laboratory."

> Marie Curie, researcher on radioactivity and first woman to win the Nobel Prize (1867–1934), referring to a wedding dress in correspondence, 1894

Christian Bale, who played Batman, said that a cape isn't really <u>practical</u> for a superhero. He said that he often stepped on the cape, and when he threw a punch, the cape would fly up and cover his whole head.

> Matt Pais, "Acting Is Simple!" chicagotribune.com, Sept. 2007

✳ *Pragmatic*

A question for Anne Hathaway: "Do you step up and act when the chips are down, or do you panic?"
Anne Hathaway: "I'm pretty good at remaining calm during an emergency. My house burned down when I was twelve, which made me really <u>pragmatic</u> about what needed to be done."

> Anne Hathaway, interviewed by Angelina Jolie in interviewmagazine.com, 2004

"I'm much more <u>pragmatic</u> about romance than I used to be....I wanted to be the princess. Now I'm much more willing to see myself as human and flawed, and [to] accept...the whole picture [about someone else]."

> Jennifer Garner, award-winning American actress and film producer, interviewed in *InStyle* magazine, reported in "Jennifer Garner Realistic About Ben Affleck Marriage," wenn.com, Aug. 22, 2005

These three words are related in meaning, but there are distinctions between them. Let's start with *practical* and *practicable*. They look similar and their meaning can overlap, so they're easy to confuse.

Something is *practicable* if it's feasible, if it can be done or used. A route or passage is *practicable* if it can be traversed.

Practical has several meanings. The one that could be confused with *practicable* is "useful, able to be put to good use in practice," "reasonable to do or use."

It's not hard to decide which of these two words to use, though, because there are key differences between them. First, *practicable* never describes people, while *practical* is used of both people and things. Second, not everything that's *practical* is *practicable*. For instance, although it might be very *practical* to be able to change a flat tire, you might not have the time or opportunity to learn how. So a plan to learn tire-changing skills wouldn't be *practicable* for you. And, to use the example above, a detailed knowledge of how the brain works could be wonderfully *practical* in treating diseases. But the research project to map the functions of the brain might not be *practicable,* given the available time and resources.

Practically comes from *practical*. It means "for practical purposes, in a practical manner."

Practically also means "for all intents and purposes" or "virtually, almost":

> "Insanity runs in my family. [It] <u>practically</u> gallops!"
> Cary Grant, Academy Award–winning English-American actor (1904–1986), in the 1944 film *Arsenic and Old Lace*

> "I recently turned sixty. <u>Practically</u> a third of my life is over."
> Woody Allen, quoted in *Observer,* Mar. 10, 1996

Several twentieth-century usage critics condemned this sense of the word as too loose. It's been part of the language for over 250 years, though, and excellent writers have used it. **This meaning of the word is fully standard, so I suggest that you feel free to use it.**

A pragmatic person is practical as opposed to idealistic. She deals with facts and events in a reasonable and down-to-earth way instead of depending on theories.

Which version of the sentence below is correct?

(A) "Hearts will never be <u>practical</u> until they can be made unbreakable."

(B) "Hearts will never be <u>practicable</u> until they can be made unbreakable."

> Frank Morgan as the Wizard in the 1939 film *The Wizard of Oz*

The Wizard is saying that hearts aren't sensible and efficient, or *practical*.

Pragmatic has been one of the most looked-up words online in recent years. In fact, Merriam-Webster chose it as the Word of the Year for 2011, concluding that *pragmatism* is a quality that people value and want to learn more about.

PREROGATIVE

"Intuition, however illogical, Mr. Spock, is recognized as a command <u>prerogative</u>."

> William Shatner, Emmy Award– and Golden Globe Award–winning Canadian actor, musician, writer, and director, as Captain Kirk in "Obsession," episode from the original TV series *Star Trek*, Dec. 15, 1967

In her song "Man! I Feel Like a Woman!" Shania Twain says that the <u>prerogative</u> to have fun is the best thing about being a woman.

Prerogative comes from the Latin for "to ask first," which referred to asking someone's opinion before anyone else's. In that sense, a group with the *prerogative* voted first. The word then came to mean "a special right or privilege exercised by the monarch." In late Middle English it developed the much broader meaning that it still has:

A prerogative is a special right or privilege accorded to any person, group, or class of people.[65]

So in Shania Twain's song, being a woman confers certain privileges, especially the right to have fun. That's okay, but speaking for us men, I think that this right should belong to all people, which means that it's no one's prerogative.

Which version of the sentence below is correct?

(A) "The first <u>perogative</u> of an artist in any medium is to make a fool of himself."

(B) "The first <u>prerogative</u> of an artist in any medium is to make a fool of himself."
   Pauline Kael, National Book Award–winning American film critic (1919–2001), "Is There a Cure for Film Criticism?," published in 1962, reprinted in Pauline Kael, *I Lost It at the Movies* (1965)

In the passage above, version B is correct.

Prerogative is often misspelled and mispronounced *perogative*. It may help to remember the history of the word as meaning "having **pr**eference and **pri**vilege," words that begin with *pr*.

QUOTE or QUOTATION

"It is my belief that nearly any invented <u>quotation</u>, played with confidence, stands a good chance to deceive."
   Mark Twain, *Following the Equator* (1897)

"<u>Quote</u> me as saying I was <u>misquoted</u>."
   Groucho Marx, quoted in Leo Rosten, "I Remember Groucho," readersdigest.com, May 1983

"Quotations, when engraved upon the memory, give you good thoughts. They also make you anxious to read the authors and look for more."
　　Winston Churchill, *My Early Life* (1930)

To quote has been a verb meaning "to reproduce a passage or a statement" for nearly five hundred years. In the 1880s, though, people started to use the word *quote* in a new sense, as a noun meaning "a quotation." That usage was rare until the 1940s, but it's very familiar today in casual speech and writing. Stylists used to object to it in formal contexts, but it's gained widespread approval recently. In 2009, for example, 80 percent of the *American Heritage* Usage Panel accepted sentences that referred to a *quote* from the Bible or *quotes* from Marx Brothers movies.

In both informal and formal use, say either *quotation* or *quote*.[66]

Also in the 1880s, the word *quotes* started to be used to mean "quotation marks." This sense is well established in informal American English, but traditionalists don't like it.

In formal contexts, say *quotation marks*.

SPLIT INFINITIVES: "TO BOLDLY GO"

"Space—the final frontier. These are the voyages of the starship *Enterprise*. Its five-year mission … to boldly go where no man has gone before."
　　Star Trek, TV series, NBC (1966)

"Far back in the mists of ancient time, in the great and glorious days of the former Galactic Empire, life was wild, rich, and largely tax free.... And all dared to brave unknown terrors, to do mighty deeds, to boldly split infinitives that no man had split before."
　　Douglas Adams, *The Hitchhiker's Guide to the Galaxy* (1979)

Let's start with a few definitions.

An **infinitive** is a verb in its simplest form, such as *love, laugh, forget,* or *sing*. It's the entry that you see in a dictionary. The word *to* often appears in front of it:[67]

"<u>To err</u> is human. <u>To blame</u> someone else is politics."
> Hubert Humphrey, U.S. vice president 1965–69, quoted in Sara B.
> Hobolt and James Tilley, *Blaming Europe? Responsibility Without
> Accountability in the European Union* (2014)

to err
to blame

A **split infinitive** has one or more words between *to* and the verb. These words are usually adverbs like *ever, just, really,* and *actually.* Here are some examples:

I didn't expect <u>to ever love</u> someone new.
My dad told me <u>to just forget</u> about being a rock star.
It's a relief <u>to really laugh</u>.
My dream is <u>to actually sing</u> with Britney Spears.

Split infinitives like these sound natural, and if you to try to "fix" them, the results may be awkward and clunky:

Awkward: I didn't expect <u>ever to love</u> someone new.
Awkward: I didn't expect <u>to love</u> someone new <u>ever</u>.
Awkward: My dad told me <u>just to forget</u> about being a rock star.

What's more, unsplitting a split can change the meaning of a sentence:

My dream is <u>to actually sing</u> with Britney Spears

means something a little different from

My dream is <u>actually to sing</u> with Britney Spears.

Split infinitives first appeared in English in the thirteenth century, though most writers didn't use them much or at all for more than five hundred years after that. Writers then started splitting infinitives again, and in the nineteenth century grammarians decided that it was a sty-listic error.[68] Many commentators now say that splits often are natural and useful, though. Some style guides say that it's fine to split infinitives, as long as they sound natural to the ear.

There's nothing grammatically wrong with splitting infinitives, but keep your intended readers in mind. In the passage below, Raymond Chandler actually insists on keeping the infinitives split in his detective fiction:

> "Would you convey my compliments to the purist who reads your proofs and tell him or her that I write in a sort of broken-down patois which is something like the way a Swiss waiter talks, and that when I split an infinitive, God damn it, I split it so it will stay split."
>
> Raymond Chandler, British American novelists and screenwriter (1888–1959), letter to the editor of *Atlantic Monthly* magazine, Jan. 18, 1948

But many purists still consider split infinitives to be inferior in formal English. Several of the major style manuals advise you to avoid them when you can. This is changing, though. In 2005, 70 percent of the *American Heritage* Usage Panel thought that the split infinitive "to legally pay" is okay, and 91 percent accepted "to more than double."

So, in formal speech and writing, the choice is up to you. Feel free to boldly split an infinitive. Keep in mind, though, that some readers will object. If you want to be conservative, you can place the adverb before or after the infinitive, as long the unsplit version sounds natural and clear.

The important thing is that your sentence should say what you mean and sound right to the ear. **Don't use splits that sound awkward or stilted.**

Awkward: He wanted to forever be the champion.
Better: He wanted to be the champion forever.

And generally avoid creating wide splits that pile adverbs between *to* and the verb.

Awkward: No modern grammarian was willing <u>to dogmatically, pedantically, and invariably condemn</u> split infinitives.

Better: No modern grammarian was willing <u>to condemn</u> split infinitives <u>dogmatically, pedantically, and invariably.</u>[69]

Which version of the sentence below sounds more natural?

(A) We hope <u>to very quickly, easily, and honestly double</u> our money.

(B) We hope <u>to double</u> our money <u>very quickly, easily, and honestly.</u>

Version A puts a string of adverbs between *to* and the infinitive. The result is clumsy. With the three adverbs at the end of the sentence, version B sounds more graceful.

Here's a hint: as a matter of style, I suggest that you normally put adverbs at the end of a clause, not in front of the verb, even if there's no infinitive in the sentence. That's generally a graceful way to write.

SUBSTITUTE or REPLACE

"It is never a good idea to <u>substitute</u> anyone's judgment <u>for</u> your own."

> Dr. Phil (Phil McGraw), American TV host, psychologist, and author, *Self Matters: Creating Your Life from the Inside Out* (2001)

Rolling Stones guitarist Keith Richards, asked whether he still enjoyed playing live: "There's no <u>substitute for</u> live work to keep a band together."

> *Keith Richards on Keith Richards: Interviews and Encounters,* ed. Sean Egan (2013)

Have you ever heard anyone say *substituted by* to mean "replaced by"? The traditional use of *substitute* is with *for, in (the) place of,* or *instead of,* meaning "to put or use someone or something in the place of another":

<u>substitute</u> anyone's judgment <u>for</u> your own
there's no substitute for live work

> *Substitute* also can be used as a verb in this sense without a preposition:

> "I like pasta. It's pretty good. I'll even <u>substitute</u> wheat pasta in
> there to make it more healthy."
>> Prince Fielder, American professional baseball player, in "Swapping
>> Vegetarian Recipes with Prince Fielder," sports.yahoo.com, Mar. 21,
>> 2008

For over three hundred years, though, the phrase *substitute by* has been
used to mean "replace by":

> "Good brandy being <u>substituted by</u> vile whiskey."
>> *Life in the South* (1863) (*OED*)

Substitute with, meaning "replace with," has been used since the nineteenth century:

> "I tried to take off the Dover sole, which is $65, and <u>substitute</u> it
> <u>with</u> gray sole or lemon sole for $24."
>> *New York Magazine,* Sept. 29, 2008 (*OED*)

Substitute also has been used without a preposition to mean "replace":

> "Refined sal oil is rapidly <u>substituting</u> cocoa butter in making
> chocolates."
>> *Leicester Mercury,* June 2, 1999 (*OED,* citing Lexis)

For most of the twentieth century the *Oxford English Dictionary* called
this newer use of *substitute* incorrect, and Fowler insisted in 1926 that
either the older usage or the newer one had to go. But there's been a
change recently: the current edition of the *OED* says that *substitute with*
and *substitute by* are now generally considered Standard English. Some
major style guides disagree, though, and edited English normally
requires *substitute for.*

**I suggest that in formal contexts you use *substitute* in its tradi-
tional sense.**

Let's say I'm in a game and the coach decides to send you in instead.

The coach *replaces* me.
or
The coach *replaces* me *with* you.
or
You *replace* me.
or
The coach *substitutes* you *for* me.

THAT or WHICH

* ## *That*

"I say, beware of all enterprises <u>that</u> require new clothes."
Henry David Thoreau, American writer, poet, activist,
transcendentalist (1817–1862), *Walden* (1854)

"I stand by all the misstatements <u>that</u> I've made."
Dan Quayle, U.S. vice president 1989–93, Aug. 17, 1989, quoted in
Esquire, Aug. 1992

"I truly believe in the glamorous lifestyle <u>that</u> I present to the
outside world."
Lady Gaga, quoted in John Dingwall, "Lady Gaga Used Tough
Times as Inspiration for Her New Album," *Daily Record*
(Glasgow), Nov. 27, 2009

* ## *Which*

"You ought never to knock your little sisters down with a club. It
is better to use a cat, <u>which is soft</u>."
Mark Twain, "Advice for Good Little Boys," written in 1865, *Early
Tales and Sketches* (1981)

"Your time is limited, so don't waste it living someone else's life. Don't be trapped by dogma, <u>which</u> is living with the results of other people's thinking."

> Steve Jobs, commencement address at Stanford University, June 12, 2005

"I got married at 45.... Forty-five is late to get married. Clearly, I had some issues, <u>which</u> I was enjoying while I had them."

> Jerry Seinfeld, "I Had Issues" stand-up routine, 2008, jerryseinfeld. com

Here's a quick and easy way to decide whether to start a clause with *that* or *which,* according to the traditional rule:

(1) **If you can cross out the clause without changing the basic meaning of the sentence, start the clause with *which*.**
(2) **If you can't, begin the clause with *that*.**

(Remember, a clause is a group of words that includes a subject and a verb.)

According to this rule, a clause that begins with *which* isn't essential to the main point of the sentence, so it's called a **nonessential clause**. It just provides additional information. It's also called a **nonrestrictive clause** because it doesn't narrow or restrict the subject. **Put a comma in front of it:**

a cat, which is soft
dogma, which is living with the results of other people's thinking
issues, which I was enjoying

A clause starting with *that*, by contrast, *is* essential to the meaning of the sentence. Don't put a comma in front of it:

all enterprises that require new clothes
all the misstatements that I've made
the glamorous lifestyle that I present to the outside world

Another way to say this is that a *that* clause tells us something essential by narrowing or defining the subject it refers to. It's called an **essential clause** or a **restrictive clause**.

In Thoreau's passage above, for example, if we dropped "that require new clothes," the sentence would lose its meaning. It would tell us to beware of all enterprises. The *that* clause narrows down what kind of enterprises Thoreau has in mind: those that require new clothes.

In the second passage, if we dropped the *that* clause, the meaning of the sentence would be incomplete. Quayle would be saying that he stands by all misstatements. The *that* clause defines which misstatements he stands by: the ones that he's made.

The main point of Lady Gaga's quotation, too, would be incomplete without the *that* clause. The *that* clause tells us what sort of glamorous lifestyle she believes in: the one that she presents to the outside world.

In each case, *that* opens a clause that is essential to the sentence and defines or restricts the preceding subject.

That's not true of the *which* clauses. In Twain's passage, for example, "which is soft" simply adds information about cats in general—they're soft. It isn't essential to the main meaning, and the sentence can stand without it. If it were a *that* clause without a comma, it would advise boys to knock down their sisters "with a cat that is soft"—in other words, with a soft cat, as opposed to a hard one. That would narrow the subject. But it wasn't Twain's meaning.

If we dropped the *which* clause from Jobs's passage, it would say, "Don't be trapped by dogma." That makes sense on its own. The next clause only gives us his definition of *dogma*, and the sentence can stand without it.

In Seinfeld's quotation, if you threw out the *which* clause, the sentence wouldn't be as funny, but it would still be complete and would make its main point.

By the way, you often can drop the word *that* in a clause that provides essential information. If we do that in two of the passages at the top of this lesson, they'll still be grammatical:

I stand by all the misstatements I've made.

I truly believe in the glamorous lifestyle I present to the outside world.

You can't do that with *which* in nonessential clauses.

✳ *Exceptions to the Rule*

Four hundred years ago, writers often used *which* where the strict modern distinction requires *that,* and *that* where the rule calls for *which.* This verse from the King James Version of the Bible (1611) uses *that* and *which* as if there's no difference between them:

> "Then saith he unto them, Render therefore unto Caesar the things <u>which</u> are Caesar's; and unto God the things <u>that</u> are God's."
>   Matthew 22:21

By the late nineteenth and early twentieth centuries, language commentators were insisting on the distinct functions for *that* and *which.* But very many people continue to use *which* where the rule requires *that,* both in speech and in edited writing:[70]

> "We have a criminal jury system <u>which</u> is superior to any in the world; and its efficiency is only marred by the difficulty of finding twelve men every day who don't know anything and can't read."
>   Mark Twain, "Americans and the English," speech, July 4, 1872

> "Everyone is a moon, and has a dark side <u>which</u> he never shows to anybody."
>   Mark Twain, *Following the Equator* (1897)

> "Conscience is the inner voice <u>which</u> warns us that someone may be looking."
>   H. L. Mencken, American journalist, satirist, and editor (1880–1956), in *A Mencken Chrestomathy* (1949)

> "My fellow Americans, I am pleased to tell you I just signed legislation <u>which</u> outlaws Russia forever. The bombing begins in five minutes."

> President Ronald Reagan, joking without realizing that sound
> equipment was being voice-checked, quoted in "Reagan Said to
> Joke of Bombing Russia Before Radio Speech," *New York Times,*
> Aug. 13, 1984

Commentators on language don't agree about this. Many usage guides strictly state the traditional rule. Strunk and White said that careful writers go "which-hunting," replacing the word *which* with *that* whenever it opens a clause that is essential to the meaning of a sentence. *The Chicago Manual of Style* and the Associated Press and *New York Times* stylebooks also state the rule. But other usage books allow *which* in essential clauses, and some language commentators and stylists don't follow the rule themselves.[71]

I recommend that in formal writing you use *that* to introduce a clause that contains information that is essential to a sentence.

I suggest that you say *which* only to open clauses that add nonessential information. Put a comma in front of it.

✳ That *or* Which *vs.* Who

Strictly, *that* or *which* refer to things and *who* refers to people. So in formal speech and writing, I suggest that you use *who* for people. *That* is often used to refer to people, though, especially in a conversational tone:[72]

> "Man is the only animal <u>that</u> blushes."
> Mark Twain, *Following the Equator* (1897)

THERE IS or THERE ARE

✳ *There Is*

> "<u>There's</u> a sucker born every minute."
> Attributed to American showman and businessman P. T. Barnum,
> probably mistakenly

"Every time a child says, 'I don't believe in fairies' <u>there is</u> a little fairy somewhere that falls down dead."

> J. M. Barrie, *Peter Pan* (1928 ed.)

"<u>There is</u> nothing like a dame."

> Oscar Hammerstein II, Tony Award– and Academy Award–winning librettist and theater producer and director (1895–1960), title of a song in the 1949 Broadway musical *South Pacific*

"<u>There is</u>, of course, no reason for the existence of the male sex except that sometimes one needs help with moving the piano."

> Rebecca West, English writer and critic (1892–1983), in *Sunday Telegraph*, June 28, 1970

✳ *There Are*

"<u>There are</u> more things in heaven and earth, Horatio, than are dreamt of in your philosophy."

> Shakespeare, *Hamlet* (1599–1602)

"<u>There are</u> several good protections against temptations, but the surest is cowardice."

> Mark Twain, *Following the Equator* (1897)

"<u>There are</u> two tragedies in life. One is not getting your heart's desire. The other is to get it."

> George Bernard Shaw, *Man and Superman* (1903)

"In America <u>there are</u> two classes of travel—first class, and with children."

> Robert Benchley, American humorist and actor (1889–1945), *Pluck and Luck* (1925)

"At every party <u>there are</u> two kinds of people—those who want to go home and those who don't. The trouble is, they are usually married to each other."

Ann Landers, pen name of American advice columnist Eppie
Lederer, *International Herald Tribune,* June 19, 1991

About *Seinfeld*: "And then <u>there are</u> the big questions, like what
you do when your girlfriend suggests sharing a toothbrush."
Bruce Handy, writer and producer, "Television: It's All about
Timing," time.com, Jan. 12, 1998

When a clause begins with a phrase like *there is* or *there are,* the word
there is what's called a **dummy subject**. That's because the real subject
doesn't appear until after the verb. In "there is a little fairy somewhere
that falls down dead," for example, the real subject is the little fairy. That
also applies to phrases like *there seems to be* or *there appear to be.* **The
standard rule is that the verb should be singular if the real subject
that follows it is singular, and it should be plural if the real subject is.**
So if the real subject is singular, say *there's.*

The reality, though, is that people often say *there's* when they refer
to plural nouns, especially in casual speech. I sometimes hear myself
saying something like "There's still several things to do" (and I'm usually unbearably stuffy about grammar rules). In fact, in conversation,
people actually say *there's* before a plural noun more often than they say
there are.[73]

In formal writing, especially academic writing, on the other hand,
people normally follow the standard rule strictly. But they often don't do
that in everyday writing.

The standard rule may be weakening, at least in some contexts. The
large majority of the 1995 *American Heritage* Usage Panel rejected a sentence like "<u>There's</u> only three things you need to know." But the panelists
were much more open to saying *there is* if it referred to two singular
nouns.[74]

Now, this brings us to the question of whether you should use a dummy
subject at all. I always tell my students to aim for economy and dyna-
mism in their writing, and one way to economize is to eliminate *there is*
or *there are* when you can. Most of the quotations at the top of this
lesson are fine with those phrases. But instead of "there is a little fairy
somewhere that falls down dead," you could say "a little fairy somewhere

falls down dead." It's a matter of style and personal taste, so use your judgment.

THIS or THAT KIND, THESE or THOSE KINDS

✳ *This Kind*

"I welcome <u>this kind of examination</u> because . . . I'm not a crook."
  President Richard M. Nixon, after agents of his reelection committee were arrested at the Watergate Hotel, quoted in *New York Times,* Nov. 18, 1973

"<u>This Kind of 'Picky Eater'</u> Is Made, Not Born."
  Sally Sampson, parenting.blogs.nytimes.com, Feb. 19, 2014

✳ *These or* Those Kinds

"I honestly don't have a clue. I'm amazed that at my age <u>these kinds of parts</u> are still coming to me."
  Richard Gere, award-winning American actor, on the source of his appeal, and on being cast in the 2012 film *Arbitrage*, quoted in John Hiscock, "Richard Gere interview for *Arbitrage*," telegraph.co.uk, Feb. 8, 2013

"I use <u>those kinds of films</u> to get leverage."
  John Cusack, American actor, producer, and screenwriter, on making big-budget films, quoted in Ryan Gilbey, "Being John Cusack," *Guardian,* Sep. 6, 2007

"<u>Those Kinds of Things</u>" was the title of the first episode in season 6 of the Showtime TV series *Dexter,* on October 2, 2011.

"You read statistics all the time like 'Thirteen million people are at risk because of the severe drought in East Africa,' but I think <u>those kinds of numbers</u> fall on deaf ears. There's so much devastation in the world that it's a bit overwhelming for people."
  Scarlett Johansson, quoted in interviewmagazine.com, Dec. 2011

Most American usage books prescribe this traditional pattern:

This kind of and *that kind of* **are singular and refer to a singular subject.**

These kinds of and those kinds of **are plural and refer to a plural subject.**

So a standard sentence might say *This kind of man is hard to find* or *These kinds of men are hard to find.* That also applies to *this sort of, these types of,* and similar phrases.

Starting in the fourteenth century, though, a strange variant arose mixing singular and plural forms. It includes phrases like *all kind of, these kind of,* or *those kind of.* So instead of *these kinds of men,* someone could say *these kind of men.* Shakespeare wrote, "These kind of knaves" in *King Lear,* and John Milton, Jonathan Swift, Alexander Pope, and Winston Churchill, among others, used similar constructions. British grammarians have been more tolerant of this sort of locution than American language commentators have, but eminent style experts on both sides of the Atlantic have called it illogical. The overwhelming majority of the *Harper Dictionary* Usage Panel opposed saying *these kind of* in speech or writing, though a few admitted apologetically that they sometimes slip and use it when they speak. More than eight in ten of the *American Heritage* usage panelists also rejected this usage in 2005. Despite this opposition, the construction *these kind of* is very common colloquially, and it appears at times in print, even in America.[75]

I suggest that you follow these guidelines in formal speech and writing: Never say *these kind of.* **If you say** *this kind of* **or** *that kind of* **followed by a singular noun, use a singular verb afterward.**

This kind of Batman comic book is very valuable.

If you say *these kinds of* **or** *those kinds of,* **follow it with a plural verb.**

Those kinds of animated movies are often in 3-D.

The same guidelines apply to *type of, sort of,* **etc.**

UNIQUE, PERFECT: COMPARING
ABSOLUTE ADJECTIVES

"The British nation is <u>unique</u> in this respect: they are the only people who like to be told how bad things are, who like to be told the worst."
> Winston Churchill, speech in House of Commons, June 10, 1941

"Each of us is a <u>unique</u> person, with a <u>unique</u> perspective on the world, a member of a class of one."
> W. H. Auden, Anglo-American poet (1907–1973), quoted in *New York Times Biographical Service* 4 (1973)

Question: "You didn't believe you were an addict?"
Charlie Sheen: "I just didn't believe I was like everybody else. I thought I was <u>unique</u>."
> Charlie Sheen, quoted in playboy.co.za, Apr. 2011

"People in their twenties are trying to be <u>unique</u> in every way. [They say,] 'I don't listen to the same records as you! My earrings are vintage—you can't buy them anywhere!'"
> Lena Dunham, interview in *GQ*, Apr. 30, 2012

Can a person be very unique? Can a thing be more perfect or the most infinite? Starting in the eighteenth-century, some grammarians reasoned that certain adjectives describe states or conditions that can't be compared. Over time this opinion was elevated to a rule and the number of adjectives that it affected grew. Those adjectives are called **absolute** or **incomparable**. The word *unique* is one of them.

✳ *Unique*

Unique entered English from French about four hundred years ago meaning "the only one of its kind" and "without parallel, unequalled." The grammarians were right about not comparing *unique* in those senses of the word: something can't be *more unique*, meaning "more one-of-a-kind" or "more without equal."

Here's how to apply the traditional rule to *unique*. Something can be <u>nearly</u> unique or <u>almost</u> unique in the sense of not quite unique. If it truly is one of a kind, you can say that it's <u>surely</u> unique. It also can be "unique in every way," as in the passage by Lena Dunham above. But in the strict sense of the original meanings of the word, a unique thing can't be measured or compared. That means that there can't be degrees of uniqueness: a person or thing can't be <u>more</u> unique than another. And something can't be <u>completely</u> unique, <u>very</u> unique, or <u>the most</u> unique. It's just unique.

This rule is based on the early meanings of *unique,* as we've seen. But about 150 years ago, people began to use the word more loosely, to mean "unusual, remarkable, rare." Once that happened, it was only natural to say that something is *more unique* or *very unique,* in the sense of "more unusual" or "very rare." That usage is common in casual speech and even in good prose today. But many careful writers and language critics regard it as incorrect in formal speech and writing.[76]

In formal contexts, I recommend that you avoid the looser, disputed sense of *unique:* don't say *more unique, very unique,* etc., to compare degrees of uniqueness. If you want to compare levels of excellence or rarity, use a synonym, such as *excellent, rare,* or *unusual.*

✳ Perfect

"As perfect a film as it gets."
Excerpt of a review used in an ad for the 2013 film *American Hustle*

The ad above quotes from a rave review of a great film. As far as I'm concerned, any movie that has Jennifer Lawrence and Amy Adams in it might even be perfect. But can it be more perfect than another film? The ad illustrates the difference between how people often use the word *perfect* and the traditional rules about absolute adjectives. Logically, if something really is perfect, it can't get any better, right? But since the fourteenth century, people have compared degrees of perfection. They've called things *more perfect* and *most perfect,* and for centuries writers used the words *perfecter* and *perfectest.* The *Middle English*

Dictionary and the *Oxford English Dictionary* say that *more perfect* has the sense of "more nearly ideal" and "approaching" a state of perfection. The phrase *more perfect* even appears in the preamble to the U.S. Constitution ("We the People of United States, in order to form a <u>more perfect</u> Union…"). Some language commentators consider it pedantic to criticize this usage, since the founding fathers clearly meant "a more nearly perfect union." This remains controversial, though. Even the phrases "near perfect" and "almost perfect" aren't acceptable to everyone. Only half (52 percent) of the *Harper Dictionary* Usage Panel accepted those phrases, and some of those who did expressed reluctance.

In formal writing, I recommend that you be conservative and consider *perfect* to be an absolute adjective that can't be compared or measured by degrees.

✳ *Other Absolute Adjectives*

Other adjectives that, according to the traditional rules, can't be compared by degree include:

absolute	perpendicular
universal	circular
pregnant	eternal
ultimate	infinite
unanimous	

People may use these adjectives in an approximate sense rather than with their strict, absolute meanings. And they may say something like *very unique, completely unanimous,* or *totally universal* for emphasis. **I recommend that you avoid such expressions in formal speech and writing.**

Which version of the old television ad below is correct according to the strict rules of usage?

(A) "In the dull and commonplace occurrences of day-to-day living, one thing stands out as <u>a completely unique</u> experience: Colt 45 Malt Liquor."

(B) "In the dull and commonplace occurrences of day-to-day living, one thing stands out as <u>a unique</u> experience: Colt 45 Malt Liquor."
    TV ad in 1960s

In formal speech and writing, *unique* is an incomparable adjective, so version B is correct ("a unique experience"). The ad, however, said "completely unique."

WHEN, WHERE

✳ *Is When, Is Where*

People often say *is when* or *is where* to define something when they're speaking casually. The examples below are in relaxed, colloquial English, and they're fine in those contexts:

"A love scene to Cagney <u>was when</u> he let the other guy live."
    Bob Hope, award-winning English-born American comedian, vaudevillian, actor, singer, dancer, writer, and athlete (1903–2003), speaking about James Cagney, quoted in *Films in Review* 25 (1974)

"A recession <u>is when</u> a neighbor loses his job. A depression <u>is when</u> you lose yours."
    Ronald Reagan, speech, 1980

"A team <u>is where</u> a boy can prove his courage on his own.... A gang <u>is where</u> a coward goes to hide."
    Mickey Mantle, American star baseball player for the New York Yankees (1931–1995), *The Quality of Courage* (1999)

"A development deal <u>is where</u> they're giving you recording time and money to record, but not promising that they'll put an album out."
    Taylor Swift, quoted in Chris Willlman, "Swift Rise," ew.com, July 25, 2007

Saying *is when* and *is where* to frame definitions seems to have been common in the eighteenth century. Starting around 1850, though, grammarians began to object to those constructions, and several recent usage books still do.[77] This locution shows up once in a while in writing, but I suggest that you avoid it in formal contexts.

In formal English, say *where* to refer to places and *when* to refer to times.

Don't use either to frame definitions.

Here's how the passages above could be rewritten in formal English:

A love scene to Cagney was one <u>in which</u> he let the other guy live.

<u>In a recession</u>, a neighbor loses his job. <u>In a depression</u>, you lose yours.

<u>On a team</u> a boy can prove his courage on his own.... A coward goes to hide <u>in a gang</u>.

<u>In a development deal</u> they give you...

✳ *Where*

The word *where* typically refers to physical locations:

> "Hollywood is a place <u>where</u> they'll pay you a thousand dollars for a kiss and fifty cents for your soul."
>
> Marilyn Monroe, in Marilyn Monroe and Ben Hecht, *My Story* (2006)

> "Well, that's all the news from Lake Wobegon, <u>where</u> all the women are strong, all the men are good-looking, and all the children are above average."
>
> Garrison Keillor, award-winning American radio personality, storyteller, writer, and humorist, closing words of his monologue on the public radio show *A Prairie Home Companion*

People often say *where* to refer to logical locations, rather than physical ones. In these cases, *where* means "in which" or "when," and it refers to circumstances, times, experiences, fields of knowledge or skill, stages of development, examples, etc.:

"Baseball is the only field of endeavor <u>where</u> a man can succeed three times out of ten and be considered a good performer."
> Ted Williams, American star baseball player for the Boston Red Sox (1918–2002), *The ESPN Baseball Encyclopedia* (2006), citing "widely quoted" sources

"I've always been attracted to more revolutionary changes… because they're harder. They're much more stressful emotionally. And you usually go through a period <u>where</u> everybody tells you that you've completely failed."
> Steve Jobs, quoted in *Rolling Stone,* June 16, 1994

"I took a speed-reading course <u>where</u> you run your finger down the middle of the page and was able to read *War and Peace* in twenty minutes. It's about Russia."
> Woody Allen, attributed in Phyllis Mindell, letter to *New York Times,* Sep. 3, 1995

"I go through long periods <u>where</u> I don't listen to things, usually when I'm working."
> Bruce Springsteen, award-winning American singer-songwriter, quoted in Nick Hornby, "A Fan's Eye View," theguardian.com, July 16, 2005

Saying *where* to refer to logical locations is standard, and it's especially common in academic writing.[78] But many stylists don't approve of it. In 2001, only 44 percent of the *American Heritage* Usage Panel, for example, accepted a sentence containing the phrase *a situation where*.

I suggest that in formal writing, you say *in which* or *when* instead.

If the passages above were intended for formal contexts, they might read,

the only field of endeavor <u>in which</u> a man can succeed

a period <u>when</u> (or <u>in which</u>) everybody tells you that you've completely failed

a speed-reading course <u>in which</u> you run your finger down the middle of the page

long periods <u>when</u> (or <u>in which</u>) I don't listen to things

WHO or WHOM

* *Who*

"She's the kind of girl <u>who</u> climbed the ladder of success, wrong by wrong."
> Mae West, in the 1933 film *I'm No Angel*

"A professor is one <u>who</u> talks in someone else's sleep."
> W. H. Auden, quoted in *The Treasury of Humorous Quotations,* ed. Evan Esar and Nicolas Bentley (1951)

"The chief problem about death, incidentally, is the fear that there may be no afterlife—a depressing thought, particularly for those <u>who</u> have bothered to shave."
> Woody Allen, *Without Feathers* (1975)

"The moonwalk came from these beautiful black kids <u>who</u> live in the ghettos in the inner cities, <u>who</u> are brilliant."
> Michael Jackson, award-winning American singer, actor, and producer (1958–2009), interview with Oprah Winfrey, Feb. 10, 1993, quoted in "The Michael Jackson Interview: Oprah Reflects," oprah.com, Sept. 16, 2009

"Why is McDonald's still counting? How insecure is this company? 40 million, 80 jillion billion zillion killion…<u>Who</u> cares?"
> Jerry Seinfeld, *I'm Telling You for the Last Time,* 1998 stand-up comedy special

"Julia Child was a young woman <u>who</u> was six foot two. She was great-looking, but she was outsized in her world, and that was a handicap in the days when the main reason to go to Smith College was to get a husband."
> Meryl Streep, award-winning American actress, quoted in Marisa Fox, "Ladies Who Lunch," lhj.com, Aug. 2009

✳ *Whom*

"Any man's death diminishes me, because I am involved in mankind; and therefore never send to know for <u>whom</u> the bell tolls; it tolls for thee."

John Donne, English poet, satirist, lawyer, and cleric (1572–1631), "Meditation XVII," *Devotions upon Emergent Occasions* (1624)

"Acquaintance, *n.*: A person <u>whom</u> we know well enough to borrow from, but not well enough to lend to."

Ambrose Bierce, *The Devil's Dictionary* (1911)

"Marriage is the alliance of two people, one of <u>whom</u> never remembers birthdays and the other never forgets [them]."

Ogden Nash, American poet famous for his comic verse (1902–1977), "I Do, I Will, I Have," 1948

"He mobilized the English language and sent it into battle to steady his fellow countrymen and hearten those Europeans upon <u>whom</u> the long dark night of tyranny had descended."

Edward R. Murrow, award-winning American journalist and broadcaster (1908–1965), speaking of Winston Churchill, Nov. 30, 1954, quoted in *In Search of Light,* ed. Edward Bliss (1967)

Linda Evangelista, Christy Turlington, and Naomi Campbell were women about <u>whom</u> the term *supermodel* was used in the late 1980s.

"My parents, both of <u>whom</u> came from impoverished backgrounds and neither of <u>whom</u> had been to college, took the view that my overactive imagination was an amusing personal quirk that would never pay a mortgage, secure a pension."

J. K. Rowling, commencement address at Harvard, June 5, 2008

"I was 13 years old. [My mother] had been married for almost 20 years, and I watched her go through a tough time, trying to date, trying to figure things out. She dated some horrible men <u>whom</u> I had to kick out of the house."

Ellen DeGeneres, quoted in David Hochman, "Nice Girls Finish First," *Good Housekeeping*, Oct. 2011

"My parents thought all actors were secretly drug addicts, except for Clint Eastwood, <u>whom they admired</u>."

Ethan Hawke, American actor, writer, and director, quoted in nypost.com, Mar. 24, 2012

When was the last time you said *whom* in conversation? I say it every now and then, but I'm very peculiar that way. Most of us don't use it much, if at all, when we speak.

Whom has a long history, and an ancestry that dates back to Old English. The word is increasingly rare, though, especially in speech. People often say *who* when the traditional rules prescribe *whom,* but that's nothing new. *Whom* was used as the subject of a sentence as early as the 1300s. By the sixteenth century, Shakespeare and others felt free to say *who* where the traditional rules now require *whom,* and *whom* where we normally would expect *who*.[79] Of course, those strict rules weren't formally established until the eighteenth century and later. And even then some grammarians argued that formal usage should be left loose to reflect what people actually said.

The grammarians don't seem to have had much of an impact on everyday speech in any case. Today we say *who* instead of *whom* in pretty much the same ways that Shakespeare did, especially at the beginning of a sentence or a clause. When asking questions in casual conversation, for example, people very rarely or never say *whom*.[80] Since the nineteenth century, in fact, some language commentators have been predicting—or hoping—that *whom* is going to disappear from English altogether. The eminent psychologist and linguist Steven Pinker says that the *who/whom* distinction is going the way of the phonograph record.[81]

He may be right. And yet many music lovers treasure vinyl records and buy millions of them every year. And *whom* is still with us. In conversation, it does sound very formal and maybe even pretentious, especially to Americans and Australians. But in a letter of application, a student essay, a professional publication, a job inquiry, or any other writing aimed at educated readers, it's still important to know when to use *who* and *whom*.

In formal use, *whom* is common after prepositions (*to whom, of whom, for whom*, etc.). Many letters to committees or organizations still begin with <u>*To whom*</u> *it may concern.* (Opening a job application with *To who it may concern* would be a really bad idea.) It's normal in casual conversation to ask a question like <u>*Who*</u> *did you give it to?* But people would think that something was wrong with you if you asked, *To who did you give it?* And a statement like *I have three brothers,* <u>*two of who*</u> *served in Iraq* would be conspicuously bad. So would *I'd like to thank my two favorite teachers,* <u>*both of who*</u> *are here today.*

In all styles of speech and writing, use *who* to refer to someone who is doing something or being described.

the kind of girl <u>who</u> climbed
a professor is one <u>who</u> talks
<u>who</u> cares

In formal writing, use *whom* when you put a preposition immediately in front of it. *Whom* in that context is called the **object of a preposition.**

<u>for whom</u> the bell tolls
<u>upon whom</u> the long dark night of tyranny had descended
neither <u>of whom</u> had been to college

Whom* can be the object of a preposition even if the preposition appears later in the clause.** In sentences like that, people often say *who,* and that's fine, even in some formal contexts. **But if you're writing for critical readers, I suggest that you say *whom, as James Franco does here:

> "I'm actually turned off when I look at an account and don't see any selfies, because I want to know <u>whom</u> I'm dealing <u>with</u>."
>
> James Franco, Golden Globe Award–winning American actor, director, screenwriter, producer, teacher, and writer, "The Meaning of the Selfie," nytimes.com, Dec. 26, 2013

In formal contexts, use *whom* when someone is receiving action:

a person <u>whom</u> we know well enough to borrow from
horrible men <u>whom</u> I had to kick out of the house
<u>whom they admired</u>

Here's a hint: *who* **is typically followed by a verb.**

who climbed
who cares
who talks
who was

And here's a silly trick for remembering when to use *whom:*

> During a pledge drive for National Public Radio, Click and Clack,
> the hosts of *Car Talk,* said that NPR depends on listeners' donations.
> Click: From <u>whom</u>?
> Clack: From youm.
>   Tom and Ray Magliozzi, *Car Talk,* NPR, May 18, 2013

Sometimes nonsense words can be easy to remember. If you can recall
From whom? From youm, you'll have the model in your mind that *whom*
follows *from* and other prepositions.

✳ *A Trick for Deciding When to Use* **Who** *or* **Whom**

Take a shortcut to the right answer in formal speech and writing by following these three steps:

   (1) **Invert the sentence.**
   (2) **Substitute** *he* or *him* **for** *who* or *whom.*
   (3) **If** *he* **is correct, use** *who.* **If** *him* **is right, use** *whom.*

The right answer will usually be obvious.
   Remember, you don't necessarily need to follow the rules for using
whom in casual conversation or informal or creative writing. If we were

to transform the passages below into formal English, though, here are the steps we could take:

Which versions of the quotation below would be correct in formal writing?

(A) "Who [are] you going to believe, me or your own eyes?"
(B) "Whom [are] you going to believe, me or your own eyes?"
>   Chico Marx, American comedian and actor (1887–1961), in the 1933 film *Duck Soup*

(1) Invert the sentence: "you're going to believe who" or "you're going to believe whom."
(2) Substitute *he* or *him:* "you're going to believe he" or "you're going to believe him."
(3) The correct choice is obvious: *him.* So *whom* is correct, as in version B. (Chico actually said, "Who you gonna believe…")

Here's a passage from Woody Allen's 1969 film *Take the Money and Run.* In formal English, which is right, *who* or *whom*?

(A) "He never made the Ten-Most-Wanted list. It's very unfair voting. It's <u>who</u> you know."

(B) "He never made the Ten-Most-Wanted list. It's very unfair voting. It's <u>whom</u> you know."

(1) Invert the sentence, giving you "you know whom."
(2) Substitute *he* or *him:* "you know he" or "you know him."
(3) The right choice is *him.* So it's also *whom* as in version B.

The line in the film was actually "It's who you know." In conversation, that's much more natural than saying *whom.*

One more thing: **You may choose to drop the word *whom* after some prepositions, including *in.* Just move the preposition to the end of the clause or sentence, and add the word *that:***

"The more famous you are, the harder it becomes...to create a character <u>in whom</u> people suspend belief."

can become

"The more famous you are, the harder it becomes...to create a character <u>that</u> people suspend belief <u>in</u>."

> Vera Farmiga, American actress and director, quoted in Elizabeth Day, "Vera Farmiga: 'I Demand a Lot from Myself,'" theguardian. com, Mar. 26, 2011. Farmiga actually said "in whom." Either version would be correct, though.

WHOEVER or WHOMEVER

✻ *Whoever*

"<u>Whoever</u> named it necking was a poor judge of anatomy."
> Groucho Marx, attributed

"<u>Whoever</u> you are, I have always depended on the kindness of strangers."
> Blanche DuBois, in Tennessee Williams, *A Streetcar Named Desire* (1947)

"<u>Whoever</u> wants to know the heart and mind of America had better learn baseball."
> Jacques Barzun, French-born American historian of ideas and culture (1907–2012), *God's Country and Mine* (1954)

"When I sing I don't feel like it's me. I feel I am fabulous, like I'm 10 feet tall. I am the greatest. I am the strongest. I am Samson. I'm <u>whoever</u> I want to be."
> Cyndi Lauper, award-winning American singer-songwriter and actress, quoted in Beth Mann, "Cyndi Lauper Graces the Tropicana," examiner.com, Dec. 6, 2010

"*Quien bien te quiere te hará llorar:* <u>Whoever</u> really loves you will make you cry."
> Spanish proverb

"Whoever said money can't buy happiness simply didn't know where to go shopping."

> Anonymous, sometimes attributed to Bo Derek, American actress, film producer, and model

✳ *Whomever*

"I always have a wonderful time, wherever I am, whomever I'm with."

> James Stewart, Academy Award–winning American actor (1908–1997), in the 1950 film *Harvey,* quoted in imdb.com

One good thing about Internet dating is that you're sure to click with whomever you meet.

> Anonymous bad pun

Knowing when to use *whomever* may be the trickiest grammar problem that I present to my students. *Whomever* has been part of English for about seven hundred years, but it's extremely rare today. When it does appear, it's very frequently misused, even in prominent edited publications. Yet the rule for how to use *whomever* isn't hard.

Choose between *whoever* and *whomever* in generally the same way that you do between *who* and *whom*: **If the pronoun stands for someone who is being described or doing something, say** *whoever.* **If that person is receiving action or is the object of a preposition, say** *whomever.*

The tricky part is that you'll often use *whoever* or *whomever* in a clause (a group of words that include a subject and a verb), and the entire clause may receive the action or be the object of a preposition. That means that **you should choose between *whoever* and *whomever* inside the clause and ignore the words that precede it.** Here are two tips for how to do that:

TIP 1: If *whoever* or *whomever* appears at the beginning of a clause, substitute *he* or *him.*

If *he* is correct, choose *whoever.*

If *him* is right, use *whomever.*

Groucho's passage above begins with "<u>Whoever</u> named it necking." We can substitute *he* for *whoever:* "<u>He</u> named it necking." So *whoever* is correct.

The same is true of "<u>Whoever</u> really loves you" and "<u>Whoever</u> said money can't buy happiness." In both cases, you can substitute *he:* "<u>He</u> really loves you" and "<u>He</u> said money can't buy happiness." So *whoever* is the right choice in both.

Now, even careful speakers rarely begin a sentence with *whomever*. It does appear in that position occasionally, though, as in this translation from the biblical book of Job:

"<u>Whomever</u> He imprisons cannot be set free."
  Job 12:14 (Tanakh)

In this passage, if you invert the sentence and substitute *he* or *him,* you get "He imprisons he" or "He imprisons *him*." Since *him* is right, *whomever* is too.

TIP 2: If *whoever* or *whomever* appears in the middle of a sentence, go through these three steps:

(1) **Cross out all words in the sentence before the word *whoever* or *whomever*.**
(2) **Invert the sentence.**
(3) **Substitute *he* or *him*. If *he* is grammatically correct, so is *whoever*. If *him* is correct, so is *whomever*.**

In the sentence "I always have a wonderful time, wherever I am, *whomever* I'm with," cross out all of the words before *whomever*. That leaves you with "whoever I'm with" or "whomever I'm with." Next, invert the sentence and substitute *he* or *him*. The choice then is between "I'm with he" and "I'm with him." Since *him* is obviously correct, *whomever* is, too.

Here are some more examples:

I'll vote for (whoever/whomever) you prefer.

(1) Cross out *I'll vote for*, then invert the sentence. That results in *you prefer whoever* or *you prefer whomever*.

(2) Next, substitute *he* or *him*.

(3) The obvious choice is *you prefer him*. So, *whomever* is right.

I'll vote for (whoever/whomever) is the best candidate.

    (1) Cross out *I'll vote for*. Then invert the sentence.

    (2) Substitute *he* or *him*. That gives you *he/him is the best candidate*.

    (3) Obviously, the right choice is *he is the best candidate*. So *whoever* is correct.

I'll get the name of the nearest sushi place from (whoever/whomever) is at the front desk of our hotel.

    (1) Cross out all of the words before *whoever/whomever*.

    (2) Substitute *he* or *him*. That produces *he is at the front desk* or *him is at the front desk*.

    (3) The right choice is *he*, so *whoever* is correct.

I'll ask for directions from (whoever/whomever) we see on the street.

    (1) Cross out all of the words before *whoever/whomever*.

    (2) Substitute *he* or *him* and invert the sentence. That produces *we see he on the street* or *we see him on the street*.

    (3) Since *we see him* is correct, so is *whomever*.

Be sure that you trust the character of (whoever/whomever) you marry.

    (1) Cross out the words before *whoever/whomever*.

    (2) Substitute *he* or *him* and invert the sentence. That produces *you marry he* or *you marry him*.

    (3) Since *you marry him is right*, *whomever* is the correct choice.

Just as people often say *who* when the strict rules prescribe *whom*, it's very common for people to say *whoever* for *whomever* in everyday speech. It often sounds more natural to do that.

Which version of the statement below is appropriate in formal writing?

(A) "Had it simply been lost in the sixteen years that had elapsed since it had been written, or had it been taken by <u>whoever</u> had searched the room?"

(B) "Had it simply been lost in the sixteen years that had elapsed since it had been written, or had it been taken by <u>whomever</u> had searched the room?"

J. K. Rowling, *Harry Potter and the Deathly Hallows* (2007)

(1) Cross out the words before *whoever/whomever*. That leaves "whoever had searched the room" or "whomever had searched the room."

(2) There's no need to invert the sentence.

(3) Substitute *he* or *him* ("he had searched the room" or "him had searched the room").

The correct version, obviously, is "he had searched the room." So *whoever*, in version A, is correct.

CHAPTER 4

Tricky Words of The Twentieth Century and Today

Some words in this section of the book were coined in the twentieth century and there's disagreement about what they mean or how to use them. Others are old words that have become especially significant in recent years. Some have developed new senses that many language commenters and stylists have resisted. Still others have been used in new ways grammatically: they're nouns that are used as verbs, for example, or plural words that are treated as singular.

ACCESS

"For eight years I was sleeping with the president, and if that doesn't give you special <u>access</u>, I don't know what does!"
    Nancy Reagan, U.S. First Lady 1981–89, with William Novak, *My Turn* (1989)

"I've been blessed with the opportunity to express the views of Black people who otherwise don't have <u>access</u> to power and the media. I have to take advantage of this while I'm still bankable."
    Spike Lee, American film director, producer, writer, and actor, quoted in *Mother Jones* magazine, Sept. 1989

Dumbledore warned Harry that Lord Voldemort had realized the dangerous <u>access</u> to his thoughts and feelings that Harry had been enjoying.

J. K. Rowling, *Harry Potter and the Half-Blood Prince* (2005)

"There are 4 billion cell phones in use today. Many of them are in the hands of market vendors, rickshaw drivers, and others who've historically lacked <u>access</u> to education and opportunity. Information networks have become a great leveler, and we should use them together to help lift people out of poverty and give them a freedom from want."

Hillary Clinton, U.S. First Lady 1993–2001, senator, and secretary of state, speech at the Newseum, Washington, D.C., Jan. 21, 2010

Access is one of several words whose meaning has been changing during my lifetime, and maybe during yours. Since the 1300s, *access* has been a noun in English. Some six hundred years later, in the mid-twentieth century, people began to use it as a verb as well.[1]

Access is the ability, the right, or the opportunity to come near or enter. In the twentieth century, its meaning evolved, especially in the high-tech world. **Access came to mean "an opportunity or way to enter a system, retrieve information, etc."**

By the 1950s, people who worked with computers were also using *access* as a verb. **It means "to gain access to (a computer file, etc.)":**

"Edward Snowden <u>accessed</u> some secret national security documents by assuming the electronic identities of top NSA officials, said intelligence sources."

"Snowden Impersonated NSA Officials, Sources, Say," nbcnews.com, Oct. 16, 2013

Soon people were using *access* as a verb in new contexts: they were speaking of ways to access the beach, medical care, cable TV, etc. Using *access* this way still disturbs many careful writers.

In formal speech and writing, I recommend that you use *access* as a verb only when you speak about computers or electronics. But keep in mind that there's still opposition even to that.[2]

AVATAR

"[Martha] Stewart's image as the <u>avatar</u> of modern American domesticity helped Kmart draw in upwardly mobile shoppers who previously would not have darkened the door."

> Leslie Kaufman and Constance L. Hays, "Blue Lights or Not, Martha Stewart Remains Calm," nytimes.com, Jan. 26, 2002

"For legions of Rolling Stones fans, Keith Richards is not only the heart and soul of the world's greatest rock 'n' roll band, he's also the very <u>avatar</u> of rebellion...and the coolest dude on the planet."

> Michiko Kakutani, Pulitzer Prize–winning American literary critic, "A Writing Stone: Chapter and Verse," *New York Times,* Oct. 25, 2010 (Lexis)

"When Gloria Steinem, the <u>avatar</u> of the women's movement, was featured on an August 1971 cover [of *Newsweek*], the text called her 'The New Woman: Liberated Despite Beauty, Chic, and Success.'"

> Eleanor Clift, American journalist, commentator, and author, "When Women Said 'No,'" *Newsweek,* Dec. 31, 2012 (Lexis)

Of John Wayne:
"Whether he was a gunfighter, a cowboy, or a cavalry officer, he became, for many moviegoers, the very <u>avatar</u> of the American frontier."

> Michiko Kakutani, "He Acted Like the Man You Wanted to Be," nytimes.com, Mar. 24, 2014

Many young people know the word *avatar* from its use in computer games and the 2009 film *Avatar*. It's an ancient word, though, with religious associations. It comes from a Sanskrit term meaning "descent" and refers to the descent to earth of a Hindu deity who takes on bodily form. Translations have focused on that manifestation or incarnation. **So an *avatar* is the embodiment of something**. The passages above illustrate that sense of the word.

In the late twentieth century, though, *avatar* took on a new meaning, and the word has continued to evolve. **In current usage, an *avatar* can be a digital icon or figure representing a person or a character in a computer game, Internet forum, etc.**[3]

This retains the earlier sense of taking on a new form in a different environment. But as a digitized image, an *avatar* is actually the opposite of an incarnation:

> "When most people need a break, they take out their cellphones and begin pushing buttons to command <u>avatars</u> to run, jump, and shoot other <u>avatars</u>."
> Jon Methven, "How to Daydream," nytimes.com, June 23, 2013

A very recent use of *avatar* refers to a robot surrogate that can be controlled by a computer:

> "Because the slightest cold virus could kill him, Lyndon Baty almost never leaves the house.... A robot <u>avatar</u> now goes to classes and wanders school hallways for Lyndon.... The teen controls his <u>avatar</u> robot through the laptop on his desk at home."
> Linda Carroll, today.com, Feb. 17, 2011

Taking the meaning of the word one step further, an *avatar* also can be a body into which a human's mind has been projected. This was popularized as science fiction by the film *Avatar*. But people now are thinking in terms of creating real avatars in this sense of the word.

> "A conference in New York City...called the Global Future 2045 International Congress is working toward building <u>avatars</u> for us to upload our brains into in 32 years."
> Joel Stein, "Man vs. Machine," time.com, June 17, 2013

COULDN'T CARE LESS

"It looks like the Wii U may be sold out, my friends, which means it's time to put on black and go into mourning. Gnash your teeth. Shrug if you <u>couldn't care less</u>."
   Matt Peckham, "Watch Out, Here Come the Wii U Vultures," time.com, Nov. 14, 2012

If you *couldn't care less,* **you're completely uninterested.** This expression is pretty new: the first example cited in the *Oxford English Dictionary* is from 1946. Since around 1960, though, the expression *could care less,* meaning "couldn't care less," has become popular, mainly in colloquial American English. Usage commentators absolutely hate this phrase: the editors of the *Harper Dictionary of Contemporary Usage* call it "an ignorant debasement of the language."[4] The *Harper Dictionary* Usage Panel rejected it overwhelmingly in casual speech and by an even larger margin in writing. Panel member Isaac Asimov commented, "I don't know people stupid enough to say this."[5] That was a little harsh, I think, since many people who use this phrase are just trying to be ironic and a little cool in casual conversation. But you get the point: this isn't an expression that you want to use in a college application or job inquiry. In 1980, William Safire declared that *could care less* was beginning to die out, and wrote, "Farewell, 'could care less'! You symbolized the exaltation of slovenliness, the demeaning of meaning."[6] This phrase still survives in conversation today, however.

Could care less meaning "don't care" is nonstandard. It is inappropriate in formal English.

For that matter, *couldn't care less* **is a cliché.** As a matter of style, even though it's Standard English, **I suggest that you restrict it to conversation and informal writing.**

   Which version of the sentence below is grammatically correct?

(A) "I've learned to let things roll off my back. If [people] say negative things, I <u>couldn't care less</u>."
(B) "I've learned to let things roll off my back. If [people] say negative things, I <u>could care less</u> ."

Leighton Meester, American actress and singer, from *Teen* magazine, reprinted in people.com, Feb. 28, 2008

Version A is the correct choice. (However, Meester was quoted as having said version B.)

DATA

✳ The Data Are, *Etc. (Plural)*

"The <u>data imply</u> that moving…from the city with the 30th coldest climate in the United States (Chicago) to the city with the warmest (Honolulu) lowers the probability of September-to-April depression by some 40 percent."
  Seth Stephens-Davidowitz, "Dr. Google Will See You Now," nytimes.com, Aug. 9, 2013

"Between 1988 and 2010 (the latest year for which <u>data are</u> available), the percentage of never-married males between the ages of 15 and 19 who reported ever having had sex dropped from 60 percent to 42 percent."
  Nick Gillespie, "Society Is Coarser—but Better," time.com, Oct. 9, 2013

"In 2011, an Associated Press poll found that 8 in 10 Americans believed in angels.…In 2009 the Pew Research Center reported that 1 in 5 Americans experienced ghosts and 1 in 7 had consulted a psychic.…One interpretation of <u>these data</u> is that belief in the supernatural is hard-wired."
  T. M. Luhrmann, American psychological anthropologist, "Conjuring Up Our Own Gods," nytimes.com, Oct. 14, 2013

✳ The Data Is, *Etc. (Singular)*

"I've really been amazed by some of the <u>data that's</u> out there, especially with [regard] to tendencies of hitters, and certainly tendencies of pitchers as well."

David Cone, former major league baseball pitcher, quoted in nymag.com, May 26, 2011

"Think of it this way: Facebook has two assets: data and members. <u>Data</u>, by <u>itself, is</u> worthless."
Dan Lyons, "The Facebook Bubble," *Newsweek,* June 6, 2011 (Lexis)

"Within the United States, the NSA has been collecting not just records of Americans' phone calls, but of their e-mails as well. E-mail <u>data is</u> often even more revealing than phone data."
David Cole, "The Three Leakers and What to Do About Them," *New York Review of Books,* Feb. 6, 2014

Data refers to factual or statistical information, often in digital form.
The word *data* came into English in the seventeenth century but was rarely used until the twentieth. Now, as we hear so much about data plans, big data, data collection, etc., the word appears quite often.

Should you say *the data is* or *the data are*? How about *this data* or *these data*? *Data* is the plural of *datum* in Latin, and logically, since English borrowed the word from Latin, it should be plural in English too. So we should say *these data are.* But not many English speakers know Latin, and most of us don't spend a lot of time thinking about logical consistency in language. As a result, people often treat *data* like the word *information,* giving it a singular verb and referring to it as *this data* or *it.* In fact, computer specialists have treated *data* as singular since the 1940s:

"The <u>data is</u> stored in the memory...with the points numbered in sequence."
C. N. Moore, *The 1946 Moore School Lectures* (1985, *OED*)

Usage guides are split about this. Some treat *data* as plural, and editors at publishing houses often apply this guideline. Other language commentators put *data* in the same category as *agenda* and *opera*—plural words that are now considered singular. The plural construction is more common in print, possibly because of the influence of editors.[7]
Both the singular and plural senses of *data* are standard in formal speech and writing. In fact, the same journal can treat the word as both

singular and plural. I have to admit that I personally could never say *The data is.* As a stuffy professor, I firmly believe that, since *data* is plural in Latin, it should be plural in English, too. **But you're free to use *data* as either singular or plural. Just be consistent.**

Some terms involving the word *data* have become part of the fabric of our lives, including these:

A *data plan* is an arrangement with a service provider that gives you access to the Internet, email, etc., on a smartphone, laptop, or other mobile device without using a Wi-Fi connection.

Big data **refers to the study of massive amounts of computer-generated information, often to determine how people will act in the future.**

> <u>Big data</u> doesn't deal with people's motives. Instead, it looks for patterns in the data. Walmart executives found, for example, that people buy lots of Strawberry Pop-Tarts when hurricanes approach, so they put Pop-Tarts at the front of stores with storm supplies.
>
> David Brooks, discussing the book *Big Data*, in "What You'll Do Next," nytimes.com, Apr. 15, 2013.

> "<u>Big data</u> is suddenly everywhere.... Whether we're talking about analyzing zillions of Google search queries to predict flu outbreaks, or zillions of phone records to detect signs of terrorist activity, or zillions of airline stats to find the best time to buy plane tickets, <u>big data</u> is on the case.... [But] it never tells us which correlations are meaningful."
>
> Gary Marcus and Ernest Davis, "Eight (No, Nine!) Problems with Big Data," nytimes.com, Apr. 6, 2014

***Metadata* is information about data.** Metadata may include, for example, data indicating where messages came from, when they were sent, and to whom, but not their actual contents.

> "For some communications, <u>metadata</u> matters more than content.... 'You can text political donations. The <u>metadata</u> shows

your political leanings; the content just shows the amount you gave. Calling a cell tower away from my house in the middle of the night indicates I'm not sleeping at home.'"

Quentin Hardy, "Intelligence Agencies and the Data Deluge," bits. blogs.nytimes.com, June 9, 2013

The word *metadata* first appeared around 1969. Its use increased dramatically from the mid-1990s until 2008, according to Google Books Ngram Viewer. Since the revelation in 2013 that the National Security Agency has been collecting vast amounts of metadata about Americans' phone calls, email, and Internet usage, the word has appeared quite often in the news media.

DISINTERESTED or UNINTERESTED

✳ *Disinterested*

"Disinterested love for all living creatures [is] the most noble attribute of man."

Charles Darwin, English naturalist and geologist (1809–1882), *The Descent of Man* (1871)

"Rare and precious is the truly disinterested man."

Winston Churchill, *The River War: An Historical Account of the Reconquest of the Soudan*, 1899

"No one ever complains if a great artist says that he was driven to create a masterpiece by a hunger for recognition and money. But a scientist . . . is meant to be disinterested, pure, his ambition merely to [discover] the cement of the universe. He isn't meant to use it to start laying his own patio."

Will Self, English novelist and journalist, in *The Quantity Theory of Insanity* (1991)

✻ *Uninterested*

> "Luna did not seem to have noticed; she appeared singularly <u>uninterested</u> in such mundane things as the score."
> J. K. Rowling, *Harry Potter and the Half-Blood Prince* (2005)

> "America can breathe a sigh of relief to know that the President…is <u>uninterested</u> in the lives and loves of the Kardashian clan."
> Allison Berry, "President Obama Doesn't Want to Keep Up with the Kardashians," time.com, Oct. 19, 2011

A question for you, dear reader: if you're innocent of a crime, do you want the judge at your trial to be disinterested or uninterested? The answer is at the bottom of this lesson.

The traditional distinction between these words is that if you're *disinterested,* **you're impartial or unbiased, while if you're** *uninterested,* **you just don't care.**

These two words didn't always have these meanings, though. In fact, in their earliest appearances each meant what the other means now. But *disinterested* has had its current sense for over 350 years, and *uninterested* took on its present meaning in the eighteenth century. So by that point their meanings were set. Then for some reason, in the first quarter of the twentieth century, people again began to say *disinterested* in the sense of "not interested." Some usage guides accept that usage, but others don't. *American Heritage* usage panels have overwhelmingly rejected that meaning of *disinterested* in survey after survey. And 100 percent of the *Harper Dictionary* Usage Panel did the same.

The distinction between these words is useful and I recommend that you observe it in formal speech and writing: use *disinterested* **in its traditional sense of "unbiased, impartial."** As an alternative, if you want to avoid confusion, you can say *impartial* instead.

So, if you want a fair-minded judge, you want one who's *disinterested,* in the Standard English sense of these words. An *uninterested* judge wouldn't care about you or your case.

FINALIZE

President Dwight D. Eisenhower, on his plans to campaign for reelection: "That kind of thing is the subject of a great deal of conversation and talk, but nothing has been <u>finalized</u>."
     News conference, Aug. 31, 1956

Finalize is one of the words that a lot of usage commentators and stylists hate. That may be partly because it's a recent word, born in the twentieth century, and partly because some people think that coining new words by adding *-ize* is awkward and overdone. But a lot of the hostility to *finalize* seems to focus on the fact that bureaucrats and other government officials use it.

Finalize means "to put in final form, to complete." The word appears to have first been established in the 1920s in Australia and New Zealand. It evidently was adopted by the U.S. Navy and then became common in American bureaucratic circles. Many people took an instant dislike to the new word, and opposition to it peaked in the 1950s, especially after President Eisenhower used it. Some usage books now consider *finalize* to be standard, or close to it. But that doesn't mean that most language commentators and careful writers like it. Strunk and White called it "a peculiarly fuzzy and silly word."[8] More than 70 percent of the *American Heritage* Usage Panel didn't accept *finalize* as a word, and about 80 percent of the *Harper Dictionary* Usage Panel said that they wouldn't use it. Some of the *Harper Dictionary* panelists called it government gobbledygook. Others said that it's a dreadful and unnecessary word. Still others complained that its use is bastardizing the English language and is helping to send America to hell. That's a little intense, but you get the idea. In the face of all that hostility, if you really want to say *finalize,* **restrict it to bureaucratic or commercial prose. But a better idea would be to say** *complete* **or** *finish* **instead.**

FLAMMABLE or INFLAMMABLE

"<u>Flammable</u> liquids have flashpoints below 100°F. The flashpoint is the temperature at which a liquid produces enough vapors to be ignited."
> "Safe Use of Flammable, Combustible Liquids Is a Basic Part of Fire Prevention," J. J. Keller's Workplace Safety, June 28, 2010

"This week's worst-dressed celebrities wore fabrics that were not only unflattering, but also highly <u>flammable</u>."
> Christina Anderson, "Worst-Dressed List," huffingtonpost.com, Dec. 14, 2012

The U.S. Coast Guard publishes the "Manual for the Safe Handling of <u>Inflammable</u> and Combustible Liquids."

These two words look like they should be opposites, but they have exactly the same meaning. That's the problem. *Inflammable* is related to the verb *inflame* and, starting in the seventeenth century, it was the word commonly used to mean "combustible." But in the 1920s, insurers and others concerned with fire safety feared that people might think that *inflammable* means "not flammable," just as *indecent* means "not decent." So, to avoid confusion, they began a campaign to put the nineteenth-century word *flammable* on trucks and other containers of combustible fluids.

Some people still prefer the older word *inflammable,* though. About three-fourths of the *Harper Dictionary* usage panelists did, but many of them nonetheless recommended using *flammable* in all warnings about combustibility.

I suggest that you use *flammable* in warnings that something can catch fire easily.

But say *inflammable* in the sense of "easily inflamed emotionally":

> "The Englishman was in a strange, <u>inflammable</u> state; the German was excited. It was a contest of words, but it meant a conflict of spirit between the two men."
> > D. H. Lawrence, English writer and painter (1885–1930), *Women in Love* (1920)

FORTUITOUS or FORTUNATE

✳ *Fortuitous*

"Movies come together at different points for <u>fortuitous</u> reasons. You do them as you get the opportunity, as opposed to doing them when you choose to or design to."

> Ethan Coen, writer, producer, and director; quoted in artvoice. com, Oct. 29, 2009

Lightning struck St. Peter's Basilica in the Vatican City a few hours after Pope Benedict XVI announced his retirement. Some people speculated in social media about whether the lightning strike was a <u>fortuitous</u> act of nature or a sign from God.

> Elizabeth Tenety, "On Day Pope Benedict Resigns, Lightning Strikes St. Peter's," washingtonpost.com, Feb. 12, 2013

✳ *Fortunate*

"Do not speak of your happiness to one less <u>fortunate</u> than yourself."

> Plutarch, Greek historian and biographer (ca. AD 45–120), quoted by the American theologian Tryon Edwards in *A Dictionary of Thoughts* (1908)

"Luck is everything.... My good luck in life was to be a really frightened person. I'm <u>fortunate</u> to be a coward...because a hero couldn't make a good suspense film."

> Alfred Hitchcock, English film director and producer (1889–1980), quoted in Elizabeth Drake, "Alfred Hitchcock: 10 Quotes on His Birthday," csmonitor.com

"If you are successful, it is because somewhere, sometime, someone...started you in the right direction. Remember also that you are indebted to life until you help some less <u>fortunate</u> person, just as you were helped."

> Melinda Gates, co-founder of the Bill and Melinda Gates Foundation, valedictory speech, Ursuline Academy, 1982

"What I do for a living is go to work and pretend I'm somebody else.... Acting is what I do and, <u>unfortunately</u>, I can't do much of anything else."

Tom Hanks, American actor, producer, writer, and director, quoted in Roy Trakin, *Tom Hanks: Journey to Stardom* (1995)

Fortuitous and *fortunate* are related to the same Latin root, meaning "chance." The classical and medieval image of Lady Fortune spinning her wheel, making the king a beggar and a beggar the king, personified the idea that chance is unpredictable. (The song "Luck, Be a Lady" from the 1950 musical *Guys and Dolls* gave that idea a twentieth-century twist.)

Fortuitous* captures that meaning. It refers to something that happens purely by chance or accident, rather than by design. The outcome may be good or bad. It's had that meaning for over 350 years, but the word took on a new sense in the twentieth century:

Since about 1920, and especially since World War II, *fortuitous* often has been used to mean "a happy accident" or "a lucky result." In this sense, it has become a synonym for *fortunate* and has lost its reference to capricious fortune. This meaning of the word is common in casual English and frequently appears in newspapers and magazines:

A mistake proved <u>fortuitous</u> for one lady in Georgia when she asked for a Mega Millions ticket at a food mart, but the clerk inadvertently gave her a Powerball ticket. That night she discovered that she had won a $25 million Powerball grand prize. She woke up her family with shrieks of joy.

Allison Berry, "Clerk Error Lands Georgia Woman $25 Million in Powerball Jackpot," time.com, Oct, 5, 2011

Some of the major usage guides point out that this new sense of the word may lead to confusion or objections.

In formal speech and writing, I recommend that you use *fortuitous* in its traditional sense: to describe something that happens purely by chance or accident. Since other people will use the word with its more recent meaning, though, be sure that the context makes your meaning clear.

Fortunate **means "lucky, prosperous, favored by fortune."**
Which version of the sentence below is correct?

(A) "I believe there is something out there watching us.
<u>Unfortunately</u>, it's the government."
(B) "I believe there is something out there watching us.
<u>Fortuitously</u>, it's the government."
Attributed to Woody Allen

This sentence doesn't refer to something that's happened by chance. So version A is correct.

FUNDAMENTALISM

"A <u>fundamentalist</u> is just an evangelical who is angry about something."
Jerry Falwell, televangelist and co-founder of the Moral Majority (1933–2007), quoted by Rick Walston, "Fundamentalist Evangelical?," columbiaseminary.edu[9]

The term *fundamentalism* is so common today that you might be surprised to hear that it was coined only in 1920. It came from a series of pamphlets called *The Fundamentals*. They were written in response to liberal understandings of the Bible, Darwin's challenge to the biblical concept of creation, and other aspects of modernist culture. These pamphlets were intended to affirm beliefs that the conservative Protestant authors considered to be fundamental to their faith, including the inerrancy of the Bible, the authenticity of miracles, and the bodily Resurrection. People who were willing to fight to defend those beliefs were called *fundamentalists*.

Fundamentalism is a religious movement that upholds beliefs that its conservative Christian adherents consider fundamental to their faith.

When applied to other religions, especially Islam, *fundamentalism* is used to signify "a strict adherence to ancient or fundamental doctrines."

An economic or political doctrine also can be called *fundamentalist.*
Fundamentalism is a contested term. Critics often use it as a label for
believers who feel threatened by modernity and cling to "old-time religion." The word is often applied to Islamic extremists, but scholars
debate whether it makes sense to use it of any religious group other than
Christians. The quotations below capture some of the range of meanings
with which the term is used:

> "Fundamentalists are not just religious conservatives;
> they are conservatives who are willing to take a stand
> and to fight."
>> George Marsden, American historian of religion and
>> culture, *Understanding Fundamentalism and
>> Evangelicalism* (1991)

> "*Fundamentalism*... may be described as a 'religious way of
> being'... by which beleaguered believers attempt to preserve
> their distinctive identity as a people or group in the face of
> modernity and secularization."
>> Malise Ruthven, Anglo-Irish expert on religion, especially
>> fundamentalism and Islamic affairs, *Fundamentalism: The Search
>> for Meaning* (2004)

> "Every fundamentalist movement I've studied in Judaism,
> Christianity, and Islam is convinced at some gut, visceral level
> that secular liberal society wants to wipe out religion, wants to
> wipe them out."
>> Karen Armstrong, English writer and commentator on
>> comparative religion, interviewed by Bill Moyers on *Now*, PBS,
>> Mar. 1, 2002

> "I'm a fundamentalist in the true sense. That is to say, I follow
> the fundamentals of religion—and the fundamentals of the
> Muslim religion are actually very good: they advocate
> peace... friendship, brotherhood, and tolerance."
>> Mahathir Mohamad, prime minister of Malaysia (1981–2003),
>> quoted in bbc.co.uk, Oct. 13, 2003

HOPEFULLY

"Will we carry Ohio?" the candidate asked <u>hopefully</u>.

***Hopefully* has meant "with hope, in a hopeful manner" for nearly four hundred years.**

In the 1930s, a new meaning of *hopefully* appeared in the United States: "I hope, let's hope." By the early 1960s this new sense of the word had caught on. People say it in sentences like these:

"Hopefully, it will be a good year."
"Hopefully, I'll get a good job."

The word *hopefully* is a classic example of the tension between what language commentators and teachers say and the way most people actually speak. Starting in the 1960s, just as the new meaning of *hopefully* was spreading in the United States, American language critics launched a sustained attack against it. It's not clear why this particular word attracted so much hostility, but many stylists still condemn the new sense of *hopefully*. One main objection goes something like this: since the historical meaning of the word is "in a hopeful manner," to say "Hopefully the mosquitos won't be biting" means that the mosquitos will be full of hope when they decide not to bite us. Traditionalists may oppose this usage largely because it's new.

The newer meaning of *hopefully* is firmly established in informal American speech, though. Some style guides now accept it, as the *Associated Press Stylebook* did in 2013. *The New York Times Manual of Style and Usage,* by contrast, still recognizes only the older meaning of the word. The *Harper Dictionary* Usage Panel overwhelmingly dismissed the newer sense of *hopefully,* with panelists calling it a sloppy, sleazy vulgarism. In fact, the *Harper* panelists' opposition actually increased over time. The same hardening of opinion appeared in surveys of *American Heritage* usage panels. That suggests that resistance to the new sense of *hopefully* is stiffening in some circles as the usage becomes more popular. Now, I accept that the new meaning of *hopefully* has won in everyday speech. It's even found in some news and academic writing.[10] **Opposition to it is so strong, though, that I suggest you avoid the word *hopefully* in the newer sense of "I hope" or "we hope" in formal speech and writing. Say *I hope* or *we hope* instead.**

Which version of the sentence below is appropriate in formal contexts?

(A) "<u>Hopefully</u>, the Mets will win the World Series this year," he said with a deranged look in his eyes.
(B) "<u>I hope</u> that the Mets win the World Series this year," he said with a deranged look in his eyes.

If this sentence is intended as formal English, version B is the wiser choice, though version A is fine colloquially. The Mets' chances of becoming world champions anytime soon don't look good at the time of this writing, though.

THE INTERNET or THE WORLD WIDE WEB

✳ *The Internet*

"The <u>Internet</u> is becoming the town square for the global village of tomorrow."

> Bill Gates, American business magnate, investor, programmer, philanthropist, chairman of Microsoft, *Business @ the Speed of Thought* (1999)

"Vice President Gore defended on Thursday his statement that he invented the <u>Internet</u>: 'The day I made that comment, I was tired from staying up all night inventing the camcorder,' Gore said, deadpan."

> Chuck Raasch, "Vice President Plays Up Role as Net 'Evangelist,'" usatoday.com, Mar. 19, 1999

"The trick to <u>Internet dating</u> is to weed the losers from the potential partners by emailing each other for as long as possible before meeting up."

> *Asiana*, Spring 2005 (*OED*)

"The <u>Internet's</u> like one big bathroom wall with a lot of people who anonymously can say really mean things."

> Zooey Deschanel, American actress, singer-songwriter, and musician, quoted in Elizabeth Day, "Zooey Deschanel: 'I Don't Have Control over What's on Screen, and That's Terrifying,'" theguardian.com, Apr. 24, 2010

✳ *The World Wide Web*

"When I took office [in January 1993], only high energy physicists had ever heard of what is called the <u>World Wide Web</u>.... Now even my cat has its own <u>Web page</u>."

> Bill Clinton, U.S. president, 1993–2001, "Excerpts from Transcribed Remarks by the President and the Vice President to the People of Knoxville on Internet for Schools," Oct. 10, 1996

"In 1989, at the European Particle Physics Laboratory in Geneva, Switzerland, Sir [Timothy] Berners-Lee first proposed a 'global hypertext project' to be known as the <u>World Wide Web</u>. He wanted researchers like himself to be able to easily and automatically combine their knowledge in a web of hypertext documents."

> Chris Oakes, "Interview with the Web's Creator," wired.com, Oct. 23, 1999

"The world's urban poor and the illiterate are going to be increasingly disadvantaged and are in danger of being left behind. The <u>Web</u> has added a new dimension to the gap between the first world and the developing world. We have to start talking about a human right to connect."

> Timothy Berners-Lee, British inventor of the World Wide Web, quoted in John Naish, "The NS Profile: Tim Berners-Lee," newstatesman.com, Aug. 15, 2011

Many people speak of the Internet and the World Wide Web as if they're the same thing, but they're not. The Web is one way of accessing information by using the Internet, but the Internet includes email and other features that the Web can't access.

The Internet is a global computer network consisting of interconnected networks. It grew out of a program that the U.S. Defense Department established in 1969. By 1971 email was being sent over a distributed network, and twenty years later the World Wide Web was made available to the public. The word *Internet* has increased in use dramatically since the early 1990s, and by 2008 it appeared in print more often than *phone, television,* and the words for many other everyday items.[11] It's given us phrases like *Internet addiction, Internet café, Internet dating,* and *Internet service provider* (*ISP*).

When you refer to the global Internet, capitalize the *I*.

The World Wide Web is a multimedia information system that allows searches on the Internet through the use of hyperlinks. Capitalize *World Wide Web*.

As of this writing, many of the major style guides have no entries for *Internet* or *World Wide Web*. A few recommend capitalizing *Web, Website,* and *Web page.* The *Chicago Manual of Style* now considers those terms to be generic, so it doesn't capitalize them. **I recommend that when you use *Web* by itself, you capitalize it in order to distinguish it from any other kind of web. The word *website* is so common, though, that I put it in lowercase. Whichever style you choose, be consistent.**

> "I was making Facebook the week before finals, and there was a class [in which] you had to learn all these pieces of art.... A few days before the exam...I took all the images and made a <u>website</u>, where you could add notes to each image, and it was a 'study tool' where everyone else filled in all the notes that I needed to pass the class.... That was my first social hack."
>
>   Mark Zuckerberg, quoted in Jason Kincaid, "Startup School: An Interview with Mark Zuckerberg," washingtonpost.com, Oct. 23, 2009

Which version of the passage below is correct?

(A) "Now, think about the <u>Internet</u>, how rapidly it's become a part of our lives. In 1969 the government invested in a small computer network that eventually become the <u>Internet</u>.... The day is coming when every home will be connected to it...changing the way we relate to one another, the way we send mail, the way we hear news, the way we play."

(B) "Now, think about the <u>internet</u>, how rapidly it's become a part of our lives. In 1969 the government invested in a small computer network that eventually become the <u>internet</u>.... The day is coming when every home will be connected to it...changing the way we relate to one another, the way we send mail, the way we hear news, the way we play."

> President Bill Clinton, "Excerpts from Transcribed Remarks by the President and the Vice President to the People of Knoxville on Internet for Schools," Oct. 10, 1996

The global *Internet* should be capitalized, so version A is the right choice.

IRREGARDLESS or REGARDLESS

"People who use '<u>irregardless</u>' with a straight face are misguided souls who are trying to add emphasis to 'regardless.' They are the same people who think that 'penultimate' is an even-more-ultimate form of 'ultimate.' Unfortunately, 'penultimate' means 'next-to-last.'"

> Bob Levey, "Regardless, There's No Irregardless," *Washington Post,* Apr. 27, 1987

"I think there's something wrong with me—I like to win in everything I do, <u>regardless</u> of what it is. [If] you want to race down the street, I want to beat you. If we're playing checkers, I want to win."

> Derek Jeter, American professional baseball player, quoted in Mark Feinsand, "Yankees' Derek Jeter Says TV Booth Is Not for Him," nydailynews.com, Feb. 22, 2013

The word *irregardless* came into existence in American dialectal speech a little over a hundred years ago, possibly when somebody blended the words *irrespective* and *regardless*. Whatever its origin may have been, *irregardless* is a double negative: *ir-* is a negative marker (as in *irrespective* and *irresponsible*) and so is *-less*. Lookups of *irregardless* spiked on the Merriam-Webster online dictionary in 2012 when an emailed list of "Top 10 Grammar Peeves" said that it isn't a word. It is a word, but it's a non-standard one that's often mocked or used humorously. Virtually the entire *Harper Dictionary* Usage Panel rejected the use of *irregardless* in serious writing. Panelists called it barbarous, utterly useless, and an amusing illiteracy that should only be used as a joke. It's mainly used orally but sometimes shows up in transcribed speech or casual journalism.[12]

Say *regardless* instead in formal contexts. It means "without regard to (something), in spite of (the consequences)."

Which version of the passage below is correct?

(A) "My job is to play quarterback, and I'm going to do that the best way I know how, because I owe that to my teammates <u>irregardless</u> of who is out there on the field with me."

(B) "My job is to play quarterback, and I'm going to do that the best way I know how, because I owe that to my teammates <u>regardless</u> of who is out there on the field with me."

Tom Brady, American professional football quarterback, quoted in profootballtalk.nbcsports.com, July 23, 2013

Version B of Brady's statement is the right choice, and it's what he actually said.

ISLAMIC or ISLAMIST

✳ *Islamic*

"In 622 the Prophet Muhammad and his followers moved from the city of Mecca to Medina, where they established the first

Islamic community. This famous journey, known as the Hijrah, marked the beginning of Year One of the Islamic calendar."

> John L. Esposito, director of the Center for Muslim-Christian Understanding, Georgetown University, "Calendar, Islamic," in *The Islamic World* (2004)

"Rising oil wealth is lifting Islamic banking—banking that adheres to the laws of the Koran and its prohibition against charging interest—into the financial mainstream.... In Islamic banking, financiers are required to share borrowers' risks, meaning that depositors are treated more like shareholders, earning a portion of profits."

> Wayne Arnold, "Adapting Finance to Islam," *New York Times,* Nov. 22, 2007 (*Lexis*)

"This is a good time to ask apologists for the Islamic regime, who degrades Islam? Who imposes stoning, forced marriage of underage girls and flogging for not wearing the veil? Do such practices represent Iran's ancient history and culture, its ethnic and religious diversity?... What makes the guardians of the Islamic Republic more Muslim or more Iranian than others?"

> Azar Nafisi, Iranian American writer and professor of English literature, "Iran's Women: Canaries in the Coal Mine," huffingtonpost.com, Dec. 9, 2010

✳ *Islamist*

"The enemy is not just 'terrorism.' It is the threat posed specifically by Islamist terrorism, by Bin Laden and others who draw on a long tradition of extreme intolerance within a minority strain of Islam that does not distinguish politics from religion, and distorts both."

> The 9/11 Commission Report, Executive Summary, July 22, 2004

The word *Islam* means "submission" or "surrender." Its central religious text, the Qur'an (also spelled *Koran*), uses *Islam* to describe obedience to God and the universal acceptance of the natural laws of the universe.

Islamic means "characteristic of Islam, Muslim." It's been used in English since the eighteenth century.

Islamism is an older term that originally denoted the Muslim religion. It was first recorded in English over three hundred years ago. In the twentieth century it was displaced in that sense by the word *Islam*.

Islamism in its current sense refers to a set of ideologies that have appeared over the last century claiming to speak for Islam. The word has been used in English with increasing frequency since the time of the Iranian revolution in 1979. It and the related word *Islamist* are controversial and contested terms, but Islamists generally assert that Islam should guide social, political, and personal life. *Islamism* is often called *political Islam*.

The word *Islamist* is often used to describe Islamic extremism or fundamentalism.[13] With the Arab Spring in 2011, however, the phrase *moderate Islamist* appeared more frequently in the popular media, at least for while:

> "Morocco's King Mohammed on Tuesday appointed Abdelilah Benkirane as the new prime minister after his <u>moderate Islamist</u> Justice and Development Party (PJD) won the most seats in a parliamentary election last week."
>> Souhail Karam, "The Rise of Morocco's <u>Moderate Islamist</u> PJD Party to the Prime Minister's Office," reuters.com, Nov. 29, 2011

> "As <u>Moderate Islamists</u> Retreat, Extremists Surge Unchecked"
>> Headline to story by David D. Kirkpatrick, nytimes.com, June 18, 2014

Which version of the passage below is correct?

(A) "<u>Islamic</u> law is clearly against terrorism, against any kind of deliberate killing of civilians or similar 'collateral damage.'"

(B) "<u>Islamist</u> law is clearly against terrorism, against any kind of deliberate killing of civilians or similar 'collateral damage.'"
> Feisal Abdul Rauf, Kuwaiti-born Egyptian American Sufi imam, writer, and activist, *What's Right with Islam Is What's Right with America* (2005)

Imam Feisal refers here to Muslim, or *Islamic,* law. Version A is the right choice.

> In 2014 a panel of advisors to the new National September 11 Memorial Museum in New York objected to a film that used the terms *Islamist* and *jihad* to describe the ideology of the 9/11 attackers. The panelists worried that unsophisticated visitors to the museum would mistakenly think that *Islamist* and *jihadist* refer to all Muslims. Several scholars of Islam have rejected the term *Islamic terrorist* but have said that *Islamist* and *jihadist* can be used to refer to Al Qaeda.
>
> Sharon Otterman, "Film at 9/11 Museum Sets Off Clash over Reference to Islam," nytimes.com, Apr. 23, 2014

JIHAD

"Today jihad continues to have multiple meanings. It is used to describe the personal struggle to lead a good or virtuous life, to fulfill family responsibilities, to clean up a neighborhood, to fight drugs, or to work for social justice. Jihad is also used in wars of liberation and resistance as well as acts of terror."

John L. Esposito and Dalia Mogahed, *Who Speaks for Islam? What a Billion Muslims Really Think* (2007)

We've heard the word *jihad* a lot in the news since 9/11, but the term is widely misunderstood in the West. *Jihad* comes from an Arabic root meaning "to strive, to exert effort." It actually entered the English language in the nineteenth century, but I'm including it in this section of the book because it has become common in the last several decades. The *Oxford English Dictionary* defines the Islamic concept of jihad as "a religious war of Muslims against unbelievers." *Jihad* does include that meaning for Muslims, but it's much broader.

The *greater jihad* is striving to live a good life, according to God's will:

> The greater jihad is "the inner battle to purify the soul."
>
> Seyyed Hossein Nasr, Iranian-born scholar of Islam, Muslim expert on the West, and professor at George Washington University, *The Heart of Islam* (2002)

> "It might be said that all of life, according to Islam, is a jihad, because it is a striving to live according to the Will of God, to exert oneself to do good and to oppose evil."
>
> Ibid.

The *lesser jihad* is outward struggle or war against people whom one considers to be oppressive or corrupt. Islamist groups often use *jihad* in this sense. Western media and many commentators generally use the word only in this way, to refer to holy war. Terrorists often attempt to justify violent acts as defensive, and thus in accordance with the rules of jihad. A *jihadi* or *jihadist* is someone who conducts armed jihad, and *jihadism* describes this ideology:[14]

> "Jihad implies a struggle against the self, against one's passions and instincts and the temptations that oppress the soul. Yet in a religion obsessed with social justice, the idea of jihad as an internal struggle quickly expanded to include the physical struggle against oppression...against the internal and external enemies of Islam, even against unbelief."
>
> Reza Aslan, Iranian American writer and scholar of religions, *How to Win a Cosmic War* (2009)

> "As for the lesser jihad, in the sense of outward struggle and battle...all Shi'ite and most Sunni jurists...believe that jihad is legitimate only as defense...and cannot be originated as aggression.... Those who carry out terror in the West or elsewhere in the name of jihad are vilifying an originally sacred term, and their efforts have not been accepted by established and mainstream religious authorities."
>
> Seyyed Hossein Nasr, *The Heart of Islam* (2002)

"There is no solution to the Palestinian problem except by <u>jihad</u>. The initiatives, proposals and international conferences are but a waste of time, an exercise in futility."

> The Hamas Charter (1988)

"Sons of Islam everywhere, the <u>jihad</u> is a duty to establish the rule of Allah on earth and to liberate your countries and yourselves from America's domination and its Zionist allies. It is your battle—either victory or martyrdom."

> Sheikh Ahmed Yassin, who was the spiritual leader of Hamas (1937–2004), public letter, quoted in Ibrahim Barzak, "Hamas' Spiritual Leader Urges Jihad," Associated Press, Feb. 19, 2002

"Prime Minister Manuel Valls declared Saturday that France was at war with radical Islam.... 'It is a war against terrorism, against <u>jihadism</u>, against everything that is aimed at breaking fraternity, freedom, solidarity,' Mr. Valls said."

> Dan Bilefsky and Maia de la Baume, "French Premier Declares 'War' on Radical Islam as Paris Girds for Rally," nytimes.com, Jan. 10, 2015

Since the late nineteenth century, the term *jihad* also has been used loosely, sometimes in secular contexts. The *Oxford English Dictionary* defines this sense as "a war or crusade for or against some doctrine, opinion, or principle; war to the death":

"What I think is highly inappropriate is what's going on across the Internet, a kind of political <u>jihad</u> against Dan Rather and CBS News that is quite outrageous."

> Tom Brokaw, former anchor of NBC News, quoted in "Brokaw and Jennings Defend Rather," foxnews.com, Oct. 5, 2004

In 2011, Tamerlan Tsarnaev, who later became one of the accused Boston Marathon bombers, reportedly discussed jihad in a phone call with his mother. The Russians intercepted the call and warned the FBI that Tsarnaev had become a strong believer in radical Islam. But they didn't mention the reference to jihad in the call until after the Boston bombing, according to a report by an inspector general.[15]

"LIKE" AS A SPACE FILLER, TO
INDICATE DIRECT SPEECH, ETC.

> "I've had grand pianos that are more expensive than, <u>like</u>, a year's worth of rent."
>> Lady Gaga, quoted in Vanessa Grigoriadis, "Growing Up Gaga," in nymag.com, Mar. 28, 2010

It's not true that Valley Girls from California were the first to stick the word *like* intrusively into sentences. It's not even fair to blame mid-twentieth-century hipsters. That colloquial habit was born in England, and you may be surprised to hear that it was first noted in the writing of an eighteenth-century Englishwoman, the writer Fanny Burney:

> "Father grew quite uneasy, <u>like</u>, for fear of his Lordship's taking offence."
>> *Evelina* (1778, *OED*)

It became extremely common in colloquial use in the second half of the twentieth century, so I've put it in this section of the book.

Today, in informal speech, young people (and others) frequently use *like* as a verbal hiccup or a filler, in the way that a speaker might pause by saying "um" or "you know." Or they use *like* to set off the main focus of a sentence. They also say *like* to show that what they're saying is approximate and not strictly accurate. Speakers use *like* to soften a request ("Can I have, <u>like</u>, ten dollars?") or to diplomatically soften the blow before saying something the listener may not like.[16] And they often use it before reporting what someone said, or at least an approximation of what was said. It can emphasize the attitude behind the statement ("He asked me out and <u>I'm like</u>, 'No way!'").

Many language purists condemn this sense of *like* as a vulgarism. Don't use it in formal writing.

Wikihow.com offers tips for teens and others who want to stop using *like* in this way, including:[17]

- Stop using *like* before a quotation:
  Nonstandard: "He was <u>like</u>, 'Where are you going?" and she was
  <u>like</u>, 'None of your business!"
  Standard: "He asked, "Where are you going?" and she yelled,
  "None of your business!"
- Don't use *like* to approximate:
  Nonstandard: "She's, <u>like</u>, five feet tall."
  Standard: "She's about five feet tall."
- Stop using *like* before adjectives and adverbs:
  Nonstandard: "He was, <u>like</u>, *so* tall."
  Standard: "He was very tall."

RACISM and BIGOTRY

"I refuse to accept the view that mankind is so tragically bound
to the starless midnight of <u>racism</u> and war that the bright
daybreak of peace and brotherhood can never become a reality."
  Martin Luther King Jr., Nobel Peace Prize acceptance speech, Oslo,
  Dec. 10, 1964

"I was raised to believe that excellence is the best deterrent to
<u>racism</u> or sexism."
  Oprah Winfrey, American actress, talk-show host, producer, and
  media entrepreneur, quoted in *The African Guardian* 7 (1992)

"Homophobia is like <u>racism</u>, and anti-Semitism, and other forms
of <u>bigotry</u> in that it seeks to dehumanize a large group of people,
to deny their humanity, their dignity, and personhood."
  Coretta Scott King, widow of Martin Luther King Jr. (1927–
  2006), quoted in *Chicago Defender,* Apr. 1, 1998

"<u>Racism</u> isn't born, folks. It's taught. I have a 2-year-old son. You
know what he hates? Naps! End of list."
  Attributed to Denis Leary, American actor, comedian, director,
  writer, and film producer

"A study in the Jan. 9 issue of the journal *Science* presents strong evidence that even people who aspire to tolerance—who would consider themselves <u>non-racist</u>—still harbor unconscious biases powerful enough to prevent them from confronting overt <u>racists</u> or from being upset by other people's <u>racist</u> behavior."

> Eben Harrell, 'Study: Racist Attitudes Are Still Ingrained," time.com, Jan. 8, 2009

Racism and *bigot* are among the most frequently looked-up words in online dictionaries. Bigotry is a key aspect of racism, but the words *bigot* and *racism* were born in very different times and circumstances.

✳ *Racism*

Racism is a relatively new word, though people have long divided themselves and others into groups based on appearance and ethnic background, and attributed certain qualities to those groups. The English word *race* was used in that sense in the seventeenth century. But the first known use of the word *racism* in English was recorded only in 1903, when a group called Friends of the Indian denounced segregating people by class or race. The word remained very rare until the civil rights movement in the 1960s, after which its use increased dramatically.[18]

Racism is the belief that all or virtually all members of a race have inherent abilities and qualities that are determined by their race.

Racists usually assume that one race is superior to another. As a result, *racism* denotes prejudice, antagonism, and discrimination toward people of other races.

Racism also can refer to a racist political program or doctrine.

✳ *Bigotry*

Bigot is a medieval French term for a religious hypocrite. It sounds like "by God," and it actually may be related to that phrase. The word was first recorded in English in the sixteenth century, and within a hundred years it had taken on the broader meaning that it has today:

Bigotry **is an obstinate attachment to one's own group, religion, race, politics, or other convictions, with prejudice against others.**

> The understanding of race has become quite sophisticated since the mapping of the human genome. Many scientists now say that the genetic differences among the major human groups are so subtle and slight that they can only be determined statistically. For example, variants of particular genes may appear more often in people of European descent than in they do in Africans. These genetic distinctions fall into clusters that let scientists link a person's genome to its place of origin.[19]

SCHIZOPHRENIA

"Why is it that when we talk to God, we're said to be praying, but when God talks to us, we're <u>schizophrenic</u>?"
   Lily Tomlin, quoted in *Concise Columbia Dictionary of Quotations* (1989)

"The ever-quickening advances of science made possible by the success of the Human Genome Project will also soon let us see the essences of mental disease. Only after we understand them at the genetic level can we rationally seek out appropriate therapies for such illnesses as <u>schizophrenia</u> and bipolar disease."
   James D. Watson, Nobel Prize–winning co-discoverer of the structure of DNA, quoted in nytimes.com, Oct. 25, 2007

Schizophrenia is a comparatively new word. It was invented by a Swiss psychiatrist in the early twentieth century, based on the Greek for "split" and "mind."[20] That doesn't mean that *schizophrenia* refers to a split personality, though. That's how people often use the word popularly, but it isn't its technical meaning.

Schizophrenia **is a psychotic disorder that is defined by delusions, hallucinations, or disorganized thinking and speech.[21] In formal English, use *schizophrenia* only in the technical psychiatric sense.**

Does the passage below use the word *schizophrenic* in its technical sense?

"Roses are red, violets are blue, I'm a <u>schizophrenic</u> and so am I!"
Bill Murray, American actor and comedian, in the 1991 film *What About Bob?*

Bill Murray's character uses the word in its popular sense, not its psychiatric meaning.

TERRORISM

"The purpose of <u>terrorism</u> lies not just in the violent act itself. It is in producing terror. It sets out to inflame, to divide, to produce consequences which they then use to justify further terror."
British prime minister Tony Blair, speech in House of Commons, Mar. 18, 2003

"<u>Terrorism</u>, to me, is the use of terror for [a] political purpose...indiscriminate murder of civilians to make a point."
Senator Al Franken, quoted in forbes.com, Sept. 8, 2006

The word *terrorism* is more than two hundred years old, but terrorist acts and the responses to them have become so consequential in recent decades that I've put this lesson in this section of the book.

The word *terrorism* first appeared in English in 1795, referring to the Reign of Terror during the French Revolution. In 1793, the revolutionary leader Maximilien Robespierre and the delegates to the French National Convention had decided that terror through repression and bloodshed was legitimate state policy. In 1794, however, the delegates had begun to fear that Robespierre would turn on them. They accused him of a criminal abuse of power, which they called *terrorisme,* and sent him to the guillotine.[22]

So in late nineteenth-century France, terrorism was a legal instrument of the state. Nowadays in the West, we tend to think of it as an illegal tactic used by nonstate groups and individuals. In many areas of the world, though, people still speak of state terrorism. It's a question of who's talking and how they understand the term.

The dictionary definition of *terrorism* is usually simple and clear. It goes something like this: "**the use of violence, or the threat of violence, to frighten people in order to achieve a political, social, or religious goal.**" That seems straightforward enough. So you may be surprised to hear that there's no consensus about what terrorism actually is. The League of Nations first proposed a legal definition of the word as far back as 1937, but there's still no international agreement about what qualifies as terrorism.

Instead, there are hundreds of definitions of the term focusing on its different facets. They note, for example, that terrorism targets civilians and noncombatants and creates a climate of fear. It disregards the rules of war. It's asymmetric, involving the weak vs. the strong, the armed vs. the unarmed. Sometimes it's used to provoke an overreaction, other times to avenge a perceived wrong or to undermine public order and security. Terrorism is typically premeditated. It's normally intended as a message meant to influence an audience, with the goal of advancing a political, social, or religious project. That makes it different from the general crime of murder or sabotage.

Terrorism is a familiar word today, but it was rare until the turn of the twenty-first century. By 2008 the word occurred more than thirty times more often in English books than it did a little more than a century before. It appeared more than twice as often in 2008 as it did in 2000, before the 9/11 attacks, according to Google Books Ngram Viewer.

But who gets to decide what is terrorism, as opposed to legitimate opposition to an oppressive government? What distinguishes terrorism from assassination or guerrilla warfare? And who are noncombatants? People have disputed these points for decades.

That's because *terrorism* is a loaded term that stigmatizes and delegitimizes a group, with legal as well as moral consequences. Dissident organizations usually reject the term *terrorist,* even if they use violence against civilians. Instead they choose words like *revolutionary, freedom fighter,* or *martyr.* Journalists may refer to them as *militants* or *suicide bombers.* An autocratic government may call all opponents terrorists in order to elevate itself morally and justify a severe crackdown. And state officials normally don't say that their own forces have committed acts of terrorism. When soldiers kill a large number of innocent civilians, government or military spokesmen may call it *collateral damage.* The mainstream media may label an extreme case an *atrocity.* But they rarely use the word *terrorism* to describe their own government's actions.

CHAPTER 5

Look-Alikes

Several words are tricky because they look alike. Some were born from the same word, but they have different meanings and minor differences in spelling today. That leads to lots of mistakes, especially when people write in a hurry. This chapter deals with some word pairs that are frequently confused with each other in spelling or meaning.

ADAPT or ADOPT

✳ *Adapt*

"Enjoying success requires the ability to <u>adapt</u>.... Only by being open to change will you have a true opportunity to get the most from your God-given talent."
    Nolan Ryan, former major-league pitcher and CEO of the Texas Rangers, in *Nolan Ryan's Pitcher's Bible* (1991)

"My career should <u>adapt</u> to me. Fame is like a VIP pass wherever you want to go."
    Leonardo DiCaprio, American actor and film producer, quoted in Brian J. Robb, *The Leonardo DiCaprio Album* (1997)

"I'm not trying to keep up or <u>adapt</u>. I'm allowing myself to grow, evolve and create new music."

LL Cool J (short for Ladies Love Cool James), American rapper, entrepreneur, and actor, interview in *Billboard,* Aug. 7, 2004

"Guys don't <u>adapt</u> as well as women do to getting their heart broken for the first time. It's tragic."

Jamie Foxx, American actor, comedian, and musician, quoted in "The *Django Unchained* Interview with Kam Williams," euroweb. com, Dec. 25, 2012

✳ *Adopt*

"The radical of one century is the conservative of the next. The radical invents the views. When he has worn them out, the conservative <u>adopts</u> them."

Mark Twain, *Notebook* (1898)

"The thing I want more than anything else? I want a baby! I want to have children! I used to feel [that] for every child I had, I would <u>adopt</u> another."

Marilyn Monroe, quoted in George Barris, *Marilyn—Her Life in Her Own Words* (2001)

"There are techniques of Buddhism, such as meditation, that anyone can <u>adopt</u>."

Dalai Lama, high lama of Tibetan Buddhism, in "Oprah Talks to the Dalai Lama," *O, the Oprah Magazine,* oprah.com, Aug. 2001

"I get letters from little girls begging me to <u>adopt</u> them."

Kim Kardashian, quoted in Michael Solomon, "Kim Kardashian's Motherhood Guide," dailybeast.com, Jan. 4, 2013

The difference between these words is that if you *adapt* something, you change it; if you *adopt* it, you accept it and use or include it. If your friend comes up with a way to make a great pizza and you ask for the recipe, do you <u>adapt</u> it or <u>adopt</u> it? The answer is below.

When you *adapt* something, you change or modify it for a new purpose.

You also can adapt your own behavior *to* a new situation.

When you *adopt* an idea, an approach, or a suggestion, you accept it or start to use it.

To *adopt* children is to bring them up as your own legally.

So, if you follow your friend's pizza recipe, you've <u>adopted</u> it. But if you try to improve it, you're <u>adapting</u> it.

Which version of the sentence below is correct?

(A) The 2012 film *The Hunger Games* was <u>adopted</u> from the 2008 science fiction novel of the same name by Suzanne Collins.

(B) The 2012 film *The Hunger Games* was <u>adapted</u> from the 2008 science fiction novel of the same name by Suzanne Collins.

Since the film *The Hunger Games* was an <u>adaptation</u> of the novel, a change for a new purpose, *adapted* is the right choice. Version B is correct.

ADVERSE or AVERSE

✳ *Adverse, Adversity*

"I didn't like the play, but then I saw it under <u>adverse</u> conditions—the curtain was up."

> Groucho Marx, in Peter Hay, *Broadway Anecdotes* (1989); this is a variation on Groucho's actual statement, spoken in 1931

Michael Jordan was known for his clutch performances, even in <u>adverse</u> circumstances.

Your doctor should explain the potential <u>adverse</u> side effects of any medicine that she prescribes for you.

"A review of reports...found that communication failure (rather than a provider's lack of technical skill) was at the root of over 70 percent of serious <u>adverse</u> health outcomes in hospitals."

　　Nirmal Joshi, "Doctor, Shut Up and Listen," nytimes.com, Jan. 4, 2015

"By trying we can easily learn to endure <u>adversity</u>. Another man's, I mean."

　　Mark Twain, *Following the Equator* (1897)

＊ *Averse, Aversion*

During the Great Recession, many business executives became risk-<u>averse</u>.

"I'm not <u>averse</u> to being in big commercial films."

　　Sienna Miller, English actress, model, and fashion designer, quoted in Jonathan Van Meter, "Sienna Miller: Seriously Sienna," vogue. com, July 1, 2009

"First Lady Michelle Obama cajoled Jay Leno into nibbling on apples, sweet potato fries, and a pizza made with eggplant, green peppers, and zucchini on *The Tonight Show,* breaking his long-held <u>aversion</u> for all-things-healthy in his diet."

　　"First Lady Pushes Jay Leno to Eat Healthy," AP, Feb. 1, 2012

"If there's anything baby boomers hate more than aging, it's the idea of being considered senior citizens. [They have] a collective <u>aversion</u> to asking for 'senior' discounts or specials."

　　Martha C. White, "Senior Discounts That Really Aren't," time. com, Aug. 14, 2012

If you have a hard time remembering the difference between *adverse* and *averse,* you're not alone. These words sound alike because they both ulti-mately come from the same Latin root. And both have unpleasant meanings. One main difference between them is that usually it's a circumstance, a condition, or something else that's *adverse,* while it's a person who's *averse to* something.

Adverse effects, circumstances, or conditions are unfavorable. The word comes from the Latin for "against, opposite." So *adverse* conditions, circumstances, etc., are against you. *Adversity* is the noun form.

If someone is *averse* to something, he is opposed to it or feels a strong dislike toward it. The word ultimately comes from the Latin for "turned away from." So if you're *averse* to something, you've turned your mind away from it. That feeling is an *aversion.*

Here's a memory trick:

Adverse events can cause **advers**ity.

If someone is **aver**se to something, it's as if he wants to **avert** a bad thing that it will cause.

Another hint:

Adverse frequently appears in front of a noun (*adverse conditions, adverse effects,* etc.). *Averse* almost never does.

Which version of the sentence below is correct?

(A) I wouldn't be <u>averse</u> to having some chocolate gelato.
(B) I wouldn't be <u>adverse</u> to having some chocolate gelato.

In the sentence above, the speaker wouldn't be opposed, or *averse,* to eating some gelato. Version A is correct.

ADVICE or ADVISE

✳ *Advice*

"Fools need <u>advice</u> most, but wise men only are the better for it."
Benjamin Franklin, *Poor Richard's Almanack,* Jan. 1758

"I always pass on good <u>advice</u>. It is the only thing to do with it. It is never of any use to oneself."
Oscar Wilde, Irish writer (1854–1900), *An Ideal Husband* (1895)

"'All children must look after their own upbringing.' Parents can only give good <u>advice</u> or put them on the right paths, but the final forming of a person's character lies in their own hands."

> Anne Frank, German Jewish writer and Holocaust victim (1929–1945), entry of July 15, 1944, *The Diary of Anne Frank: The Revised Critical Edition* (2003)

Great baseball pitcher Leroy "Satchel" Paige's classic bit of <u>advice</u>: "Don't look back. Something may be gaining on you."

> Quoted in *Collier's* magazine, June 13, 1953

"Wall Street is the only place that people ride to in a Rolls-Royce to get <u>advice</u> from those who take the subway."

> Warren Buffett, quoted in Mary Buffett and David Clark, *The Tao of Warren Buffett* (2006)

✳ *Advise*

"The best way to give <u>advice</u> to your children is to find out what they want and then <u>advise</u> them to do it."

> Harry S. Truman, U.S. president, 1945–53, interview with Edward R. Murrow, CBS-TV, May 27, 1955

"Streets flooded. Please <u>advise</u>."

> Robert Benchley, American humorist (1889–1945), in a telegram he sent from Venice, quoted in *The Algonquin Wits,* ed. Robert E. Drennan (1968)

"The Wizarding community is currently under threat from an organization calling itself the Death Eaters.... You are <u>advised</u> not to leave the house alone."

> J. K. Rowling, *Harry Potter and the Half-Blood Prince* (2005)

Jennifer Lawrence, on an article in *Cosmopolitan* that gave tips on how to interview for jobs: "They <u>advise</u> you to say things like, 'I'm really bad about organization, so I'm taking organization classes to get better!' and stuff like that that shows initiative. So this article in *Cosmo* basically helped me in no way whatsoever."

> Jennifer Lawrence, quoted in interviewmagazine.com

It's easy to distinguish between these two words: *advice* is a noun, while *advise* is a verb.

When you give *advice*, you're offering guidance or a recommendation.

When you *advise* people, you recommend or inform them about something, or you give suggestions.

Which version of the sentence below is correct?

(A) The ring "may have other powers than just making you vanish when you wish to.... If you take my <u>advice</u>, you will use it very seldom, or not at all."

(B) The ring "may have other powers than just making you vanish when you wish to.... If you take my <u>advise</u>, you will use it very seldom, or not at all."

> Gandalf, advising Frodo, in J. R. R. Tolkien, *The Lord of the Rings: The Fellowship of the Ring* (1954)

Gandalf's recommendation, or <u>advice</u>, to Frodo, is the right choice, as in version A. If you've read Tolkien, you know that it's good advice.

AFFECT or EFFECT

Affect and *effect* are very familiar words, but people often confuse them. That's probably why these words have been among the most looked-up in the Merriam-Webster online dictionary. There's a pretty simple rule for telling them apart, though:

Affect is almost always a verb and *effect* is almost always a noun.

✳ *The Usual Meanings of* Affect *and* Effect

Affect

> "My voice is so bad, nothing can <u>affect</u> it."
> Bob Dylan, American musician, singer-songwriter, and writer, interview in *Rolling Stone*, June 21, 1984

"Never hate your enemy. It <u>affects</u> your judgment."

> Al Pacino, Academy Award–winning American actor and director, as Michael Corleone in the 1990 film *Godfather III*

"A changing environment will <u>affect</u> Alaska more than any other state, because of our location. I'm not one, though, who would attribute it to being man-made."

> Sarah Palin, former governor of Alaska and candidate for U.S. vice president, quoted in Mike Coppock, "Palin Speaks to Newsmax About McCain, Abortion," newmax.com, Aug. 29, 2008

" 'There is the fame monster, as you can see,' she says, gesturing outside, 'but it also comes from within. It will only change you and <u>affect</u> you if you allow it to.' "

> Lady Gaga, referring to the effects of her fame on her excited fans on the street, and potentially on herself, quoted in Jonathan Van Meter, "Lady Gaga: Our Lady of Pop," *Vogue,* Mar. 2011

"I'm not here to <u>affect</u> you politically or socially. I'm here to make you laugh."

> Stephen Colbert, American political satirist, writer, comedian, and TV host, quoted in Lisa Rose, "Stephen Colbert Interview," nj.com, Oct. 26, 2009

Effect

"The great thing about the United States and the historically magnetic <u>effect</u> it has had on a lot of people like me is its generosity…[its] broadness of mind, curiosity, [and] willingness to accept strangers. [However,] there is a tremendously cramped feeling now."

> Christopher Hitchens, British American author and journalist (1949–2011), interview in telegraph.co.uk, Apr. 13, 2011

"Life unravels the way it does, and it has an <u>effect</u> on you, but you have to take responsibility for dealing with it.…I am not happy not singing. I want to sing."

> Shania Twain, on the tragedies in her life and her inability to sing, quoted in "Shania Twain Speaks Out," oprah.com, May 3, 2011

"The Angelina <u>Effect</u>" was the title of *Time* magazine's May 27, 2013, cover story after Angelina Jolie chose to have a prophylactic double mastectomy. The story discussed the likelihood that many more women would get tested for breast cancer in reaction, and maybe overreaction, to Jolie's decision.

In most cases, *affect* means "to influence" or "to have an effect on":

can <u>affect</u> my voice
change you and <u>affect</u> you
<u>affects</u> your judgment

To affect also can mean "to pretend to be, to have, or to feel (something)." This is a different verb from *affect* in the sense of "to influence."

"I <u>affected</u> an even deeper sincerity."
Gore Vidal, American writer and public intellectual (1925–2012), *Kalki* (1978)

***Effect* is almost always used as a noun meaning "result," "influence," or "outward sign."**

the Mozart <u>effect</u>
the butterfly <u>effect</u>

✳ *Less Common Meanings of* Affect *and* Effect

In rare cases these words take on different meanings. The quotations below gives examples of those less common uses of *affect* and *effect*.

Affect as a Noun

"The act of birth is the first experience of anxiety, and thus the source and prototype of the <u>affect</u> of anxiety."
Sigmund Freud, in *The Interpretation of Dreams,* 2nd ed., 1909

The patient showed flat <u>affect</u>, with no expression of emotion at all.

"I have all of the worst qualities of being a nerd—all of the <u>affect</u> and none of the smarts. I'm a useless nerd! That's pretty bad."

> Claire Danes, American actress, quoted in James Mottram, "Claire Danes: I Have All the Qualities of a Nerd," independent.co.uk, Dec. 4, 2009

In a psychological context, *affect* is noun. It refers to the expression of an emotion, such as sadness, elation, anger, or, as in Freud's passage above, anxiety.[1]

Effect as a Verb

"There is a godless grace, and snap, and style about a born-and-bred New Yorker which mere clothing cannot <u>effect</u>."

> Mark Twain, *Life on the Mississippi* (1883)

"I think that the Internet is going to <u>effect</u> the most profound change on the entertainment industries."

> Steven Spielberg, American film director, writer, and producer, on NBC's *Today* show, Dec. 3, 1999, quoted on imdb.com

Review of Michael Moss's book *Salt Sugar Fat*: "Moss's revelation that pink slime was a component of America's most commonly eaten ground beef…set off a countrywide furor.…By dint of good old-fashioned reporting, Moss <u>effected</u> real change, a big win for the consumer."

> David Kamp, *New York Times Book Review,* Mar. 17, 2013

***Effect* can be a verb meaning "to bring about, accomplish."**

clothing cannot <u>effect</u>
<u>effected</u> real change

Which version of the sentence below is correct?

(A) "Oh, I will always be honest with my music.…I've never let people's opinions <u>affect</u> the way I write."

(B) "Oh, I will always be honest with my music.... I've never let
people's opinions <u>effect</u> the way I write."
> Katy Perry, American singer-songwriter and actress, quoted in
> theguardian.com, Aug. 6, 2010

In this statement, the verb means "to influence," so the right choice is
affect, as in version A.

AID or AIDE

✳ *Aid*

"Learn to do good.
Devote yourselves to justice;
<u>Aid</u> the wronged.
Uphold the rights of the orphan;
Defend the cause of the widow."
> Isaiah 1:17 (Jewish Publication Society)

"In my family, there was one cardinal priority—education.
College was not an option; it was mandatory.... I signed up for
financial <u>aid</u>, Pell Grants, work-study, anything I could."
> Eva Longoria, American actress, speech at Democratic National
> Convention, Charlotte, N.C., Sept. 6, 2012

In 2013, Congress passed the Violence Against Women Act, expanding federal assistance in <u>aiding</u> victims of domestic and sexual abuse.

✳ *Aide*

Ten days before the 2008 presidential election, several <u>aides</u>
to Senator John McCain accused vice-presidential nominee
Sarah Palin of "going rogue." A Palin associate replied that she
was simply trying to "bust free" of a mismanaged campaign
roll-out.

"The average tenure of a White House senior <u>aide</u> is 18 to 20 months. I was there for nearly seven years."

> Karl Rove, former senior adviser and deputy chief of staff to President George W. Bush, interview by Wolf Blitzer, quoted in "Interview with Karl Rove," realclearpolitics.com, Mar. 10, 2010

A nurse's <u>aide</u>, or certified nursing assistant, helps patients perform day-to-day tasks, including dressing, bathing, and eating.

The word *aid* has been in the language for six hundred years, but *aide* came into English from French only 250 years ago. *Aides* at that time were typically military officers and assistants. The meaning of the word has expanded since then, especially in the United States, where it now refers to many different kinds of assistants

When you write these two words, the main thing to remember is that you can *aid* people, but you can't *aide* them.

When you *aid* people, you help or assist them.

***Aid* as a noun means "assistance" or "means of assistance."**

***An aide* is a person who assists or helps, especially in the military, politics, or government. In the United States an *aide* also can be someone who works as an assistant in any of many capacities, especially with sick or disabled people.**

Which version of the sentence below is correct?

(A) The sentence "Now is the time for all good men to come to the <u>aid</u> of the party" has been used as a typing drill since at least 1889.

(B) The sentence "Now is the time for all good men to come to the <u>aide</u> of the party" has been used as a typing drill since at least 1889.

Since the sentence above refers to assistance to one's party, the right choice is *aid,* as in version A.

ALL READY or ALREADY

❋ *All Ready*

The Wizard sent for "a big clothes basket, which he fastened with
many ropes to the bottom of the balloon. When it was all ready,
Oz sent word to his people that he was going to make a visit to a
great brother Wizard who lived in the clouds."

> L. Frank Baum, *The Wonderful Wizard of Oz* (1900)

"I've brought a big bat.
I'm all ready, you see.
Now my troubles are going
To have trouble with *me*!"

> Dr. Seuss, American writer and cartoonist (1904–1991), *I Had
> Trouble in Getting to Solla Sollew* (1965)

"Harry stifled a yawn behind his hand.
"'Bed,' said an undeceived Mrs. Weasley at once. 'I've got Fred
and George's room all ready for you.'"

> J. K. Rowling, *Harry Potter and the Half-Blood Prince* (2005)

"A lot of aspiring writers are all ready to write a novel, but they
don't know how to write sentences."

> American novelist Tom Robbins, quoted by Colette Bancroft,
> "Author Tom Robbins to Sign Books in St. Petersburg," tampabay.
> com, Feb. 16, 2013

❋ *Already*

"The Publicity Department was already on the ball. The
magazines seemed to be celebrating a perpetual Marilyn Monroe
week. My picture was on nearly all of their covers."

> Marilyn Monroe, on how 20th Century-Fox launched her
> career, quoted in Marilyn Monroe and Ben Hecht, *My Story*
> (2006)

"Advice is what we ask for when we <u>already</u> know the answer but wish we didn't."

>Erica Jong, American writer and teacher, *How to Save Your Own Life* (1977)

As far back as 1980, *Time* magazine ran a cover story saying that the use of robots was <u>already</u> transforming American industry.

"Most important, have the courage to follow your heart and intuition. They somehow <u>already</u> know what you truly want to become. Everything else is secondary."

>Steve Jobs, commencement address at Stanford University, June 12, 2005

"Look at the way celebrities and politicians are using Facebook <u>already</u>. When Ashton Kutcher posts a video, he gets hundreds of pieces of feedback."

>Mark Zuckerberg, quoted in Fred Vogelstein, "The Wired Interview: Facebook's Mark Zuckerberg," wired.com, June 29, 2009

If you confuse *all ready* with *already,* it's probably a slip in spelling, not a problem understanding the difference between them.

As two words, ***all ready* can mean "prepared for as an entire group."** ***All ready* also can mean "completely prepared":**

When it was <u>all ready</u>, Oz sent word to his people
I've got Fred and George's room <u>all ready</u> for you

This sense of the phrase actually just means "ready," with *all* acting an intensifier. It mainly appears in conversation and casual writing, though in edited texts it may show up in transcribed speech.

***Already* means "before" or "by now, by then":**

The Publicity Department was <u>already</u> on the ball.

Which version of the sentence below is correct?

(A) "When you are discontent, you always want more, more, more. Your desire can never be satisfied. But when you practice contentment, you can say yourself, "Oh yes—I <u>all ready</u> have everything that I really need."

(B) "When you are discontent, you always want more, more, more. Your desire can never be satisfied. But when you practice contentment, you can say to yourself, "Oh yes—I <u>already</u> have everything that I really need."

The Dalai Lama, quoted in "Oprah Talks to the Dalai Lama," *O, the Oprah Magazine,* oprah.com, Aug. 2001

The Dalai Lama is saying that we can practice contentment by telling ourselves that we have everything that we really need by now, or *already*. So version B is the right choice.

ENOUGH ALREADY!

"<u>Enough already</u> with these crazy kids and their wacky dances."

Vanity Fair, Mar. 1992 (*OED*)

Since the early twentieth century, especially in casual Jewish speech in the United States, *already* has been used in phrases ranging from *Enough already!* to *All right already!* to *Shut up already!* Based on Yiddish, these phrases suggest various degrees of irritation, sometimes humorously. They're roughly equivalent to *That's enough now, I've had it!,* or *Stop bugging me!* To some extent they've become Americanisms.[2]

ALL RIGHT or ALRIGHT

"If I were to try to read, much less answer, all the attacks made on me, this shop might as will be closed for any other business…If the end brings me out <u>all right</u>, what is said against me won't amount to anything."

> Abraham Lincoln, quoted in *"Abe" Lincoln's Yarns and Stories,* ed. Alexander K McClure (1901)

"<u>All right</u>, then, I'll go to hell."

> Mark Twain, *The Adventures of Huckleberry Finn* (1884)

"'You paid us more than if you'd been telling the truth,' he explained blandly, 'and enough more to make it <u>all right</u>.'"

> Private eye Sam Spade, in American crime writer Dashiell Hammett's *The Maltese Falcon* (1930)

"Don't Think Twice, It's <u>All Right</u>"

> Bob Dylan, 1963 song title

"'Are you <u>all right</u>, dear?'
"'Oh yes,' said Voldemort quietly. 'Yes, I'm very well... .'"

> J. K. Rowling, *Harry Potter and the Half-Blood Prince* (2005)

Is *alright* ever okay as a spelling of *all right*? No, in formal writing it isn't. It was first recorded in print a little over a hundred years ago as a fused spelling of *all right*.[3] *Already, altogether,* and *always* also fuse *all* with another word, and they're accepted as Standard English. But *alright* isn't.

Alright is common in correspondence, though, and it sometimes appears in comic strips, magazines, newspaper articles, and business publications.[4] Gertrude Stein, James Joyce, and Langston Hughes used it. But it's been strongly criticized by almost all recent style guides. One major usage authority says, for instance, that if somebody uses the spelling *alright,* that reveals his background, upbringing, and education as much as any other word in English—and not in a good way! Almost nine out of every ten *Harper Dictionary* usage panelists objected to *alright* as a general substitute for *all right*.[5]

Use *all right* in formal writing.
Which version of the sentence below is standard?

(A) "<u>All right</u>, everybody, line up alphabetically according to your height."

(B) "<u>Alright</u>, everybody, line up alphabetically according to your height."

> Attributed to Casey Stengel on the Official Site of Casey Stengel, caseystengel.com

"All right" in version A of Casey Stengel's quotation above is correct, even if his logic wasn't.

ALL TOGETHER or ALTOGETHER

✳ *All Together*

The Beatles released the song "<u>All Together</u> Now" on the soundtrack for their 1968 film *The Yellow Submarine*.

"It's a new era in fashion. There are no rules. It's all about individual and personal style, wearing high-end, low-end, classic labels, and up-and-coming designers <u>all together</u>."

> Alexander McQueen (1969–2010), British fashion designer and couturier, quoted in Lauren Smith, "35 Best Fashion Quotes of All Time," glamourmagazine.co.uk, Mar. 26, 2013

"To me, teamwork is the beauty of our sport, where you have five acting as one.... I tell my players, 'A basketball team is like five fingers on your hand. If you can get them <u>all together</u>, you have a fist. That's how I want you to play.'"

> Mike "Coach K" Krzyzewski, head men's basketball coach at Duke University, quoted in www.achievement.org, Aug. 26, 2008

"When you make a movie, you do it piecemeal. You're doing it not only scene by scene, out of order, but shot by shot, line by line. And there's this idea that the director has the whole thing in his head and they're going to somehow weave it <u>all together</u> in the end."

Jason Reitman, Canadian American director of films including *Juno* and *Up in the Air,* quoted in Molly Creeden, "Live from New York: Jason Reitman on His Table Reading Series," vogue.com, Apr. 26, 2012

✳ *Altogether*

"First, however, she waited for a few minutes to see if she was going to shrink any further.... 'For it might end, you know,' said Alice to herself, 'in my going out <u>altogether</u>, like a candle.'"
  Lewis Carroll, *Alice's Adventures in Wonderland* (1865)

"The judgments of the Lord are true, and righteous <u>altogether</u>."
  Abraham Lincoln, correspondence, Mar. 20, 1865 (referring to Psalm 19:10)

"I do not think it <u>altogether</u> inappropriate to introduce myself to this audience. I am the man who accompanied Jacqueline Kennedy to Paris, and I have enjoyed it."
  President John F. Kennedy, speech, Paris, June 2, 1961

The comedian and actor Tim Allen warns men never to comment on certain aspects of a woman's figure: "Just avoid the area <u>altogether</u>. Trust me."
  Tim Allen, American comedian, actor, and writer, *Don't Stand Too Close to a Naked Man* (1994)

Lena Dunham, the creator of the HBO series *Girls,* says that positive, healthy, loving relationships are rare for people in their twenties. People either commit "aggressively because they're scared of what an uncertain time it is, or they're avoiding commitment <u>altogether</u>."
  Lena Dunham, interviewed by Lauren Bans, "Lena Dunham on *Girls*'s Kinky Sex and Why Her Grandmother Loves Her Show," gq.com, Apr. 30, 2012

If you sometimes confuse *altogether* and *all together,* don't feel too bad. That mix-up wasn't even considered a mistake until the eighteenth century, and the *Oxford English Dictionary* cites lots of historical examples of it, including one by Shakespeare.[6] It's still fairly common for people to write *altogether* when the normative rule calls for *all together*. But in formal writing it's regarded as an error, so don't do it.

All together means "all in one place," "in a group," or "all at the same time."

All and *together* can have words between them, as in this famous line:

> "We must <u>all</u> hang <u>together</u>, or most assuredly we shall all hang separately."[7]
> Attributed to Benjamin Franklin, July 4, 1776

To _have it (all) together_ and _get it (all) together_ are colloquial terms in which _together_ means "organized, confident, able to cope."

Brooke Shields on being a working mom in Hollywood: "It's never easy. I don't ever feel like I <u>have it all together</u>.... But as long as my kids are first and taken care of, that allows me to pursue some of my artistic needs."
Brooke Shields, American actress and model, quoted in "Brooke Shields Cozies Up to Skunks and Mosquitoes in *Furry Vengeance*," news.moviefone.com, Apr. 28, 2010

"We may not <u>have it all together</u>, but together we have it all."
Anonymous saccharine saying on the Internet

Altogether as one word means "entirely, completely, in all."

<u>altogether</u> inappropriate
avoid the area <u>altogether</u>

Which version of the sentence below is correct?

(A) "I know, to banish anger <u>altogether</u> from one's breast is a difficult task."

(B) "I know, to banish anger <u>all together</u> from one's breast is a difficult task."
    Mahatma Gandhi

Gandhi is speaking of banishing anger completely, or *altogether,* as in version A.

Colloquially, since the late nineteenth century, *(in) the altogether* has meant "naked."

"The king is <u>in the altogether,</u>
But <u>altogether the altogether.</u>
He's <u>altogether</u> as naked as the day that he was born."
    Danny Kaye's song about the emperor's new clothes, from the 1952 film *Hans Christian Andersen,* lyrics and music by Frank Loesser

"'<u>(In the) Altogether</u> Now, Onstage': It wasn't long ago that Daniel Radcliffe made headlines and sparked wand jokes because of his brief nude scene in *Equus....* [Now] *Leaves of Grass* is being performed, as flyers promised, 'without irony or clothing.'"
    Joe Dziemianowicz, New York *Daily News,* Aug. 14, 2009

A LOT or ALLOT

✳ *A Lot*

"I don't look at myself as a commodity, but I'm sure <u>a lot</u> of people have."
    Marilyn Monroe, quoted in Richard Meryman, "Fame May Go By," *Life* magazine, Aug. 17, 1962

"You can observe <u>a lot</u> by watching."
>Yogi Berra, quoted in *New York Times,* Oct. 25, 1963

"I watch <u>a lot</u> of baseball on radio."
>President Gerald R. Ford, quoted in Eldon L. Ham, *Broadcasting Baseball* (2011)

"You can tell <u>a lot</u> about a fellow's character by his way of eating jellybeans."
>Ronald Reagan, *New York Times,* Jan. 15, 1981

"It costs <u>a lot</u> of money to look this cheap."
>Attributed to Dolly Parton, American singer-songwriter, actor, philanthropist, and writer

"Poverty is <u>a lot</u> like childbirth—you know it is going to hurt before it happens, but you'll never know how much until you experience it."
>J. K. Rowling, quoted in *Mail on Sunday,* June 16, 2002

✳ *Allot*

"This is the portion of the food offerings presented to the Lord that were <u>allotted</u> to Aaron and his sons."
>Leviticus 7:35 (New International Version)

"The founders of a new colony, whatever Utopia of human virtue and happiness they might originally project…invariably…<u>allot</u> a portion of the virgin soil as a cemetery, another portion as the site of a prison."
>Nathaniel Hawthorne, American writer (1804–1864), *The Scarlet Letter* (1850)

"Airlines differ as to how much space they <u>allot</u> passengers, especially in coach class.…Ask the airline or your travel agent for the…distance from the back of the passenger's seat to the seat ahead—33 inches is acceptable."

Morton Hunt, "Was Man Meant to Fly?," *New York Times,* Nov. 1, 1987 (since the time this was written, several airlines have reduced legroom in coach to 31 inches or less, and some <u>allot</u> only 28 inches)

A lot of people make the mistake of spelling *a lot* without a space between the words, especially in memos and correspondence. Stylists overwhelmingly reject this as an error, though a few confess that they've made it themselves.[8] Just remember, *alot* isn't accepted in formal writing.

A *lot* means "many, much, a great deal."
To *allot* means "to apportion, assign, distribute."
Which version of the sentence below is correct?

(A) "I've learned that there are <u>allot</u> of things in your life that really benefit from being private."
(B) "I've learned that there are <u>a lot</u> of things in your life that really benefit from being private."
> Ashton Kutcher on his relationship with Mila Kunis, quoted in Mickey Rapkin, "Nobody's Fool," elle.com, Mar. 20, 2013

Ashton Kutcher is speaking of a great many things, or *a lot* of them. Version B is correct.

ALTAR or ALTER

* *Altar*

"Then Noah built an <u>altar</u> to the Lord and . . . he sacrificed burnt offerings on it."
> Gen. 8:20 (KJV)

"I wanted to be a priest at one point. I was pretty religious. I was an <u>altar</u> boy, and I was good at it. Then I started meeting girls."
> Jimmy Fallon, American TV host, comedian, actor, singer, and producer, quoted in Sia Mitchell, "Jimmy Fallon Comes Alive," *Spin* magazine interview, www.saturday-night-live.com

✳ *Alter*

"We hold these truth to be self-evident: that all men are created equal; that they are endowed by their Creator with certain unalienable rights; that among these are life, liberty, and the pursuit of happiness.... Whenever any form of government becomes destructive of these ends, it is the right of the people to <u>alter</u> or to abolish it."

Declaration of Independence, July 4, 1776

"Horribly familiar, dreadfully <u>altered</u>, it raised a wasted arm, pointing at Harry. 'No!' Harry shouted.... 'No! It wasn't us! We didn't kill you—'"

J. K. Rowling, *Harry Potter and the Deathly Hallows* (2007)

Kobe Bryant, speaking about basketball and hockey: "One person can control the tempo of a game [and] completely <u>alter</u> the momentum of a series."

Kobe Bryant, American basketball player, quoted in Adrian Wojnarowski, "Kobe Still Tough, with Assists from the Greats," sports.yahoo.com, Nov. 23, 2010

Altar and *alter* are very different words with different histories, but people sometimes confuse their spellings. That's understandable. Each was spelled both *-ar* and *-er* for centuries. By the 1600s the spellings settled down to their modern forms, though, and you need to know the difference between them.

An *altar* is a table used for religious purposes:

"an <u>altar</u> to the Lord"

It can be used figuratively:

"I [offer] you the consolation that may be found in the thanks of the Republic they died to save ... and the solemn pride that must be yours to have laid so costly a sacrifice upon the <u>altar</u> of freedom."

President Abraham Lincoln, letter of condolence to a mother he mistakenly thought had lost five sons in the Civil War, Nov. 21, 1864 (she had lost two)

"A likeable, shy young man happiest before the <u>altar</u> of his PlayStation."
New York Review of Books, June 24, 2010 (*OED*)

When you *alter* something, you change or affect it.

People and things also can *alter* in the sense of changing in some way:

"Love is not love
Which <u>alters</u> when it alteration finds."
Shakespeare, Sonnet 116 (published 1609)

Which version of the sentence below is correct?

(A) "The past is always dozing in the ice, waiting to <u>alter</u> the present."
(B) "The past is always dozing in the ice, waiting to <u>altar</u> the present."
Roger Rosenblatt, American author, commentator, editor, journalist, and professor, in *U.S. News & World Report,* Oct. 24, 1988

In Professor Rosenblatt's quotation above, the past is waiting to change, or *alter,* the present, as in version A.

ALUMNUS, ALUMNI, ALUMNA, ALUMNAE

Two Cornell University <u>alumni</u>, a husband and wife, have donated $133 million to help launch Cornell Tech, an applied-sciences research university that will be located in New York City.

Vassar <u>alumna</u> Meryl Streep gave the commencement address at Vassar in 1983. Lisa Kudrow, another <u>alumna</u>, was the speaker at Vassar's commencement ceremony in 2010.

Alumnus is a Latin word meaning "foster son, protégé, or pupil." It comes from a verb meaning "to nourish." So, in a sense, alumni are people who have been nourished by learning.

An *alumnus* is a male graduate or former student of a school, college, or university. The plural is *alumni*. By extension, former members of any group can be called *alumni*.

An *alumna* is a female graduate or former student of a school, college, or university. The plural is *alumnae*.

We use the masculine noun *alumni* to refer all graduates or former students of an institution, even if they are both male and female. It's sexist, I know, but we don't have a good alternative. Some people say *alum,* a slangy, casual form of the word. It has the advantage of avoiding the question of gender, but it's not accepted in formal English.

AMBIGUOUS or AMBIVALENT

✳ *Ambiguous*

> Val Kilmer, pointing a gun to threaten a gunman: "I want you to picture a bullet inside your head right now."
>
> The gunman, defiantly: "[Expletive]! Anyway, that's <u>ambiguous</u>."
>
> Val Kilmer: "<u>Ambiguous</u>? No, no, I don't think so."
>
> Robert Downey Jr.: "No, I think that what he means is that when you say 'Picture it *inside your head*' ... a bullet will be inside your head. Or *picture it in your head* [meaning "imagine it with your mind"].... He's got a point."
>
> Val Kilmer portraying Gay Perry and Robert Downey Jr., as Harry in the 2005 film *Kiss Kiss Bang Bang,* quoted in imdb.com

"The performances I enjoy are the ones that are hard to read or <u>ambiguous</u>...because it makes you look closer, and that's what humans are like—quite mysterious creatures, hard to pinpoint."

    Emily Blunt, Golden Globe Award–winning English actress, quoted in guardian.co.uk, June 20, 2009

"I look for <u>ambiguity</u> when I'm writing because life is <u>ambiguous</u>.... Suggestion and insinuation [are] a deeper way of touching people than trying to be explicit."

    Keith Richards, quoted in Jessica Pallington West, *What Would Keith Richards Do?* (2010)

"All people are paradoxical. No one is easily reducible, so I like characters who have contradictory impulses or shades of <u>ambiguity</u>.... It's fun because it's hard."

    Edward Norton, American actor, screenwriter, film director, and producer, quoted in dvrgmagazine.com, Aug. 15, 2012

✳ *Ambivalent*

"They say the definition of <u>ambivalence</u> is watching your mother-in-law drive over a cliff in your new Cadillac."

    David Mamet, award-winning American playwright, essayist, screenwriter, and film director, *Guardian,* Feb. 19, 2000

"I've always been profoundly <u>ambivalent</u> about fame. I think it just eats the reality out of you, and it can be intoxicating because I like some of it."

    Jane Pauley, American TV anchor and journalist, interviewed on *20/20,* abcnews.go.com

Jess, Zooey Deschanel's character on the TV series *New Girl,* will be with a new guy for a couple of weeks. Jess's three roommates are <u>ambivalent</u> about this. They're happy she's in a relationship, but they're afraid that her boyfriend might hang around all the time.

    David Hinckley, "*New Girl* Will Keep Zooey in Single File," New York *Daily News,* Nov. 5, 2111 (Lexis)

"We all parent the best we can. Being human, we're <u>ambivalent</u>. We want perfection for our babies, but we also need sleep."
> Erica Jong, American author whose books include *Fear of Flying,* nytimes.com/roomfordebate, May 1, 2012

"The snobby French are <u>ambivalent</u> about being the No. 1 [tourist] destination of the 21st century. The erstwhile Napoleonic Empire is a little embarrassed about its reliance on something as fluffy as tourism."
> Maureen Dowd, Pulitzer Prize–winning American columnist and author, "Can Valérie Seduce the French?," nytimes.com, July 16, 2013

> It's a little surprising, but *ambiguity* and *ambivalence* are two of the most looked-up words in the Merriam-Webster online dictionary. In fact, *ambivalence* ranked number two among all words that were looked up on that site in 2011. That may have reflected the public mood that year. Lookups spiked again in January 2012 when news reports said that Republicans were ambivalent about Mitt Romney's victories in early GOP presidential primaries.

Both of these words describe uncertainty and duality, and they sometimes are used in similar contexts. But it's usually easy to decide which to choose when you write. *Ambiguity* refers to doubtfulness or uncertainty in words, things, or events. *Ambivalence* describes someone's internal conflict.

Ambiguous derives from the Latin for "to drive both ways, to wander about." So something is *ambiguous* if its meaning goes in more than one direction.

Language is *ambiguous* when it has more than one possible interpretation.

Something is *ambiguous* if it is doubtful, obscure, or uncertain.

***Ambiguity* is the noun form.**

The word *ambiguity* has been in English for about six hundred years. *Ambivalence,* by contrast, is much newer. It was coined as a

German word early in the twentieth century by combining the Latin for "both" and "strength, vigor." So it suggests two strong feelings or points of view. The word entered English as a technical term in psychiatry through translations of Jung and Freud, then found a place in popular usage.[9]

People are *ambivalent* when they have contradictory or mixed emotions, actions, relationships, opinions, etc.

***Ambivalence* is the noun form of the word.**

Which version of the sentence below is correct?

(A) He was <u>ambiguous</u> in his feelings about golf.

(B) He was <u>ambivalent</u> in his feelings about golf.

In this sentence, someone has contradictory feelings, or is *ambivalent,* about golf. Version B is correct.

AMEND or EMEND

✳ *Amend, Amendment*

"Thus says the Lord of hosts, the God of Israel: <u>Amend</u> your ways and your deeds, and I will let you dwell in this place."
   Jeremiah 7:3 (English Standard Version)

"The best in this kind are but shadows, and the worst are no worse, if imagination <u>amend</u> them."
   Theseus, in *A Midsummer Night's Dream* (1590–96)

Ronald Reagan said in 1980 that 80 percent of air pollution is caused by plants and trees. He later <u>amended</u> that to 93 percent.

The city officials were ready to <u>amend</u> the budget if the economy didn't improve.

✳ *Emend, Emendation*

The editor <u>emended</u> the grammar book author's incredibly dumb error.

> "The time-honored etiquette of the situation…is this: an author's MS [manuscript] is not open to any editor's uninvited <u>emendations</u>. It must be accepted as it stands, or it must be declined.…Any alteration of it—even to a word—closes the incident, & that author & that editor can have no further literary dealings with each other."
>
> Mark Twain, objecting when an editor tried to make "improvements" in a text he had written, letter written Aug. 27, 1900, in *The Autobiography of Mark Twain* (2010)

Amend and *emend* both come from the Latin for "to remove a fault," and both refer to correcting or reforming something. But *emend* is a specialized term used mainly by textual editors, while *amend* is used more widely and with a broader meaning.

Amend means "to change or modify a document, a motion, or a law."[10]

An *amendment* is a change in a law or document, such as a constitution:

> "I believe there ought to be a constitutional amendment outlawing Astroturf."
>
> Kevin Costner, Academy Award–winning American actor, singer, producer, and director, as Crash Davis in the 1988 film *Bull Durham*

You also can *amend* your behavior, in the sense of reforming it.

To *emend* is to correct or remove errors from a text. Typically, an editor will *emend* a word or phrase to correct an error or recapture an author's original intention. That kind of editorial change is called an **emendation.**

Which version of the sentence below is correct?

(A) "The real fault is to have faults and not to <u>emend</u> them."
(B) "The real fault is to have faults and not to <u>amend</u> them."
> Confucius, Chinese philosopher (551–479 BC), *Analects,* tr. Winberg Chai, quoted in *International Thesaurus of Quotations: Revised Edition*

Confucius's statement urges people to reform (*amend*) their faults, as in version B.

AMIABLE or AMICABLE

✳ *Amiable*

"Dogs are indeed the most social, affectionate, and <u>amiable</u> animals of the whole brute creation."
> Edmund Burke, Irish statesman, author, political theorist, and philosopher (1729–1797), in *A Philosophical Enquiry into the Origin of Our Ideas of the Sublime and Beautiful* (1757)

"There is, indeed, nothing that so much seduces reason from vigilance, as the thought of passing life with an <u>amiable</u> woman."
> Samuel Johnson, letter, Dec. 21, 1762, recorded in James Boswell's *Life of Samuel Johnson* (1791)

"Elton John is 63, but feels, he says, 'like a 20-year-old.' ... His mood is <u>amiable</u> and relaxed. He is an engagingly lively conversationalist, quick to make jokes, often at his own expense."
> Interview with Elton John, award-winning English rock singer-songwriter, pianist, composer, record producer, and actor, in telegraph.co.uk, Oct. 25, 2010

The 2011 film *Kung Fu Panda 2* "has a bright palette, an <u>amiable</u> vibe and enough vivacity to keep kids entertained and any accompanying moms from bolting for *Bridesmaids.*"
> Richard Corliss, American editor and author, "*Kung Fu Panda 2: The Bear Necessities,*" time.com, May 25, 2011

✳ *Amicable*

"Conversation appeared <u>amicable</u>, but what they said was anyone's guess."
> Describing a meeting between Sen. Hillary Clinton and Sen. Barack Obama in 2008, "Clinton, Obama Reunite on Senate Floor," time.com, Mar. 13, 2008

"Is it possible to have an <u>amicable</u>—truly <u>amicable</u>—divorce?"
> Lisa Belkin, "Lessons from Divorce," *New York Times,* July 26, 2010

"I am sad to inform my fans that after 7 years, Paul and I have decided to <u>amicably</u> end our marriage."
> Danica Patrick, NASCAR racer, model, and advertising spokesperson, quoted in nydailynews.com, Apr. 26, 2013

These are two lovely words. *Amiable* ultimately derives from Latin words meaning "friendly" and "lovable." And *amicable* derives from the Latin for "friend," which is related to "love." But they're used in different ways in English.

Amiable people are friendly, likeable. An *amiable* mood, conversation, behavior, nature, etc., is friendly, kindly, likeable.

Amiability is friendliness, likeability.

Amicable relationships, talks, agreements, etc. are characterized by goodwill and a polite and friendly desire not to disagree.

To do something *amicably* is to do it cordially, without quarreling.

Which version of the sentence below is correct?

(A) In May 2010, Arnold Schwarzenegger and Maria Shriver announced that they were "<u>amiably</u> separating."
(B) In May 2010, Arnold Schwarzenegger and Maria Shriver announced that they were "<u>amicably</u> separating."

Divorces may be *amicable,* or marked by goodwill, as in version B. Interest in the word *amicable* spiked after this announcement, and many people looked it up in Merriam-Webster's online dictionary.

ANY MORE or ANYMORE

✳ *Any More*

"Foreigners cannot enjoy our food I suppose, <u>any more</u> than we can enjoy theirs.... I might glorify my bill of fare until I was tired; but after all, the Scotchman would shake his head and say, 'Where's your haggis?' and the Fijian would sigh and say, 'Where's your missionary?'"

Mark Twain, *Mark Twain's Helpful Hints for Good Living* (2004)

"Things are terribly dull now. We won't have <u>any more</u> serious comedy until Congress meets."

Will Rogers, in Joseph Carter and Larry Gatlin, *The Quotable Will Rogers* (2005)

"I do not like broccoli.... I'm President of the United States, and I'm not going to eat <u>any more</u> broccoli."

George H. W. Bush, U.S. president, 1989–93, quoted in *New York Times,* Mar. 23, 1990

"New rule: If the guy who makes up the poll questions at CNN doesn't want to do <u>any more</u>, he should just quit. This is an actual recent poll question: 'Would you like to live on the moon?' And the shocking results: No, as it turns out, we would not like to live on the moon."

Bill Maher, American comedian, TV host, commentator, author, and actor, *The New New Rules* (2011)

✳ *Anymore*

"I'm mad as hell, and I'm not going to take this <u>anymore</u>!"

Peter Finch as Howard Beale in the 1976 film *Network*

"So Harry says, 'You don't like me <u>anymore</u>. Why not?'

"And he says, 'Because you've [gotten] so terribly pretentious.'

"And Harry says, 'Pretentious? *Moi?*'"

> John Cleese, British comic, actor, writer, producer, and member of Monty Python, in "The Psychiatrist" episode of the BBC sitcom *Fawlty Towers,* 1979

"Nobody goes there <u>anymore.</u> It's too crowded."

> Yogi Berra, in *The Yogi Book* (1998)

"A nickel ain't worth a dime <u>anymore.</u>"

> Yogi Berra, ibid. (In formal English, of course, say *isn't,* not *ain't.*)

"'Truthiness' is tearing our country apart.... It doesn't seem to matter what facts are. It used to be, everyone was entitled to their own opinion but not their own facts. But that's not the case <u>anymore</u>. Facts matter not at all. Perception is everything."

> Stephen Colbert, quoted in Nathan Rabin, avclub.com, Jan. 25, 2006

"New rule: Since nobody reacts to car alarms <u>anymore</u>, stop putting alarms in cars."

> Bill Maher, *The New New Rules* (2011)

***Any more* compares amounts. It refers to any additional things or people. In this sense, it can mean "even the smallest amount."**

***Any more* also can mean "to any greater degree."**

***Anymore* refers to time. It means "any longer."** It would be nice if the single word *anymore* were the only spelling in this sense, but it's not: most authors and printers in the United Kingdom still use the phrase *any more* to mean "any longer."

Use *anymore* in the United States (or *any more* in Britain) in these contexts:

(1) **In negative statements:**
    Nobody goes there anymore.
(2) **In questions that call for yes-or-no answers:**
    Do you go there anymore?
(3) **In hypothetical statements with *if* or *whether:***
    I wonder if she goes there anymore.
    If you go there anymore, you're crazy.

Which version of the passage below is correct?

(A) "Toto, I've a feeling we're not in Kansas <u>any more</u>."
(B) "Toto, I've a feeling we're not in Kansas <u>anymore</u>."
　　　Judy Garland, award-winning American actress and singer
　　　(1922–1969), as Dorothy in the 1939 film *The Wizard of Oz*

In the United Kingdom, this is a trick question: either form is correct, because both are used in the sense of "any longer." Outside of Britain, though, the preference would be for *anymore*.

> In American English and some Irish dialects, *anymore* can mean "nowadays." It's heard in positive statements, such as "This is very expensive anymore." The *Dictionary of Regional English* dates it back to 1859 in the United States. It's widespread now except in New England, but many people consider it controversial, and stylists strongly oppose its use in Standard English: 96 percent of the *Harper Dictionary* Usage Panel objected to it in writing, for example, and 91 percent opposed it in speech.
>
> **Avoid this usage in formal writing and speech.**

ANY ONE or ANYONE

✳ *Any One*

> "Now, there is one invisible guest here.... That is my wife, and she has a good many personal friends here, and I think it won't distress <u>any one</u> of them to know that, although she is going to be confined to that bed for many months to come ... there is not any danger and she is coming along very well."
> 　Mark Twain, "Sixty-Seventh Birthday" speech, New York, Nov. 28, 1902

"All television ever did was shrink the demand for ordinary movies. The demand for extraordinary movies has increased. If any one thing is wrong with the movie industry today, it is the unrelenting effort to astonish."

> Clive James, Australian writer and critic, quoted in *Observer,* June 16, 1979, repr. in *Flying Visits* (1984)

"Most of us no longer watch television; we graze, zapping back and forth between channels.... No one does any one thing at a time. A new culture has taken shape which caters for people with the attention span of a flea."

> Michael Ignatieff, Canadian writer and critic, *Three-Minute Culture,* BBC 2, Jan. 15, 1989 [notice how long ago he made this observation]

✳ *Anyone*

"Whenever I hear anyone arguing over slavery, I feel a strong impulse to see it tried on him personally."

> Abraham Lincoln, speech, Mar. 17, 1865

"Have you ever noticed that anybody driving slower than you is an idiot, and anyone going faster than you is a maniac?"

> George Carlin, Grammy Award–winning American comedian, writer, social critic, and actor (1937–2008), quoted in "Classic George Carlin Jokes," dailynews.com, June 23, 2006

Larry King: "Do you know anyone without flaws?"
Jerry Seinfeld: "Besides you and [me]? No."

> *Larry King Live,* CNN, Nov. 1, 2007

"What I'm really trying to say is, I want the deepest, darkest, sickest parts of you that you are afraid to share with anyone, because I love you that much."

> Lady Gaga, speaking of her song "Bad Romance," on *It's On with Alexa Chung,* MTV, Nov. 3, 2009

Don't feel too bad if you confuse these two. They were both spelled *any one* until fairly recently.[11] **Now the phrase *any one* is used only to refer to any single person or thing.**

it won't distress <u>any one</u> of them to know

Anyone means "anybody."

<u>anyone</u> going faster than you is a maniac

Remember, if you can substitute "any single one," then *any one* is the right choice. If you can substitute the word *anybody,* then *anyone* is the right choice.

Which version of the sentence below is correct?

(A) We moved to New York City, where I didn't know <u>anyone</u>.
(B) We moved to New York City, where I didn't know <u>any one</u>.

In the sentence above, *anyone* in the sense "anybody" is correct, as in version A.

ANYONE...HE or *ANYONE...THEY?*

Since the mid-eighteenth century, a traditional rule has been that when you say *anyone* or *anybody,* you should refer back to that person with *he* or *him.* But in actual use, people very often say *they* or *them* instead. The same is true of *everyone, everybody,* and other pronouns that don't refer to any specific person or thing. See "HE or THEY after ANYBODY, EVERYONE, SOMEBODY, A PERSON, ETC.," on pages 89–93.

ANY WAY or ANYWAY

✳ *Any Way*

"No free man shall be taken, or imprisoned, or dispossessed, or outlawed, or exiled, or in <u>any way</u> destroyed."
    Magna Carta (1215)

"No man can call himself liberal, or radical, or even a conservative advocate of fair play, if his work depends in <u>any way</u> on the unpaid or underpaid labor of women."
    Gloria Steinem, American feminist, journalist, and activist, quoted in *New York Times,* Aug. 26, 1971

"Harry couldn't see <u>any way</u> out of his situation."
    J. K. Rowling, *Harry Potter and the Chamber of Secrets* (1998)

Question in a letter to the *Boston Globe:* "Is there <u>any way</u> to prevent a skunk from staking out territory in my backyard? I could do without his daily visits."

Answer: "The staff at the State Fisheries and Wildlife Service [say] they do not know of <u>any way</u> of fending off a skunk."
    Boston Globe, Oct. 25, 1984

✳ *Anyway*

"This land is your land and this land is my land—sure, but the world is run by those that never listen to music <u>anyway</u>."
    Bob Dylan, *Tarantula* (1970)

"I do about 90 percent of my own stunts, and the things I can't do for insurance reasons, like swinging out of a flying helicopter, I wouldn't want to do <u>anyway</u>."
    LL Cool J, interviewed in *Redbook,* Oct. 2010

On twerking: "It was one thing for Miley Cyrus to do it on national television, but a California mom warned her daughter before a school dance that it wasn't okay for the 11-year-old.... When [she] learned that her daughter had defied her and twerked <u>anyway</u>, she punished her pre-teen."

Maia Szalavitz, "Twerking Pre-Teen's Public Punishment: Why It May Backfire," time.com, Sept. 11, 2013

***Any way* as two words means "any manner."**

in <u>any way</u> destroyed
<u>any way</u> of fending off a skunk

***Anyway* as one word means "in any case":**

those that never listen to music <u>anyway</u>

***Anyway* can mean "in spite of something else, just the same, anyhow":**

her daughter . . . defied her and twerked <u>anyway</u>

***Anyway* can be tagged on to the end of a question with the sense "anyhow," "would you say?," or "more to the point." It can indicate emphasis, skepticism, or exasperation:**

"How often does a house need to be cleaned, <u>anyway</u>? As a general rule, once every girlfriend."

P. J. O'Rourke, American humorist and journalist, *The Bachelor Home Companion* (1987)

In casual use, *anyway* can return to the point or direct the conversation in a particular direction:

"But, <u>anyway</u>, I remember talking to one of these math guys, and he said, 'Geez, this computer stuff, you know, you're really good at that.' I said, 'Yes, but the courses here are so easy,' and I never signed up."

Bill Gates, quoted in Lev Grossman, "Bill Gates, the Early Years: Damn, This Thing Works!" time.com, June 8, 2007

APOCALYPTIC or APOCRYPHAL

✳ *Apocalyptic*

"With the detonation of the first atomic bomb, the catastrophic vision of the Christian <u>Apocalypse</u> seemed to take on a whole new meaning. One need not, after all, be a believer to shudder at the words of the second epistle of Peter: "But the day of the Lord will come as a thief in the night...the heavens shall pass away with a great noise, and the elements shall melt with fervent heat, the earth also...shall be burned up."
>   Stephen D. O'Leary, citing 2 Peter 3:10 (King James Version) in *Arguing the Apocalypse* (1994)

"At the hint of a dirty bomb or some other <u>apocalyptic</u> onslaught, societies could become 'decivilized.'"
>   *Observer*, Sept. 11, 2005 (*OED*)

"Survivors...of a zombie <u>apocalypse</u> use creative means to dispatch the undead."
>   Description of the 2009 film *Zombieland*, FIOS TV

"I'm...getting these crazy opportunities, like being in a production of *Company* with Stephen Colbert and the New York Philharmonic. I can't imagine Jon Cryer performing with the New York Philharmonic isn't one of the signs of [the] <u>Apocalypse</u>."
>   Jon Cryer, Emmy Award–winning American actor, screenwriter, and film director and producer, quoted in "Jon Cryer: I Thought Charlie Sheen Was Going to Die," hollywoodreporter.com, Sept. 19, 2011

In discussing climate change, Jon Stewart pointed out that fossil fuel companies would say that any restrictions on them would lead to an economic <u>apocalypse.</u> Meanwhile, scientists would say that not acting would lead to an <u>apocalypse</u> in the climate.

Stewart concluded, "I guess my question is, which <u>apocalypse</u> should I prepare for?"

The Daily Show, Comedy Central, Apr. 21, 2014

✳ *Apocryphal*

Several of the <u>apocryphal</u> books tell stories that aren't in the Bible, including what Mary and Jesus did as children.

Oscar Wilde's last words were supposedly "This wallpaper is killing me. One of us has got to go." This story may be <u>apocryphal</u>, though.

It also may be <u>apocryphal</u> that Dolly Parton said, "It takes a lot of money to look this cheap."

Otto von Bismarck, the nineteenth-century German chancellor, is supposed to have said, "Laws are like sausages. It's better not to see them being made." The story may be <u>apocryphal</u>, however.

"There's a humbling story, perhaps <u>apocryphal</u>, that Gandhi was once asked, *What do you think of Western civilization*? He supposedly responded, *I think it would be a good idea.*"

Nicholas Kristof, "Is Islam to Blame for the Shooting at Charlie Hebdo in Paris?" nytimes.com, Jan. 7, 2015

These two words have both religious and secular meanings.

The word *apocalyptic* refers to prophetic revelation.

The *Apocalypse* particularly refers to the vision of the end of days in the Book of Revelation in the New Testament. If you use the word in this sense, capitalize *Apocalypse.*

By the early twentieth century, though, any cataclysmic disaster, especially a global calamity, could be called *apocalyptic.*

a dirty bomb or some other <u>apocalyptic</u> onslaught
zombie <u>apocalypse</u>

There's enormous interest in the end-times. There's even a website called raptureready.com that matches recent events to biblical prophecies to see if the Apocalypse is coming. Interest peaked in 2012, the year of the so-called Mayan Apocalypse. Since the Mayan Long Count calendar ended a "world age" on December 21, 2012, many people took that as a sign of impending doom. One headline read, "Mayan Apocalypse: Panic Spreads as December 21 Nears." Some experts refuted the whole idea, and obviously they were right, since we're still here. Still, according to one analysis of global trends in word usage, *apocalypse* was the top English noun in 2012.[12]

The word *apocryphal* refers to Jewish and Christian books that were not accepted into the official canon of the Bible.

the <u>apocryphal</u> books tell stories that aren't in the Bible

***Apocryphal* has taken on a broader sense to describe anything that is of doubtful authenticity, false, or counterfeit.**

this story may be <u>apocryphal</u>
there's a humbling story, perhaps <u>apocryphal</u>

Which version of the sentence below is correct?

(A) The quotation "Better to keep you mouth shut and appear stupid than to open it and remove all doubt," attributed to Mark Twain, may be <u>apocalyptic</u>.

(B) The quotation "Better to keep you mouth shut and appear stupid than to open it and remove all doubt," attributed to Mark Twain, may be <u>apocryphal</u>.

The claim that Twain said the quotation above is disputed, so it may be apocryphal, as in version B.

ASSURE, ENSURE, or INSURE

✳ *Assure*

"Do not worry about your difficulties in mathematics. I can <u>assure</u> you, mine are still greater."
  Albert Einstein, letter to junior high school girl who had trouble with math, Jan. 7, 1943, in *The New Quotable Einstein* (2005)

"Let every nation know, whether it wishes us well or ill, that we shall pay any price, bear any burden, meet any hardship, support any friend, oppose any foe to <u>assure</u> the survival and the success of liberty."
  President John Kennedy, inaugural address, Jan. 20, 1961

"It's a bit startling to achieve global recognition (if that's the right word) before the age of 30, on account of your sister, your brother-in-law, and your bottom.... I can <u>assure</u> you that it feels even stranger to me than it probably does to you."
  Pippa Middleton, sister of Catherine, Duchess of Cambridge, quoted in *Parade* magazine, Oct. 28, 2012

✳ *Ensure*

"Mr. Wickham is blessed with such happy manners as may <u>ensure</u> his *making* friends—whether he may be equally capable of *retaining* them is less certain."
  Jane Austen, English novelist (1775–1817), *Pride and Prejudice* (1813)

"Evolution has <u>ensured</u> that our brains just aren't equipped to visualize in 11 dimensions directly. However, from a purely mathematical point of view, it's just as easy to think in 11 dimensions as it is to think in three or four."
  Stephen Hawking, award-winning English theoretical physicist, cosmologist, and writer, quoted in Emma Brockes, "Return of the Time Lord," *Guardian,* Sept. 26, 2005

To help <u>ensure</u> that your readers understand your point, write simply and naturally, and present your ideas clearly and directly.

✳ *Insure*

Michael Caine, explaining why he doesn't drive: "I didn't own a car until I was 30, and that was a Rolls-Royce. So it was cheaper to <u>insure</u> a chauffeur."
> Michael Caine, English actor and writer, interviewed by John Hind in theguardian.com, Sept. 12, 2009

"You cannot drive a system that's going to be aiming at preventing illness if everyone is not in it. The whole gaming of health insurance and health care in America is based on that fundamental principle: <u>insure</u> people who aren't sick and you don't have to pay more money on them."
> Dr. Mehmet Oz, Turkish American cardiothoracic surgeon, author, and TV host, interviewed on *Piers Morgan Tonight,* cnn.com, May 20, 2012

These three words all address certainty, assuredness, and security, and there is some overlap between them. But here's a quick way to remember their main meanings:

We <u>assure</u> people (about something).
We <u>ensure</u> events or outcomes (will or won't happen).
And we <u>insure</u> things and ourselves financially (through insurance).

Assure means "to give an assurance in order to remove doubt, fear, etc."
Assure also can mean "to make (something) certain."
Ensure means "to guarantee, make sure" that something will or won't happen, or that it will or won't be provided.
Insure refers to underwriting financial risk through insurance.
So you can *assure* people about something but not *ensure* them about it. Which version of the sentence below is correct?

(A) "I will not ever run for political office, I can <u>assure</u> you."

(B) "I will not ever run for political office, I can <u>ensure</u> you."

> David Petraeus, former American general and CIA director,
> quoted in politicalticker.blogs.cnn.com, Mar. 25, 2010

General Petraeus's statement removes doubt, or gives *assurance*. Version A is correct.

AWHILE or A WHILE

∗ *Awhile*

The *Canterbury Tales* pilgrims stopped <u>awhile</u> to drink some ale.

> "He took his vorpal sword in hand.
> Long time the manxome foe he sought.
> So rested he by the Tumtum tree
> And stood <u>awhile</u> in thought."
>
> Lewis Carroll, "Jabberwocky," in *Through the Looking Glass and What Alice Found There* (1871)

∗ *A While*

> "You don't win once in <u>a while</u>; you don't do things right once in <u>a while</u>; you do them right all the time."
>
> Vince Lombardi, American football player, head coach, and executive (1913–1970), quoted in Dick Schaap and Jerry Kramer, *Instant Replay: The Green Bay Diary of Jerry Kramer* (1968)

> "Creativity is just connecting things. When you ask creative people how they did something, they feel a little guilty because they didn't really *do* it; they just saw something. It seemed obvious to them after <u>a while</u>."

Steve Jobs, quoted in Gary Wolf, "Steve Jobs: The Next Insanely Great Thing," wired.com, Feb. 1996

"Sexiness wears thin after <u>a while</u> and beauty fades. But to be married to a man who makes you laugh every day, ah, now that's a real treat."

Joanne Woodward, Academy Award–winning American actress and producer, quoted in *Glamour* 106 (2008); she was married to Paul Newman

"We're still in a recession and we're not going to get out of it for <u>a while</u>. But we will get out of it."

Warren Buffett, quoted in Alex Crippen, "Warren Buffett to CNBC: 'We're Still in a Recession,'" cnbc.com, Sept. 23, 2010

It's easy to confuse these two spellings, and writers have done it for centuries. There's usually no problem with phrases like *after a while, for a while,* and *in a while:* people almost always separate *a* from *while*. But after verbs they use both *a while* and the solid spelling *awhile*.[13] In the 1920s, grammarians set down a rule to distinguish between these two forms. **The distinction is useful, and I recommend that you follow the two parts of this rule in formal writing:**

Part 1: The solid word *awhile* means "for a short time, for a while."

Here's a hint: since *awhile* has *for* as part of its meaning ("for a while"), you don't need the word *for* in front of it. That would be saying "for for a while." So write *a while* after the word *for,* or after any other preposition.

Here are some examples. Notice that *awhile* follows a verb.

stopped <u>awhile</u>
stood <u>awhile</u>

Part 2: *A while* is a noun meaning "a period of time." It often follows a word like *after, for,* or *in.*

once <u>in a while</u>
<u>after a while</u>
<u>for a while</u>

Remember, when it follows a preposition like *after, in,* or *for, a while* is two words.

Here's a quick review: a preposition is a word like *for, from, in, on, to, under,* or *with* that positions nouns or pronouns with respect to other words. Prepositions often indicate location, direction, or time.

The Day <u>After</u> Tomorrow
Midnight <u>in</u> Paris
Star Trek <u>into</u> Darkness
The Girl <u>with</u> the Dragon Tattoo

See page 13 for a list of prepositions.

Which version of the passage below is correct?

(A) "And the idea of just wandering off to a café with a notebook and writing, and seeing where that takes me for <u>a while</u>, is just bliss."

(B) And the idea of just wandering off to a café with a notebook and writing, and seeing where that takes me for <u>awhile</u>, is just bliss."

> J. K. Rowling, after the release of the film *Harry Potter and the Deathly Hallows, Part 2,* quoted in Carol Memmott, "J. K. Rowling Still Hinting about Future Books," usatoday.com, July 12, 2011

Rowling is referring to "a period of time" after the preposition *for.* So "a while" is correct, as in version A.

BACKWARD or BACKWARDS

"Life must be understood <u>backwards</u> but...it must be lived forwards."

> Søren Kierkegaard, Danish philosopher, theologian, and poet (1813–1855), *Diary* (1843)

"You might as well fall flat on your face as lean over too far <u>backward</u>."

James Thurber, American humorist (1894–1961), "The Bear ` Who Let It Alone," *New Yorker,* Apr. 29, 1939

"A reactionary is a somnambulist walking <u>backwards</u>."
Franklin D. Roosevelt, U.S. president 1933–45, radio address, Oct. 26, 1939

"*Diaper* <u>backward</u> spells *repaid*. Think about it."
Marshall McLuhan, Canadian communications and media theorist (1911–1980), speech, quoted in *Sun* (Vancouver), June 7, 1969

About Fred Astaire: "Sure, he was great. But don't forget that Ginger Rogers did everything he did backwards…and in high heels!"
Bob Thaves, American cartoonist (1924–2006), caption to a cartoon in Ginger Rogers, *Ginger: My Story* (1991)

"You can't connect the dots looking forward; you can only connect them looking <u>backwards</u>. So you have to trust that the dots will somehow connect in your future."
Steve Jobs, commencement address at Stanford University, June 12, 2005

"When I was first learning songs…I'd learn the chords and then play them <u>backward</u>. That was my first experimenting with writing a song."
Alicia Keys, American Grammy Award–winning R&B singer-songwriter, musician, actress, and record producer, quoted in Shannon Doyne, "How Did You Start Doing Something You Love?," learning.blogs.nytimes.com, Oct. 1, 2012

"You're from Australia, and…I've read that the toilets work <u>backwards</u> [there]."
Zach Galifianakis, speaking to Naomi Watts on the Internet comedy show "Between Two Ferns: Oscar Buzz Edition Part 1," funnyordie.com, Feb. 12, 2013

Use either *backward* or *backwards* to describe the direction of actions.[14]

understood <u>backwards</u>
lean over too far <u>backward</u>
<u>backwards</u>...and in high heels

Say *backward* when you describe people, places, or things.

a backward glance

Backward can mean "behind the times, primitive" or "late or retarded in development."

In this example, former sex symbol Brigitte Bardot, now an animal rights activist, uses *backward* to mean "culturally retarded":

> "I only want to protect animals from barbarous, cruel, inhuman, and <u>backward</u> rituals."
>
> Brigitte Bardot, French actress, quoted in "Brigitte Bardot's Shifting Passions," *Los Angeles Times,* Sept. 6, 2010

Here Professor Steven Pinker argues that major developed nations haven't gone to war with each other since World War II:

> "Today we take it for granted that war is something that happens in smaller, poorer, and more <u>backward</u> countries."
>
> Steven Pinker, *The Better Angels of Our Nature: Why Violence Has Declined* (2011)

BESIDE or BESIDES

✳ *Beside*

> "'Thank you very much,' said the Scarecrow, when he had been set down on the ground.... Dorothy was puzzled at this, for it sounded queer to hear a stuffed man speak, and to see him bow and walk along <u>beside</u> her."
>
> L. Frank Baum, *The Wonderful Wizard of Oz* (1900)

"I always wear beige, black or white.... When I'm <u>beside</u> a star at a fitting, and she looks into the mirror, I don't want to be competing in any way."

> Edith Head, Academy Award–winning American costume designer (1897–1981), quoted in *People* magazine, Mar. 31, 1975

The headline: "Standing <u>Beside</u> Jackie Robinson: Reese Helped Change Baseball." The story: A group of mostly southern Dodgers drew up a petition stating they wouldn't play baseball with Jackie Robinson, a black man. Pee Wee Reese refused to sign it. Many people believe that Reese's decision ended the matter.

> Headline from story by Ira Berkow, Pulitzer Prize–winning American journalist and author, *New York Times,* Mar. 31, 1997

✳ *Besides*

"Underwear makes me uncomfortable. And <u>besides</u>, my parts have to breathe."

> Jean Harlow, American actress and "blonde bombshell" of the 1930s (1911–1937), quoted in David Bret, *Jean Harlow: Tarnished Angel* (2009)

"When I was a kid, my dream was to be a farmer and marry Charlie Brown. I wanted to rescue him and make him happy. <u>Besides</u>, he was always lusting after the 'little red-haired girl.'"

> Alicia Witt, American actress and singer, quoted in *Seventeen* magazine, 1996

"Knowles admits that she eats the whole tub of ice cream, even though she worries about maintaining her curvy but toned physique.... 'I mean, we all have our imperfections,' Knowles said. 'But I'm human and, you know, it's important to concentrate on other qualities <u>besides</u> outer beauty.'"

> Beyoncé Knowles-Carter, quoted in "Beyoncé: Behind the Scenes of *Pink Panther*," abcnews.go.com, June 4, 2004

"I think as an actor you have to be open to your emotions. That's how you tap into other characters. <u>Besides</u>, by being so open I've come to terms with how screwed up I am!"
> Jake Gyllenhaal, American actor, quoted in dailymail.co.uk, Oct. 22, 2007

Beside and *besides* have been interchangeable over the years. Since the mid-nineteenth century, though, usage commentators have tried to keep their meanings distinct, and people generally use these words now in these different ways:

Beside usually means "by the side of, alongside."

In phrases like *beside the point*, *beside* means "away from, apart (to the side of)." *To be beside yourself* means "to be extremely excited or agitated" (with joy, grief, etc.).

"Which actress <u>was beside herself</u> when she chopped off her gorgeous flowing locks? Was it Anne Hathaway, Charlize Theron, or Portia de Rossi?"
> celebuzz.com, July 14, 2012

Besides means "in addition to, moreover."

Now, *beside* has been used since the fourteenth century to mean *besides* in the sense of "in addition to," and, despite what usage books say, it sometimes still is, even by good writers. **But in formal speech and writing, don't say *besides* to mean *beside* in the sense of "next to."**

Which version of the passage below is correct?

(A) "<u>Beside</u> the fact that I make movies, there's nothing interesting about my life at all, unfortunately."

(B) "<u>Besides</u> the fact that I make movies, there's nothing interesting about my life at all, unfortunately."
> Jonah Hill, American actor, screenwriter, producer, and comedian, interview, June 16, 2009, quoted in collider.com

Jonah Hill is saying "In addition to," or *besides,* as in version B.

BIANNUAL or SEMIANNUAL,
BIWEEKLY or SEMIWEEKLY

About the change to Daylight Saving Time: "The entire United States will join you in the <u>biannual</u> time change with the exception of Hawaii and Arizona."
    Nick Carbone, "Spring Forward into Daylight Saving Time," time. com, Mar. 31, 2011

Ad by a roofing company: "Our preventive-maintenance services are available as a <u>biannual</u> roof-inspection program.... Our twice-yearly visits will keep you informed through photos and reports as to the current condition of your roofing system."

This lesson deals with an issue that's so messy it's ridiculous: the confusion in words about time that begin with *bi-*.

You might think this would be simple. In Latin *bi-* means "twice, having two" and *semi-* means "half." So, strictly, *biweekly* means "every two weeks" and *semiweekly* means "twice a week" (that is, "every half week"). *Bimonthly* means "every two months" and *semimonthly* means "twice a month (that is, "every half month").

But these *bi-* words often leave us guessing. The word *biyearly,* for example, has been used in three different senses: "occurring every two years," "lasting for two years," or "occurring twice a year." There's similar craziness with the words *biweekly* and *bimonthly*.

Biannual has been used mostly in the sense of "twice a year."

The much older word *biennial* means "lasting for two years," but it also has a very different meaning: "happening every two years." A biennial, for example, is a plant that completes its life cycle in two growing seasons. Especially in the United States, though, a biennial also can be an event that takes place every other year.

Semiannual means "twice a year" (every half year), but it's also been used to mean "lasting for half a year."

Since the *bi-* words are so chaotic, aim for clarity. If you use them, let the context leave no doubt about your meaning. Or say "every

two weeks," "every two months," "every two years," "half-yearly," etc.,
instead.

In the first passage at the top of this lesson, *biannual* refers to a time
change that happens twice a year, so the meaning should be obvious to
most Americans. In the next passage, too, the context makes the meaning
of *biannual* clear.

BIBLE: CAPITALIZED OR NOT

✳ Bible (Capitalized)

"I have spent a lot of time searching through the <u>Bible</u> for
loopholes."
> W. C. Fields, during his last illness, attributed

"When the missionaries first came to Africa, they had the <u>Bible</u>
and we had the land. They said, 'Let us pray.' We closed our eyes.
When we opened them, we had the <u>Bible</u> and they had the land."
> South African bishop Desmond Tutu, quoted in Steven Gish,
> *Desmond Tutu: A Biography* (2004)[15]

"I've read the last page of the <u>Bible</u>. It's all going to turn out all
right."
> Billy Graham, American Christian evangelist, quoted in Harold
> Myra and Marshall Shelley, *The Leadership Secrets of Billy Graham*
> (2005)

✳ bible *(Not Capitalized)*

Track and Field News calls itself "the <u>bible</u> of the sport since 1948."

"You'd listen to the masters and you'd hear the timing,
and…you'd understand what Nichols and May were doing live

on Broadway.... Then the Two-Thousand-Year-Old Man became my <u>bible</u>."

> Billy Crystal, referring to Mike Nichols and Elaine May, and to Mel Brooks's character of the Two-Thousand-Year-Old Man, interviewed on *Charlie Rose,* PBS, aired Sept. 20, 2013

The *DSM-V* (*Diagnostic and Statistical Manual of Mental Disorders,* fifth edition) is the <u>bible</u> of psychiatric diagnosis.

The word *Bible* derives from the Greek word for "the books."

Capitalize the word *Bible* when it refers to the holy book.

Capitalize the titles of its books or other constituent parts, but don't italicize or put quotation marks around them:

Genesis
the Hebrew Bible
the Prophets
the Old Testament
the New Testament
Matthew
the Synoptic Gospels
Revelation

Use lowercase for the word *biblical*.

Use lowercase when you use the word *bible* to refer to a secular authoritative source of information.

Which version of the sentence below is correct?

(A) "At the beginning, on television, you don't improvise. At least in any experience I've ever had, you stick to the script. The script is [the] <u>bible</u>."

(B) "At the beginning, on television, you don't improvise. At least in any experience I've ever had, you stick to the script. The script is [the] <u>Bible</u>."

American actress and film producer Jennifer Garner, press
conference, quoted in Rebecca Murray, "Jennifer Garner Gets
Back into Action in *The Kingdom*," movies.about.com, 2007

Garner is saying that the script is authoritative in making television
shows, so *bible* is correct. Version A is the right choice.

BLOC or BLOCK

✳ *Bloc*

The religious right has formed a powerful voting <u>bloc</u> in the United
States since the 1970s.

The <u>bloc</u> of European nations that use the euro as their currency is
called the euro zone.

The six thousand people who vote for the Academy Awards
include actors, screenwriters, and several other groups. These
different factions don't vote as <u>blocs</u>, but they do share tastes, and
the editors, sound designers, cinematographers, and effects artists
were said to be rooting for *Gravity* to win as Best Picture in 2014.
Melena Ryzik, "In Oscar Voting, All Politics Is Local," nytimes.
com, Feb. 27, 2014

✳ *Block*

"Everybody in Spain is sick of me. But in America, there's
curiosity about the new kid on the <u>block</u> who doesn't speak
English very well."
Javier Bardem, Academy Award–winning Spanish actor, quoted in
Rene Rodriguez, "Javier Bardem Comes Across," nytimes.com,
Dec. 17, 2000

"My God is a God who wants me to have things. He wants me to
bling. He wants me to be the hottest thing on the <u>block</u>."

Mary J. Blige, American singer-songwriter, record producer, and actress, interviewed in *Blender* magazine, May 2006, quoted in msnbc.com, Apr. 18, 2006

A *bloc* is a combination of countries, parties, groups, or individuals joined together for a common purpose:

a <u>bloc</u> vote
a voting <u>bloc</u>
the European Union is a twenty-eight-nation <u>bloc</u>

The word *block* originally referred to a hard piece of wood, but now it can refer more generally to a solid material, usually with flat surfaces and a square or rectangular shape.

One meaning of *block* is a rectangular area bounded by four streets. This was originally an American usage. **So a *block* can refer to a person's neighborhood in a town or city.**

The word *block* also can be applied insultingly to somebody's head. A *blockhead* is a dope. Here are some examples:

"I myself am a recovering <u>blockhead</u>."
Diablo Cody, American screenwriter, producer, and director, quoted in "The Right Stuff," ew.com, Feb. 8, 2008

A threat to punch someone in the head: "Yo, Derek, I swear I'm about to knock your <u>block</u> off."
Urbandictionary.com

Which version of the sentence below is correct?

(A) "'Jenny from the <u>Block</u>' wants the <u>block</u> to buy Verizon phones from her. Singer and actress Jennifer Lopez on Wednesday announced she's opening a chain of 15 cell phone stores."

(B) "'Jenny from the <u>Bloc</u>' wants the <u>bloc</u> to buy Verizon phones from her. Singer and actress Jennifer Lopez on Wednesday announced she's opening a chain of 15 cell phone stores."

Peter Svensson, "Jennifer Lopez to Open Cellphone Stores," AP, May 23, 2013

JLo's nickname is "Jenny from the <u>Block</u>," or from the <u>neighborhood</u>, as in version A.

BORN or BORNE

* *Born*

"I was <u>born</u> modest; not all over, but in spots."
Mark Twain, *A Connecticut Yankee in King Arthur's Court* (1889)

"There's a sucker <u>born</u> every minute."
P. T. Barnum, founder of Ringling Bros. and Barnum & Bailey Circus (1810–1891), attributed

"A career is <u>born</u> in public, talent in privacy."
Marilyn Monroe, quoted in *Ms.* magazine, Aug. 1972

"Leaders are made, not <u>born</u>."
Vince Lombardi, quoted in David Maraniss, *When Pride Still Mattered: A Life of Vince Lombardi* (1999)

"<u>Born</u> in the USA"
Bruce Springsteen, title of 1984 song and album

"Be yourself and love who you are, and be proud, because you were <u>born</u> this way."
Lady Gaga, on the TV show *The View,* quoted in thedailybeast.com/newsweek, May 29, 2011

* *Borne*

"Let us strive on to finish the work we are in: to bind up the nation's wounds, to care for him who shall have <u>borne</u> the battle, and for his

widow and his orphan, to do all which may achieve and cherish a just and lasting peace among ourselves and with all nations."
    Abraham Lincoln, second inaugural address, Mar. 4, 1865

"Joy comes not out of infliction of pain on others but out of pain voluntarily <u>borne</u> by oneself."
    Mahatma Gandhi, quoted on the Official Mahatma Gandhi eArchive (mahatma.org.in)

"All sorrows can be <u>borne</u> if you put them into a story or tell a story about them."
    Isak Dinesen, pen name of Karen von Blixen-Finecke, Danish author (1885–1962), spoken in 1957, then included in her *Daguerreotypes and Other Essays* (1979)

Born means "having come into existence through birth."
    Figuratively, when referring to ideas, experiences, or things, *born* can mean "having come into existence."
    Borne means "carried" or "sustained, endured."
Which version of the sentence below is correct?

(A) "Life would be infinitely happier if we could only be <u>borne</u> at the age of eighty and gradually approach eighteen."
(B) "Life would be infinitely happier if we could only be <u>born</u> at the age of eighty and gradually approach eighteen."
    Mark Twain, quoted in William Lyon Phelps, *Autobiography with Letters* (1939)

Twain is speaking of birth, so version B is the right choice.

CAPITAL or CAPITOL

✳ *Capital*

Quick, what's the <u>capital</u> of North Dakota?

"New York is one of the <u>capitals</u> of the world and Los Angeles is a constellation of plastic; San Francisco is a lady, Boston has become Urban Renewal, Philadelphia and Baltimore and Washington wink like dull diamonds in the smog of Eastern Megalopolis."

> Norman Mailer, American author, actor, and political candidate, *Miami and the Siege of Chicago* (1969)

"We will rebuild, renew, and remain the <u>capital</u> of the free world."

> New York mayor Michael R. Bloomberg's inaugural address, less than four months after 9/11, quoted in cnn.com, Jan. 1, 2002

"My father probably thought that the <u>capital</u> of the world was wherever he was at the time.... Where he and his wife were in their own home, that, for them, was the <u>capital</u> of the world."

> Bob Dylan, *Inspirations* (2005)

✳ *Capitol*

"It would be great if politics were fact-based, but it is not, and it is surely not nuance-based. What works in a classroom or a think tank does not work on <u>Capitol</u> Hill or the White House."

> Jon Meacham, editor, political commentator, and Pulitzer Prize–winning author, in "The Trouble with Barack," newsweek.com, Jan. 21, 2010

"From the U.S. <u>Capitol</u> Building to the White House, our national symbols that represent freedom to so many of us were built by people who were anything but free."

> Former U.S. congressman Gary Ackerman, quoted in Kunbi Tinuoye, "Rep. Gary Ackerman Calls on Obama to Honor Slaves Who Built White House," thegrio.com, Feb. 10, 2012

When Jimmy Stewart's character filibusters to fight corruption in the 1939 film *Mr. Smith Goes to Washington*, is he in the <u>capital</u> or the <u>Capitol</u>? Actually, he's in both.

The word *capital* has several meanings. One of those meanings is easy to confuse with *capitol* because these words look so similar and because both relate to government. The difference between them is that a *capital* in this sense is a city and a *capitol* is a building.

Capital derives from the Latin for "head." **A *capital* is a head city, especially one that serves as the seat of government for a country, state, etc.**

The word *capitol* referred to the temple of the god Jupiter in Rome on the site that later was called Capitoline Hill. Any citadel on top of a hill could also be called a *capitol*.

The *Capitol* is the building in Washington, D.C., where the U.S. Congress meets. It sits on Capitol Hill. It's used as a kind of shorthand to refer to Congress.

So Jimmy Stewart enacts his dramatic filibuster in the <u>Capitol</u> Building, which is in the nation's <u>capital</u>.

There also are *capitol* buildings in some American state *capitals*. Which version of the sentence below is correct?

(A) Brasilia, the <u>capitol</u> of Brazil, is the largest city in the world that didn't exist a hundred years ago.

(B) Brasilia, the <u>capital</u> of Brazil, is the largest city in the world that didn't exist a hundred years ago.

The city Brasilia is the seat of government, or <u>capital</u>, of Brazil. Version B is correct.

CITE or SITE

✳ *Cite*

"The devil can <u>cite</u> Scripture for his purpose."
Antonio, speaking of Shylock in *The Merchant of Venice* (1596–98)

"Be able to <u>cite</u> three good qualities of every relative or acquaintance you dislike."

Marilyn Vos Savant, American columnist, author, and playwright, *Growing Up: A Classic American Childhood*, ch. 2 (2002)

"Nanny Eva knew her Bible as well as any scholar. She knew it cold and hot. Quote a phrase from the Bible and she could <u>cite</u> chapter and verse."

William Melvin Kelley, "Moses Mama," in *Pow-Wow: Charting the Fault Lines in the American Experience*, ed. Ishmael Reed (2009)

"As Hannah Rosin has recently pointed out in *The End of Men*…women today are attending college in record numbers…surging into graduate programs…and sailing with relative ease into the workforce.… Yet, despite these successes, which Rosin <u>cites</u> as evidence of women's ascent, the harsh reality is that this…has still not translated into either parity on the home front or power at the top."

Debora Spar, president of Barnard College, "American Women Have It Wrong." newsweek.com, Oct. 8, 2012

✳ *Site*

"The minute I get into a hotel room, I scatter my stuff everywhere. It's like a bomb <u>site</u> within a minute. So I suppose that means I'm trying to nest."

Carey Mulligan, English actress, quoted in *Interview Magazine*, Apr. 2009

"The World Trade Center <u>site</u> will forever hold a special place in our city, in our hearts."

Michael R. Bloomberg, quoted in Adam Lisberg, "Mayor Bloomberg Stands Up for Mosque," nydailynews.com, Aug. 3, 2010

"The thing about Brooklyn [is that] we always felt different. We were loyal.…I've taken my boys to…the <u>site</u> of Ebbets Field, where the Dodgers used to play.…I have infused them with New York spirit."

Larry King, award-winning TV and radio host, quoted in Camilla Webster and Laura L. M. Hill, "Larry King: Can't Take Brooklyn out of the Boy," huffingtonpost.com, Dec. 20, 2011

"I've had an unbelievable life. I've been very lucky.... I never forget where I'm from. Whenever I pass a building <u>site</u> or see somebody digging a ditch, I always think, 'That's real work.'"

> Irish actor Liam Neeson, quoted in Gill Pringle, "Liam Neeson—'A Sex Symbol? Flattering, but I Don't Think So,'" independent.co.uk, Apr. 6, 2012

It's surprising how often people confuse these two little words when they write. *Cite* and *site* sound exactly the same, of course, but they have completely different meanings and they come from very different Latin words.

To *cite* is to quote a text.

the devil can <u>cite</u> Scripture
she could <u>cite</u> chapter and verse

Or *cite* can mean "make reference to" something or someone as an example or proof.

<u>cite</u> three good qualities of every relative or acquaintance

A *site* is a physical place or setting:

a bomb <u>site</u>
the World Trade Center <u>site</u>
a building <u>site</u>

A site also can be a location on the Internet (an abbreviation for *website*):

> "People who appear to be working at their screens could be... contributing to the Star Trek fan club or visiting *Playboy* magazine's <u>site</u>."
> *Computer Weekly*, Oct. 5, 1995 (*OED*)

To keep these two words straight, just remember that *cite* is a verb related to re**cit**e and **cit**ation; *site* is a noun related to **sit**uation. People sometimes misspell *site* as *sight*. Your spell-checker may not pick up that mistake, so be careful to distinguish between those words.

Which version of the sentence below is correct?

(A) "The emphasis is on what is called 'dwell time'—how long the visitor can be kept on the <u>site</u> to view those all-important advertisements."

(B) "The emphasis is on what is called 'dwell time'—how long the visitor can be kept on the <u>cite</u> to view those all-important advertisements."

> *Computer Weekly,* Apr. 20, 2000 (*OED*)

The passage refers to a website, so version A is the right choice.

COMPLEMENT or COMPLIMENT

✳ *Complement*

"Jails and prisons are the <u>complement</u> of schools."

> Horace Mann, American education reformer (1796–1859), making the point that if we have fewer schools we'll need more jails and prisons, quoted in "Report of the Superintendent of Public Instruction of the Commonwealth of Pennsylvania" (1881)

"Chinooks are American forces' preferred helicopters in Afghanistan because they are powerful enough to fly over mountains while carrying a full <u>complement</u> of troops."

> Joe Pappalardo, "3 Questions About SEAL Team Six Helicopter Crash," popularmechanics.com, Aug. 7, 2011

"How can we ensure that our makeup <u>complements</u> our wardrobe? If your outfit is making a statement, then your makeup should act as the accessory."

> Jennifer Ennion, "Bold and the Beautiful," *Hobart Mercury* (Australia), Oct. 19, 2012

"Dear Carolyn,

"My mom and I…clash about one BIG thing: whom she dates.
She tells me all about what kind of guy she likes and how she
wants a man who <u>complements</u> her lifestyle (classy and
adventurous), yet she keeps bringing home losers."

    Letter to Carolyn Hax, *Washington Post*, Oct. 22, 2012

"As difficult as being a father is, it's entirely <u>complementary</u> with
everything else in your life."

    David Letterman, on *CBS This Morning*, quoted in usmagazine.
com, Dec. 20, 2013

The headline: "Opposites Attracting (and <u>Complementing</u>)."
The story: "For almost as long as Jay-Z and Beyoncé have been a
couple, they have been collaborators, one artist enhancing the
other by bringing things the other doesn't have."

    Jon Caramanica, nytimes.com, June 26, 2014

✳ *Compliment*

Praise is fine, <u>compliments</u> are fine, "but affection—that is the
last, and final, and most precious reward that any man can win."

    Mark Twain, "Books, Authors, and Hats," speech, London, June 25,
1907

"There is nothing you can say in answer to a <u>compliment</u>. I have
been <u>complimented</u> myself a great many times, and they always
embarrass me—I always feel that they have not said enough."

    Mark Twain, speech in Jamestown, Virginia, Sept. 23, 1907

"If you are flattering a woman, it pays to be a little more subtle.
You don't have to bother with men; they believe any <u>compliment</u>
automatically."

    Alan Ayckbourn, English playwright, in *Round and Round the
Garden* (1975)

"The highest <u>compliment</u> you can pay me is to say that I work hard every day…and that I never dog it."

> Wayne Gretzky, Canadian former professional ice hockey player and head coach, in Wayne Gretzky and Rick Reilly, *An Autobiography* (1990)

"It's an honor and an overwhelming <u>compliment</u>, but it's also a kind of bizarre thing. All of a sudden you're at these parties and everybody's famous, and you feel like a loser."

> Jennifer Lawrence, on the Academy Awards ceremony, quoted in wmagazine.com, Oct. 2012

Complement and *compliment* sound the same, but the small difference in spelling makes a big difference in what they mean. There's usually no problem with *compliment*. But people evidently aren't sure about how to use *complement:* it was one of the most looked-up words in the online Oxford Dictionaries a few years ago.

A *complement* is something that completes something else or makes it perfect. It can describe each of two parts that supply each other's deficiencies.

jails and prisons are the <u>complement</u> of schools.

A *complement* is also the number or amount needed to make something complete.

a full <u>complement</u> of troops

To *complement* means "to complete or enhance; to form the complement to."

our makeup <u>complements</u> our wardrobe
a man who <u>complements</u> her lifestyle
opposites attracting (and <u>complementing</u>)

Something is *complementary* when it completes or perfects something else.

it's entirely <u>complementary</u> with everything else in your life

A *compliment* is an expression of approval, praise, or flattery.

the highest <u>compliment</u> you can pay me
it's an honor and an overwhelming <u>compliment</u>

When you *compliment* people you pay them compliments.

I have been <u>complimented</u> myself a great many times

When these words are confused, it's usually a matter of spelling. Here's a memory trick: a **comple**ment **comple**tes something.
    Which version of the sentence below is correct?

(A) "I can live for two months on a good <u>complement</u>."
(B) "I can live for two months on a good <u>compliment</u>."
        Mark Twain, quoted in Albert Bigelow Paine, *Mark Twain: A Biography* (1912)

Twain is saying how good it feels to receive praise, or a *compliment,* as in version B.

CONNOTATION or DENOTATION

✳ *Connotation*

"Whenever I hear someone describe something as a kids' movie or a family movie, it immediately has a negative <u>connotation</u> in my mind because I think…it's purely for children…and it's simplistic."
    Steve Carell, Golden Globe Award–winning American actor, comedian, director, producer, and writer, on why *Evan Almighty* isn't a kids' movie, quoted in craveonline.com, June 22, 2007

The creators of Yelp chose its name as a combination of "yellow pages" and "help." They had doubts because the word *yelp* has a negative <u>connotation</u>, as a cry of pain or alarm. But they decided that the name works well.

> Jeremy Stoppelman, CEO and co-founder of Yelp, Inc., interviewed on *Charlie Rose,* August 19, 2013

❋ *Denotation*

The dictionary definition of a word is its <u>denotation</u>.

> According to the *Oxford English Dictionary*, the word *gaga* <u>denotes</u> a senile, crazy, or dotty state of mind. But in Lady Gaga's name the word suggests a wild enthusiasm that describes her fans and fits her image.

The implications or associations of a word beyond its literal meaning are its *connotations*. The verb form is *to connote*.

> "Freedom is not worth having if it does not <u>connote</u> freedom to err."
> Mahatma Gandhi, in *Young India,* Dec. 3, 1931

***Denotation* refers to the primary or literal meaning of a word. The verb form is *denote*.**

COUNCIL or COUNSEL

❋ *Council*

> During the genocide in Darfur, George Clooney warned the United Nations Security <u>Council</u>, "After September 30, you won't need the UN. You will simply need men with shovels and bleached white linen and headstones."
>
> George Clooney, address to the UN Security Council, quoted in *Washington Post,* Sept. 14, 2006

> "In high school, I was on the youth advisory <u>council</u> for the mayor's office of Los Angeles.... I was still naive, 15 or 16, thinking you could change the world."

Rashida Jones, American actress, comic book-author, screenwriter, and singer, quoted in Sam O'Neal, "Rashida Jones," avclub.com, Apr. 8, 2009

✳ *Counsel*

"Where no <u>counsel</u> is, the people fall, but in the multitude of counselors there is safety."
>   Proverbs 11:14 (King James Version)

"If your determination is fixed, I do not <u>counsel</u> you to despair. Few things are impossible to diligence and skill."
>   Samuel Johnson, *The History of Rasselas, Prince of Abissinia* (1759)

"Do not go to the elves for <u>counsel</u>, for they will say both no and yes."
>   Frodo, in J. R. R. Tolkien, *The Lord of the Rings: The Fellowship of the Ring* (1954)

"Let none now reject the <u>counsels</u> of Gandalf, whose long labors against Sauron come at last to their test."
>   Aragorn, in J. R. R. Tolkien, *The Lord of the Rings: The Return of the King* (1955)

If you have trouble remembering which spelling is which for these words, don't feel too bad about it. It took the English more than three hundred years to decide that. But since the sixteenth century, when they did settle on fixed spellings for these two words, *council* has been used to refer to an advisory or administrative assembly.

A *council* is an assembly that meets for discussion or consultation.

A *council* is also a body appointed or chosen to advise, deliberate, or legislate.

Any group that serves in an administrative capacity can be called a *council,* including a student council, a church council, a town council, and the United Nations Security Council.

***Counsel* is advice or direction that comes from consultation.**

Where no <u>counsel</u> is, the people fall
Do not go to the elves for <u>counsel</u>
Let none now reject the <u>counsels</u> of Gandalf

Counsel also can refer a lawyer or a body of legal advisers:

"On the advice of <u>counsel</u>, I respectfully assert my right to remain silent."

When you _counsel_ people, you advise them.

I do not <u>counsel</u> you to despair

Remember, _council_ isn't a verb. You can _counsel_ people, but you can't _council_ them.

Which version of the sentence below is correct?

(A) "I didn't run for student <u>counsel</u>. I don't see myself in any elected office. I love policy. I'm not particularly fond of politics."

(B) "I didn't run for student <u>council</u>. I don't see myself in any elected office. I love policy. I'm not particularly fond of politics."
   Former secretary of state Condoleezza Rice, quoted in Dana Hughes and Jonathan Karl, "Condoleezza Rice Still Not Interested in VP Slot," ABC News, abcnews.go.com, July 13, 2012

Dr. Rice is referring here to an elected student advisory or governing body, or council. Version B is correct.

DISCREET or DISCRETE

* _Discreet_

"Lady, lady, should you meet
One whose ways are all <u>discreet</u>,
One who murmurs that his wife

Is the lodestar of his life,
One who keeps assuring you
That he never was untrue,
Never loved another one…
Lady, lady, better run!"

    Dorothy Parker, American writer and humorist (1893–1967),
    "Social Note" (1926)

"You know what I never [understand about] the limo: the
tinted windows. Is that so people don't see you? Yeah, what
better way not to have people notice you than taking a
30-foot Cadillac with a TV antenna and a uniformed driver.
How <u>discreet</u>."

    Jerry Seinfeld, quoted in "What's the Deal with…: 15 Jokes from
    Jerry Seinfeld on His Birthday," wcbsfm.cbslocal.com, Apr. 29,
    2013

"I think Joan's advice would be: always know more than
anyone else, always be as <u>discreet</u> as possible, and never cry at
work."

    Christina Hendricks, American actress, on her character on *Mad
    Men,* quoted in Andy Morris, "Christina Hendricks Reveals All,"
    gq-magazine.co.uk, Aug. 2, 2010

✳ *Discrete*

In 2011, Netflix split its online streaming and its DVD rentals into
two <u>discrete</u> programs.

Reported advice from Steve Jobs: "Keep your secrets: Nobody at
Apple talks. Everything is on a need-to-know basis, with the
company divided into <u>discrete</u> cells. The secrecy allows Jobs to
generate frenzied interest for his surprise product
demonstrations."

    Leander Kahney, "The 10 Commandments of Steve," *Newsweek,*
    Sept. 5, 2011 (Lexis)

✳ *Discretion*

"The better part of valor is <u>discretion</u>."
  Falstaff, in *Henry IV Pt. 1* (1597)

Discreet means "prudent, circumspect, tactful."
Discretion is the noun form.
Discrete means "distinct, separate, individual."

These two words have separate (or *discrete*) meanings and spellings today, but they're actually close relatives. They ultimately derive from the same Latin word, *discrēt-us*. In classical Latin, it meant "separate, distinct," which gave us the English word *discrete*. In late Latin, the word had come to mean "prudent, discerning." That was the source of our word *discreet*.

Here's a memory trick: *discreet* keeps its *ee* tucked discreetly between the *r* and the *t*, but *discrete* keeps the *e*'s separate from each other, which illustrates the meaning of the word.

Which version of the sentence below is correct?

(A) Marriage "is not by any to be entered into unadvisedly or lightly;
    but reverently, <u>discreetly</u>, advisedly, soberly, and in the fear of God."
(B) Marriage "is not by any to be entered into unadvisedly or lightly;
    but reverently, <u>discretely</u>, advisedly, soberly, and in the fear of God."
  Book of Common Prayer, "Solemnization of Matrimony" (1928 ed.)

This passage advises you to enter marriage with good judgment, or *discreetly*. Version A is correct.

DIVED or DOVE

✳ *Dived*

"It was time to go to the whales' help. The *Nautilus* <u>dived</u> under the water."
  Jules Verne, *Twenty Thousand Leagues Under the Sea* (1870)

"There is a pretty good chance that you're going to go down when you're on a motorcycle or if you're skydiving or whatever, but that happened before I even got this job and I haven't <u>skydived</u> since."

> Charisma Carpenter, American actress on the TV series *Buffy the Vampire Slayer* and *Angel,* asked about doing dangerous sports, quoted on bbc.co.uk

✳ *Dove*

"Straight into the river [he]...<u>dove</u> as if he were a beaver."

> Henry Wadsworth Longfellow, American poet and professor (1807–1882), *Hiawatha* (1855)

On riding a whale: "Frank Junior happened by just then, and Mr. Johnson asked him how it felt to ride a whale. Without batting an eye he replied: 'I thought I was a goner. I felt him moving under me. I was on him until I was maybe 20 yards from my dory. Then I stood up and <u>dove</u>.'"

> "Cape Codders Say Boy Rode Whale and <u>Dived</u> Off Big 'Willie' at Sea," *New York Times,* June 28, 1948

"He disregarded warnings for his own safety and refused to believe bystanders who said it was a lost cause. Instead, 19-year-old Andy Hart pulled off his leather work boots and <u>dove</u> into a murky stock pond, searching blindly until he pulled two women from a submerged van."

> "Young Hero <u>Dived</u> Despite Warnings," *Austin American Statesman,* Apr. 22, 1998

"Astronomers are marveling at the death and apparent resurrection of Comet ISON, which <u>dove</u> close to the sun on Thursday."

> Kenneth Chang, "Comet, Presumed Dead, Shows New Life," nytimes.com, Nov. 29, 2013

Quick, which is right: *she <u>dived</u> off the high board* or *she <u>dove</u> off the high board*? Unless you come from some areas in the United States or Canada, you probably chose *dived*. That's been the past tense of this verb since

Early Modern English, and it derives from the word's early origins in Old English. But in the mid-nineteenth century *dove* began to appear instead in North America and in some British dialects. *Dove* is now the prevalent past tense in the northern United States and parts of Canada, and it's also common in California, Nevada, and other states. So both forms are now well established in American English. Some usage guides prefer *dived,* but most accept either form as standard in American English.

The passages above from 1948 and 1998 use both forms in the same story. The headlines say "dived" while the stories themselves use "dove." In the case of the article in the *New York Times, dove* appears within a quotation.

Which version of the passage below is correct?

(A) "He <u>dived</u> in and saved her life."
(B) "He <u>dove</u> in and saved her life."
       F. Scott Fitzgerald, *The Last Tycoon* (1941)

Fitzgerald lived for years in New York and New Jersey, where the verb *dove* is common, and in this passage, he actually wrote *dove.* Some language critics might object, but many would consider either choice to be correct. Having spent most of my life on Long Island, I think that *dove* sounds fine. It may sound weird to people who live in places where *dived* is the past tense form, though.

E-MAIL or EMAIL

The letter *e* stands for "electronic." *E-mail* and *email* are both acceptable.

EMIGRATE, EMIGRATION, IMMIGRATE, IMMIGRANT

✳ *Emigrate, Emigration*

Since late 1989, more than a million people have <u>emigrated</u> from the former Soviet Union to Israel.

Mark Twain proposed that to empty out the red-light district of Manhattan, poets should read their most soulful poetry to the sketchy people who lived there. "The plan would be very effective in causing an <u>emigration</u> of the depraved element," he said.

Mark Twain, "Poets as Policemen," speech, New York, Mar. 24, 1900

✳ *Immigrate, Immigrant*

Each year for the past twenty years, about one million people who have <u>immigrated</u> to the United States have received green cards, giving them permanent residency status.

> "My fellow Americans, this is an amazing moment for me. To think that a once-scrawny boy from Austria could grow up to become governor of California and stand in Madison Square Garden to speak on behalf of the president of United States. That is an <u>immigrant's</u> dream."
>
> Arnold Schwarzenegger, then governor of California, speech at the Republican National Convention, Aug. 31, 2004

Whether somebody is *emigrating* or *immigrating* depends entirely on the speaker's point of view.

Seen from the perspective of the country a person is leaving, she *emigrates* <u>**from**</u> **her old home** <u>**to**</u> **her new own.**

Seen from the perspective of her new country, she *immigrates* <u>**to**</u> **the new land and becomes an immigrant.**

Which version of the sentence below is correct?

(A) "When New Zealanders <u>emigrate</u> to Australia, it raises the average IQ of both countries."
(B) "When New Zealanders <u>immigrate</u> to Australia, it raises the average IQ of both countries."

Robert Muldoon, New Zealand statesman, attributed, 1991–92

You need to figure out the perspective of the speaker in order to decide if *emigrate* or *immigrate* is the right choice here. Notice that this passage was spoken or written by a New Zealander. In addition, it's a funny insult to Australia (and to people who move there). So we can assume that it refers to people who <u>emigrate</u> from New Zealand to Australia, as in version A.

EMPATHY or SYMPATHY

✳ *Empathy*

"<u>Empathy</u> is the spark of human concern for others, the glue that makes social life possible. It may be fragile, but it has, arguably, endured throughout evolutionary times and may continue as long as humans exist."
> Martin L. Hoffman, American psychologist, *Empathy and Moral Development: Implications for Caring and Justice* (2001)

About Lord Voldemort: "He's really sort of the devil....He's completely emotionally detached. He has no <u>empathy</u>. You find that in psychopaths."
> Ralph Fiennes, English actor, speaking of the character he played in the Harry Potter films, quoted in usatoday.com, Dec. 6, 2010

"The struggle of my life created <u>empathy</u>....I could relate to pain...being abandoned, having people not love me."
> Oprah Winfrey, American talk show host, actress, producer, entrepreneur, and philanthropist, quoted in "Sheryl Sandberg, Facebook COO, Interviews Oprah Winfrey Online," huffingtonpost.com, Sept. 9, 2011

From a study of doctors' communication with patients in one hospital: "A lack of <u>empathy</u> was often apparent: in one instance, after a tearful patient had related the recent death of a loved one, the physician's next sentence was, 'How is your abdominal pain?'"
> Nirmal Joshi, "Doctor, Shut Up and Listen," nytimes.com, Jan. 4, 2015

"The ship captain being played by Tom Hanks in a Hollywood movie said on Tuesday...that he never felt <u>empathy</u> for the Somali pirates who hijacked his vessel and took him captive four years ago. 'That never entered my mind,' Richard Phillips said in an interview. 'We were always adversaries.'"

Lisa Rathke, "Vt.'s Captain Phillips Says He Never Empathized," Associated Press, Oct. 2, 2013

✳ *Sympathy*

"My heart goes out in <u>sympathy</u> to anyone who is making his first appearance before an audience.... I recall the occasion of my first appearance.... My knees were shaking so that I didn't know whether I could stand up."

Mark Twain, speech in Norfolk, CT, Oct. 5, 1906

"I know there was a major screw-up. I've hurt my wife. I've hurt the kids. I take the responsibility....I'm not looking for <u>sympathy</u> at all."

Arnold Schwarzenegger, quoted in "Schwarzenegger: I Deserve Public, Family Anger," politico.com, Oct. 7, 2012

Empathy and *sympathy* play essential roles in the ways that we relate to each other as human beings. People evidently are very curious about that, since *empathy* has been one of the most frequently looked-up words in online dictionaries in recent years. These words have overlapped in meaning, with *sympathy* having been used for what is now often called *empathy*.

The word *empathy* came into English in its current sense in the twentieth century.

Empathy involves feeling what another feels, or understanding what the other is experiencing. *Empathy* is typically a passive and involuntary response in children and adults, though you also can make a deliberate effort to *empathize*.[16] The passage below illustrates how *empathy* can involve consciously projecting yourself inside someone else's skin:

"I've always thought of acting as more of an exercise in <u>empathy</u>, which is not to be confused with <u>sympathy</u>.... [In acting,] you try to get inside [someone else's] emotional reality or motivational reality...so you can represent it."

    Edward Norton, American actor, screenwriter, director, and producer, in Peter Howell, "Edward Norton Comes to Grips with De Niro and The Boss," thestar.com (*Toronto Star*), Sept. 9, 2010

Sympathy is a much older word than *empathy,* having been used in English since the sixteenth century. It comes from the Greek for having a feeling in common with someone else.[17]

**   *Sympathy* can mean having a relationship in which what affects one affects the other similarly. In this sense, it denotes sharing the feelings or interests of the other.**

**   *Sympathy* involves compassion for someone else's suffering: feeling *for* another.**

**   Being *in sympathy with* means agreeing with or supporting someone or something:**

"I am most emphatically <u>in sympathy with</u> the movement, now on foot in Russia, to make that country free. I am certain that it will be successful, as it deserves to be."

    Mark Twain, speech in New York, Apr. 11, 1906

ENERGIZE or ENERVATE

✳ *Energize*

"<u>Energize</u>!"

    Captain Kirk's command to Mr. Scott to activate the transporter in "Where No Man Has Gone Before," *Star Trek,* Sept. 22, 1966

"Self-confidence <u>energizes</u>, and it gives your people the courage to stretch, take risks, and achieve beyond their dreams. It is the fuel of winning teams."

Jack Welch, former chairman and CEO of General Electric, *Winning* (2005)

"The first voice you hear in 'Star Trek: The Video Game' is Capt. James T. Kirk screaming 'Ambush!'.... Co-publishers Paramount Pictures and Namco Bandai hope to <u>re-energize</u> the [*Star Trek*] franchise by turning to one of the most successful gaming genres of the last decade: the third-person duck-and-cover shooter."
Todd Martens, "Light Years Off," *Los Angeles Times*, Apr. 30, 2013 (Lexis)

The Energizer Bunny is so <u>energized</u> that, according to his online biography at energizer.com, his turn-ons are marathons and hot air balloons, and his pet peeves are stop signs and waiting rooms.

✷ *Enervate*

"My Dearest Emma,
    "It is a relief to me to take up the pen and write you a line, for I...had, about four o'clock this morning, one of my dreadful spasms, which has almost <u>enervated</u> me.... I am...quite weak."
Horatio Nelson, British naval commander famous for his victories over the French during the Napoleonic Wars (1758–1805), letter written Oct. 1, 1805, quoted in *The Letters of Lord Nelson to Lady Hamilton* (2006)

Describing Andy Murray's 2012 victory at the U.S. Open:
"It wasn't easy.... It wasn't swift either. The first set alone took a full hour and 27 minutes, and the <u>enervating</u> tug-of-war ate up four hours and 54 minutes of a chilly, windy afternoon and evening."
"When Pigs Flew," www.tennis.com, Sept. 11, 2012

Doctors say that pollen is "contributing to a rise in seasonal hay fever and allergic asthma in the USA, where the pollen season has lengthened up to 16 days since 1995.... For Carol

Leopold and her 13-year-old twin sons, the pollen count is personal. She says their allergies have worsened in the past couple of years and they hit their peak in May, when spring comes alive. 'Anything that blooms <u>enervates</u> us. It wears us down,' says Leopold."

Wendy Koch, "Pollen Plague," *USA Today,* May 31, 2013

Don't be fooled by the fact that these two words look almost alike. They mean the exact opposite of each other, and they derive from totally different sources. **Energize** is related to the word *energy*, which descends from the Greek word for "active." **Enervate**, by contrast, comes from the Latin for cutting the tendons out of something in order to hamstring it. That's because one early meaning of the word *nerve* was "sinew or tendon." So to *enervate* meant to remove those body parts.[18] The word soon took on a broader sense of weakening someone or something,

To *energize* means "to infuse with energy, to activate."
To *enervate* means "to weaken."
Which version of the passage below is correct?

(A) "Leaders can't have an iota of fakeness. They have to know themselves—so that they can be straight with the world, <u>enervate</u> followers, and lead with the authority born of authenticity."

(B) "Leaders can't have an iota of fakeness. They have to know themselves—so that they can be straight with the world, <u>energize</u> followers, and lead with the authority born of authenticity."

Jack Welch, *Winning* (2005)

Welch, who was the chairman of General Electric, wants leaders to fill followers with energy, or *energize* them, as in version B.

ENVELOP or ENVELOPE

✳ *Envelop*

Harry, Ron, and Hermione entered Honeydukes and "were <u>enveloped</u> by warm, toffee-scented air."
> J. K. Rowling, *Harry Potter and the Half-Blood Prince* (2005)

"I felt a sudden blaze of fire <u>envelop</u> me."
> Walter Restrepo, describing the blast when a coal mine exploded in Colombia in 2010, quoted in Simon Romero, "Colombian Coal Mine Blast Kills at Least 18," nytimes.com, June 10, 2010

✳ *Envelope*

"*Why* do you sit there looking like an <u>envelope</u> without any address on it?"
> Mark Twain, *The American Claimant* (1892)

"One of the phrases that kept running through their conversation was 'pushing the outside of the <u>envelope</u>.' The '<u>envelope</u>' was a flight-test term referring to the limits of the particular aircraft's performance."
> American author and journalist Tom Wolfe, describing test pilots, *The Right Stuff* (1979)

"'Pushing the <u>envelope</u>' sort of implies that you're inside the <u>envelope</u> with everyone else, and you're trying to find the edges on the outside.'"
> Louis C.K., American comedian, TV and film writer, director, producer, editor, and actor, in Austin L. Ray, "Louis C. K. on Twitter and Tracy Morgan," cnn.com, June 21, 2011

Envelop is an Old French word that Chaucer was evidently the first writer to use in English, in the late fourteenth century. In the *Canterbury Tales* he had one pilgrim accuse another of being "<u>enveloped</u> in sin." The next English author to use the word spoke of being "<u>enveloped</u> in crime" a few years later. These early usages weren't a promising beginning for the word *envelop,* but it managed to hang on in English.

A little more than three hundred years later the noun *envelope* came into English from modern French. There's been some debate about how to pronounce this word. Some people in the eighteenth century pronounced it in a way that they thought recalled its French origin, with a nasalized first syllable, as in *encore.* Some language commentators have denounced that as a pseudo-French or bargain-basement French mispronunciation. Still, a lot of us (including me sometimes) still pronounce it that way without even thinking about it. The word has been fully Anglicized, though, and both pronunciations are common.

To *envelop* means to "enclose, cover."

An *envelope* is something that envelops, covers, or contains. It's often a flat paper sheet folded and gummed so it can serve as a cover for a letter.

It can be used figuratively, as in "pushing the envelope."

Which version of the sentence below is correct?

(A) Michelle Obama opened the <u>envelop</u> that held the name of the Academy Award winner for the Best Picture of 2012, *Argo.*

(B) Michelle Obama opened the <u>envelope</u> that held the name of the Academy Award winner for the Best Picture of 2012, *Argo.*

Mrs. Obama opened an *envelope,* as in version B.

EVERY DAY or EVERYDAY

✳ *Every Day*

> "We have a criminal jury system which is superior to any in the world; and its efficiency is only marred by the difficulty of finding twelve men <u>every day</u> who don't know anything and can't read."
>
> Mark Twain, "Americans and the English," speech, London, July 4, 1872

"Start <u>every day</u> off with a smile and get it over with."
 W. C. Fields, attributed

"Okay, maybe nobody has as much as I do, but, girls, come on!
Each and <u>every day</u> you can find something that makes you feel
pretty, flirty, fun, happy."
 Paris Hilton, American socialite, actress, model, and celebrity, and
 Merle Ginsberg, *Your Heiress Diary: Confess It All to Me* (2005)

"I am a walking piece of art <u>every day</u>, with my dreams and my
ambitions forward at all times in an effort to inspire my fans to
lead their life in that way."
 Lady Gaga, quoted in Horacio Silva, "The World According to
 Gaga," tmagazine.blogs.nytimes.com, Mar. 4, 2010

"I wear jeans and loafers <u>every day</u>...but when I really turn it on,
I like a classic, simple look."
 Allison Williams, American actress, comedian, and musician, and a
 star of the HBO series *Girls,* quoted in Rachel Brown, "Allison
 Williams: From *Girls* to 'It' Girl?," wwd.com, Sept 24, 2012

✳ *Everyday*

"I have an <u>everyday</u> religion that works for me. Love yourself first
and everything else falls into line."
 Attributed to American actress and comedian Lucille Ball (1911–1989)

"The advance of technology is based on making it fit in so that
you don't really even notice it, so it's part of <u>everyday</u> life."
 Bill Gates, quoted in news.bbc.co.uk, Dec. 7, 2001

"In our <u>everyday</u> experience, if something has never happened
before, we are generally safe in assuming it is not going to happen
in the future. But the exceptions can kill you, and climate change
is one of those exceptions."
 Former U.S. vice president Al Gore, quoted in *Spiegel Online,* Nov.
 2, 2009

"Fast food has become the <u>everyday</u> meal."
> Michelle Obama, U.S. First Lady (2009–), quoted by AP, Feb. 8, 2011

"My <u>everyday</u> beauty routine is always rushed and pretty simple. I put on SK-II Skin Signature Moisturizing Cream, which is great under makeup as a base because it creates a dewy finish."
> Cate Blanchett, Academy Award–winning Australian actress and global ambassador for SK-II, quoted in "Cate Blanchett on Philanthropy and Beauty," marieclaire.com, Apr. 1, 2011

People confuse these two a lot, even in newspapers and magazines, not to mention online. Just remember, *every day* **means "each day."**

finding twelve men <u>every day</u>
start <u>every day</u> off with a smile

Everyday, written as one word, means "ordinary, usual, daily."

it's part of <u>everyday</u> life
the <u>everyday</u> meal
my <u>everyday</u> beauty routine

Which version of the lyric below is correct?

(A) "Thank heaven for little girls!
For little girls get bigger <u>everyday</u>."
(B) "Thank heaven for little girls!
For little girls get bigger <u>every day</u>."
> "Thank Heaven for Little Girls," song by Alan Jay Lerner and Frederick Loewe, performed by Maurice Chevalier in the 1958 film *Gigi*

In this song, *every day* is correct because it means "each day." Version B is the right choice.

EVERY ONE or EVERYONE

* *Every One*

"But, jesting aside, Mr. President, woman is lovable, gracious, kind of heart, beautiful—worthy of all respect, of all esteem, of all deference.... Each and <u>every one</u> of us has personally known, and loved, and honored the very best one of them all—his own mother."
  Mark Twain, address: "Eulogy of the Fair Sex," quoted in the *Washington Star,* Jan. 13, 1868

"We are a rare as well as an endangered species. <u>Every one</u> of us is, in the cosmic perspective, precious. If a human disagrees with you, let him live. In a hundred billion galaxies, you will not find another."
  Carl Sagan, *Cosmos* (1985)

In 2012, for the first time in history, <u>every one</u> of the 204 delegations to the Olympics included women athletes.

"Walmart to U.S. Veterans: We'll Hire <u>Every One</u> of You Who Wants a Job"
  Headline of a story by Anne D'Innocenzio, Associated Press, Jan. 15, 2013

* *Everyone*

"I want to thank <u>everyone</u> who made this day necessary."
  Yogi Berra, on Yogi Berra Day, St. Louis, 1947, quoted in Bruce Bohle, *Home Book of American Quotations* (1967)

"I'm a bit of a P. T. Barnum. I make stars out of <u>everyone</u>."
  Donald Trump, American business magnate and TV personality, on the women in his life, quoted in *Observer* (London), July 7, 1991

"I touch people. I think <u>everyone</u> needs that. Placing a hand on a friend's face means making contact."

> Diana, Princess of Wales, interview in *Le Monde,* Aug. 27, 1997 (four days before she died)

"These days, <u>everyone</u> wants John Lennon's sunglasses, accent, and swagger, but no one is prepared to…stand naked, [as] he did in his songs."

> Bono, Irish singer-songwriter, lead singer of the rock band U2, businessman, and philanthropist, interview in *Guardian,* Mar. 4, 2000

"If slaughterhouses had glass walls, <u>everyone</u> would be vegetarian."

> Paul McCartney, ad for PETA, 2012

Every one as two words means "each one (of the ones in a group)." It's often followed by *of* and it takes a singular verb.

<u>every one</u> of you <u>has</u>
<u>every one</u> of us <u>is</u>
<u>every one</u> of you who <u>wants</u> a job

Everyone as one word means "everybody." It also takes a singular verb.

<u>everyone needs</u> that
<u>everyone wants</u> John Lennon's sunglasses
<u>everyone</u> would be vegetarian

If you can substitute *everybody*, the right choice is the single word *everyone*.

Which version of the sentence below is correct?

(A) "I told my psychiatrist that <u>every one</u> hates me. He said I was being ridiculous. <u>Every one</u> hasn't met me yet."

(B) "I told my psychiatrist that <u>everyone</u> hates me. He said I was being ridiculous. <u>Everyone</u> hasn't met me yet."

Rodney Dangerfield, American comedian (1921–2004), quoted in
Bob Fenster, *Laugh Off: The Comedy Showdown Between Real Life
and the Pros* (2005)

Since Rodney Dangerfield was saying that everybody hates him, the
right choice is *everyone,* as in version B.

Historically, people have said *everyone... they* and *everybody... they.*
In both casual and formal English, they frequently still do. It's one
way to avoid the sexism of using *he* to represent both genders. Also,
we may tend to think that *everyone* and *everybody* represent a group,
so the plural *they* may sound right. Some style guides state flatly that
saying *everyone... they* is simply wrong. Others allow it. People can
get pretty intense about this. I suggest that, when writing formal
English, you use the strategies listed in "HE or THEY after
ANYBODY, EVERYONE, SOMEBODY, A PERSON, ETC.," on
page 92–93.

EVOKE or INVOKE

✳ *Evoke*

"Good writing is supposed to <u>evoke</u> sensation in the reader—not
the fact that it's raining, but the feeling of being rained upon."
  E. L. Doctorow, American author, quoted in Charles Ruas,
  Conversations with American Writers (1985)

"A lot of the stuff that I do with Betty is in the eyes. A lot of the
feelings that I <u>evoke</u> with her are unspoken, so that's been fun to
play with."
  January Jones, American actress and model, speaking of playing
  Betty Draper on the TV series *Mad Men,* interviewed by Bruce
  Handy, "Mad Men Q&A: January Jones," *Vanity Fair,* Aug. 5, 2009

On the sexiest kind of voice: "Researchers in London have [found that] the most attractive type of female voice is...breathy and high-pitched.... This sound <u>evokes</u> a woman of relatively small body size, which...is most desired by men."

> Kent Sepkowitz, "Dirty Talk: Why Do Some Voices Turn Us On?," *Newsweek*, May 3, 2013 (Lexis) [this is a summary of a scientific study and isn't necessarily my own opinion]

"Few things <u>evoke</u> panic like last-minute shopping for holiday gifts."

> Hitha Prabhakar, "7 Last-Minute Holiday Shopping Tips," usnews. com, Dec. 19, 2013 (Lexis)

✳ *Invoke*

In Book I of the *Iliad*, the narrator <u>invokes</u> the Muse's help.

President John F. Kennedy, on the United States and its adversaries: "Let both sides seek to <u>invoke</u> the wonders of science instead of its terrors. Together let us explore the stars, conquer the deserts, eradicate disease, tap the ocean depths, and encourage the arts and commerce."

> Inaugural address, Jan. 20, 1961

"Alex Rodriguez is expected to be suspended by Major League Baseball on Sunday or Monday.... [Commissioner of Major League Baseball Bud] Selig could <u>invoke</u> the broad powers outlined in the Basic Agreement to impose a suspension in the best interests of the sport."

> Teri Thompson, Bill Madden, and Michael O'Keefe, "Alex's Options: A Lifetime Ban or a 200-Game Suspension," *Daily News* (New York), Aug. 3, 2013 (Lexis)

"Lincoln did not create Thanksgiving from nothing.... Early Americans celebrated Thanksgiving not as a fixed annual event, but as a series of ad hoc holidays called in response to specific events. These were religious occasions intended to <u>invoke</u> God's help to cope with hardships, or to offer God thanks for positive developments."

> Paul Quigley, "The Birth of Thanksgiving," *New York Times* blogs, Nov. 28, 2013 (Lexis)

About the CW TV series *Star Crossed:* "With a premise involving well-intentioned aliens who crash-land on Earth and are herded into a concentration camp, the show <u>invokes</u> film and television predecessors from *E.T.* to *Roswell* to *District 9*."

> Mike Hale, "A Romance from Beyond Mars and Venus," *New York Times,* Feb. 17, 2014 (Lexis)

These two words are easy to confuse. *Evoke* and *invoke* come from the same Latin root meaning "to call," and they sometimes overlap in meaning. But *evoke* comes from the Latin for "to call out, call forth." *Invoke*, by contrast, comes from a Latin word meaning "to call on or call in." That slight difference gives these words very distinct meanings in English.

To *evoke* is "to elicit, call forth, summon up."

You can *evoke* feelings, memories, sensations, responses, etc. In this sense, *to evoke* is to bring something <u>out</u>.

to <u>evoke</u> sensation in the reader
the feelings that I <u>evoke</u> with her
<u>evoke</u> panic

Invoke has many meanings, and they all retain the sense of "call on, call in." The word originally referred to calling on, appealing to, or summoning God or a divine being. One can *invoke* a deity or spirit for inspiration, help, or protection, or as a witness. ***To invoke* in this sense means "to call on, solicit, appeal to, or petition for help or support."**

the narrator <u>invokes</u> the Muse's help

***To invoke* can mean "to implement."**

<u>invoke</u> the broad powers outlined in the Basic Agreement

To *invoke* also can mean "to cite, mention, refer to (in order to influence people)."

to <u>invoke</u> the wonders of science

To *invoke* a law or a right is to cite it in order to make use of it.

The official <u>invoked</u> his Fifth Amendment right to remain silent.

Which version of the passage below is correct?

(A) "Do not <u>evoke</u> the names of other gods; do not let them be heard on your lips."
(B) "Do not <u>invoke</u> the names of other gods; do not let them be heard on your lips."
　　　Exodus 23:13 (King James Version)

In this passage, God forbids mentioning or calling on other gods. *Invoke* is the right choice, as in version B.

EXPLICIT or IMPLICIT

✳ *Explicit*

On sex: "As soon as you deal with it <u>explicitly</u>, you are forced to choose between the language of the nursery, the gutter, and the anatomy class."
　　　C. S. Lewis, British novelist, poet, scholar, critic, and lay theologian (1898–1963), quoted in Kenneth Tynan, *In Search of C. S. Lewis* (1975)

"A cardinal principle that we must not stray from—no exceptions—is that your genetic information is your business in terms of who sees it. Nobody should be gaining access to that information without your <u>explicit</u> permission. And nobody should be requiring you to take a genetic test unless you decide that that's what you want to do."

> Francis Collins, then director of the Human Genome Project and currently director of the National Institutes of Health, quoted in "Religion & Ethics Newsweekly," pbs.org, June 16, 2000

What to do when adult children come back to live at home: "Be upfront and <u>explicit</u> about your expectations and about the rules of the house.... Conversation is key, about boundaries, about shared spaces in the house."

> Robert Bornstein, coauthor of *How to Age in Place,* quoted in *USA Today*, Oct. 22, 2013 (Lexis)

✳ *Implicit*

"An <u>implicit</u> respect paid to the laws of the land."

> Thomas Jefferson, letter, Sept. 27, 1786 (*OED*)

"'And through all this we are supposed to believe Dumbledore has never suspected you?' asked Bellatrix. 'He has no idea of your true allegiance, he trusts you <u>implicitly</u> still?'

"'I have played my part well,' said Snape."

> J. K. Rowling, *Harry Potter and the Half-Blood Prince* (2005)

"Everyone wants to give the perfect gift.... I asked people to share with me the most memorable, special, or just plain best gifts they've received over the years. Here's what they said... and <u>implicit</u> in each story is a lesson... about what makes a gift truly great."

> Kit Yarrow, "Here's How to Give the Perfect Gift This Holiday," time.com, Dec. 14, 2013

"During past downturns, Congress has usually been willing to vote for extended unemployment benefits, with the <u>implicit</u> assumption that most of those who cannot find jobs are unfortunate victims of a poor economy.... But now... the political climate has become less friendly."

> Floyd Norris, "Fewer Layoffs, but Not Much Hiring," nytimes. com, Feb 14, 2014

These two words come from the same Latin root meaning "to fold." When something is *explicit*, it's unfolded, laid open for people to see. *Implicit* is the opposite of that. It means "folded in," in the sense that its meaning is covered or contained within something else and isn't explicit.

If something is *explicit*, it's clear, definite, and not concealed. The adverb is *explicitly*.

as soon as you deal with it <u>explicitly</u>

An *explicit* statement makes a point distinctly, openly, and unambiguously.

without your <u>explicit</u> permission
upfront and <u>explicit</u> about your expectations

An *explicit* picture, book, film, etc. depicts nudity or sexuality openly and graphically.

"I see <u>explicit</u> covers on magazines, and they're getting even more <u>explicit</u>.... Are women being empowered or is this just what sells magazines?"

> Rosie Perez, American actress, dancer, choreographer, and director, quoted in Mim Udovitch, "Naked Truths," guardian.co.uk, July 15, 2000

When something is *implicit*, it's implied, not plainly stated.

<u>implicit</u> in each story is a lesson
the <u>implicit</u> assumption

***Implicit belief, implicit confidence, implicit faith,* etc., involve having no doubts or reservations.**

an <u>implicit</u> respect

***Implicitly* is the adverb:**

he trusts you <u>implicitly</u>

> Which version of the poem below is correct?
>
> (A) If no thought your mind does visit,
>   Make your speech not too <u>explicit</u>.
> (B) If no thought your mind does visit,
>   Make your speech not too <u>implicit</u>.
>   Piet Hein, "The Case for Obscurity," in *Grooks* (1966)

This little poem advises people not to openly, or *explicitly,* reveal that they have nothing to say. Version A is correct.

FAZE or PHASE

∗ *Faze*

> American actress and model Emma Stone, on not being <u>fazed</u>: "I always think it's funny when people feel they have to be delicate with me.... On *Superbad,* people would say absolutely anything every single day. After that, nothing could <u>faze</u> me."
>   Quoted in John Powers, "Emma Stone: Playing It Cool," vogue. com, Mar. 2011

> "Bucs' Best Efforts Don't <u>Faze</u> Peyton Manning."
>   Headline in tampabay.com, Dec. 2, 2012

> "All of the marquee singer-actors—even Hugh Jackman, known Broadway star—auditioned live for Tom Hooper's film [*Les Misérables*] in a variety of rundown, run-of-the-mill audition

studios.... It didn't <u>faze</u> Mr. Jackman, though, as he tried out for Valjean."

> Melena Ryzik, "In a Dingy Studio, Making Hugh Jackman Audition," carpetbagger.blogs.nytimes.com, Jan. 18, 2013

On Ashton Kutcher: "Kutcher doesn't have much time.... He moves from dance rehearsal to read-through to walk-through rehearsal and blocking, skips lunch, and presses on with rewrites through the afternoon.... He has dinner at 6:00 with a venture-capital client. It doesn't <u>faze</u> him, this schedule, and he doesn't expect that it should <u>faze</u> anyone else."

> Tom Chiarella, "The All-New Ashton Kutcher Story," *Esquire,* Mar. 1, 2013 (Lexis)

✳ *Phase*

"The Chinese people...are the oldest civilized people on earth. Their civilization passes through <u>phases</u>, but its basic characteristics remain the same. They yield, they bend to the wind, but they do not break."

> Pearl S. Buck, Pulitzer Prize– and Nobel Prize–winning American writer, *China, Past and Present* (1972)

"I think it's important to have closure in any relationship that ends—from a romantic relationship to a friendship.... You need that in your life to move cleanly into your next <u>phase</u>."

> Jennifer Aniston, American actress, film director, and producer, quoted in accesshollywood.com, Sept. 8, 2009

"I think that people in the <u>phase</u> between being someone's kid and being someone's parent have always been uniquely narcissistic, but that social media and Twitter and LiveJournal make it really easy to navel-gaze in a way that you've never been able to before."

> Lena Dunham, interview on avclub.com, Feb. 15, 2012

Marion Cotillard on motherhood as a <u>phase</u>: "'Suddenly...you're not the most important person anymore.' But this new <u>phase</u> in her life has positive repercussions on her career as well.... 'I have this huge energy that I've never experienced before,'" she says.

> Marion Cotillard, Academy Award–winning French actress and singer, quoted in Marlow Stern, "A Beautiful Mind," *Newsweek*, Dec. 10, 2012 (Lexis)

Faze is such a familiar word that I was surprised to learn as I researched this lesson that it was born in the United States and is less than two hundred years old. It's a variant of *feeze* ("to drive off"), a word that dates back to Old English but has dropped out of use except in some dialects. In the early twentieth century, *faze* was still a new Americanism, and some commentators warned against using it. It's fully standard now, of course. It's used mainly in negative contexts:

nothing could <u>faze</u> me
efforts don't <u>faze</u> Peyton Manning
it didn't <u>faze</u> Mr. Jackman

> *Faze* is sometimes misspelled *phase,* but they're totally different words.
> **To *faze* is to disturb, embarrass, or upset someone.**
> **A *phase* is a distinct stage or period of development.**
> **As a verb, to *phase* is to do something in stages, often with *out* or *in*:**

"The German Parliament approved a plan to <u>phase out</u> nuclear power over the next two decades."

> Victor Homola, "Germany Nuclear Phase-Out Approved," *New York Times,* Dec. 15, 2001 (Lexis)

Which versions of the passages below are correct?

(A) "Puberty is a <u>faze</u>.... Fifteen years of rejection is a lifestyle."
(B) "Puberty is a <u>phase</u>.... Fifteen years of rejection is a lifestyle."
> Willie Garson, American actor, as Stanford on "The Turtle and the Hare," *Sex and the City,* 1998

(A) "It's quite hard to <u>faze</u> me. I'm fairly un-shockable."
(B) "It's quite hard to <u>phase</u> me. I'm fairly un-shockable."
> Emily Blunt, English actress, quoted in Donna Freydkin, "Emily Blunt Is a Big Fish in Acting Pond with 3 Films Due," usatoday.com, Mar. 9, 2012

In the first passage, puberty is a stage of development, or *phase*. Version B is the right choice.

In the second passage, Emily Blunt says that she isn't easily disturbed, or *fazed*. Version A is correct.

FLAUNT or FLOUT

✳ *Flaunt*

> "That's it, baby. When you['ve] got it, <u>flaunt</u> it."
> Zero Mostel, in the 1968 film *The Producers*

> Mark Twain, denouncing a reviewer: "His grammar is foolishly correct, offensively precise. It <u>flaunts</u> itself in the reader's face."
> Mark Twain, "Comment on Tautology and Grammar," May 6, 1898, in *Autobiography of Mark Twain,* vol. 1 (2010)

✳ *flout*

> "The best way to drive out the devil, if he will not yield to texts of Scripture, is to jeer and <u>flout</u> him, for he cannot bear scorn."
> Martin Luther, seminal figure in the Protestant Reformation (1483–1546), in a translation used by C. S. Lewis in his first epigram opening *The Screwtape Letters* (1942)

> "Prof. Dumbledore, these boys have <u>flouted</u> the Decree for the Restriction of Underage Wizardry."
> Severus Snape, in J. K. Rowling, *Harry Potter and the Chamber of Secrets* (1998)

Flaunt and *flout* are so similar that people often say *flaunt* when they mean *flout,* and the results can be embarrassing. The *Oxford English Dictionary* lists several examples of that since the 1920s, including a slip by the brilliant playwright and composer Noël Coward and a gaffe by a prime minister. American leaders aren't immune, either. In 1979, President Jimmy Carter, asking the UN for sanctions against Iran, declared that Iran could not "flaunt…the will of the world community."[19] Even the usage expert Eric Partridge admitted to having written *flaunt* for *flout* in one of his books on language, and to having noticed it with horror later.[20]

Flaunt means to "show off or display ostentatiously."

To *flout* **is to "treat with disdain or openly disregard (a law, etc.)."**

Which version of the sentence below is correct?

(A) The freshmen flouted all of the rules of student conduct.

(B) The freshmen flaunted all of the rules of student conduct.

It's more likely that freshmen will disregard rules than that they will display them ostentatiously. Version A is probably the right choice.

HARDY or HEARTY

✳ *Hardy*

> "The sage-brush is a singularly hardy plant, and grows right in the midst of deep sand, and among barren rocks, where nothing else in the vegetable world would try to grow."
>
> Mark Twain, *Roughing It* (1872)

> "The river's earliest commerce was in great barges…. In time this commerce increased until it gave employment to hordes of rough and hardy men: uneducated, brave, suffering terrific hardships with sailor-like stoicism."
>
> Mark Twain, *Life on the Mississippi* (1883)

It takes a hardy athlete to complete the Iron Man Triathlon.

✳ *Hearty*

"When Johnny comes marching home again, hurrah, hurrah,
We'll give him a <u>hearty</u> welcome then, hurrah, hurrah."
"When Johnny Comes Marching Home" (1863)

"One <u>hearty</u> laugh together will bring enemies into a closer
communion of heart than hours spent on both sides in inward
wrestling with the mental demon of uncharitable feeling."
William James, American philosopher and psychologist (1842–
1910), "The Gospel of Relaxation," talk (1899)

Dorothy "ate a <u>hearty</u> breakfast and watched a wee Munchkin
baby, who played with Toto and pulled his tail."
L. Frank Baum, *The Wonderful Wizard of Oz* (1900)

"Mr. Roosevelt ... is so <u>hearty</u>, so straightforward, outspoken, and
so absolutely sincere. These qualities endear him to
me ... but ... they make of him a sufficiently queer president."
Mark Twain, speaking of President Theodore Roosevelt, in
Autobiography of Mark Twain, vol. 1 (2010)

These two words are easy to confuse, especially for those of us who pronounce them as if they were spelled the same. But they have different
origins and different meanings:

Hardy comes from an Old French word meaning "to harden, to make
bold."

Hearty comes from *heart,* an Old English word.

**Hardy suggests that something is hard in the sense of "not soft":
"strong, vigorous, bold," or "able to endure harsh conditions."**

a <u>hardy</u> plant
a <u>hardy</u> athlete

Hearty means "heartfelt, warm, enthusiastic, vigorous, or cheerful."

a <u>hearty</u> welcome
one <u>hearty</u> laugh

***Hearty* also means "nourishing."**

a <u>hearty</u> meal

And it means "having a good appetite."
Which is correct?

(A) In his book *Anatomy of an Illness* (1979), Norman Cousins wrote
that <u>hearty</u> belly laughter can give hours of pain-free sleep.
(B) In his book *Anatomy of an Illness* (1979), Norman Cousins
wrote that <u>hardy</u> belly laughter can give hours of pain-free sleep.

This passage refers to laughter that is heartfelt, or *hearty*. Version A is
correct.

HOLOCAUST: CAPITALIZED OR NOT?

Oprah: "After living through such an atrocity, was it possible for
you to be normal again—to go on with your life?"

Elie Wiesel: "What is abnormal is that I am normal. That I
survived the <u>Holocaust</u> and went on to love beautiful girls, to
talk, to write, to have toast and tea and live my life—that is what
is abnormal."

Elie Wiesel, Nobel Peace Prize–winning Romanian-born Jewish
American writer, professor, and activist, interviewed in "Oprah
Talks to Elie Wiesel," *O, the Oprah Magazine,* oprah.com, Nov.
2000

"AIDS: the new <u>holocaust</u>."
Sunday Telegraph, Nov. 15, 1987 (*OED*)

A *holocaust* was originally a sacrifice to God that was entirely consumed by fire. The word, which derives ultimately from the Greek for "burnt whole," came into English in the early 1300s. By the seventeenth century, *holocaust* came to refer more generally to any complete destruction, especially by fire or slaughter. In the early 1940s, the word *Holocaust* was being applied to the Nazi atrocities against the Jews, which were happening at that time.

Capitalize *Holocaust* when referring to the Nazi campaign of genocide against the Jews.

In other contexts, put *holocaust* in lowercase to describe massive destruction by fire or the large-scale killing of people.

Which version of the sentence below is correct?

(A) "For while the threat of nuclear <u>holocaust</u> has been significantly reduced, the world remains a very unsettled and dangerous place."

(B) "For while the threat of nuclear <u>Holocaust</u> has been significantly reduced, the world remains a very unsettled and dangerous place."
   William S. Cohen, testimony as secretary of defense–designate, before the Senate Armed Services Committee, Jan. 22, 1997

In this passage, *holocaust* refers to a possible future destruction, so it should be in lowercase, as in version A.

HURDLE or HURTLE

✳ *Hurdle*

"As in most pursuits, one's self is one of the biggest <u>hurdles</u> to get over."
   American actress, comedian, writer, and producer Lisa Kudrow, commencement address at Vassar College, May 24, 2010

"Players taunted them, slapped them with towels, and poured water over them.... Such attacks were routine for female sportswriters in the late '60s and '70s. Even as journalism opened up to allow women to cover professional athletics, they faced formidable <u>hurdles</u>."

> Adrienne Vogt, "A Girl in the Locker Room?!" *Newsweek*, July 17, 2013 (Lexis)

"City public school students and teachers could be downloading their textbooks from an iTunes- or Amazon-like platform, under a bid put out by the city. But the effort faces major <u>hurdles</u>, given some classrooms' slow Internet speeds, critics charge."

> Rachel Monahan, "Putting Mega-Bite on Schools," New York *Daily News*, Sept. 9, 2013 (Lexis)

✳ *Hurtle*

"Neck and neck they <u>hurtled</u> toward the Snitch."

> J. K. Rowling, *Harry Potter and the Sorcerer's Stone* (1997)

"Scientists are trying to find a way to protect Earth from the giant rocks which travel around the Milky Way.... The project, though, is a little late as a chunk of rock 400 times the [size of] the City of London is set to <u>hurtle</u> closer than a rock of its size has in a very long time."

> "Monster Rock, 400 Times the City of London, Hurtling Past Earth This Week," *Korea Times,* Jan. 29, 2012

Hurdle and *hurtle* are very different words with totally different linguistic origins, but a lot of people, including me, pronounce them as if they were exactly the same. And that makes it easy to confuse them.

A *hurdle* is a frame that runners jump over in a race, or an obstacle or barrier.

To *hurdle* is to run a race over hurdles, or to overcome obstacles as if they were hurdles.

one of the biggest <u>hurdles</u> to get over
they faced formidable <u>hurdles</u>

To *hurtle* means "to move or fall with great speed, especially noisily."

they <u>hurtled</u> toward the Snitch
is set to <u>hurtle</u> closer

Which version of the sentence below is correct?

(A) "San Jose State has already achieved remarkable results with online materials from edX, a nonprofit online provider, in its circuits course, a long-standing <u>hurdle</u> for would-be engineers."

(B) "San Jose State has already achieved remarkable results with online materials from edX, a nonprofit online provider, in its circuits course, a long-standing <u>hurtle</u> for would-be engineers."
Tamar Lewin, "Colleges Adapt Online Course to Ease Burden," nytimes.com, Apr. 29, 2013

In this sentence, *hurdle* is used figuratively to show that the course on circuits has been an obstacle for students. Version A is correct.

IMMANENT, IMMINENT, or EMINENT

✳ *Immanent*

"The Lord Himself beholds all; His <u>immanent</u> presence is pervading everywhere."
Shri Guru Granth Sahib (2008)

✳ *Imminent*

"Three times today you have defended me from <u>imminent</u> death."
Shakespeare, *Henry VI, Part 2* (1591)

"It is a curious fact about the British Islanders...that as danger comes nearer and grows they become progressively less nervous; when it is <u>imminent</u> they are fierce; when it is mortal they are fearless."

> Winston Churchill, *The Second World War* (1948)

"Since the 18th century, many Western intellectuals have predicted religion's <u>imminent</u> demise. Yet...in Britain three in four people, and in America four in five, declare allegiance to a religious faith."

> Jonathan Sacks, English former chief rabbi of the United Hebrew Congregations of the Commonwealth, in "The Moral Animal," nytimes.com, Dec. 23. 2012

Big budget cuts were <u>imminent</u>, but the candidates didn't say a word about them.

✳ *Eminent*

"I saw an old friend of mine at breakfast a while ago...and he gave me a lot of notices of my New York lecture delivered 18 months ago. I inflict them on you—for why shouldn't I?.... The *Tribune* notice is by Ned House, who ranks as the most <u>eminent</u> dramatic critic in the Union."

> Mark Twain, sending his wife the reviews of his 1866 lecture in New York, correspondence, Nov. 28, 1868

These three words sound almost alike and they're easy to confuse, but they have very different meanings.

An *eminent* person is distinguished, dignified in rank or station.

the most <u>eminent</u> dramatic critic in the Union

Eminently **means "notably, to a high degree."**

"The Emperor of Russia and his family conducted us all through the mansion themselves.... We spent half an hour idling through the palace, admiring the cozy apartments and the rich but <u>eminently</u> home-like appointments of the place, and then the Imperial family bade our party a kind goodbye, and proceeded to count the spoons."

Mark Twain, *The Innocents Abroad* (1869)

Immanent is a specialized word used mainly in philosophy and theology. It often describes God as **"inherent," "remaining in or pervading the universe."**

his <u>immanent</u> presence is pervading everywhere

Imminent refers to something hanging over your head, ready to happen, usually (but not always) in a threatening way.

defended me from <u>imminent</u> death

Which version of the sentence below is correct?

(A) "Censure is the tax a man pays to the public for being <u>imminent</u>."
(B) "Censure is the tax a man pays to the public for being <u>eminent</u>."
    Jonathan Swift, Anglo-Irish satirist, poet, cleric, and political pamphleteer (1667–1745), *Thoughts on Various Subjects* (1706)

In this passage, Swift's rather bitter point is that eminence attracts criticism. Version B is the right choice.

IN TO or INTO

✳ *In To*

He dropped <u>in to</u> see if she was feeling better.
I'm just popping <u>in to</u> offer my best wishes.
You must be logged <u>in to</u> post a comment.

✳ *Into*

"When you gaze long <u>into</u> an abyss, the abyss also gazes <u>into</u> you."

>Friedrich Nietzsche, German philologist, philosopher, social critic, and poet (1844–1900), *Beyond Good and Evil,* aphorism 146 (1886)

"This memory of ours stores up a most perfect record of the most useless facts and anecdotes and experiences. . . . Now, things that I have remembered are constantly popping <u>into</u> my head. And I am repeatedly startled by . . . their utter uselessness in being remembered at all."

>Mark Twain, "Morals and Memory," speech at Barnard College, Mar. 7, 1906

"Men buy <u>into</u> the idea that there is a path up to success. I think—speaking for myself—that women are more 360. We're looking all around—behind, in front, to the side. And we take a lot of other people <u>into</u> account in our decisions."

>Meryl Streep, interview in *Ladies' Home Journal,* Aug. 2009

Write *in to* as two words when *in* is part of a phrase (*broke in, came in, dropped in, looked in, walked in, stopped in,* etc.) and *to* means "in order to."

"They <u>stopped in to</u> wish us a happy anniversary" means that they paid us a quick visit in order to wish us a happy anniversary.

***Into* indicates movement or direction.** The movement can be literal or figurative.

You can <u>break into</u> song, or you can <u>break in to</u> rescue a pet from a fire.
You can <u>come into</u> a fortune, or you can <u>come in to</u> join a party.
You can <u>turn yourself into</u> a professional violinist by practicing, or you can <u>turn yourself in to</u> the police.

Which version of the sentence below is correct?

(A) "If you run <u>into</u> a wall, don't turn around and give up. Figure
out how to climb it, go through it, or work around it."

(B) "If you run <u>in to</u> a wall, don't turn around and give up. Figure
out how to climb it, go through it, or work around it."
Michael Jordan, quoted in csmonitor.com, Feb. 17, 2013

To <u>run into</u> something is to hit it while moving fast. So version A is
right.

Into also has the colloquial meaning of being "avidly interested in,
involved with, or knowledgeable about":

"Sorry, but I'm not <u>into</u> that."
urbandictionary.com

He's Just Not That <u>into</u> You
Title of a 2009 film based on Greg Behrendt and Liz
Tucillo's self-help book of the same name

Obviously, you should say this only in informal contexts.

IT'S or ITS

✳ *It's*

Groucho Marx, asked if he was enjoying a cricket match that had
been going on for hours, replied, "<u>It's</u> great. When does it start?"
Groucho Marx, attributed in *Daily Telegraph,* Dec. 13, 2005

"<u>It's</u> nice to be included in people's fantasies, but you also like to
be accepted for your own sake."
Marilyn Monroe, interview in *Life* magazine, Aug. 3, 1962

Oprah Winfrey, explaining that her name comes from the Bible: "<u>It's</u> misspelled. <u>It's</u> supposed to be *Orpah*."

> Oprah Winfrey, quoted in "The Ultimate O Interview," from the May 2010 issue of *O, the Oprah Magazine,* oprah.com

"I don't consider my own clothing to be outrageous.... The truth is that people just don't have the same references that I do. To me <u>it's</u> very beautiful and <u>it's</u> art, and to them <u>it's</u> outrageous and crazy."

> Lady Gaga, quoted in "35 Best Fashion Quotes of All Time," glamourmagazine.co.uk, Mar. 2013

✳ *Its*

"All happy families resemble one another; each unhappy family is unhappy in <u>its</u> own way."

> Leo Tolstoy, Russian writer and philosopher (1828–1920), *Anna Karenina* (1875–77)

"A lie will fly around the whole world while the truth is getting <u>its</u> boots on."

> Mark Twain, attributed

"Baseball—with <u>its</u> lore and legends, <u>its</u> cultural power and seasonal associations, <u>its</u> native authenticity, <u>its</u> simple rules and transparent strategies... was the literature of my boyhood."

> Philip Roth, award-winning American novelist, "My Baseball Years," op-ed, *New York Times,* Apr. 6, 1973

"I don't like clutter. I firmly believe there is a place for everything and everything should be in <u>its</u> place. And I know there's a name for people like me: neat."

> Ellen DeGeneres, quoted in David Hochman, "Ellen DeGeneres: Nice Girls Finish First," goodhousekeeping.com, Oct. 2011

If you've ever confused *it's* and *its,* that's understandable. These two forms came into regular use in the seventeenth century, and for two hundred years people couldn't decide which of them should show possession. Shakespeare apparently didn't use *its* for that purpose: he seems to have written *it* to mean "its":

> "It had <u>it</u> head bit off."
> *King Lear* (from the 1608 quarto)

The distinction that we use today didn't become standard until the nineteenth century and into the twentieth. Even now, you can see *it's* and *its* confused online, in people's correspondence, in ads, and just about everyplace else where there's no grammar checker to catch the error. One reason for the confusion is that *-'s* indicates possession after nouns. With pronouns, though, it doesn't. So **its shows possession, while *it's* is a contraction of *it is* or *it has*.**

It's easy to mix them up, especially when you're writing quickly. Just remember, when you show possession in pronouns, there's no apostrophe in *his, hers, ours,* or *yours,* and there's none in *its.* The same applies to *whose.*

Which versions of the sentences below are correct?

(A) "Well, all comedy starts with anger. You get angry and <u>it's</u> never for a good reason, right?"
(B) "Well, all comedy starts with anger. You get angry and <u>its</u> never for a good reason, right?"
> Jerry Seinfeld, quoted in David Steinberg, "Takes One to Know One," latimes.com, Nov. 30, 2008

(A) Justin Bieber's mom "is wary of show business and <u>its</u> potential consequences: 'We don't have yes-men around him. I don't want him being a diva.'"
(B) Justin Bieber's mom "is wary of show business and <u>it's</u> potential consequences: 'We don't have yes-men around him. I don't want him being a diva.'"
> Quoted in vanityfair.com, Jan. 4, 2011

Version A of Jerry Seinfeld's quotation above is right because *it's* is a contraction for *it is*.

Version A of the passage about Justin Bieber is correct because *its* refers to the potential consequences of show business.

The original draft of the U.S. Constitution reflected the uncertainty about *it's* and *its* in the eighteenth century. It said *it's* where our current rules call for *its:* "No State shall...lay any imposts or duties on imports or exports, except what may be absolutely necessary for executing <u>it's</u> inspection laws" (Article I, section 10).

LOOSE or LOSE

✳ *Loose*

"In Los Angeles all the <u>loose</u> objects in the country were collected, as if America had been tilted and everything that wasn't tightly screwed down had slid into Southern California."
 Saul Bellow, Canadian-born American Pulitzer Prize– and Nobel Prize–winning writer (1915–2005), *Seize the Day* (1956)

"The ideal attitude is to be physically <u>loose</u> and mentally tight."
 Arthur Ashe, champion American professional tennis player (1943–1993), quoted posthumously in *New York Times,* Feb. 8, 1993

"With animation, because you can draw anything, and do anything, and have the characters do whatever you want, the tendency is to be very <u>loose</u> with the boundaries and the rules."
 Matt Groening, American cartoonist, animator, screenwriter, producer, comedian, voice actor, and musician, quoted in Robert Lloyd, "*Futurama* Ends: The Matt Groening Interview, Part 2," latimes.com, July 24, 2013

✳ *Lose*

"To <u>lose</u> one parent, Mr. Worthing, may be regarded as a misfortune; to <u>lose</u> both looks like carelessness."
   Oscar Wilde, *The Importance of Being Earnest* (1895)

"You must not <u>lose</u> faith in humanity. Humanity is an ocean. If a few drops of the ocean are dirty, the ocean does not become dirty."
   Mahatma Gandhi, quoted in Anil Dutta Mishra, *Inspiring Thoughts of Mahatma Gandhi* (2008)

"What a waste it is to <u>lose</u> one's mind, or not to have a mind. How true that is."
   Dan Quayle, U.S. vice president, 1989–93, speech to United Negro College Fund (which had the slogan "A mind is a terrible thing to waste"), quoted in *New York Times,* May 26, 1989

If something is *loose*, it's not firmly fixed or it doesn't fit tightly. *Loose* also can mean "relaxed," "not strict, unrestrained." *Lose* can mean "to be deprived of" or "to suffer loss." When you *lose*, you are unsuccessful.
Which version of the sentence below is correct?

   (A) "Success is a lousy teacher. It seduces smart people into thinking they can't <u>lose</u>."
   (B) "Success is a lousy teacher. It seduces smart people into thinking they can't <u>loose</u>."
      Bill Gates, in *Impatient Optimist: Bill Gates in His Own Words* (2012)

Gates is warning against the feeling that you can't fail to win, or can't *lose.* Version A is correct.

MEAN or MEDIAN

"After Medicare was created in 1965, doctors' salaries actually increased, as demand for physicians' services skyrocketed. In

1940 ... the <u>mean</u> income for American physicians was about $50,000. By 1970, it was nearly $250,000."

> Sandeep Jauhar, "Out of Camelot, Knights in White Coats Lose Way," nytimes.com, Jan. 31, 2011

A question: "The *Washington Post* ran a front-page story on how half the country lives on less than the <u>median</u> income. Is this headline for real, or is it (as I suspect) a made-up anecdote?"

The reply: "By definition half the people are above and half are below the <u>median</u>. That's how <u>medians</u> work."

> Snopes.com, Jan. 9, 2012

"<u>Median</u> wages of production workers, who comprise 80% of the workforce, haven't risen in 30 years, adjusted for inflation."

> Robert Reich, American political economist, professor, author, and former secretary of labor, quoted in Sean Williams, "5 Reasons U.S. Wages Aren't Rising," www.fool.com, Nov. 6, 2012

If you're like me, your eyes nearly cross when you see discussions of statistics, especially when terms like *median* or *mean* appear. The fact that these words are somewhat similar makes it even harder to remember what each means. They're useful terms, though. And if you're not a specialist in math or the social sciences, you're likely to make a big impression if you get a chance to use one of them. The differences between these terms are fairly straightforward.

The *median* is the midpoint, with half of the numbers falling above it and half falling below it.

If the numbers are 1, 2, 3, 4, 5, the *median* is 3 (with two numbers above it and two below it).

The *arithmetic mean* is the average.

If the numbers are 1, 2, 3, 4, and 10, the *mean* is 4 (the total, 20, divided by 5, since there are five numbers in the set).

MYSTERIOUS or MYSTICAL

* *Mysterious*

"'As a rule,' said Holmes, 'the more bizarre a thing is the less <u>mysterious</u> it proves to be. It's your commonplace, featureless crimes which are really puzzling.'"

    Arthur Conan Doyle, *Adventures of Sherlock Holmes* (1892)

"There is a <u>mysterious</u> cycle in human events. To some generations much is given. Of other generations much is expected. This generation of Americans has a rendezvous with destiny."

    President Franklin D. Roosevelt, speech at 1936 Democratic National Convention, Philadelphia, June 27, 1936

"People always ask me, 'What do you think of Britney Spears? What do you think of this group or that one?' I always say, 'Well, they're great.' But...I think they all went too far. Their jeans got too low, their tops got too see-through. Personally, I think that [being] sexy is keeping yourself <u>mysterious</u>."

    Stevie Nicks, Grammy Award–winning American singer-songwriter and member of Fleetwood Mac, quoted in *Rolling Stone,* Oct. 10, 2002

* *Mystical, Mysticism*

"<u>Mysticism</u>...is essentially a movement of the heart, seeking to transcend the limitations of the individual standpoint and to surrender itself to ultimate Reality...purely from an instinct of love."

    Evelyn Underhill, *Mysticism* (1911; 1961 ed.)

"In <u>mysticism</u>...the attempt is given up to know God by thought, and it is replaced by the experience of union with God."

    Erich Fromm, *The Art of Loving* (1956)

"In my tradition, one must wait until one has learned a lot of Bible and Talmud and the Prophets to handle <u>mysticism</u>. This isn't instant coffee. There is no instant <u>mysticism</u>."

> Elie Wiesel, quoted in Jeff Chu, "10 Questions for Elie Wiesel," time.com, Jan. 22, 2006

"There are a lot of things that didn't kill the Mayans, [such as] global cataclysms prophesied by shamans and etched into ancient calendars. What did wipe them out was likely something that is far less <u>mystical</u>…climate change."

> Jeffrey Kluger, "Did Climate Change Kill the Mayans?" time.com, Nov. 9, 2012

Mysterious and *mystical* sound alike for a good reason: they come from the same Greek root, and they both deal with things that are hidden. The word *mystery* derives from the Greek for "secret thing." *Mystic* comes from the Greek for someone who has been initiated into secret rites and spiritual matters. *Mysticism* refers to the knowledge of spiritual mysteries or the experience of God or the Absolute. The term originated in ancient Greece, but *mysticism* is a vital element in Christianity, Judaism, Islam, and Eastern religious traditions and practices.[21]

Something is *mysterious* if it is very hard or impossible to explain, understand, or discover; obscure.

a <u>mysterious</u> cycle in human events

A *mysterious* person can be enigmatic, elusive, secretive.

being sexy is keeping yourself <u>mysterious</u>

If something is *mystical*, it has a spiritual nature or meaning that is beyond ordinary human understanding.

***Mysticism* involves learning hidden spiritual truths. Practitioners of *mysticism* often seek to transcend reason and have a direct experience or knowledge of God.**

Which version of the passage below is correct?

(A) "Not even the visionary or <u>mystical</u> experience ever lasts very
     long. It is for art to capture that experience."
(B) "Not even the visionary or <u>mysterious</u> experience ever lasts very
     long. It is for art to capture that experience."

> Salmon Rushdie, Booker Prize–winning British Indian novelist
> and essayist, "Is Nothing Sacred?," Herbert Read Memorial
> Lecture, London, Feb. 6, 1990

Since Rushdie's passage refers to visionary experience, he is speaking in a
spiritual sense. So the right choice is *mystical,* as in version A.

PASSED or PAST

✳ *Passed*

> "Let the word go forth from this time and place, to friend and
> foe alike, that the torch has been <u>passed</u> to a new generation of
> Americans."
>
> President John F. Kennedy, inaugural address, Jan. 20, 1961

In 2013, an asteroid <u>passed</u> within 17,200 miles of the surface of the
Earth, the closest approach ever recorded for an object of that size.

"In terms of actual laws or bills <u>passed</u>, the 113th Congress
[January 2013–January 2015] is headed toward historic levels of
unproductivity."

> Chris Cillizza, "Yes, President Obama Is Right. The 113th Congress
> Will Be the Least Productive in History," washingtonpost.com,
> Apr. 10, 2014

✳ *Past*

> "The <u>past</u> is never dead. It's not even <u>past</u>."
>
> William Faulkner, *Requiem for a Nun* (1950)

"For the <u>past</u> 33 years, I have looked in the mirror every morning and asked myself: 'If today were the last day of my life, would I want to do what I am about to do today?' And whenever the answer has been 'No' for too many days in a row, I know I need to change something."

Steve Jobs, commencement address at Stanford, June 12, 2005

"The only way to see the end of the hill is to go <u>past</u> it and realize you're going down."

Jerry Seinfeld, on why he ended his TV series while it was still rated number one, in *O, the Oprah Magazine,* oprah.com, Nov. 2007

Passed and *past* were originally the same word, which explains why they have the same sound. They both came from the verb *to pass.* In fact, until about 150 years ago, the spelling *past* could be used to mean "passed." We now write only *passed* as a verb, and we write *past* in all other uses of the word.

***Passed* refers to onward motion that has already happened. It has many meanings, some of which relate to physical movement, a satisfactory performance on a test, a missed opportunity, or the approval of a proposal or law.**

the torch has been <u>passed</u>
an asteroid <u>passed</u>
laws or bills <u>passed</u>

***Past* relates to a former time. It refers to something that is over, gone by, or previous.**

the <u>past</u> is never dead. It's not even <u>past</u>
the <u>past</u> 33 years

***Past* also can refer to a position or a distance that is beyond some point of reference.**

to go <u>past</u> it

Which version of the sentence below is correct?

(A) In February 2013, Congress <u>past</u> the Violence Against Women Act, expanding federal assistance in aiding victims of domestic and sexual abuse.

(B) In February 2013, Congress <u>passed</u> the Violence Against Women Act, expanding federal assistance in aiding victims of domestic and sexual abuse.

In the sentence above, since Congress voted to approve an act, *passed* is the right choice, as in version B.

PRINCIPAL or PRINCIPLE

✳ *Principal*

"Adam and Eve had many advantages, but the <u>principal</u> one was, they escaped teething."
  Mark Twain, *Pudd'nhead Wilson* (1894)

"If you pick up a starving dog and make him prosperous, he will not bite you. This is the <u>principal</u> difference between a dog and a man."
  Ibid.

"All animals, except man, know that the <u>principal</u> business of life is to enjoy it."
  Samuel Butler, English author (1835–1902), *The Way of All Flesh* (1903)

✳ *Principle*

"Cats seem to go on the <u>principle</u> that it never does any harm to ask for what you want."
  Joseph Wood Krutch, American naturalist (1893–1970), *Twelve Seasons* (1949)

"Those are my <u>principles</u>. If you don't like them, I have others."
> Attributed to Groucho Marx in *Legal Times,* Feb. 7, 1983, though
> the joke is old

"At the center of nonviolence stands the <u>principle</u> of love."
> Martin Luther King Jr., "Nonviolence and Racial Justice," *Christian
> Century*, Feb. 6, 1957

"I had many teachers that were great, positive role models and
taught me to be a good person and stand up and be a good man.
A lot of the <u>principles</u> they taught me still affect how I act
sometimes, and it's 30 years later. You think school ends when
it ends, but it doesn't."
> Kevin James, American actor, comedian, writer, and producer,
> quoted in sun-sentinel.com, Oct. 8, 2012

Have you ever noticed that *principal* has the sound of the word *prince* in
it? That's because it derives from the Latin word for *prince,* which had the
sense of "the first in importance." That gave *principal* its meaning today:

**Principal refers to the main, most important, or most excellent
person or thing.**

the <u>principal</u> difference
the <u>principal</u> business of life

A school's *principal* is its chief administrator.

> "My grandmother was a teacher, my sister was a teacher, my
> daughter was a teacher…and my son-in-law is a high school
> <u>principal</u>. I am surrounded."
> American actress Loni Anderson, interview in abilitymagazine.com

**More generally, a *principal* is a person in authority or in a leading
role or position.**

> In research projects, the lead scientist or engineer is called the PI,
> which stands for "<u>principal</u> investigator."

In later Latin, the word came to mean **the main or original sum that was invested or lent to someone.** That gives us the sense of the *principal* of a loan.

The word *principle* ultimately derives from the same Latin word as *principal,* but it has a very different meaning today.

A *principle* is a belief, rule, standard, truth, conviction, theory, law, or code.

I probably don't have to tell you that these two words are really easy to confuse. People mix them up a lot, and a word processor may not catch the mistake. So you need to be able to distinguish them on your own. One difference between them is that *principle* is a noun, not an adjective, while *principal* can be either. So you can be the *principal* player in a trade or a *principal* of a school.

Which are the correct versions of the passages below?

(A) Thomas Jefferson was the <u>principle</u> author of the Declaration of Independence.

(B) Thomas Jefferson was the <u>principal</u> author of the Declaration of Independence.

(A) Adam, explaining why he ate the forbidden fruit in Eden: Eve "brought some of those apples. I was obliged to eat them, I was so hungry. It was against my <u>principals</u>, but I find that <u>principals</u> have no real force except when one is well fed."

(B) Eve "brought some of those apples. I was obliged to eat them, I was so hungry. It was against my <u>principles</u>, but I find that <u>principles</u> have no real force except when one is well fed."

Mark Twain, *Extracts from Adam's Diary* (1904)

Since President Jefferson was the main, or *principal,* author of the Declaration of Independence, version B is correct in the first passage above.

In the quotation by Twain, Adam is referring to his convictions, or *principles,* as in Version B.

A tired old way to remember the spelling of *principal* is that the school *principal* is your **pal**. That memory trick is pathetic, I know. So it might be better to imagine that a **prince** is your **pal**, since the prince is the person in charge.[22]

PROPHECY or PROPHESY

✳ *Prophecy*

"If I have the gift of <u>prophecy</u> and can fathom all mysteries and all knowledge, and if I have a faith that can move mountains but have not love, I am nothing."
  1 Corinthians 13:2 (New International Version)

"<u>Prophecy</u> is a good line of business, but it is full of risks."
  Mark Twain, *Following the Equator* (1897)

"The visions we offer our children shape the future.... Often they become self-fulfilling <u>prophecies</u>. Dreams are maps."
  Carl Sagan and Ann Druyan, *Pale Blue Dot: A Vision of the Human Future in Space* (1994)

✳ *Prophesy*

"It was from Jaffa that Jonah sailed when he was told to go and <u>prophesy</u> against Nineveh, and no doubt it was not far from the town that the whale threw him up when he discovered that he had no ticket."
  Mark Twain, *The Innocents Abroad* (1869)

"I always avoid <u>prophesying</u> beforehand, because it is much better policy to <u>prophesy</u> after the event has already taken place."
  Winston Churchill, press conference, Cairo, Feb. 1, 1943

Prophecy and *prophesy* come from the Greek for "speaker for or before (someone)." A prophet was a divinely inspired spokesman or interpreter of the will or intentions of God or a divinity.

One of these two English words is a noun and the other is a verb, but don't feel too bad if you're not sure which is which. It took the English centuries to agree about that. Both were spelled either *prophecy* or *prophesy* until about the year 1700, when the modern spellings started to become fixed. The distinction is now standard: **prophecy is the noun and *prophesy* is the verb.**[23]

Prophecy refers to divinely inspired speech or writing. It is a declaration of God's intentions or a prediction of the future as a revelation from God.

Prophecy also can refer to a prediction based on intuition or conjecture.

To *prophesy* is to speak or write through divine inspiration, or to foretell an event that way.

Someone also can *prophesy* in a secular sense, predicting the future based on intuition or conjecture.

Prime Minister Churchill, for example, made no claim of divine assistance when he spoke about *prophesying* "after the event" in the quotation near the top of this lesson.

Remember, *prophesy* ends with the sound of the word **sigh**, and rhymes with *on* **high**.

Which version of the sentence below is correct?

(A) "<u>Prophesy</u> upon these bones, and say to them, 'O ye dry bones, hear the word of the Lord.'"

(B) "<u>Prophecy</u> upon these bones, and say to them, 'O ye dry bones, hear the word of the Lord.'"

Ezekiel 37: 4 (King James Version)

In this passage, God is telling the prophet Ezekiel to foretell events, or *prophesy*, as in version A.

RAVAGE or RAVISH

✻ *Ravage*

In her 1970 hit song "Big Yellow Taxi," Joni Mitchell personifies the earth as our beautiful sister and asks what people have done to her. They've ravaged and plundered her, ripped her and stuck her with knives, she answers.

"Citrus Disease with No Cure Is Ravaging Florida's Groves"
Headline, *New York Times,* May 10, 2013 (Lexis)

"After nearly a decade, David Bowie re-emerged bleak and brittle with *The Next Day,* an album that confronts mortality with bitter fury…as he sees time ravage youth, idealism, love, and hope."
Jon Pareles, "And a Teenager Shall Lead Them," nytimes.com, Dec. 15, 2013

✻ *Ravish*

"Some things can't be ravished. You can't ravish a can of sardines."
D. H. Lawrence, *Lady Chatterley's Lover* (1928)

"For a Viking of character, it seems to have been all in a good day's work to bash in the head of a peasant, desecrate a church, humiliate a king, ravish a maid, and discover America."
Mark Stevens, "Viking Booty and Beauty," *Newsweek,* Oct. 6, 1980 (Lexis)

"The problem…is that a vampire who doesn't ravish young virgins, or at least scarily nuzzle their flesh, isn't much of a vampire or much of an interesting character."
Manohla Dargis, American film critic, review of *The Twilight Saga: New Moon,* in "Abstinence Makes the Heart…Oh, You Know," *New York Times,* Nov. 20, 2009 (Lexis)

In their earliest English uses, *ravage* and *ravish* signified violent, harmful acts. They came from the same Old French word that meant "to seize, carry away," and in English they referred to powerful and destructive forces and actions. But they developed in very different ways. Today, to *ravage* still involves inflicting great harm. But *ravish* now usually means to "carry away" in a romantic sense. Strange as it may seem, from those harsh origins came the word *ravishing*.

To *ravage* means "to plunder" or "to cause extensive and severe damage."

they've <u>ravaged</u> and plundered her
<u>ravaging</u> Florida's groves
he sees time <u>ravage</u> youth

To *ravish* is "to carry (a woman) off by force," "to rape." This sense is now archaic and it has a literary quality that masks the brutality of rape.

After *ravish* had been in the language for several decades, it came to refer figuratively to a very different kind of carrying away: transporting the mind by the force of an emotion, especially delight or ecstasy. That gave us the adjective *ravishing*, meaning "exciting ecstasy or sensuous pleasure, entrancing."

In a weakened sense, *ravishing* commonly means "very beautiful, gorgeous":

> "An actress…usually dresses in the very latest fashion and has her photographs airbrushed into superhuman oblivion. Julianne Moore, while she looks <u>ravishing</u> in films and on the red carpet, and even in her sweatpants at morning drop-off…is not such an actress."
>
> Deborah Needleman, "The Taste Divide," *New York Times,* Apr. 12, 2013 (Lexis)

Which version of the passage below is correct?

(A) "Rejoice in the wife of thy youth…and be thou <u>ravished</u> always with her love."

(B) "Rejoice in the wife of thy youth...and be thou <u>ravaged</u> always with her love."

> Proverbs 5:18–19 (American Standard Version)

In the proverb above, men are told to be filled with delight, or *ravished,* as in version A.

REGARD or REGARDS

✳ *Regard*

"Simply seek happiness, and you are not likely to find it. Seek to create and love <u>without regard to</u> your happiness, and you will likely be happy much of the time."

> M. Scott Peck, American psychiatrist and author (1936–2005), *The Different Drum: Community Making and Peace* (1987)

"It is capitalist America that produced the modern independent woman. Never in history have women had more freedom of choice <u>in regard to</u> dress, behavior, career, and sexual orientation."

> Camille Paglia, American feminist social critic and professor, *Sex, Art, and American Culture: Essays* (1992)

"In the past 30 years, officials of the Iranian regime and its apologists have labeled criticism, especially <u>with regard to</u> women's rights, as anti-Islamic and pro-Western, justifying its brutalities by ascribing them to Islam and Iran's culture."

> Azar Nafisi, "Iran's Women: Canaries in the Coal Mine," huffingtonpost.com, May 28, 2013

✳ *Regards*

"<u>As regards</u> intellectual work, it remains a fact, indeed, that great decisions in the realm of thought, and momentous discoveries, and solutions of problems are only possible to an individual working in solitude."

Sigmund Freud, *Group Psychology and the Analysis of the Ego* (1921)

In regard to, with regard to, without regard to, and *as regards* **are all Standard English.** Some twentieth-century commentators criticized these phrases as too wordy and suggested that we say *about, on,* or *concerning* instead. **The choice is purely a matter of style, though, so use your own judgment.**

In regards to or *with regards to* are mainly used orally and are rare in edited texts.[24] American critics in particular condemn these phrases. Only 6 percent of the *American Heritage* Usage Panel accepted *in regards to* in phrases like "in regards to health care."

Which version of the sentence below is correct?

(A) "I have placed you at the head of the Army of the Potomac.... And yet I think it best for you to know that there are some things <u>in regards to</u> which I am not quite satisfied with you."

(B) "I have placed you at the head of the Army of the Potomac.... And yet I think it best for you to know that there are some things <u>in regard to</u> which I am not quite satisfied with you."

Abraham Lincoln, letter to Gen. Joseph Hooker, Jan. 26, 1863

Version B is the right choice.

ROUT or ROUTE

✳ *Rout*

"Where's the old love, Apple? Wall Street has turned viciously on its one time iDarling. The <u>rout</u> in Apple's share price...has many wondering when, and where, all of this will end."

Nathaniel Popper and Nick Wingfield, "After Apple's Rise, A Bruising Fall," nytimes.com, Apr. 18, 2013

"Getting back to the NBA Finals isn't nearly enough to satisfy [LeBron] James or the Miami Heat. For the third straight year, the Heat are headed to the title round.... It could have ended on Monday, of course, with the Heat coming off their worst offensive outing of the year in Game 6. They responded with a <u>rout</u>.... 'By any means necessary...we took care of business,' James said."

Tim Reynolds, "Heat Top Pacers for East Title and Date with Spurs," Associated Press, June 3, 2013

"The worst emerging market <u>rout</u> in five years has raised fresh fears of global contagion."

Ambrose Evans-Prichard, "Record Market Rout Punctures Feelgood Factor in the Alps," *Daily Telegraph* (London), Jan. 25, 2014 (Lexis)

❋ *Route*

Oprah Winfrey: "Where does your strong work ethic come from?"
Sean Combs: "My mother worked three jobs and my grandmother worked two. At an early age, I started my own paper <u>route</u>. Once I saw how you could service people and do a good job and get paid for it, I just wanted to be the best I could be in whatever I did."

Sean Combs, American rapper, record producer, entrepreneur, and actor, quoted in "Oprah Talks to Sean Combs," *O, the Oprah Magazine,* oprah.com, Nov. 2006

The president of San Jose State University predicts, "Traditional teaching will be disappearing in five to seven years...as more professors come to realize that lectures are not the best <u>route</u> to student engagement, and cash-strapped universities continue to seek cheaper instruction."

Tamar Lewin, "Colleges Adapt Online Course to Ease Burden," nytimes.com, Apr. 29, 2013

NBC took a logical <u>route</u> in choosing Jimmy Fallon to replace Jay Leno as host of *The Tonight Show*. Fallon's videos and use of social media appeal to younger viewers.

A *rout* is a disorderly retreat or a resounding defeat.

the worst emerging market <u>rout</u> in five years

A *rout* also be the act of decisively defeating an enemy or an opponent.

they responded with a <u>rout</u>

A *route* is a course taken from one point to another.
Figuratively, a *route* is a way of doing or achieving something.

the best <u>route</u> to student engagement
NBC took a logical <u>route</u> in choosing Jimmy Fallon

Route can be pronounced either with the sound of the word *root* or rhyming with *out*. Even if you normally say *route* so it rhymes with *out*, the chances are good that you say it in *Route 95* and *en route* so it sounds like *root*.[25]

Which version of the sentence below is correct?

(A) Google Maps offers real-time traffic reports and public transportation <u>routes</u>.
(B) Google Maps offers real-time traffic reports and public transportation <u>routs</u>.

This sentence refers to courses from one place to another, or *routes*. Version A is correct.

SET or SIT

✳ *Set*

"Whoever undertakes to <u>set himself up</u> as a judge of Truth and Knowledge is shipwrecked by the laughter of the gods."

> Albert Einstein, in *Essays Presented to Leo Baeck on the Occasion of His Eightieth Birthday* (1954)

"Here men from the planet Earth first <u>set foot upon</u> the moon, July 1969, A.D. We came in peace for all mankind."

> Plaque left on the moon by Neil Armstrong

"Despite the fact that he had spent every waking moment of the past few days hoping desperately that Dumbledore would indeed come to fetch him, Harry felt distinctly awkward as they <u>set off</u> down Privet Drive together."

> J. K. Rowling, *Harry Potter and the Half-Blood Prince* (2005)

"The thing you fear most has no power. Your fear of it is what has the power. Facing the truth really will <u>set you free</u>."

> Oprah Winfrey, quoted in forbes.com, Sept. 27, 2012

✳ *Sit*

"I have a dream that one day on the red hills of Georgia, sons of former slaves and sons of former slave-owners will be able to <u>sit</u> down together at the table of brotherhood."

> Martin Luther King Jr., "I Have a Dream" speech, Washington, D.C., Aug. 28, 1963

"I was a strange, loud little kid who could <u>sit</u> at the piano and kill a Beethoven piece."

> Lady Gaga, quoted in Jonathan Van Meter, "Lady Gaga: Our Lady of Pop," *Vogue*, Mar. 2011

To *set* means "to cause to sit" or "to cause to be in a certain position."

To *sit* means "to be seated."

Since about the year 1300, though, *set* also has been used to mean "sit." Thomas Jefferson used it in that sense. So did Dickens and Thackeray, though they put it in the mouths of rural and less educated characters.[26] *Set* meaning "sit" is now mainly found in speech, not edited writing. It's generally considered dialectal and uneducated, as in the phrase *set a spell,* meaning "sit for a while." In some contexts, though, it's standard. The sun *sets,* for example. So do plaster and concrete. It's also standard to say that a chicken *sets* on an egg—though I have to confess that I've never said that and don't ever expect to.

Also, since about 1300, *sit* has sometimes been used to mean *set* in the sense of causing someone to sit.[27] It's now standard to say this in sentences like *They <u>sat</u> us at the children's table.*

There are many phrases involving *set,* including *set a trap, set up, set in motion, set in place,* and these from the passages at the top of this lesson:

<u>set himself up</u>
<u>set foot upon</u>
<u>set forth</u>
<u>set off</u>
<u>set free</u>

There are also many phrases containing *sit,* including *sitting pretty, sit in judgment, sit for an exam, sit around, sit on one's hands, sit tight,* and *sit in.*

Remember, in standard usage, you tell a dog to <u>sit</u>, but you can <u>set</u> a bone in front of him.

Which version of the sentence below is correct?

(A) "By and by it got sort of lonesome, and so I went and <u>set</u> on the bank and listened to the current swashing along."
(B) "By and by it got sort of lonesome, and so I went and <u>sat</u> on the bank and listened to the current swashing along."

    Huck, in Mark Twain, *Adventures of Huckleberry Finn* (1885)

Twain has Huck speak colloquially when he says that he "set on the bank." The correct form in Standard English would be *sat*, as in version B.

> *Set* is a different word from *sit* because of a pattern in grammar that's older than English. In the language spoken by the ancestors of the Angles and the Saxons, if you changed a vowel sound you could give certain verbs the meaning of making something happen. That's why to *lay* means to make something *lie* down. Strange as it may seem, it's why to *drench* means to cause something to *drink* up a liquid. It's also why *set* means to make something *sit*.[28]

STATIONARY or STATIONERY

✳ *Stationary*

"All is flux; nothing is <u>stationary</u>."
> Heraclitus, Greek philosopher, ca. 500 B.C., quoted in Aristotle, *De Caelo*

"Since the sun remains <u>stationary</u>, whatever appears as a motion of the sun is really due rather to the motion of the earth."
> Nicolaus Copernicus, Polish mathematician and astronomer (1473–1543), in *De Revolutionibus Orbium Coelestium* (1543), translation in Jean Dietz Moss, *Novelties in the Heavens* (1993)

There are two kinds of home generators: portable models, which can be stored until they are needed, and <u>stationary</u> models, which are installed permanently outside the home and start automatically during an electrical outage.

✳ *Stationery*

"I've written on legal pads, hotel <u>stationery</u>, anything I can get my hands on. I have no finickiness about anything like that."

> Woody Allen, on writing down ideas for his movies, interviewed
> by Michiko Kakutani, "Woody Allen: The Art of Humor No. 1,"
> parisreview.org, Fall 1995

These words look alike because they both derive from the same Latin word. They had different histories, though, and they came into English with different meanings. *Stationary* means "being in a fixed position." *Stationery*, by contrast, referred to items bought from a station**er**, a tradesman who sold writing materials in a fixed station or shop (rather than as a traveling salesman).

A *stationary* thing stays in one place. It's unmoving or fixed in one spot. *Stationery* refers to paper, envelopes, and other writing materials.

Here's one way to remember the distinction: the **-er** toward the end of *stationery* can remind you of *lett**er*** or *pap**er***.

Which version of the sentence below is correct?

(A) We need envelopes and other <u>stationary</u>.
(B) We need envelopes and other <u>stationery</u>.

The sentence above refers to writing and office materials, or *stationery,* so version B is the right choice.

Here's a joke:

> "I saw a <u>stationery</u> store move."
>> Jay London, American comedian, cited in Wikiquote.com

The joke is that the store selling *stationery* wasn't *stationary*. It's a pun. (I didn't say it was funny.)

THAN or THEN

✳ *Than*

> "In the new code of laws which I suppose it will be necessary for
> you to make, I desire you would remember the ladies, and be

more generous and favorable to them <u>than</u> your ancestors. Do not put such unlimited power into the hands of the husbands."

> Abigail Adams, letter to her husband, John Adams, Mar. 31, 1776

"They spell it *Vinci* and pronounce it *Vinchy;* foreigners always spell better <u>than</u> they pronounce."

> Mark Twain, *The Innocents Abroad* (1869)

"Income tax has made more liars out of the American people <u>than</u> golf."

> Will Rogers, "Helping the Girls with Their Income Taxes," *The Illiterate Digest* (1924)

"I had a better year <u>than</u> he did."

> Babe Ruth, on why he demanded a higher salary than President Herbert Hoover's in 1930, quoted in *New York Times,* Aug. 19, 1948

"I'd rather be dead <u>than</u> sing 'Satisfaction' when I'm 45."

> Mick Jagger, English musician, singer, songwriter, actor, and founding member of the Rolling Stones, quoted in *People* magazine, June 9, 1975

"At the end of the day there's probably nothing that makes me feel better <u>than</u> junk food and reality TV."

> Jennifer Lawrence, quoted on The Insider at Yahoo, celebrity .yahoo.com, Jan. 30, 2014

✳ *Then*

"If at first you don't succeed, try, try, again. <u>Then</u> quit. There's no use being a damn fool about it."

> W. C. Fields, attributed

"If you have an important point to make…don't try to be subtle or clever. Use a pile driver. Hit the point once. <u>Then</u> come back and hit it again. <u>Then</u> hit it a third time—a tremendous whack."

> Winston Churchill, 1936, quoted by Edward, Duke of Windsor, "A King's Story, Part I," *Life,* May 22, 1950

"If you are lucky enough to have lived in Paris as a young man, <u>then</u> wherever you go for the rest of your life, it stays with you, for Paris is a moveable feast."
    Ernest Hemingway, *A Moveable Feast* (1964)

"Sure, I've done movies in which I was embarrassed by my performance, or might not have cared for a co-star.... <u>Then</u> I'd have to tell lies, like, 'Oh we loved each other; everything was perfect!'"
    Sandra Bullock, Academy Award–winning American actress and producer, quoted in Guy Adams, "Sandra Bullock: America's $56m Sweetheart," independent.co.uk, Aug. 7, 2010

"An unemployed graphic designer named Charlie Schmidt recorded his cat Fatso playing a keyboard in 1986. It wasn't until 2009, however, that Fatso—by <u>then</u> deceased—gained fame on YouTube as 'Keyboard Cat.'"
    Dashka Slater, "Cat Videos," nytimes.com, June 9, 2013

If you've ever looked at online conversations or users' comments, you may have noticed that people confuse *than* and *then* a lot. I admit, it drives me a little crazy when a student does that repeatedly. But the confusion is understandable, since these words look very similar to each other, and they have almost the same sound in some American dialects. In fact, *than* and *then* were originally the same word. The spelling distinction between them has been settled for about four hundred years, though, so follow these simple rules:

Than is used in comparisons or contrasts.

It also commonly appears in phrases like *other than, rather than,* and *different(ly) than.*

See COMPARISONS; DIFFERENT FROM or DIFFERENT THAN; and I or ME in the Tricky Words section.

Then means "at that time" or "next."

<u>then</u> quit
<u>then</u> come back
<u>then</u> hit it a third time

Then also can mean "therefore, in that case."

<u>then</u> wherever you go

Which version of the sentence below is correct?

(A) "Get your facts first and <u>then</u> you can distort them as much as you please."
(B) "Get your facts first and <u>than</u> you can distort them as much as you please."
> Mark Twain, quoted in Rudyard Kipling's *From Sea to Sea: Letters of Travel* (1899)

In this sentence, Twain is saying "at that time," or *then*. Version A is correct.

THEIR, THERE, or THEY'RE

✳ *Their*

> "Dear Charley,
> "The Committee of the Public Library of Concord, Mass., have … expelled Huck from <u>their</u> library as 'trash and suitable only for the slums.' That will sell 25,000 copies for us."
> > Mark Twain, referring to *Adventures of Huckleberry Finn*, correspondence, Mar. 18, 1885

> "It's the great secret of doctors, known only to <u>their</u> wives but still hidden from the public: most things get better by themselves; most things, in fact, are better in the morning."
> > Lewis Thomas, American physician, writer, researcher, and policy adviser (1913–1993), quoted in *New York Times Magazine*, July 4, 1976

> "The oppressed and the oppressor alike are robbed of <u>their</u> humanity."
> > Nelson Mandela, *Long Walk to Freedom* (1995)

"You can question [people's] views and <u>their</u> judgment without questioning <u>their</u> motives or their patriotism."

> President Barack Obama, commencement address at the University of Michigan, May 1, 2010

About Emma Stone: "A throwback to the giddily verbal screen actresses of the 1930s, Stone has that quality audiences have always loved in <u>their</u> stars: she seems to be enjoying herself. Not only does she know her way around a wisecrack…she exudes a fresh-faced decency that makes her instantly likeable."

> John Powers, "Emma Stone: Playing It Cool," *Vogue*, Mar. 2011

✳ *There*

"You've got to be careful if you don't know where you're going, [be]cause you might not get <u>there</u>."

> Yogi Berra, *The Yogi Book* (1998)

"It gets late early out <u>there</u>."

> Ibid.

About Lady Gaga: "<u>There are</u> plenty of comparisons that could be made with Madonna, such as the Italian parentage, her Catholic upbringing, and being signed to a major label as a teenager."

> John Dingwall, "The Fear Factor," *Daily Record* [Glasgow, Scotland], Nov. 27, 2009

"Ladies and gentlemen…as I set off for exciting new career opportunities, I just want to make one thing clear to everyone listening out <u>there</u>: I will do nudity."

> Conan O'Brien, American TV host, comedian, writer, producer, and musician, last monologue as host of the *Tonight Show*, Jan. 22, 2010

✳ *They're*

"That's the way with these directors: <u>they're</u> always biting the hand that lays the golden egg."

Samuel Goldwyn, mixing metaphors, quoted in Alva Johnston, *The Great Goldwyn* (1937)

About mothers: "There's always been something mystical and reverent about them. They're the Walter Cronkites of the human race."

Erma Bombeck, *If Life Is a Bowl of Cherries, What Am I Doing in the Pits?* (1978); Walter Cronkite (1916–2009) was a widely trusted American broadcast journalist, anchorman of the *CBS Evening News* for nineteen years

"Heroes may not be braver than anyone else. They're just braver five minutes longer."

President Ronald Reagan, "Remarks on Presenting the 1980 and 1981 Young American Medals for Bravery and Service," Dec. 22, 1982

People "with dementia are still people, and they still have stories, and they still have character, and they're all individuals, and they're all unique."

Carey Mulligan, quoted in Adam Brimelow, "Carey Mulligan Supports Bid to Raise Dementia Awareness," BBC News, bbc.co.uk, May 21, 2012

It's not unusual to see *their, there,* and *they're* confused with each other in casual writing. Here are some simple guidelines for when to use each:

Their indicates possession:

their wives
their humanity
their motives

There means "in or at that place," "to that place," "not here."

you might not get there
it gets late early out there

It also can mean "in that respect or in that matter."

You've got me there means that you've made a valid point and I can't respond to it.

The phrases *there is* and *there are* indicate that something exists.

> "There <u>is</u> no place <u>like home</u>."
> Dorothy, in L. Frank Baum, *The Wonderful Wizard of Oz* (1900)

<u>There are</u> plenty of comparisons that could be made with Madonna.

***They're* is a contraction of *they are*.**

they're always biting the hand

Here are ways to be sure you've chosen the right one of these three words:

(1) If you can substitute "they are" for the word, *they're* is correct.
(2) Remember that ***their*** has the word ***heir*** inside it. That can remind you that *their* indicates possession. I know, this idea is pretty lame, but it might work.
(3) In every other case, *there* is the right choice. Keep in mind that it has the word ***here*** in it.[29]

Which version of the sentence below is correct?

(A) "I don't trust books. <u>Their</u> all fact, no heart."
(B) "I don't trust books. <u>There</u> all fact, no heart."
(C) "I don't trust books. <u>They're</u> all fact, no heart."
> Stephen Colbert, on *The Colbert Report,* Oct. 17, 2005

In the sentence above, Stephen Colbert is saying *they are,* or *they're,* as in version C.

WHO'S or WHOSE

✳ *Who's*

"<u>Who's</u> on First?"
> Comedy routine made famous by American comedy duo Bud Abbott and Lou Costello, ca. 1937

"I've been in <u>*Who's*</u> *Who,* and I know what's what, but it'll be the first time I ever made the dictionary."
> Mae West, letter to Royal Air Force, 1941, after the RAF's term for inflatable life jackets, "Mae Wests," was entered into a dictionary, *Goodness Had Nothing to Do with It* (1959)

"How can you expect a man <u>who's</u> warm to understand one <u>who's</u> cold?"
> Alexander Solzhenitsyn, Russian novelist, *One Day in the Life of Ivan Denisovich* (1962)

"Anyone <u>who's</u> done a musical knows—whether you're dancing or not, physically it's the most difficult thing you can do."
> Hugh Jackman, quoted in Helen Jackson, "Hugh Jackman Went a Little Wolverine on Tom Hooper to Land *Les Misérables* Role," movieline.com, Dec. 7, 2012

✳ *Whose*

"Conscience is a mother-in-law <u>whose</u> visit never ends."
> H. L. Mencken, *A Mencken Chrestomathy,* "This and That" (1949)

"The Lord of the Ring is not Frodo, but the master of the Dark Tower of Mordor, <u>whose</u> power is again stretching out over the world!"
> Gandalf, in J. R. R. Tolkien, *The Lord of the Rings: The Fellowship of the Ring* (1954)

"A religious man is a person who holds God and man in one thought at one time... <u>whose</u> greatest passion is compassion, <u>whose</u> greatest strength is love and defiance of despair."

Abraham Joshua Heschel, Polish-born American rabbi, theologian, philosopher, and professor (1907–1972), "What Ecumenism Is," *Moral Grandeur and Spiritual Audacity: Essays* (1996)

"The reason I talk to myself is that I'm the only one <u>whose</u> answers I accept."

George Carlin, *Napalm and Silly Putty* (2001)

"Hang out with people better than you.... Pick out associates <u>whose</u> behavior is better than yours and you'll drift in that direction."

Warren Buffett, quoted in Jason Zweig, "How Do You Learn from a Master?" cnnmoney.com, May 3, 2004

Johnny Depp, <u>whose</u> character in *Pirates of the Caribbean,* Jack Sparrow, is based on Keith Richards, called Richards "the maestro, my hero, my friend."

Rolling Stone, Nov. 12, 2009

"I wanted to be a skinny little ballerina, but I was a voluptuous little Italian girl <u>whose</u> dad had meatballs on the table every night."

Lady Gaga, quoted in Paul Thompson, "'I Used to Throw Up Because I Felt Fat," dailymail.co.uk, Feb. 9, 2012

People often confuse *who's* and *whose* out of carelessness. The difference between them is simple: **Who's is a contraction for "who is" or "who has." Whose means "belonging to" or "associated with."**

Which version of the sentences below is correct?

(A) "A statesman is a politician <u>who's</u> been dead for 10 or 15 years."
(B) "A statesman is a politician <u>whose</u> been dead for 10 or 15 years."

Harry S. Truman, quoted in *New York World Telegram and Sun,* Apr. 12, 1958

In the passage above, version A is correct because President Truman used *who's* as a contraction of "who has."

* *Can Whose Refer to Things?*

The distinction between *who's* and *whose* is straightforward. A more contested issue is whether *whose* must refer only to people, or if you also can say it to refer to things. English doesn't have a word to express the possessive form of *that* or *which,* so *whose* has been used in that role since the fourteenth century. Shakespeare used the word that way. So did John Milton, Alexander Pope, and William Wordsworth, and that's pretty good company to be in. Eighteenth-century grammarians were skeptical about that usage, though, and their doubts gave rise to the folk belief that *whose* can only refer to humans. Twentieth-century commentators, led by the formidable H. W. Fowler, forcefully dismissed that idea. Good writers today often say *whose* to refer to things, since it's more graceful and economical than saying *of which*, and many stylists are open to this: 80 percent of the *Harper Dictionary* Usage Panel, for example, said that there's no merit at all to the claim that *whose* can only refer to people. About the same number of panelists thought that it's time to bury that idea for good.[30]

I recommend that you feel free to say *whose* to refer to people, animals, or things.

If you use *whose* as the first word in a question, though, it normally should refer to people or animals:

<u>Whose</u> bone is that on our new sofa, Spot's or Fido's?

YOU'RE or YOUR

* *You're*

"Don't be so humble. <u>You're</u> not that great."
   Golda Meir, Israeli prime minister, 1969–74, quoted in *New York Times,* Mar. 18, 1969

"I heard you call me immature earlier. Well, <u>you're</u> just a big poop head."

> Jon Lovitz, American comedian, actor, and singer, quoted in Norman H. Finkelstein, *Jewish Comedy Stars: Classic to Cutting Edge* (2010)

"I was performing in New York and my friends started to call me Gaga. They said I was very theatrical.... So they said, '<u>You're</u> Gaga.'"

> Lady Gaga, interviewed by Barbara Walters, quoted in ABCnews. go.com, Jan. 21, 2010

George Clooney, on having been ambushed in Africa: "You can't pull out your... 1999 Sexiest Man Alive *People* magazine and say, 'You really shouldn't kill me. <u>You're</u> doing the whole country a huge disservice.'"

> Quoted in Nigel Perry, "George Clooney's Thoughts for Today," esquire.com, Sept. 30, 2011

"Does any new parent, even if <u>you're</u> not a first-time parent, ever really know what to do?"

> Robert Downey Jr. on becoming a father, interviewed in *Esquire,* May 2012, quoted in huffingtonpost.com, Apr. 19, 2012

"VMAs 2014: What to Expect (When <u>You're</u> Expecting Beyoncé, Taylor Swift, and More)"

> Headline describing the 2014 MTV Video Music Awards, time. com, Aug. 21, 2014

✳ *Your*

"'You have still got the ring in <u>your</u> pocket,' said the wizard. "'Well, so I have!' cried Bilbo."

> J. R. R. Tolkien, *The Lord of the Rings: The Fellowship of the Ring,* ch. 1 (1954)

"Will the people in the cheaper seats clap <u>your</u> hands? All the rest of you, if you'll just rattle <u>your</u> jewelry ..."

> John Lennon, English singer-songwriter and founding member of the Beatles (1940–1980), at the Royal Variety Performance, Nov. 4, 1963

"When you're part of a team, you stand up for your teammates. <u>Your</u> loyalty is to them."

> Yogi Berra, in Yogi Berra and Dave Kaplan, *When You Come to a Fork in the Road, Take It!* (2002)

Questionnaire: "What is <u>your</u> idea of perfect happiness?"
Louis C.K.: "Not ever having to fill out this questionnaire."

> Louis C.K., referring to a questionnaire for *Vanity Fair,* in vanityfair.com, Jan. 2013

You're is a contraction of "you are."

<u>you're</u> not that great
<u>you're</u> Gaga
<u>you're</u> doing the whole country a huge disservice

Your indicates possession.

in <u>your</u> pocket
clap <u>your</u> hands
rattle <u>your</u> jewelry
<u>your</u> idea of perfect happiness

Which version of the passage below is correct?

(A) "<u>You're</u> not a star until they can spell <u>your</u> name in Karachi."
(B) "<u>Your</u> not a star until they can spell <u>you're</u> name in Karachi."

> Humphrey Bogart, quoted in *Concise Columbia Dictionary of Quotations* (1989)

This passage contains, first, the contraction of you are, or *you're;* then it refers to someone's own name as *your* name. Version A is correct.

CHAPTER 6

Plurals

Quick, how do you spell the plural of *potato*? What's the plural of *tomato*? If you're like me, there are times when you're a little unsure about spelling even some common plural words. That just illustrates how messy English can be. The usual way to pluralize a noun in written English is to add an *-s* at the end of the word, but there are lots of exceptions. Some are weird early English plural forms that have survived. Others are words that were borrowed from Latin, Greek, French, Italian, Spanish, Hebrew, and other languages, foreign plural endings and all. In some cases we use those foreign endings to pluralize these words; in others we use the regular English *-s* or *-es* ending instead. This lesson deals with these and other types of tricky plurals. It describes patterns and offers guidelines and examples, but be sure to consult a good dictionary or spell-checker if you have any doubt about a plural form.

Oh, by the way, the plural forms of *potato* and *tomato* are *potatoes* and *tomatoes*.

NATIVE ENGLISH WORDS THAT CHANGE THEIR VOWELS TO FORM PLURALS

There are seven of these:

foot   → feet
goose → geese
louse   → lice
man   → men
mouse → mice
tooth   → teeth
woman → women

MICE or MOUSES?

The Old English word *mice* has been in the language for more than eleven hundred years, but another plural form of *mouse* may be gaining traction today. Believe it or not, it's *mouses*. In the 1990s, *mouses* entered English as a term for the handheld computer devices that move a cursor. Some style guides recommend this new usage to distinguish the gadget from the rodent. It's similar to the way that *louses* and *lice* distinguish contemptible people from the parasitic insects. The *Oxford English Dictionary* cites this use of *mouses*, but the *Associated Press Stylebook* opposed it in 2009. Time and usage will tell if the word survives.[1]

NATIVE ENGLISH NOUNS THAT ADD -*EN* TO FORM PLURALS

There are only three of these in common use:

brother → brethren
child   → children
ox   → oxen

PLURALS OF WORDS THAT END IN -*F* OR -*FE*

A small and shrinking group of old nouns that end in an -*f* or -*fe* change to -*ves* in the plural:

calf → calves
elf → elves
half → halves
knife → knives
leaf → leaves
life → lives
loaf → loaves
self → selves
shelf → shelves
thief → thieves
wife → wives
wolf → wolves (*also* werewolves)

Others simply end in -*fs*:

proof → proofs

Some nouns in this category end in either -*fs* or -*ves*:

dwarf → dwarfs *or* dwarves
hoof → hoofs *or* hooves
roof → roofs *or* rooves
scarf → scarfs *or* scarves

In the United States and Britain, *roofs* appears much more often than *rooves*.[2]

DWARFS or DWARVES?

Snow White and the Seven Dwarfs
    Title of 1937 Walt Disney animated film

"Dwarves are not heroes, but calculating folk with a great idea of the value of money."
    J. R. R. Tolkien, *The Hobbit, or, There and Back Again* (1937)

In the United States and Britain, *dwarfs* is now far more common than dwarves. In fact, the *Oxford English Dictionary* lists *dwarfs* as the only plural form of *dwarf*. Fans of J. R. R. Tolkien may object that he used the word dwarves, but Tolkien actually said in *The Hobbit* that *dwarfs* is the only correct form. In his fiction, though, he spoke of the *dwarves* as a particular ancient race. Major American dictionaries list both *dwarfs* and *dwarves*. And the Google Books Ngram Viewer confirms that *dwarves* still sometimes appears in both the United States and the United Kingdom.

PLURALS OF NOUNS THAT END IN -*I*

Most nouns that end in -*i* become plural simply by adding an -*s:*

alibi	→	alibis
bikini	→	bikinis
khaki	→	khakis
kiwi	→	kiwis
rabbi	→	rabbis
yogi	→	yogis

Asked if she was obsessed with her weight, Elizabeth Hurley said: "If I were really concerned with my weight, I'd be half a stone lighter and in really good shape.... [But] I do have to squeeze myself into quite a few dresses and <u>bikinis</u>."

> Elizabeth Hurley, English actress, model, and owner of a beachwear line, quoted in Polly Vernon, "'Gosh, I've Got Quite a Lot of Clothes on Today,'" theguardian.com, Jan. 14, 2006

Three exceptions are

alkali	→	alkalis *or* alkalies
chili	→	chilies, chiles, *or* chillies
taxi	→	taxis *or* taxies

PLURALS OF NOUNS THAT END IN -*O*

Many English words that end in -*o*, such as *cargo, embargo, fiasco, mosquito,* and *studio,* are borrowings from Italian or Spanish. Some words were taken directly from Latin, including *hero, ratio,* and *veto.* Others, like *calico* and *kangaroo,* were borrowed from other languages.

The rules for how to spell the plurals of words that end in -*o* are pretty loose, and there are many exceptions and inconsistencies. Have you ever noticed, for example, that *halos* can also be spelled *haloes,* but, there's only one way to spell *vetoes*?[3] Here are some general guidelines:

If the -*o* follows a vowel, add -*s* to form the plural.

cameos	cuckoos
duos	embryos
kangaroos	portfolios
radios	ratios
rodeos	stereos
studios	tattoos
trios	videos
zoos[4]	

"I do have <u>tattoos</u> and I do wear leather, but there are other sides of me that my films express."
>   Angelina Jolie, Academy Award–winning American actress and filmmaker, quoted in *Elle,* 2000

"I have a real interest in pushing some of the limits of things that <u>studios</u> don't want to make.... I won't be able to at some point in the near future. But right now I can."
>   George Clooney, quoted in "George Clooney's Thoughts for Today," esquire.com, Dec. 13, 2011

If the -*o* follows a consonant, you also can simply add -*s* to form many plurals.

altos	casinos
dynamos	egos

kimonos	Latinos
memos	pianos
ponchos	silos[5]

"Gentlemen, start your <u>egos</u>."
> Billy Crystal, hosting the Academy Awards ceremony, Feb. 29, 2004

"I've had grand <u>pianos</u> that are more expensive than ... a year's worth of rent."
> Lady Gaga, quoted in Vanessa Grigoriadis, "Growing Up Gaga," nymag.com, Mar. 28, 2010

But some nouns that end in a consonant plus *-o* are pluralized by adding *-es*, including *potatoes* and *tomatoes*:

heroes[6]
potatoes
tomatoes
vetoes

"<u>Heroes</u> may not be braver than anyone else. They're just braver five minutes longer."
> President Ronald Reagan, "Remarks on Presenting the 1980 and 1981 Young American Medals for Bravery and Service," White House, Dec. 22, 1982

Zoë Kravitz, on her favorite comfort food: "I would fly to Los Angeles just for a cheeseburger with pickles and extra <u>tomatoes</u> from In-N-Out."
> Zoë Kravitz, American actress, singer, and model, interviewed by Arianna Davis, "How Zoë Kravitz Lives Her Best Life," *O, the Oprah Magazine,* oprah.com, June 2013

"They know they have trouble. The worst kind of trouble. Dame Trouble ... Angry <u>tomatoes</u> are not small <u>potatoes</u>."
> A parody of Dean Martin and the Rat Pack by Maureen Dowd, "Ain't Nothin' Like a Dame," nytimes.com, Dec. 10, 2013

And some have two plural forms:

buffalo(e)s	cargo(e)s
commando(e)s	desperado(e)s
domino(e)s	halo(e)s
mosquito(e)s	motto(e)s
tornado(e)s	volcano(e)s
zero(e)s	

Some Italian loanwords ending in -*o* become plural by ending in -*i*:

graffito ➡ graffiti

Other Italian loanwords are made plural with either English or Italian endings:

cello	➡	cellos or celli
libretto	➡	librettos or libretti
maestro	➡	maestros or maestri
piccolo	➡	piccolos or piccoli
solo	➡	solos or soli
tempo	➡	tempos or tempi
torso	➡	torsos or torsi
virtuoso	➡	virtuosos or virtuosi[7]

One more point about words in this category: add an -*s* to pluralize acronyms and abbreviations ending in -*o*:

Acronyms	Abbreviations
CEOs	hippos
IPOs	kilos
PCs	memos
PINs	photos
UFOs	typos

PLURALS OF WORDS THAT END IN -*Y*

If a word ends in a vowel plus -*y*, in most cases just add an -*s* to form the plural:

alley	→	alleys
boy	→	boys
chimney	→	chimneys
journey	→	journeys
joy	→	joys
key	→	keys
turkey	→	turkeys
way	→	ways

To pluralize most nouns that end in a consonant plus -*y*, drop the -*y* and add -*ies*:

ally	→	allies
baby	→	babies
cherry	→	cherries
city	→	cities
doggy	→	doggies
opportunity	→	opportunities
party	→	parties
pony	→	ponies
puppy	→	puppies
rally	→	rallies
story	→	stories
worry	→	worries

The plural of a few words that end in -*quy* also end in -*ies*:

soliloquy → soliloquies

The *y* stays in the plural forms of most names:

the Crosbys
the Kennedys
the Levys
the Three Marys

There are some exceptions, though. A few names ending in -*y* are pluralized with -*ies*:

the Alleghenies
the Ptolemies
the Rockies

PLURALS OF WORDS THAT END
WITH THE SOUND *DJ, KS, S, SH, TCH,* OR Z

Words that end with those sounds form plurals with the letters -*es*:

beach → beaches
box → boxes
bus → buses (*or* busses, *mainly U.S.*)
bush → bushes
church → churches
judge → judges
kiss → kisses
phrase → phrases
quiz → quizzes
success → successes
waltz → waltzes

That also applies to people's names:

the Adamses
the Bushes
the Joneses
the Willises

PLURALS OF LATIN AND GREEK WORDS

Many tricky English plural nouns are borrowed from Latin and Greek. Several retain their Latin or Greek plural endings. Others take either the foreign endings or the English -*s* or -*es*.

abacus → abaci *or* abacuses
alumna → alumnae (*female graduates*)
alumnus → alumni (*male graduates and all graduates*)
analysis → analyses
antenna → antennae (*sensory organs*) *or* antennas (*TV or radio aerials*)
appendix → appendices (*in books and documents*) *or* appendixes (*in surgery and zoology*)

bacillus	→	bacilli
bacterium	→	bacteria
basis	→	bases
cactus	→	cacti *or* cactuses
crisis	→	crises
criterion	→	criteria
curriculum	→	curricula *or* curriculums
focus	→	foci *(in scientific and scholarly work)* or focus(s)es *(in general writing)*
forum	→	forums *or* fora
fungus	→	fungi *or (rarely)* funguses
gymnasium	→	gymnasiums *or* gymnasia[8]
hypothesis	→	hypotheses
index	→	indices *(in scientific and scholarly work)* or indexes *(in general writing and books)*
locus	→	loci
medium	→	media *or* mediums *(people who claim to be in contact with the dead)*
memorandum	→	memoranda *or* memorandums
museum	→	museums *or (very rarely)* musea
nemesis	→	nemeses
nucleus	→	nuclei *or (very rarely)* nucleuses
oasis	→	oases
parenthesis	→	parentheses
phenomenon	→	phenomenons or phenomena
radius	→	radii *or (very rarely)* radiuses
referendum	→	referenda *or* referendums[9]
stimulus	→	stimuli
stratum	→	strata *or (very rarely)* stratums
syllabus	→	syllabi *or* syllabuses[10]
synopsis	→	synopses
thesis	→	theses
ultimatum	→	ultimatums *or* ultimata[11]

WORDS THAT DON'T TAKE LATIN PLURAL ENDINGS

Some Latin loanwords, including *albums* and *viruses,* are pluralized only with the English *-s* ending.

The plural of *hiatus* is *hiatuses* (or *hiatus*).

The word *caucus* is a special case. The best reason not to give it a Latin ending is that it's not a Latin word. It first appeared in the United States and, though its origin is uncertain, it may come from Algonquian. The plural is *caucuses* or *caucusses*.

IGNORAMUSES AND OCTOPUSES

A Funny Thing Happened on the Way to a Plural

How is an ignoramus like an octopus? The answer is that people sometimes use made-up plural forms for both of them. When an English-speaker puts the Latin plural marker *-i* at the end of *ignoramus,* some overeducated people may think that he is one. That's because *ignoramus* isn't a Latin noun at all; it's a verb meaning "we don't know." Since there never was a Latin plural noun *ignorami,* it's a mistake to use it as a noun in Standard English. The plural of *octopus* is *octopodes* in Greek. It sometimes shows up in English, but it's extremely rare. *Octopi* appears more often, but that's a made-up word. The usual plural forms of these two words in English are *ignoramuses* and *octopuses.*

PLURALS OF FRENCH WORDS

French loanwords that end in *-eau* or *-ieu* are pluralized with *-s* or *-x:*

adieu	→	adieux *or* adieus
beau	→	beaux *or* beaus
bureau	→	bureaus *or* bureaux
chateau	→	chateaux *or* chateaus
milieu	→	milieus *or* milieux
plateau	→	plateaus *or* plateaux
trousseau	→	trousseaux *or* trousseaus[12]

PLURALS OF HEBREW WORDS

A few Hebrew loanwords become plural with Hebrew endings:

goy   → goyim
midrash → midrashim

A few are made plural with either English or Hebrew endings:

cherub → cherubs *or* cherubim
kibbutz → kibbutzes *or* kibbutzim
seraph → seraphs *or* seraphim

Rabbi comes from a Latin word that derives from Greek, and ultimately from Hebrew. *Sabbath* derives from the Hebrew word *shabbat,* but it came into English through Latin and French. Their plural forms in English are *rabbis* and *sabbaths*.

PLURAL NOUNS WITH THE SAME
SPELLING AS THE SINGULAR FORMS

Only the context will tell your readers if words like these represent one thing or many:

aircraft	bison
deer	moose
offspring	salmon
series	sheep
species	swine

COLLECTIVE WORDS FOR ANIMALS

Singular form: "Vice President Dick Cheney said today that he experienced 'one of the worst days of my life' on Saturday, when he accidentally shot and injured a friend of his while the two were hunting for <u>quail</u>."

Maria Newman, "Cheney Takes Full Responsibility for Shooting Hunter," nytimes.com, Feb. 15, 2006

Plural form: "And it came to pass, that at even [evening] the <u>quails</u> came up... And when the children of Israel saw it, they said to one another, It is manna."
Ex. 16:13 (KJV)

When you think of animals like the ones below collectively, don't use a plural marker. That's especially true when you speak of them as the quarry for hunting.

End the plural with *-(e)s* **when you think of the animals as individual creatures, or as distinct species or kinds:**

antelope *or* antelopes	duck *or* ducks
elephant *or* elephants	elk *or* elks
giraffe *or* giraffes	pheasant *or* pheasant
quail *or* quails	rabbit *or* rabbits

SINGULAR NOUNS THAT HAVE PLURAL FORMS

Words in this category are two-part items. They include devices, tools, and articles of clothing, several of which can follow the phrase *a pair of.* **They take plural verbs:**

clothes	forceps
gallows	glasses (the optical device)
jeans	pajamas
pants	pliers
scissors	shorts
slacks (the garment)	tights
tongs	trousers

NOUNS THAT LOOK PLURAL BUT TAKE SINGULAR VERBS

billiards
darts *(the game)*
news

WORDS THAT LOOK PLURAL BUT TAKE EITHER SINGULAR OR PLURAL VERBS, DEPENDING ON THE CONTEXT: *ECONOMICS, POLITICS, STATISTICS* (OR, TOPICS TO AVOID OVER A ROMANTIC DINNER)

Some words, including *economics, politics,* and *statistics,* look plural but can take either singular or plural verbs.

Economics usually takes a singular verb when it refers to a field of study or endeavor, or to the management of economies.

It can take either a singular or a plural verb when it refers to economic matters, especially financial considerations.

> *Singular:* "Geography has made us neighbors. History has made us friends. <u>Economics has</u> made us partners. And necessity has made us allies."
>> President John F. Kennedy, address to the Canadian Parliament in Ottawa, May 17, 1961

> *Plural:* "<u>Economics are</u> basically the only reason to get married, but I'm very glad I did it."
>> Helen Mirren, quoted in Tim Walker, "Dame Helen Mirren Speaks for Finance and Not Romance," telegraph.co.uk, Dec. 7, 2008

Politics usually takes a singular verb when it refers to the art or science of government.

It often takes a plural verb when it refers to a particular set of political ideas or practices, or to someone's personal political convictions or sympathies.

It takes either a singular or a plural verb in other contexts.

> *Singular:* "<u>Politics is</u> supposed to be the second-oldest profession. I have come to realize that it bears a very close resemblance to the first."
>> Ronald Reagan, at a conference in Los Angeles, Mar. 2, 1977

> *Plural:* "Our <u>politics are</u> our deepest form of expression: they mirror our past experiences and reflect our dreams and aspirations for the future."

The late U.S. senator Paul Wellstone, quoted on Wellstone.org

Statistics **often takes a plural verb in the context of data or facts that are collected and classified or analyzed.**

It takes a singular verb when it refers to the science of collecting or studying those data.

> *Plural:* "Statistics are like a bikini. What they reveal is suggestive, but what they conceal is vital."
>
>> Professor Aaron Levenstein, quoted in Trish Parry, *Statistics in Clinical Research* (2004)

> *Singular:* "Statistics was developed and institutionalized in part by Karl Pearson."
>
>> *Handbook of the Psychology of Science,* eds. Gregory Feist and Michael Gorman (2012)

PLURALS OF PEOPLE'S NAMES

People's names normally add *-s* to form the plural. As noted above, the plural forms of names ending in *-y* retain the *y,* and names ending in the sound *dj, ks, s, sh, tch,* or *z* end in the spelling *-es.*

the Bushes	the Clintons
the Coolidges	the Kennedys
the Obamas	the Reagans
the Timberlakes	

PLURALS OF COMPOUND WORDS

Compounds usually become plural in the same way that the final element in the compound does. That means that in most cases, they add an *-s.* But compounds that end with words like *-man, -woman,* and *-wife* end with *-men, -women,* and *-wives,* respectively:

babysitters	baseballs
deputy sheriffs	earthquakes

footballs   Italian Americans
keyboards   redheads
sailboats   salesclerks
skyscrapers   stomachaches
superstars   thunderstorms
trade-ins   vice presidents
X-rays

but

businesswomen
firemen
midwives

The main exceptions are the compounds in which the first word is the most important element:

brothers-in-law   daughters-in-law
fathers-in-law   mothers-in-law
sisters-in-law   sons-in-law
grants-in-aid   holes in one
maids of honor   passersby
runners-up

Some word compounds came into English from French, which puts nouns before adjectives and adds the plural ending to the noun. Following that model, several constructions add an *-s* to the first word to form plurals:

aides-de-camp
attorneys general
courts-martial
heirs apparent

We sometimes add *-s* to the adjectives as well:

bêtes noires
faits accomplis

But in some cases English-speakers put the plural markers at the end of these constructions. The results may look weird to French-speakers:

bon mots
court martials

cul-de-sacs
hors d'oeuvres

Compounds ending in *-ful* normally add *-s* at the end to become plural:

armful   → armfuls
handful   → handfuls
shovelful   → shovelfuls
tablespoonful → tablespoonfuls
teaspoonful   → teaspoonfuls

In rare cases, both parts of a compound are made plural:

manservant → menservants

PLURALS OF DATES, NUMBERS, LETTERS, AND ABBREVIATIONS

You can add either *-'s* or just *-s,* but the trend is to use the *-s* without an apostrophe, as long as your meaning is clear.

the 1960s
the sixties
B52s
CDs
DVDs
IOUs
ABCs

but

5's and 6's
M.D.'s
Ph.D.'s
A's and B's
"Mind your p's and q's"
"Cross your t's and dot your i's"

Aim for clarity. With abbreviations, letters, numbers, and periods, I recommend that you use an apostrophe if there's any chance of confusion. Without an apostrophe, *A's* would appear to be the word *As* and *i*'s would look like *is*. And people wouldn't know what to make of *B*s, *p*s, *q*s, or *t*s.

Which version of the sentence below is correct?

(A) "<u>Mothers-in-law</u> who wear a black armband to the wedding are expendable."

(B) "<u>Mother-in-laws</u> who wear a black armband to the wedding are expendable."

Erma Bombeck, *I Lost Everything in the Post-Natal Depression* (1974)

The answer is version A.

Notes

INTRODUCTION

1. As Bryan A. Garner notes, linguists have identified five basic styles (or registers): intimate; casual, for everyday conversation; consultative, for business; formal; and frozen, in religious and legal contexts. See his excellent *Garner's Modern American Usage* (New York: Oxford University Press, 2009), xlv.

2. Acquiring vocabulary from context is a major focus of educational theory. Its importance is cited repeatedly in the Common Core State Standards Initiative. In addition, the new design of the SAT will test whether students understand the meaning of words in context. The SAT will focus on words that are important to know in academic and civil life, not rare or obscure vocabulary. See James S. Murphy, "The Case for SAT Words," theatlantic.com, Dec. 11, 2013.

3. The 2013 Singles in America survey examined the attitudes and behavior of 5,300 singles from age eighteen to over seventy. Funded by the dating site Match. com, it was a national study using a representative sample of Americans based on the U.S. census. I'm grateful to Dr. Helen Fisher, who created, executed, and analyzed the survey, for providing me with details about it. Good grammar in this context refers to an educated use of language. See the definition of grammar in Chapter 2, however.

4. Jessica Bennett, "When Autocorrect Goes Horribly Right," nytimes.com, Jan. 9, 2015.

CHAPTER I

1. David Crystal, *The Stories of English* (Woodstock, NY: Overlook Press, 2005), intro.; David Crystal, *The Cambridge Encyclopedia of the English Language* (Cambridge: Cambridge University Press, 1995), 110. Linguists disagree about the meaning of the term *Standard English*. Tom McArthur notes that it is "a widely

used term that resists easy definition but is used as if most educated people nonetheless know precisely what it refers to" (*Oxford Concise Companion to the English Language* [Oxford: Oxford University Press, 2005], 576–79).

2. Crystal points out that anyone who travels around the English-speaking world will be convinced that nonstandard Englishes in the form of regional and ethnic dialects are the way most people communicate (*The Stories of English*, 6).

3. *Merriam-Webster's Dictionary of English Usage* (Springfield, MA: Merriam-Webster, 1994), 60–64. See the lesson on *ain't* in this book.

4. Steven Pinker, "Steven Pinker on the False Fronts in the Language Wars," slate.com, May 31, 2012. See also Martin Stevens, "The Derivation of 'Ain't,'" *American Speech* 29 (1954), 196–201.

5. There's a controversy about this in the academic world. Many linguists are descriptivists, rather than prescriptivists. They argue that the purpose of linguistics is to describe and analyze language. Instead of making judgments about correctness, these linguists apply scientific approaches to the intricacies of language. For a brilliant descriptivist perspective, see John McWhorter, *What Language Is (and What It Isn't and What It Could Be)* (New York: Gotham Books, 2011). David Crystal notes that linguists don't make value judgments about whether one usage is better than another, but they do accept the importance of standard language. He points out that using informal language in a formal context would be inappropriate. Crystal adds that the concept of appropriateness puts a value on natural expression that doesn't attract criticism (*Cambridge Encyclopedia of the English Language*, 366–67).

6. This phenomenally successful grammar, by Lindley Murray, adopted and hardened earlier strictures, making them prescriptive. See Ingrid Tieken-Boon van Ostade, *The Bishop's Grammar: Robert Lowth and the Rise of Prescriptivism* (Oxford: Oxford University Press, 2011), ch. 1.

7. Edward R. Murrow, American broadcast journalist; broadcast, Nov. 30, 1954.

8. Fowler's approach wasn't purely prescriptive. He also had a sharp eye for actual usage, and he dismissed some prescriptive dictums as pedantry or superstition. He thought that it's better to split infinitives than to write ambiguously or artificially, for example. He had no objection to starting sentences with *But*. He also favored putting prepositions at the end of clauses, and he did it often in his own writing. See David Crystal's introduction to the republication of the first edition of Fowler's *A Dictionary of Modern English Usage* (Oxford: Oxford University Press, 2009); Jenny McMorris, *The Warden of English: The Life of H. W. Fowler* (New York: Oxford University Press, 2001), 217; and William Manchester and Paul Reid, *The Last Lion: Winston Spencer Churchill, Defender of the Realm, 1940–1965* (New York: Bantam Books, 2012), 30.

In the United States, the emphatically prescriptivist *The Elements of Style* by William Strunk Jr. and E. B. White has been the main or only style guide to which many American students have been exposed. White himself commented that Strunk's approach was to issue sharp commands about choosing between "right" and "wrong" usages. The book has been criticized for containing errors and for basing claims on intuition and prejudice rather than established literary usage. See Geoffrey K. Pullum, "50 Years of Stupid Grammar Advice," *Chronicle of Higher Education*, April 17, 2009, and "Strunk and White," episode 166 on Mignon Fogarty's wonderful website, quickanddirtytips.com.

9. Pinker, "Steven Pinker on the False Fronts in the Language Wars."

10. Steven Pinker, "Usage in *The American Heritage Dictionary*," *The American Heritage Dictionary*, 5th ed. (2011), xvi–xix.

CHAPTER 2

1. See David Crystal, *The Cambridge Encyclopedia of the English Language* (Cambridge: Cambridge University Press, 1995), 190–91.

2. Although the word order of this title is fine, the punctuation needs a little editing. Unless the speaker in the song is named Maybe, this title needs a comma after *Me,* which I've supplied.

3. Defining a noun is a little more complicated than that, though. See "Mark Twain's Snoring" on pages 131–34.

4. See Mignon Fogarty's wonderful *Grammar Girl's Quick and Dirty Tips for Better Writing* (New York: St. Martin's Press, 2008), 67.

CHAPTER 3

1. In this book, I silently emend quotations to make them conform to American spelling. I also occasionally emend punctuation for purposes of clarity.

2. The *Dictionary of American Regional English* notes that the nonstandard use of *a* before a word beginning with a vowel sound is widespread across the United States.

3. *OED* in source lines refers to the *Oxford English Dictionary*.

4. James Sledd and Wilma R. Ebbitt, *Dictionaries and That Dictionary* (Chicago: Scott, Foresman, 1962), 80–81.

5. Though *ain't* is very common in conversation, with about four hundred occurrences per million words, and appears in fictional dialogue, it is otherwise a rare and stigmatized form. (*Longman Grammar of Spoken and Written English*, Edinburgh Gate: Pearson Education Limited, 1999, 167–68.)

6. For further discussion, see *Merriam-Webster's Dictionary of English Usage* (Springfield, MA: Merriam-Webster, 1994), 82–83.

7. Members of *American Heritage Dictionary* usage panels have increasingly allowed this broader usage, and by 2009, nearly 90 percent of the panelists accepted the phrase "plenty of alternatives."

8. *Among, amid,* and *while* are actually descended from forms that are older than the *-st* variants. *Amongst and whilst* are a little more common in British than in American books today. *Amidst,* though rare now, is used about equally in the United Kingdom and America. The word *unbeknownst* is more common than *unbeknown,* especially in American English, though both versions appear infrequently. (Google Books Ngram Viewer, Jean-Baptiste Michel, Yuan Kui Shen, Aviva Presser Aiden, Adrian Veres, Matthew K. Gray, William Brockman, the Google Books Team, Joseph P. Pickett, Dale Hoiberg, Dan Clancy, Peter Norvig, Jon Orwant, Steven Pinker, Martin A. Nowak, and Erez Lieberman Aiden, "Quantitative Analysis of Culture Using Millions of Digitized Books," *Science* 331, no. 6014, 2011: 176–82.)

9. *The New Yorker,* Dec. 10, 1966 (*OED*).

10. *Harper Dictionary of Contemporary Usage* (New York: Harper and Row, 1985), 354. The panel comprised 166 distinguished consultants.

11. *The Oxford Guide to English Usage* notes that some people especially prefer *such as* to *like* if more than one example is mentioned (Oxford: Oxford University Press, 1983), 115.

12. William Strunk Jr. and E. B. White, *The Elements of Style,* 4th ed. (Boston: Pearson Education, 2000), 41.

13. *American Heritage* usage panels have never been enthusiastic about the phrase *beg the question. The American Heritage Guide to Contemporary Usage and Style* advises avoiding the phrase altogether (57).

14. This can be tricky, though, and careful writers may be conservative about applying this rule. Most of the *Harper Dictionary* Usage Panel, for example, objected to saying that negotiations were going on *between* several nations in an international organization. Because more than two nations were involved, the large majority of the Usage Panel thought that *among* was the right word. Some of them did say that *between* would be okay if the negotiations involved two people at a time.

15. Strunk and White, *The Elements of Style,* 41. The *Harper Dictionary of Contemporary English* points out that "can't help but" is a double negative (101), but Garner says that the phrase should no longer be stigmatized (*Garner's Modern American Usage* [New York: Oxford University Press, 2009], 129).

16. *Merchant of Venice,* act 2, sc. 1. Since two men are being compared, the normative usage today would be *redder.*

17. Otto Jespersen said that in ordinary use, words like *tallest* and *best* represent different ways of looking at a comparison between two things, not a higher degree

than *tall* or *better* (*A Modern English Grammar on Historical Principles* [Copenhagen: E. Munksgaard, 1909–49], vii.11.6).

18. The large majority of *American Heritage* panelists, for example, rejected a statement that the fruit and vegetables near Chernobyl were *decimated* by the nuclear accident there.

19. The *Oxford Guide to English Usage* says that *different to* sometimes sounds more natural than *different from* (101).

20. Bishop Robert Lowth is usually said to have prescribed the rule forbidding double negatives, in 1763. Lowth was actually describing the general movement away from using double negatives that was already well under way in writing and in educated speech. In 1795 the grammarian Lindley Murray turned Lowth's observation into a recommendation against using double negatives at all, even to make a positive. See Ingrid Tieken-Boon van Ostade, "English at the Onset of the Normative Tradition," in *The Oxford History of English,* ed. Lynda Mugglestone (Oxford: Oxford University Press, 2006), ch. 9; see also Tieken-Boon van Ostade's *The Bishop's Grammar: Robert Lowth and the Rise of Prescriptivism* (Oxford: Oxford University Press, 2011), ch. 1. The *Longman Grammar* notes that in conversation today, multiple negation can have a strengthening effect, as in "There's no jobs, there's no nothing" (178).

21. Otto Jespersen observed that *either of* constructions have a fundamental plurality in people's minds, so they're sometimes thought of as plural (*A Modern English Grammar on Historical Principles*, ii.172). The Google Books Ngram Viewer confirms this inconsistency. It shows, for example, that the singular *either of them is* and *either of them has* are more common than the plural forms of these phrases in printed books today; the pattern has been the other way around at times in the past, however. By contrast, today *either of you were* and *either of you have* far outnumber *either of you was* and *either of you has,* respectively.

22. The *Oxford Guide to English Usage* (177) accepts this rule but notes that, according to the *Oxford English Dictionary,* in actual practice, "at all times there has been a tendency to use the plural with two or more singular subjects when their mutual exclusion is not emphasized."

23. In 2009 nearly two-thirds of the *American Heritage* Usage Panel, for example, accepted this pattern. Burchfield prescribed a plural verb after a *neither...nor* construction, even if the first subject is plural and the second subject is singular (R. W. Burchfield, *Fowler's Modern English Usage,* 3rd ed. (Oxford: Oxford University Press, 2004), 518). The *Longman Grammar of Spoken and Written English* confirms that pattern in everyday usage (183).

24. See the list of prepositions on page 13.

25. In eighteenth-century England, there were two opposite trends in this debate, one that adhered to Latin models and another that resisted them. See

Nuria Yanez-Bouza, "Preposition Stranding in the Eighteenth Century: Something to Talk About," in *Grammars, Grammarians, and Grammar-Writing in Eighteenth-Century England,* ed. Ingrid Tieken-Boon van Ostande (Walter de Gruyter, 2008), 254–77. Bishop Lowth distinguished between speech and writing as well as different levels and style in his comments on preposition stranding. He said that it was common in conversation and was well suited to a familiar style in writing, but wasn't appropriate to an elevated writing style (Tieken-Boon van Ostade, *The Bishop's Grammar,* ch. 1).

26. H. W. Fowler, *A Dictionary of Modern English Usage* (1926; Oxford: Oxford University Press, 2009), 457–59; see David Crystal's introduction, xxi. Except in academic prose, stranded prepositions are common in questions that begin with words like *who* and *where. About, after, at, by for, from, in, like, of, on, to,* and *with* are stranded more often than other prepositions (*Longman Grammar of Spoken and Written English,* 105–8).

27. See Ingrid Tieken-Boon van Ostade, "Henry Fowler and His Eighteenth-Century Predecessors," *Bulletin of the Henry Sweet Society for the History of Linguistic Ideas,* 51 (Dec. 2009): 21–24. A phrasal verb is a verb that consists of more than one word, often a verb and a preposition. Some examples are *break down, deal with, get rid of, hold on, look after, pick on, stand up, strike out,* and, of course, *put up with.* They are idioms, and you should use the entire phrase, not just the verb. In some cases, though, you can split the verb from the preposition. So you can use the phrasal verb *strike out* as James Thurber did in "The majority of American males put themselves to sleep by striking out the batting order of the New York Yankees." Or you could say "by striking the batting order of the New York Yankees out." See Garner, *Garner's Modern American Usage,* 628–29; also Harvey Frommer, *Yankee Century and Beyond* (Naperville, IL: Sourcebooks, 2007), ch. 6.

28. Since *et al.* also stands for the neuter *et alia, Merriam-Webster's Dictionary of English Usage* says that it's not incorrect to use it to refer to things. See my recommendation in this lesson, however.

29. Paige Jackson, "APA Style," blog.apastyle,org.

30. This line was written by David Mamet and spoken by Robert De Niro, who played Capone in the 1987 film.

31. In British books, *further* now dominates over *farther* in all senses by a ratio of about 20:1, according to Google Books Ngram Viewer; in American books, the ratio is closer to 7:1. The British National Corpus shows an even more lopsided ratio of 70:1 in British English. In the Cambridge International Corpus, the ratio in American usage is 10:1 (Pam Peters, *Cambridge Guide to English Usage* [Cambridge: Cambridge University Press, 2004], 222).

32. Nearly every member of the 2009 *American Heritage* Usage Panel, for example, approved of the rule that *farther* should describe distance and *further*

should be used in figurative, nonphysical senses. In practice, though, most panelists accepted sentences in which the pattern was reversed. Between 80 and 90 percent of the *Harper Dictionary* Usage Panel approved of the rule, but several panelists admitted that they *tried* to remember it or *hoped* to remember it but often slipped. *Merriam-Webster's Dictionary of English Usage* notes that in actual usage, *farther* as an adjective has been relegated to the sense of geographic distance. It and several other major style guides note the widespread use of *further* in all senses.

33. One *Harper* panelist said that he says *bad* to describe a physical condition but *badly* for an emotional response. This was a minority view, but many people make the same distinction in everyday usage, according to *Merriam-Webster's Dictionary of English Usage,* 437–38.

34. *Middle English Dictionary* (Ann Arbor: University of Michigan Press, 1954–2001), **wel** adj., 1d. See *The Merchant of Venice,* act 3, sc. 2; *Much Ado about Nothing,* act 4, sc. 1; *The Merry Wives of Windsor,* act 1, sc. 1.

35. Cited by *Merriam-Webster's Dictionary of English Usage,* 480.

36. *Merriam-Webster's Dictionary of English Usage,* 494. The Google Books Ngram Viewer confirms the dominance of *hanged* over *hung* in the phrases *hanged to death* and *hanged by the neck.*

37. Fowler, *Dictionary of Modern English Usage,* 648. Strunk and White called the generic use of *he* simple, practical, and historically based, though they offered strategies to avoid overusing *he or she* (*The Elements of Style,* 60–61).

38. Facebook lets users choose between three pronouns: *him, her,* or *their.* It allows at least fifty-eight options for people to identify their gender, though. That reflects the belief that there are many human genders (Russell Goldman, "Here's a List of 58 Gender Options for Facebook Users," abcnews.go.com, Feb. 13, 2014).

39. Cited in the *Longman Dictionary of the English Language* (London: Longman), 1984.

40. See Strunk and White, *Elements of Style,* 60–61.

41. The American Heritage Usage Panel, which is often conservative about usage, overwhelmingly said that they used *the* before the phrase *hoi polloi.*

42. This is also the norm in fiction and news (*Longman Grammar of Spoken and Written English,* 335–36). English-speakers are used to putting subject pronouns like *I, he,* and *we* before verbs, and object pronouns like *me, her,* and *us* after verbs. Since the pronoun follows the verb in *It was I,* people tend to say *It was me* in informal speech. See Sidney Greenbaum and Randolph Quirk, *A Student's Grammar of the English Language* (Harlow, Essex: Pearson Education, 1990), 111–12.

43. *Two Gentlemen of Verona,* act 2, sc. 3; *Twelfth Night,* act 2, sc. 5. Shakespeare put this construction in the mouths of characters of both high and low rank. See F. Th. Visser, *An Historical Syntax of the English Language* (Leiden: Brill, 1970), 239–45.

44. *The Cambridge Guide to English Usage,* 341–42. *It was me* is the usual choice in British and American books today, while *It was I* has all but flatlined. *It was her* is also more common than *It was she.* But *It was he* predominates over *It was him,* which has always been very rare (Google Books Ngram Viewer). When someone asks to speak to a particular person on the phone, many people say *This is she* or *This is he,* both of which are strictly correct, rather than the more casual *This is her* or *him.*

45. Eric Donald Hirsch, *The Making of Americans* (New Haven, CT: Yale University Press, 2009), note 26.

46. *Merchant of Venice,* act 3, sc. 2; *King Lear,* act 1, sc. 1.

47. *Harper Dictionary of Contemporary Usage,* 71–72.

48. This nonstandard use of *X and me* as the subjects of sentences occurs mainly in conversation. It rarely appears in fiction or news and almost never in academic prose (*Longman Grammar of Spoken and Written English,* 337–38).

49. For example, "A man no mightier than thyself <u>or me</u>" (*Julius Caesar,* act 1, sc. 3) and "Charges she more than <u>me</u>?" (*Measure for Measure,* act 5, sc. 1). When the pronoun was the subject, Shakespeare wrote *than I* more often: "You have done more miracles <u>than I</u>" (*Henry VI, Part II,* act 2, sc. 1). He also had Cleopatra ask, "Is she <u>as tall as me</u>?" (*Antony and Cleopatra,* act 3, sc. 3).

50. This pattern occurs about half of the time in fiction but is extremely rare in news and academic writing (*Longman Grammar,* 336). There appears to be some inconsistency, depending on the context. The Google Books Ngram Viewer shows, for example, that *older than me* is more frequent than *older than I,* but *stronger than I* is much more common than *stronger than me.* (In both examples, *than I* is formally correct.) At the end of sentences, *than I* significantly outnumbers *than me,* though both are rare.

51. Kenneth G. Wilson, *The Columbia Guide to Standard American English* (New York: Columbia University Press, 1993), 243; Burchfield, *Fowler's Modern English Usage,* 748; The American Philosophical Society, "Instructions for Authors." The Google Books Ngram Viewer shows that in books, *if I were* appears more often today than *if I was* in both the United States and Britain. It's much less common than it was a hundred years ago, but its use is not very different from two hundred years ago. *I wish I were* appears a bit more often than *I wish I was* in American books, but the ratio is reversed in Britain.

52. Lexis in source lines refers to LexisNexis.

53. The authors of the *Merriam-Webster's Dictionary of English Usage,* in a subtle and nuanced reading of the evidence in the *OED,* conclude that for four hundred years *infer* was used to mean "hint, suggest" when the subject wasn't a person. That sense overlaps with *imply.* They conclude that the actual controversy is over *infer* with a personal subject, which is a recent usage in print. They note that

More's use of *infer* without a human subject still appears, but is declining because of the commentators' denunciation of the "personal infer" with a person as its subject.

54. *The Cambridge Guide to English Usage*, 270.

55. The word *irony* ultimately derives from the Greek for "feigned ignorance" or "someone who hides under a false appearance." Socrates practiced this kind of irony when he pretended to be ignorant as a tactic for getting to the truth of a matter.

56. A large majority of the *American Heritage Dictionary* Usage Panel in 1987 rejected the use of *ironically* to simply mean "by coincidence" or "improbably." But most of the panel accepted the word when it exemplified the fact that people say one thing but ironically do another (*American Heritage Guide to Contemporary Usage and Style*, 262–63).

57. See the entry for "Irony" in *The Princeton Encyclopedia of Poetry and Poetics*, 4th ed. (Princeton, NJ: Princeton University Press, 2012).

58. M. H. Abrams, *A Glossary of Literary Terms*, 7th ed. (Boston: Heinle & Heinle, 1999), 136.

59. *Merriam-Webster's Dictionary of English Usage*, 581; Burchfield, *Fowler's Modern English Usage*, 437.

60. Just as a transit is a passage across or through something, a transitive verb carries an action from an actor, or subject, to the person or thing that is acted on in a sentence. An intransitive verb, by contrast, expresses an action that is limited to the subject.

61. The Google Books Ngram Viewer shows that *lain* has always been rare. Its usage nearly flatlined in the late twentieth century.

62. See John McWhorter's *What Language Is* (New York: Gotham Books, 2011), 83–84.

63. William Safire notes other expressions that are sometimes used with *literally* but aren't literally possible: *to literally jump out of your skin, to literally sweat blood*, and *to literally fly off the handle* (*On Language* [New York: Times Books, 1981], 154).

64. Phrases with possessive subjects before *-ing* forms, like *the angel's returning, the king's coming*, and *your saying that* have been part of the language since Old English. Non-possessive subjects in *-ing* clauses haven't been in English quite as long. The first *-ing* forms in English functioned as pure nouns. Gradually they acquired most of the properties of verbs as well, and by the fifteenth century they were well developed as gerunds. The Old English variant *-ung* died out in Middle English.

65. The earlier sense of the word relating to the king or queen also survives as the *royal prerogative*.

66. Journalists and other writers tend to think of *quotes* as contemporary remarks that they can use in their writing and of *quotations* as dignified expressions of the wisdom of the ages (*The Chicago Manual of Style,* 16th ed. [Chicago: University of Chicago Press, 2010], 5.220).

67. Grammarians call *to* plus a verb a full infinitive.

68. Visser, *An Historical Syntax of the English Language,* II:1035–45. Though split infinitives are rare in Middle English, some do occur in the great poem *Sir Gawain and the Green Knight.* Here are two of them, describing the hot-blooded young King Arthur: "He louied þe lasse / Auþer to longe lye or to longe sitte,"which means, roughly, "He didn't like to long lie down or to long sit." In her elegant translation, Marie Borroff renders this as "The less he cared / To be lying for long, or long to sit" (*Sir Gawain and the Green Knight: A New Verse Translation* [New York: Norton, 1967], lines 87–88). See Henk Aertsen, "The Use of the Infinitive in *Sir Gawain and the Green Knight,*" in *This Noble Craft,* ed. Erik Kooper (Amsterdam: Rodopi, 1991), 16.

69. This is a paraphrase of a humorous passage in the *Times* (London), May 18, 1992, cited by Burchfield, *Fowler's Modern English Usage,* 737. In 2005, only 58 percent of the *American Heritage* Usage Panel accepted a sentence with three adverbs between *to* and the verb.

70. Despite the normative rule, writers of fiction, news, and academic prose use *which* far more often in essential clauses than in nonessential clauses. This is much less common in American news than in British journalism, however. By contrast, people rarely open a nonessential clause with *that* (*Longman Grammar of Spoken and Written English,* 610–17).

71. Most members of the *Harper Dictionary* Usage Panel thought that the distinction between *that* and *which* is worth preserving, but nearly a third of them said that they didn't do that in their own writing. Paul Brians says in his *Common Errors in English Usage* that he ignores the rule himself (2nd ed. [Wilsonville, OR: William, James, 2009]). *The Oxford Guide to English Usage* says that *which* sounds better in clauses that add significant information, and it can help make some sentences read more clearly. Theodore M. Bernstein points out that it's better to say "that which" than "that that" (*The Careful Writer* [1965; New York: Free Press, 1993).

72. In news and academic prose, people overwhelmingly say *who* to refer to people. In conversation, however, *that* is almost as common as *who* in reference to people (*Longman Grammar of Spoken and Written English,* 612–15). The passage by Twain has the quality of natural speech.

73. In conversation, people also often say *here's, where's,* and *how's* before plural noun phrases. They might say, for example, "Here's your shoes" (*Longman Grammar of Spoken and Written English,* 185–86).

74. Most of the panel accepted the sentences "In each of us there's a dreamer and a realist" and "There's a gas station on the left and a grocery store on the right" (*American Heritage Guide to Contemporary Usage and Style,* 463).

75. Despite the more accepting attitude of British usage experts, the frequency of locutions like *these kind of* isn't much different in Britain than it is in America. The British National Corpus shows that the normative *these kinds of* appears three times more often than *these kind of* in the United Kingdom; the ratio in American English is 4:1, according to the Cambridge International Corpus (*Cambridge Guide to English Usage,* 307). The Google Books Ngram Viewer shows a much more lopsided ratio in favor of the standard form in both the British and American books.

76. For example, 89 percent of the *Harper Dictionary* Usage Panel rejected phrases like "rather unique" or "most unique" in writing. Almost as many objected to those phrases in casual speech (1985). In 1988, the *American Heritage* Usage Panel gave a similar response to "quite unique." By 2004, though, the *American Heritage* panel's opposition had reduced to 66 percent. The tide may be turning, but opinion is still strongly opposed to comparing incomparable adjectives.

77. *Merriam-Webster's Dictionary of English Usage,* 953–55.

78. The *Longman Grammar of Spoken and Written English,* 626–27.

79. Visser, *An Historical Syntax of the English Language,* 241; *Middle English Dictionary,* **who**, pron., 6a. *Merriam-Webster's Dictionary of English Usage* notes that most of Shakespeare's speakers who switch *who* and *whom* in the examples it cites are from the upper classes (957–58).

80. *Longman Grammar of Spoken and Written English,* 214–15, 610–11. The Google Books Ngram Viewer tracks the declining use of both *who* and *whom* in printed books since the mid-nineteenth century and shows that *who* is now used more often than *whom* in all contexts by a ratio of over 12:1.

81. Steven Pinker, *The Language Instinct: How the Mind Creates Language* (New York: Harper Perennial Modern Classics, 1994), 220.

CHAPTER 4

1. Since the 1890s, *to access* has occasionally been used in the sense of "entering in the accessions register of a library, museum, etc." It's a different verb from the one discussed here.

2. In 1988, 82 percent of the *American Heritage Dictionary* Usage Panel rejected the use of *access* as a verb referring to obtaining something. By 2001 the panelists' opposition had reduced to 46 percent. So they had become much more accepting in a short time, but nearly half of them still opposed this common usage. They were even less enthusiastic about using *access* as a verb in a medical context.

3. Use of the word *avatar* in books more than tripled between 1975 and 2008 (Google Books Ngram Viewer). This is true of the word in general, though its popularity in the sense of a digitized image was no doubt a major factor.

4. William and Mary Morris, *Harper Dictionary of Contemporary Usage* (New York: Harper & Row, 1985), 144.

5. Ibid.

6. William Safire, *On Language* (New York: Times Books, 1980), 60.

7. *Merriam-Webster's Dictionary of English Usage* (Springfield, MA: Merriam-Webster, 1994) suggests that editorial influence is a main reason for the preference for the plural in printed texts. It adds that most usage writers recognize or approve of the mass singular construction of *data*. In fact, only 49 percent of the *Harper Dictionary* Usage Panel (1985) allowed a singular construction in writing (though 65 percent didn't object to it in casual speech). On the other hand, 60 percent of the *American Heritage Dictionary* Usage Panel accepted *data* with a singular verb and pronoun in 1988, and in 2005 two-thirds accepted it. So singular *data* has become a standard usage. But many more usage experts think of *data* as a plural noun: fully 92 percent of the *American Heritage* Usage Panel approved of plural *data* in 2005.

8. William Strunk Jr. and E. B. White, *The Elements of Style*, 4th ed. (Needham Heights, MA: Allyn & Bacon, 2000), 83.

9. The historian George Marsden notes that Falwell borrowed this line from him. See George M. Marsden, *Fundamentalism and American Culture* (New York: Oxford University Press, 2006), 235.

10. *Longman Grammar of Spoken and Written English* (Harlow, Essex: Pearson Education, 1999), 856–57. William Safire embraced the new sense of *hopefully*, saying that it's readily understood and time-tested, and that to begin a sentence with it is as structurally correct as to open a sentence with *fortunately, doubtlessly,* or *basically* (*On Language*, 134–35).

11. At the time of this writing, the Google Books Ngram Viewer included data on the word *Internet* only up to 2008.

12. Pam Peters, *The Cambridge Guide to English Usage* (Cambridge: Cambridge University Press, 2004), 292.

13. See Malise Ruthven, *Fundamentalism: The Search for Meaning* (Oxford: Oxford University Press, 2004), ch. 1, for a discussion of the problems with transferring the word *fundamentalism* from a Christian context to Islam. Also see "EXTREMIST or FANATIC" and "FUNDAMENTALISM" in this book, above.

14. The scholar of religion Reza Aslan says that Islamists are motivated by religious nationalism, as opposed to jihadis, who seek to erase nationalities and return to an idealized religious communalism of the past (*How to Win a Cosmic War* [New York: Random House, 2009], 29).

15. Tsarnaev's mother also reportedly sent text messages discussing his readiness to die for Islam (Bill Chappell, "Tamerlan Tsarnaev Spoke of Jihad with Mother, Reports Say," npr.org, Apr. 28, 2013; Michael S. Schmidt and Eric Schmitt, "Russia Didn't Share All Details on Boston Bombing Suspect, Report Says," nytimes.com, Apr. 9, 2014).

16. John McWhorter argues that young people's use of *like, totally,* and *lol* all exhibit a sensitive awareness of the listener's state of mind ("Like, Degrading the Language? No Way," nytimes.com, Apr. 5, 2004).

17. "How to Stop Saying the Word 'Like,'" wikihow.com/Stop-Saying-the-Word'" Like"#_note-1.

18. By 1926, *racist* was used in English to refer to the racial ideology of the Nazis and others. *Racialism,* first recorded in English in 1902, has largely been superseded by *racism,* according to the *Oxford English Dictionary.* Between 1962 and 2008, the frequency of the word *racism* in books increased by a factor of about 11 in American English and, stunningly, by a factor of over 47 in British English. There's been a significant drop in the use of the word since the turn of the twenty-first century (Google Books Ngram Viewer).

19. H. Allen Orr, "Stretch Genes," *New York Review of Books,* June 5, 2014, 18–20.

20. The term *schizophrenia* was coined by Paul Eugen Bleuler, who also invented the word *ambivalence.*

21. The disorder involves at least one of those three symptoms, and other symptoms as well ("Schizophrenia Spectrum and Other Psychotic Disorders," *Diagnostic and Statistical Manual of Mental Disorders,* 5th ed. (Washington, DC: American Psychiatric Association, 2013). Schizophrenia is not multiple personality disorder or dissociative identity disorder.

22. This and much of the rest of this lesson are indebted to Alex P. Schmid, "The Definition of Terrorism," in *The Routledge Handbook of Terrorism Research,* ed. Alex P. Schmid (Oxford: Taylor & Francis, 2011), ch. 2.

CHAPTER 5

1. "Glossary of Technical Terms," *Diagnostic and Statistical Manual of Mental Disorders,* 5th ed. (Washington, DC: American Psychiatric Association, 2013).

2. William Safire, "On Language: Enough Already! What Am I, Chopped Liver?" *New York Times,* Oct. 25, 1998.

3. R. W. Burchfield, *Fowler's Modern English Usage,* 3rd ed. (Oxford: Oxford University Press, 2004), 43. Even as two words, the phrase *all right* was very rare until the nineteenth century, as indicated by the Google Books Ngram Viewer. *Al right* appears in some manuscripts of Chaucer's *Troilus and Criseyde* (ca. 1385) in the line "Criseyde was this lady name al right" (Book 1). *Al* and *right* aren't fused

in this line, but word divisions in critical editions of Middle English texts are usually editorial decisions in any case.

4. *Alright* became steadily more common in books over the course of the twentieth century, especially in America (Google Books Ngram Viewer).

5. Perhaps surprisingly, 25 percent of the panelists said that they would use *alright* to mean "Yes, certainly!"

6. "Then altogether they fell vpon me" (*A Comedy of Errors,* act 5, sc. 1). Keep in mind, however, that modern editors often determine the word division in their editions of early texts.

7. This quotation is often attributed to Franklin at the signing of the Declaration of Independence on July 4, 1776, but there are two problems with this: Franklin may not have said it, and the Declaration of Independence wasn't actually signed until August 2 (though it was dated July 4).

8. A full 93 percent of the *American Heritage* Usage Panel in 1996 considered writing *alot* to be an error, though 13 percent of them admitted that they'd done it at some point.

9. Both *ambiguity* and *ambivalence* were used in print more often in the 1990s than at any time before or since, according to the Google Books Ngram Viewer.

10. In this sense, *amend* is sometimes applied to emending a text, though the other meanings of the word are far more common.

11. The *OED* lists only one instance of the solid form *anyone* before the twentieth century. The Google Books Ngram Viewer notes an increase in the spelling *anyone* soon after 1850.

12. This finding was reached by Global Language Monitor, which catalogues and analyzes the depth and breadth of word usage on the Internet, including the blogosphere and social media sources, as well as the top 275,000 print and electronic news sources. It included the use of *apocalypse* in reference to any cataclysmic event. The newspaper headline about the Mayan Apocalypse appeared on December 7, 2012 (telegraph.co.uk).

13. In books, the spelling *a while* appears ten times more often than *awhile* in the phrases *after a while, for a while,* and *in a while.* That's correct according to the prescriptive rule. But writers use *a while* and *awhile* almost equally after verbs like *visit* and *stay* (Google Books Ngram Viewer). The British National Corpus shows that 15 percent of the instances of *awhile* appear in the phrase *for awhile,* which doesn't follow the strict rule (Pam Peters, *Cambridge Guide to English Usage* [Cambridge: Cambridge University Press, 2004]).

14. It's usually reported that in the United States and Canada, people generally say *backward* more often than *backwards,* while the British are slightly more likely to say *backwards.* The Google Books Ngram Viewer supports that view of North American usage but not of British English.

15. An almost identical quotation, but about Native Americans, not Africans, is attributed to Chief Dan George, Canadian native chief and actor, in Gerald Walsh, *Indians in Transition: An Inquiry Approach* (Toronto: McClelland and Stewart, 1971).

16. See Martin L. Hoffman, *Empathy and Moral Development: Implications for Caring and Justice* (Cambridge: Cambridge University Press, 2001), ch. 1. I am grateful to Professor Hoffman for his assistance with this lesson. *Empathy* is taken from the German word *Einfühlung*. The *OED* notes that the meaning of *empathy* has shifted decisively since the mid-twentieth century. In the 1933 and 1972 *OED* supplements, the word was a technical term in aesthetics and psychology denoting the power of projecting one's personality into, and so comprehending, an object of contemplation. The *OED* now considers *empathy* to be a familiar everyday term meaning "the ability to understand and appreciate another person's feelings, experience, etc." (Philip Durkin, "Release Notes: The Changes in Empathy, Employ, and Empire," public.oed.com, March 2014 update).

17. The word *sympathy* is used far less often in books than it was in the nineteenth century, while *empathy* has been used with increasing frequency since the end of the Second World War (Google Books Ngram Viewer).

18. *Enervate* is similar to *eviscerate,* which came into English about the same time, meaning "to remove the internal organs or entrails from something." *Enervate* is a rare word now, but it is a hundred years older than *energize* and it was the more common of the two words until the twentieth century (Google Books Ngram Viewer).

19. William Safire quotes this as it was reported in the *New York Times* (*On Language,* New York: Times Books, 1981, 96–97). It is also cited by Gerhard Peters and John T. Woolley in *The American Presidency Project* (www.presidency.ucsb.edu).

20. Eric Partridge, *Usage and Abusage: A Guide to Good English* (1942; Harmondsworth, Middlesex: Penguin, 1973), 118.

21. Margaret Smith, "The Nature and Meaning of Mysticism," in *Understanding Mysticism,* ed. Richard Woods (Garden City, NY: Image Books, 1980), ch. 1.

22. The *Harper Dictionary of Contemporary Usage,* under "principal/principle," suggests another memory trick: if you can substitute the word *main,* use *principal.* Both contain the letter *a.* If you can substitute *rule,* use *principle,* which can mean a "rule." Both end in -*le.*

23. The Cambridge International Corpus shows that about half of the American instances of *prophesy* are nouns (Peters, *Cambridge Guide to English Usage,* 444). The *Merriam-Webster's Dictionary of English Usage* says, however, that its own files contain no examples of this spelling for the noun since 1967 (779). People sometimes say *prophesize,* but this version of the verb never caught on and is generally regarded as an error.

24. The Cambridge International Corpus says that *in* or *with regard to* appears nine times more frequently than *in* or *with regards to* in American newspapers (Peters, *Cambridge Guide to English Usage*, 466–67). The Google Books Ngram Viewer shows an even larger ratio in American books. The British National Corpus shows the opposite trend, but this is not supported in the British books scanned by the Ngram Viewer.

25. See Bryan A. Garner, *Garner's Modern American Usage* (New York: Oxford University Press, 2009), 722.

26. *Merriam-Webster's Dictionary of English Usage*, **set, sit.**

27. The Middle English Dictionary, **sitten,** 20(a).

28. John McWhorter, *What Language Is* (New York: Gotham Books, 2011), 83–84.

29. Paul Brians, *Common Errors in English Usage*, 2nd ed. (Wilsonville, OR: William, James, 2009), 228.

30. The *American Heritage* Usage Panel in 2002 was more equivocal about this than the *Harper* group was.

CHAPTER 6

1. The *Oxford English Dictionary* cites one mid-eighteenth-century instance of *mouses* in a nautical context. Its earliest citation of *mouses* meaning "computer devices" dates from 1997.

2. Based on data from the Cambridge International Corpus and the British National Corpus, cited in Pam Peters, *The Cambridge Guide to English Usage* (Cambridge: Cambridge University Press, 2004), 198. *Hooves* became more common than *hoofs* in American English in the late twentieth century, and it still is; *scarves* is the dominant plural form in both America and Britain.

3. A survey in 1998–2001 showed that people worldwide are reducing the number of *-oes* spellings of plural words. Of a list of twenty words, *-oes* was preferred only in *echoes, heroes,* and *tomatoes.* If the major dictionaries list *-oes* spellings, however, they are still correct (Peters, *Cambridge Guide to English Usage,* 385).

4. The *Oxford English Dictionary* cites one instance of *embryoes.* It lists *rodeoes* as a rare form but notes no instances of it.

5. The *Oxford English Dictionary* cites one early nineteenth-century instance of the spelling *pianoes* and one mid-nineteenth-century instance of *siloes.*

6. The *Oxford English Dictionary* also cites a couple of twentieth-century instances of the spelling *heros,* both referring to hero sandwiches.

7. The *Oxford English Dictionary* lists the plural of *cello* as *celli* but includes a note from *Grove's Dictionary of Music* saying that this Italian plural form isn't desirable. *The Cambridge Guide to English Usage* wryly observes that although the program notes at music concerts sometimes use Italian plural endings for Italian

musical words ending in *-o*, musicians pluralize them with *-s*, just as the general public does (Peters, *Cambridge Guide to English Usage,* 295–96).

8. *Gymnasiums* is slightly more common than *gymnasia* in the United States; it's the other way around in British English (Google Books Ngram Viewer).

9. *Referenda* is slightly more common in American English, while *referendums* appears somewhat more often in British English (Google Books Ngram Viewer).

10. Garner says that in American legal writing *syllabi* appears ten times more often than *syllabuses* (Bryan A. Garner, *Garner's Modern American Usage* [New York: Oxford University Press, 2009], 793). The Google Books Ngram Reader shows that in printed books, *syllabi* is far more common in the United States, while *syllabuses* appears slightly more often in British English.

11. The *Oxford English Dictionary* lists *ultimata* as the only plural form. Major American dictionaries cite *ultimatums* first. The Google Books Ngram Reader confirms the predominance of *ultimata* in British English and *ultimatums* in American use.

12. The *Oxford English Dictionary* lists *chateaux* as the only plural spelling of *chateau*. The Ngram Reader indicates that *chateaus* has been attested for a long time, though rarely, in both the United States and the United Kingdom. It also shows that *milieus* is dominant in American English, but *milieux* is more common in the United Kingdom.

(*)

Select Bibliography

BOOKS

The American Heritage Guide to Contemporary Usage and Style. Boston: Houghton Mifflin, 2005.

Burchfield, R. W. *Fowler's Modern English Usage.* 3rd ed. Oxford: Oxford University Press, 2004.

The Chicago Manual of Style. 16th ed. Chicago: University of Chicago Press, 2010.

Christian, Darrell, Sally Jacobsen, and David Minthorn, eds. *The Associated Press Stylebook and Briefing on Media Law.* New York: Basic Books, 2009.

Crystal, David. *The Cambridge Encyclopedia of the English Language.* Cambridge: Cambridge University Press, 1995.

Fowler, H. W. *A Dictionary of Modern English Usage.* Edited by David Crystal. Oxford: Oxford University Press, 2009.

Garner, Bryan A. *Garner's Modern American Usage.* New York: Oxford University Press, 2009.

Greenbaum, Sidney, and Randolph Quirk. *A Student's Grammar of the English Language.* Harlow, Essex: Pearson Education, 1990.

Jespersen, Otto. *Growth and Structure of the English Language.* New York: Free Press, 1968.

Longman Grammar of Spoken and Written English. Harlow, Essex: Pearson Education, 1999.

McArthur, Tom, ed. *The Concise Oxford Companion to the English Language.* Oxford: Oxford University Press, 2005.

Merriam-Webster's Dictionary of English Usage. Springfield, MA: Merriam-Webster, 1994.

Morris, William, and Mary Morris. *Harper Dictionary of Contemporary Usage.* New York: Harper & Row, 1985.

The Oxford Guide to English Usage. Compiled by E. S. C. Weiner. Oxford: Oxford University Press, 1983.

Peters, Pam. *The Cambridge Guide to English Usage.* Cambridge: Cambridge University Press, 2004.

The Princeton Encyclopedia of Poetry and Poetics. 4th ed. Princeton, NJ: Princeton University Press, 2012.

Siegal, Allan M., and William G. Connolly. *The New York Times Manual of Style and Usage.* New York: New York Times Company, 1999.

Strunk, William, Jr., and E. B. White. *The Elements of Style.* 4th ed. Needham Heights, MA: Allyn & Bacon, 2000.

Visser, F. Th. *An Historical Syntax of the English Language.* 4 vols. Leiden: E. J. Brill, 1970–1973.

Wilson, Kenneth G. *The Columbia Guide to Standard American English.* New York: Columbia University Press, 1993.

DICTIONARIES AND DATABASES

The American Heritage Dictionary of the English Language. 5th ed. Boston: Houghton Mifflin Harcourt, 2011.

Google Books Ngram Viewer.

Merriam-Webster Online.

Merriam-Webster's Collegiate Dictionary. 11th ed. Springfield, MA: Merriam-Webster, 2012.

The Middle English Dictionary. Ann Arbor: University of Michigan Press, 2001. Online.

The Oxford English Dictionary Online.

Webster's Third New International Dictionary of the English Language, Unabridged. Springfield, MA: Merriam-Webster, 1971.

I often turned to these excellent usage guides, hoping to be inspired by their clarity and wit:

Brians, Paul. *Common Errors in English Usage.* 2nd ed. Wilsonville, OR: William, James, 2009.

Fogarty, Mignon. *Grammar Girl's Quick and Dirty Tips for Better Writing.* New York: St. Martin's Press, 2008.

O'Connor, Patricia T. *Woe Is I: The Grammarphobe's Guide to Better English in Plain English.* 3rd ed. New York: Riverhead Books, 2009.

Strumpf, Michael, and Auriel Douglas. *The Grammar Bible.* New York: Owl Books, 2004.

Index